D1564976

3250   12 85

Uriel's Eye

Uriel's Eye

MILTONIC STATIONING
AND STATUARY IN
BLAKE, KEATS, AND SHELLEY

Nancy Moore Goslee

THE UNIVERSITY OF ALABAMA PRESS

Library of Congress Cataloging in Publication Data

Goslee, Nancy Moore, 1941–
  Uriel's eye.

  Bibliography: p.
  Includes index.
  1. English poetry—19th century—History and criticism.
2. Art and literature. 3. Landscape in literature.
4. Blake, William, 1757–1827. Milton. 5. Keats, John,
1795–1821. Hyperion. 6. Keats, John, 1795–1821. Fall
of Hyperion. 7. Shelley, Percy Bysshe, 1792–1822.
Prometheus unbound. 8. Milton, John, 1608–1674—
Influence. 9. Romanticism—England. I. Title.
PR585.A78G67   1985   821'.7'09   84-8815
ISBN 0-8173-0243-3

To my husband,
my daughter,
and my mother

Contents

Preface / ix

ONE. "Bright appearances":
Romantic Answers to *Paradise Lost* / 1

TWO. Blake's *Milton:*
From Marble Landscape to Living Form / 29

THREE. Keats's *Hyperion:*
"shap'd and palpable Gods" / 68

FOUR. Keats's *The Fall of Hyperion:*
"Like sculpture builded up upon the grave
Of . . . power" / 96

FIVE. Shelley's *Prometheus Unbound:*
"Wildernesses calm and green,
Peopled by shapes too bright to see" / 134

SIX. Sculptural Figure and a
"world of Circumstances" / 190

Notes / 197

Bibliography / 233

Index / 257

Preface

In its broad outlines the argument I develop in this book clearly emerges from the ideas of Harold Bloom, W. J. Bate, and others who have examined the "embarrassments of poetic tradition," "the burden of the past," and "the anxiety of influence." Like them, I think that the romantics felt compelled to struggle with their precursors, particularly with Milton. Each of the four long poems I discuss—Blake's *Milton*, Keats's two *Hyperion* poems, and Shelley's *Prometheus Unbound*—struggles to transform the mythic narrative of *Paradise Lost* into a new and more valid myth. Yet I diverge from the premise that these later poets use as the materials for their struggle only the texts of earlier poetry. That rivalry, I think, finds its expression and part of its resolution through metaphors of rivalry among the arts, most specifically the arts of sculpture and landscape painting. Because these analogues of the arts mediate between the conflicts of earlier and later poets, I have not directly adopted Bloom's partially Freudian theories of a psychological dynamic of influence. Instead, I have chosen to analyze the often problematic mediation of these sculptural and pictorial analogues within the poems. The framework of my critical interpretation, moreover, is drawn from historical evidence. That evidence suggests, first, that from the late seventeenth century through the early nineteenth aesthetic theorists were increasingly aware of distinctions between the plastic and pictorial arts and increasingly ready to use them as cultural metaphors. Second, it suggests that the poets who sought to emulate Milton used those distinctions and those metaphors to distinguish their own poetic art from his.

In spite of this partial rebellion against Bloom, however, my debt to him as a teacher and as a reader of romantic poetry is profound. Briefly chronicling the beginnings of the debt also will show the stages through which my own argument has developed. When I began applying my work in Louis Martz's graduate seminar on Milton to a paper on the changed locations for Keats's mythic figures and sanctuaries, Bloom—for whom I was writing the paper—suggested that I look at Douglas Bush's brief discussion in *Mythology and the Romantic Tradition* of Keats's phrase "stationing or statuary." Bush draws attention to one of Keats's marginal notes to *Paradise Lost*. Milton, says Keats, "pursues his imagination to the utmost . . . in what may be called his *stationing or statuary*. He is not content with simple description; he must station. So we see Adam *'Fair indeed and tall—under a plantane'* . . . and so we see Satan *'disfigured—on the Assyrian Mount.'* " In the first of Keats's passages from *Paradise Lost*, we share our viewpoint with Eve as she sees and nearly rejects Adam. In the second, I realized, we share Uriel's view as he spots Satan's self-revelation on Mount Niphates. The observer's response to the central, sculptural figure placed in the landscape thus generates a complex, often ambiguous, set of evaluations and actions in Milton's poem. These characteristic scenes from *Paradise Lost*, I discovered, become models for similar scenes not only in Keats's Miltonic poems but also in those of Blake and Shelley.

The dissertation I developed from that suggestion argued that similar moments of "stationing or statuary" in the Miltonic poems of Keats, Blake, and Shelley are models for the larger narrative or dramatic structures of those poems. That argument is the starting point of my new discussion; but its essentially spatial, formal pattern has been modified strongly by a temporal dimension. When I took up the project again several years after finishing the dissertation, I had become increasingly curious about the historical context of Keats's terms. My research led first to a connection of his "stationing or statuary" with the literature of the scenic picturesque. It then led to the discovery that his mythic plot in *Hyperion* followed a pattern of development from sculpturesque to picturesque stages of consciousness. Given currency by A. W. Schlegel and Coleridge in Keats's own historical era, this pattern itself describes a development from one historical era to another. Their theories contrast a classical Greek culture characterized by the serenity and objectivity of sculpture to its successor, a romantic, modern culture characterized by the restless subjectivity and the sharp contrast of painting. These historical analogues to the arts, I found, give shape to the historical myths developed by both Keats and Shelley; and they gave new structure to my readings not only of their Miltonic poems but of Blake's as well.

The first stage of my historical research, tracking down the sources of

Keats's critical vocabulary in his marginal note, already had led me to a new perspective on the traditional *ut pictura poesis* analogy. In comparing Milton's central figures to "statuary," Keats follows a conventional extension of *ut pictura poesis* theory to include comparisons of poetry to sculpture. His concept of "stationing" is tied more closely, though less obviously, to the comparison of poetry with painting. A "station" in eighteenth-century guides to picturesque landscape is a specific viewpoint for composing—whether in the mind's eye or on canvas—a paintinglike scene. Thus, although under far more serious moral pressure than the usual landscape painter, Eve and Uriel in *Paradise Lost* station the sculptural figures of Adam and Satan in the landscape; and they station themselves not simply as observers but as composers and interpreters of their scenes. All three romantic poets, I found, are aware of picturesque guidebooks to landscape; Keats and Shelley even use the term "station" in this picturesque sense, though not in the *Hyperion* poems or in *Prometheus Unbound*. Furthermore, placing Keats's term "station" in its context of picturesque practice and theory clarifies the way all three of these poets adapt Milton's poetic technique of "stationing or statuary"—his grouping of central figure, landscape, and observer. In this technique, each poet analyzes the relationships among a central godlike figure, a surrounding "world of Circumstances," and a witness who can "envisage circumstance, all calm," as Keats's Oceanus advises his Titans.

Yet in doing so, they do not simply continue the *ut pictura poesis* tradition. Instead, the poets make this scene the model for a historical transformation between sculpturesque and picturesque modes of consciousness. My discovery of this developmental pattern based on Schlegel and Coleridge prompted the second stage of my historically based criticism. Through a distinction between "statuary" (representing a classical and objective mode of cultural consciousness) and "stationing" (reflecting a romantic, picturesque, and subjective mode), each of these poets can define the relationship of his own poetic art to Milton's. If he claims that Milton's poetry is sculptural, his own is then "picturesque," in Schlegel's or Coleridge's sense. While Keats and Shelley make this claim, Blake develops an equally complex comparison of Milton's poetry to pictorial and his own to sculptural art.

In *Milton*, Blake develops this interplay among plastic and pictorial arts by associating the fallen elements of Milton's poetic vision with a pictorial naturalism. He first mimics that naturalism both in his illuminations and in his poetry. In schematic but still somewhat conventional ways, both arts "station" figures in landscape. Although both arts then subvert his apparently conventional representation, his poetry does so far more radically. To resolve this sibling rivalry and to redeem the external natural world Milton's Urizenic vision has helped to distort, Blake turns to sculpture, an art of outline and of touch.

In contrast, my analyses of the other three poems show that each moves from a "sculpturesque" stage to a more complex "picturesque" stage. Although this new, metaphysical definition of the picturesque grows out of the subjective framing of landscapes, it moves toward the reconciling of contraries characteristic of romantic theories of imagination. Both Keats and Shelley adapt these aesthetic analogues for historical development to define their answers to Milton's pattern of fallen yet providential history. In *Hyperion*, Keats shows a development from sculpturesque to picturesque consciousness in which the Titans—Saturn, then Hyperion—and the Olympian Apollo after them become subjective perceivers of universal process. In *The Fall of Hyperion*, each scene focuses upon a sculptural center, which forces the perceiving witness to develop the vexing contraries of a picturesque modern consciousness. Through that development, however, grows a recognition of the universal need for a dreamed-of Saturnian paradise. In *Prometheus Unbound*, the rigid sculptural figure of Prometheus yields the stage to the radiant mental forms generated by his renewed union with Asia. Their lyric dance of contraries radically redefines natural and cosmic landscapes and suggests—but does not complete—an apocalypse.

In working out the patterns of this argument, I have benefited from occasional but always stimulating conversations with Susan and Leslie Brisman and, above all, from discussions with my husband, David Goslee. Their encouragement and their probing questions are responsible for many of the clarifications in my thinking—but not for any obscurities that may remain.

Parts of Chapter 1 appeared, in earlier form, in *Studies in Romanticism* and in *Philological Quarterly;* a section of Chapter 2 was published in the *Journal of English and Germanic Philology* and another section has been accepted by *Blake Studies.* A shorter form of Chapter 3 appeared in the *Keats-Shelley Journal;* and a small part of Chapter 5 appeared in the *Comparatist.* I am grateful for permission to republish these.

I am also very grateful to the librarians of the Huntington, Bodleian, and Pforzheimer libraries for permission to examine and to describe the Shelley notebooks that contain passages from *Prometheus Unbound.* Several readers have made perceptive suggestions at various stages of the manuscript. Finally, the secretarial staff of the University of Tennessee Department of English has patiently and skillfully typed the manuscript: Dinah Brock, Irene Carey, Natalie Casby, and Norma Meredith.

Generous support for research and writing has come from the John C.

Hodges Better English Fund of the Department of English and from several Faculty Research Grants from the Graduate School at the University of Tennessee.

Uriel's Eye

One

𝕗𝕭

"Bright appearances"

Romantic Answers to *Paradise Lost*

Milton's "stationing or statuary"

When Adam hears that he must leave the Garden of Eden, the entire mythic narrative of *Paradise Lost* comes to a focus in a group of related images. Because the "hallow'd ground" of the garden is a place made holy by divine presence, Adam fears, though mistakenly, that both place and presence are now lost to him:

> . . . here I could frequent
> With worship, place by place where he voutsaf'd
> Presence Divine, and to my Sons relate;
> On this Mount he appear'd, under this Tree
> Stood visible, among these Pines his voice
> I heard, here with him at this Fountain talk'd
>
> . . . .
>
> In yonder nether World where shall I seek
> His bright appearances, or footstep trace?
>
> (11.317–22, 328–29)[1]

The angel Michael answers that God is in all places, not only on the sacred height of that mountain in Eden: "Yet doubt not but in Valley and in Plain / God is as here." His answer confirms the biblical insistence upon a God who transcends and yet moves through the forces and places of nature. After Michael grants him those prophetic visions of the fallen world and its redeemer that form so radical a contrast to the unfallen garden, Adam changes his lament to an intention for the future: he now wants "to walk / As in his presence" (12.562–63). To witness that presence, explains the archangel, Adam must substitute moral virtues for his

1

quest of forbidden knowledge: "then wilt thou not be loath / To leave this Paradise, but shalt possess / A paradise within thee, happier far" (12.586–88). Inhabited by these virtues, the paradise within will body forth the "bright appearances" of a "Presence Divine" and will give shape and meaning to a knowledge of "all Nature's works."²

Even for readers who share Milton's belief that this God of the mind's eye is the same transcendent presence who once "stood visible . . . under this Tree," Adam's lament remains poignant. For the romantic poets who challenged that belief in order to assert the power of their own minds' "bright appearances," the uncertainty of this new freedom may well have intensified Adam's sense of loss. Yet he recalls that loss as a powerful union of divine figure and place. In so doing, he provides a model for four major romantic poems that develop their own mythic figures and narratives to revise *Paradise Lost:* Blake's *Milton,* Keats's *Hyperion* poems, and Shelley's *Prometheus Unbound.*

These poets can place their mythic deities "among these Pines" or "on this Mount" through a poetic technique Keats describes in a marginal note to *Paradise Lost* as Milton's *"stationing or statuary."* Milton, Keats goes on to explain,

> is not content with simple description, he must station,—thus here we not only see how the Birds *'with clang despised the ground,'* but we see them *'under a cloud in prospect.'* So we see Adam *'Fair indeed and tall—under a plantane'—* and so we see Satan *'disfigured—on the Assyrian Mount.'*³

To suggest that their unorthodox visionary figures are real enough to rival Milton's God, the romantic poets follow the technique shown in these examples: they place or "station" their figures in natural settings acknowledged both as literary topoi and as actual places.

If Milton's "stationing" is Adam's precise visual location of his God "at this Fountain" or Uriel's revealing glimpse of Satan "disfigur'd . . . on the *Assyrian* mount" (4.126), his "statuary" is clearly that perceived figure itself. When Keats supplements "stationing" with this analogy to sculpture, he draws upon several other techniques for lending validity to the mythic figures of poetry. In the *ut pictura poesis* tradition that included Milton's minor poems and the eighteenth-century allegorical ode, writers frequently compared their central personifications to classical sculptures of the gods—gods who already had been rationalized to concepts.⁴ Because statues of Hercules typified strength, Keats could illustrate that concept by describing such a statue, as in *Sleep and Poetry.* His "might half slumb'ring on its own right arm" (l. 237) borrows its literal and symbolic stance either from the Farnese Hercules or from the Elgin Theseus.⁵ Designers of landscape gardens in the eighteenth century often placed statues of mythological figures at the end of vistas to convert their gardens to a series of literary allusions.[6] Through such momentary associations, both allegorical and mythic figures gain the empirical validity of "shap'd and palpable" marble forms, to use Keats's phrase from *Hyperion*.

Keats's *Hyperion* poems and Shelley's *Prometheus Unbound* intensify this association of the mythic figures with the visual, tactile, and historical reality of classical sculpture because the figures' names and to some extent their narratives come from Greek myth. The Michelangelesque human figure in Blake's illuminations for *Milton* also suggests a sculptural analogy for his poetic art. Even more important, Blake revises the second creation account in Genesis when he has Milton redeem his own ruined marble landscapes by sculpting a new form for Urizen out of Adamic red clay.

Most immediately, then, these four romantic revisions of *Paradise Lost* rely on "stationing or statuary" to suspend disbelief in their mythic figures. Yet sculpture and the fusion of figure and landscape in a pictorial composition are both powerful analogues that endanger the very verbal narratives whose figures they make credible. As critics long have complained, no dramatic external action takes place in Keats's *Hyperion* poems or in *Prometheus Unbound:* the figures are only magnificent statues, and Shelley's Titan does no more unbound than he did bound.[7] In Blake's *Milton*, on the other hand, the frenzied activity of the figures often has seemed a psychomachia without rules of conversion between mental and physical act or mental and physical place. If sculptural and pictorial analogues make vivid the objective presence of all these gods, they also seem to freeze their energy to act.

Much recent criticism argues that the poet's process of revising a precursor's narrative, more than the events of that revised narrative, constitutes its significant action. Harold Bloom's poetics of influence, in particular, describes a Freudian struggle between older and younger poet as a dramatic action beyond the stasis of the apparent narratives. In these metanarratives, the static characters of Saturn, Hyperion, and Prometheus become evidence of Milton's triumph over his later rivals; only in Blake's poem does Milton's triumph over Urizen become Blake's own.[8] In a revision of this view, I will argue that the stasis of these figures no longer need imply the impotence of their poets' struggle with Milton. Instead, these poets use the analogues of sculptural and pictorial art to surpass him. By redefining traditional theories of *ut pictura poesis*, moreover, Blake, Keats, and Shelley place their rivalry with Milton within the larger debate about which art could best transform this empirical "world of Circumstances."[9] Because this examination of rival arts takes place within Blake's *Milton* and Shelley's *Prometheus Unbound*, and because it structures both Keats's *Hyperion* and his *Fall of Hyperion*, significant action is not displaced entirely to a metanarrative. Instead, both the mythic characters and the poets struggle to realize the practical and ethical consequences of the aesthetic analogues they have developed.

When Keats's marginal note praises Milton's "stationing or statuary," he both continues and challenges the *ut pictura poesis* tradition. That theory usually identified plastic and pictorial arts with one another and then found a strong resemblance between those arts and poetry. Challenges to this theory during the romantic period most often proposed instead an analogy between music and poetry.[10] Because Keats uses his two terms not quite as synonyms, he suggests a critical distinction between the pictorial and sculptural analogues. In fact, all three of the romantic poets I consider revise the *ut pictura poesis* analogy by interpreting "statuary" or sculpture as an art strikingly different from painting. Instead of uncritically accepting a hackneyed comparison between poetry and painting, they are able to compare poetry either to painting or to sculpture. More specifically, as each shows the similarity of his own poetry either to sculpture or to painting, he shows the similarity of Milton's poetry to the other art. Blake argues that Milton's poetry is too pictorial and must be redeemed by Los's and his own more sculptural art; Keats and Shelley argue that Milton's magnificent and monumental epic must be humanized by a poetic art more like painting because it is more grounded in a world of natural limitation. As Keats's marginal note suggests, the analogues through which they challenge and reform Milton are implicit in his own poetry.

"Statuary" in this marginal note is clearly an analogue drawn from sculpture. "Stationing," Keats's other term, apparently required more emphasis, for he reiterated it: in Milton's "stationing or statuary," he "is not content with simple description, he must station." As an intensified mode of visual description, this term suggests a pictorial metaphor; and in his careful insistence upon using it, Keats may well have referred to its close association with the viewing of picturesque landscape. The category of the "picturesque" itself began as an analogy: originally an Italian adjective to describe natural scenes as "paintinglike," the concept had developed during the eighteenth century as a middle category between the sublime and the beautiful. Like those categories, it had become the subject of intense controversy over whether it was a quality of the external world or of the perceiver's or painter's mind. In contrast to the smooth, balanced order of the beautiful and the overwhelming, dislocating power of the sublime, the picturesque in nature or in art frequently was defined by roughness and by dramatic contrast.[11] In late eighteenth-century guidebooks to picturesque scenery, a "station" is a viewpoint from which the tourist or painter might compose the most effective—that is, the most paintinglike—scene.[12] Such a composition was most complete when it contained a central figure for scale and focus. In an actual landscape, the figure might be another tourist or a local shepherd; in a landscape painting, it might be local shepherd or visiting deity; and in landscape gardens, it might be the statue of a god at the end of a path.

Later in this chapter I will discuss more fully how Keats's term "stationing" enriches both his Milton criticism and his Miltonic poetry through its links to the scenic picturesque. First, however, I must briefly suggest how another, more explicitly analogical definition of the picturesque shapes both Keats's and Shelley's revisions of Milton. This more "metaphysical" picturesque—my term to distinguish it from the scenic version—uses the dramatic contrasts of the scenic picturesque to define a modern or romantic cultural era in dialectical opposition to a "sculpturesque" classical culture. Suggested in rough outline by Friedrich von Schiller, then developed by A. W. Schlegel in Germany and adopted by Coleridge in England, this theory argues that classical Greek culture and its arts shared the objective, unified, and serene qualities of Greek sculpture. Modern or "romantic" culture, in contrast, shares the subjective, dialectical, and restless qualities of painting—particularly the more modern genres of landscape and portrait painting.[13]

Both Keats and Shelley found this theory a compelling structure for organizing their challenges to Milton's epic of sacred history. In Keats's *Hyperion* poems, the conflict between Titans and Olympians dramatizes a dialectical opposition between the sculpturesque and the picturesque to explore theories of historical change. Shelley's *Prometheus Unbound* defines the binding and the release of Prometheus as a similar change from sculpturesque to picturesque historical eras. Although in quite different ways, then, both *Prometheus Unbound* and the *Hyperion* poems move from sculpturesque to picturesque as an appropriate model for modern consciousness. As they do so, they reject the grand style of an "objective" Miltonic epic in favor of his more subjective moments.

Blake, too, transforms the "objective" Miltonic epic even further than Milton himself suggests in book 9 of *Paradise Lost*. Writing slightly earlier than Keats and Shelley, Blake does not avail himself of Schlegel's developmental theory of aesthetic history. His dialectical habit of mind, however, finds expression in a similar struggle between pictorial and sculptural analogues to his own poetic art. Thus he too draws upon these analogues of the sister arts to define his vision against past historical eras. In contrast to Keats and Shelley, however, he associates Milton's poetry with a naturalistic and hence falsely objective stationing of characters in an external world—the world defined by Mosaic and Newtonian law. In his poem a sculpture or statuary based on touch becomes a metaphoric process through which both Blake and his character Milton redeem their poetic vision.

The chapter on Blake's *Milton* is the most logical place to analyze more closely his definition of sculpture as a separate art and his own critical version of an antiscenic stationing both in his illuminations and in his poetry. Similarly, the chapter on Keats's *Hyperion* will analyze Schlegel's sculpturesque and picturesque analogues and will suggest how these analogues order myth in *Hyperion, The Fall of Hyperion*, and *Prometheus Unbound*. In further sections of this introductory chapter I will, first, trace the development of "stationing" as a term from Milton, through eighteenth-century writers on landscape, to Keats. Second, I will look briefly at three lyrics that can act as test cases for the very different versions of stationing used by these poets. Blake's lyric is in fact a preface to his *Milton*, but the others too make effective prefaces for the longer poems, as their speakers translate figure and natural landscape into a redemptive architecture—for these lyrics the symbol of a redeemed human culture. Finally, I will analyze closely Keats's climactic example of Milton's "stationing or statuary," in which "Uriel's eye" discovers "Satan 'disfigured—on the Assyrian Mount.' " Because that scene is a dramatic paradigm for all four of these romantic revisions of *Paradise Lost*, I will borrow Uriel's angelic perspective long enough to survey their adaptations of it.

"Stationing" and the Scenic Picturesque

Frequent use of the term "station" during the seventeenth and eighteenth centuries manifests its close association with the changing significance of landscape and particularly with the aesthetics of the scenic picturesque. Beginning as the location of a figure temporarily static in the landscape or larger universe, "station" also develops as a synonym for a perceiver's "point of view" toward landscape or more specifically toward the conjunction of figure and landscape. Thus the term refers both to the placing of a statuelike object in the landscape and to the subjective perceiver. Further, from Milton's poetry on, these objective and subjective definitions are related to one another because the perceiver evaluates the mutually defining relationship of objective figure and natural landscape. For this reason "stationing" as a critical term might be understood in part as an anticipation of Henry James's narrative point of view. As James and later critics use it, however, point of view usually refers to a narrator's limited insight into the minds of other characters.[14] As Keats draws upon the usage of "station" from Milton and the eighteenth century, he indeed develops a version of the Jamesian meaning. He retains, however, the importance of natural landscape as problematic and yet validating context for the mythic or visionary figures located in it and for the perceivers who see them there.

Like Keats's marginal note, eighteenth-century controversies over the picturesque are haunted by Milton's descriptions of landscape. As many a philosophic gardening manual or guidebook pointed out during this period, gardeners, painters, and poets alike were attempting to regain a lost paradise.[15] To see how the pictureque, already influenced by Milton, became a way for these romantic poets to free themselves of the same influence, we first must survey the use of "station" as a specific term between Milton and Keats. That survey leads, particularly through Wordsworth's writings, to an analysis of controversial concepts in picturesque theory that can in turn clarify the use of "stationing" as a poetic technique.

Changes in the terms "station" and "stationing" reflect a broader change from a vertical and hierarchical model of the universe to a more horizontal model defined by the viewer's perspective upon landscape.[16] Milton's own use of "stationing" makes visible both the specific hierarchical levels of his universe and also the violations of that hierarchy. Although the most common meaning of "station" as a place in a hierarchy was then, as now, a definition of social status (Old English Dictionary), Milton describes physical hierarchies to illustrate his metaphysical chain of being. The divine creator first organizes this formal, spatial structure and then releases its energies: in *Paradise Lost* 3.583, the sun's "Magnetic beam . . . Shoots invisible virtue even to the deep; / So wondrously was set his Station bright"; and in 7.563, "The Planets in thir station list'ning stood."[17] Frequently this hierarchical meaning slides into the military sense of battle stations, but these military positions also moralize space as they relate unfallen to fallen figures. Raphael tells Adam in 7.146 that "far the greater part [of the angels] have kept . . . Thir station" and not rebelled. At the end of the poem Gabriel arrives to escort the fallen Adam and Eve from Eden, and "from the . . . Hill / To thir fixt Station, all in bright array, / The Cherubim descended . . ." (12.627ff.). Two other evocations of a military hierarchy, both in a hellish context, define "station" as an observation post and thus point toward eighteenth-century usage. In 2.412, Satan warns his forces of the "strict Sentaries and Stations thick / Of Angels watching round"; and in 10.535, the narrator gleefully anticipates Satan's emergence from Pandemonium as a serpent:

in "th' open Field . . . all left of that revolted Rout / Heav'n-fallen, in station stood or just array, / Sublime with expectation when to see / In Triumph issuing forth thir Glorious Chief."

In *Paradise Regained*, Milton characteristically joins spatial metaphor to theological meaning in a passage Blake later illustrated. As "Satan fell," angels "received" Christ

> From his uneasy station, and upbore
> As on a floating couch through the blithe Air,
> Then in a flow'ry valley set him down.
>
> (4.584–86)

By implication, Christ's new station "in a flow'ry valley" is far easier than his difficult physical and moral stance on the temple's pinnacle. With the possible exception of the passage from *Paradise Lost*, book 12, noted above, however, Milton uses the word "station" not so much to place his figures in natural landscapes as to measure their moral and spiritual height and depth.

Although hierarchical meanings continued well into Keats's time, "station" gradually began to describe first the location of objects in the natural world and then the perceiver's act of composing a scene of these two elements. Examples of this transitional usage come from two related groups of writers, both of whom see the excursion into the natural world as a means of discovering human value. When James Thomson and William Wordsworth write excursion poetry, they draw upon Milton's epic blank verse to establish the seriousness of their intentions. When William Gilpin and Thomas West write guidebooks for tourists in search of the picturesque, they frequently allude to Milton's scenes to give literary as well as painterly significance to their recommended views.

Borrowing Milton's style to praise the hierarchical order of nature, Thomson uses "station" almost as Milton does. In *The Seasons*, however, the visible agents of that order are not divine or angelic, but personified natural forces:

> . . . sober Evening takes
> Her wonted station in the middle air,
> A thousand shadows at her beck.[18]

In these lines Evening's intermediate station in both space and time is far more essential to her definition than is Christ's station in Milton's passage above. It is also more spatially exact than the sun's "Station bright" and is thus closer to Keats's examples from *Paradise Lost* of a "stationing or statuary" in which landscape and figure define each other's significance.

Thomson's stationing differs from those of Miltonic examples, however, because his central figure personifies a passing temporal moment. To define it, he presents Evening as a conventional goddess with a train of visual attributes as attendants. Those "thousand shadows," moreover, create an intermediate lighting analogous to her location in "middle air." He thus blends the "statuesque object of sight" with its naturalistic surroundings in a way his contemporaries found too radically fluid, but he retains the personification's hierarchical role as an intermediate ruler in nature.[19]

Wordsworth's excursion poetry also offers some striking examples of the term "station," but, because these follow and are influenced by the cult of the picturesque, we first should look at the guidebooks that promoted this cult. To point out the best vantage points for viewing a landscape as a painting, the writers of these guidebooks identified "stations" along their suggested routes. Thomas West's *Guide to the Lakes* uses this device in a way that inevitably would impress both that term and that habit of observation upon his readers. As his preface claims, "the writer has here collected . . . all the select stations and points of view, noticed by those authors who have last made the tour of the lakes, verified by his own repeated observations. He has also added remarks on the principal objects, as they appear viewed from the different stations." Later in his text, he characteristically points out a view: "Station III. A third station, on this side, will be found by keeping along the line of shore. . . . Here . . . all that is grand and beautiful in the environs, lie before you in a beautiful order and natural disposition."[20] In his wording, West maintains an uneasy balance between the possibility that the perceiver creates the scene through viewpoint and the opposing possibility that landscape already contains that arranged scene.

As his concluding phrase suggests, the search for a divine or quasi-divine order within nature has not disappeared. In fact, West emphasizes this aspect by fusing two different passages from *Paradise Lost*, quoting them—without book and line numbers—as epigraph. The first three and a half lines describe the garden as Raphael sees it on his errand of warning (5.294–97). The last one (4.247) comes from Satan's earlier approach, as he "with new wonder now . . . views . . . A Heaven on Earth" (4.205, 208):

. . . For Nature here
Wantoned as in her prime, and played at will
Her virgin fancies
Wild above rule or art [and beauteous form'd]
A happy rural seat of various view.

(4.247)

Yet West and other advocates of the picturesque, particularly William Gilpin, cannot always be satisfied by a wanton "Nature . . . wild above rule or art." Before the fall her "virgin fancies" could not disorder the universe. In this fallen world, these writers preferred that Nature follow the rules of human art.[21] To the extent that the "stations" lead to static views often carefully framed by flanking hills or by ruins, they confirm the tendency to value the composed roughness of a picture over the unexpected roughness of an actual landscape. Although West's fragmentary passages from *Paradise Lost* celebrate the observer's discovery of a paradise, the practical effect of his "stations" and the picturesque cult of landscape was to emphasize the perceiver's creative role—or at worst the perceiver's copying of the guide's creative role.

While Gilpin does not use West's formal structure of "Station I" and so on in his series of *Observations relative chiefly to picturesque beauty*, he frequently uses the term "station" both as a noun and as a verb to tell his readers where to stand. Although the frequency of the term varies from one work to another it is quite high in his early *Observations* made in the Highlands. This work, his even earlier *Observations* on the Lake Country, and West's guide might well have been consulted by Keats and Charles Brown in planning their northern trip.[22]

For Keats's purposes, however, Wordsworth provides the most significant link between the word "station" and the picturesque. Not only did he write a Lake Country guide of his own, but he also included the term's picturesque usage in poetry Keats had read. Although modern readers familiar with Wordsworth's criticism of the picturesque in *The Prelude* will find this suggestion of positive influence startling, we must remind ourselves of that poem's 1850 publication date. Even though Wordsworth included the critical passage in the 1805 *Prelude*, we have no evidence for Keats's knowing that version. Because it raises important issues about the larger significance of the picturesque, I will consider it a little later in that context. At this point, it is the origin of Keats's perspective that requires further tracing.

Wordsworth owned copies of all these Gilpin works mentioned above. From them and other such works he assimilated the term "station" to use in his own *Guide Through the District of the Lakes*, published anonymously in 1810 as the introduction to Joseph Wilkinson's *Select Views in Cumberland, Westmoreland, and Lanchashire*.[23] Mary Moorman gives the impression that the authorship of the guide was no secret.[24] If Wordsworth had not told his contemporaries of his authorship, they might have guessed from the lines of his own poetry, unpublished but unmistakable, scattered through the text. His use of "station" and its frequent synonym, a vantage or "elevated point," suggests his debt to West and Gilpin.[25] At the beginning of the

1810 introduction, for example, Wordsworth asks the reader "to place himself in imagination upon some given point . . . or rather let him suppose his station to be a cloud hanging midway between . . . two mountains."

Although the word "station" also occurs in several of Wordworth's shorter poems available to Keats, it is particularly striking in *The Excursion*. As the title suggests, this poem continues the locodescriptive tradition linked both to Milton's *L'Allegro* and *Il Penseroso* and to the picturesque. Its significance as a narrative model for all three later poets increases through the Prospectus published with it, a passage in Miltonic blank verse announcing Wordsworth's intention to rival not only the earlier poet but the earlier poet's creative god. Three passages show how emphatically Wordsworth "stations" in *The Excursion*. Early in the first book he describes the first appearance of the Wanderer: "Him had I marked the day before—alone / And stationed in the public way, with face / Turned toward the sun then setting" (1.38–40).[26] Here the Wanderer is seen as object; later he becomes perceiving subject as he remembers "What visionary powers of eye and soul / In youth were mine; when stationed on the top / Of some huge hill—expectant, I beheld / The sun rise up" (4.111–14). The term also characterizes the poem's final association of high place, visionary power, and special qualities of light in the Pastor's "vesper-service" on the "exalted station" of a "grassy mountain" (9.756).

Keats's own uses of "stationing" as a term outside his marginalia are few. With one exception, they give little hint of how we might interpret his marginal note. In a letter commiserating with Benjamin Bailey over the delay in his friend's ordination, "station" carries its frequent sense of place in a social hierarchy. Yet Keats's phrasing, converting people to abstractions of their ranks, takes on a mock-Miltonic grandeur as it echoes Satan's addresses to his cohorts: "The Stations and Grandeurs of the World have taken it into their heads that they cannot commit themselves toward and [*sic*] inferior in rank."[27] The only use of the term in his poetry, a late one, shows a similar awareness of spatial metaphor, this time to give local habitation to music: "Cunningly-station'd music dies and swells / In echoing places . . ." (*Cap and Bells*, ll. 568–71).[28] *Ut musica poesis* becomes *ut pictura poesis*, though in a poem too weak to make the case fully convincing.

More convincing is a letter written as Keats was working on the Miltonic *Hyperion*. Halfway between Milton's uses of the term and the one in Keats's note, it may even help us to date the note itself:

I feel more and more every day, as my imagination strengthens, that I do not live in this world alone but in a thousand worlds—No sooner am I alone than shapes of epic greatness are stationed around me, and serve my Spirit the office of which is equivalent to a king's bodyguard—then "Tragedy, with sceptr'd pall, comes sweeping by" According to my state of mind I am with Achilles shouting in the Trenches or with Theocritus in the Vales of Sicily.[29]

The shapes who serve as bodyguard resemble the militant angels of *Paradise Lost*. Surrounded by them, the poet sees himself as a central, throned figure like Thomson's Evening, surrounded with attendants. Both earlier and later in the passage he enters their worlds: "with Achilles shouting in the Trenches or with Theocritus in the Vales of Sicily." In so doing, he reenacts the placing of figures "in prospect," as in his marginal note. The single statuesque "shape" or figure—Achilles or Theocritus—is placed in a landscape that both typifies and extends his significance.[30]

Both kinds of images, the poet surrounded by epic shapes and the shapes or figures themselves stationed in their realms, seem to exemplify the way W. J. Bate interprets Keats's use of stationing in his own poetry: a "massive centering of image," an "ideal of poetry as 'might half slumb'ring on its own right arm.' "[31] These descriptions emphasize the central figure as "statuary"; yet the examples of "Achilles shouting in the Trenches" and "Theocritus in the Vales of Sicily," as well as Keats's examples from *Paradise Lost* in the marginal note, show that the definition also should include setting. In other words, "might half slumb'ring on its own right arm," Keats's definition of poetry in *Sleep and Poetry*, might be considered a partial example of stationing but not a full one; it includes only gesture and pose.[32] In his examples from Milton, as in this letter, the placing of figure in landscape resembles the picturesque habit of placing a figure as object in a defining scene.

Explicit in Keats's letter above and implicit in the passages he cites from *Paradise Lost* is a third element necessary to Keats's concept of stationing, the subject or observer: "I am with Achilles. . . ." As pointed out earlier, this element is essential to the "station" in West, Gilpin, and Wordsworth: a viewpoint for composing a scene as an artistic whole. The examples from these writers show that a "station" can refer either to an object placed as focus within the scene, like a piece of statuary, or to the viewpoint taken by the perceiving subject. Thus the term is a fertile one for Keats's synthesis of figure, landscape, and observer.

Keats's acquaintance with the literature of the picturesque and particularly with the guidebooks of West, Gilpin, and Wordsworth must be based on conjecture. Because the letter describing "shapes of epic greatness . . . stationed around me" and probably the marginalia as well follow his trip to the Lake Country and Scotland in the summer of 1818, this usage of "station" may well have resulted from his reading of such picturesque guides to prepare for the trip.[33] Charles Brown, his walking companion, tells friends at the end of the trip that they "can read all about [Loch Lomond] in one of the fashionable guidebooks"; and Keats repeatedly mocks the picturesque tourist in his letters. This mocking, however, often precedes his own sustained descriptions of landscape. All through the northern tour he writes attentively of its scenery to his brother Tom.[34] His mockery of the scenic picturesque as an explicit attitude and yet his adoption of its terms and some of its elements can be explained both in the context of Wordsworth's similar ambivalence and in the larger context of modern evaluations of the picturesque. Its very ambiguity, moreover, makes it useful.

In contrast to Wordsworth's recurrent use of stationing in his guide and in *The Excursion*, his earlier *Prelude* attacks picturesque habits of viewing landscape as the "barren intermeddling subtleties" of a "despotic" eye. "Through presumption," Wordsworth writes in book 12, he found himself, "giving way / To a comparison of scene with scene," and so becoming

. . . to the moods
Of time and season, to the moral power,
The affections and the spirit of the place,
Insensible. Nor only did the love
Of sitting thus in judgment interrupt
My deeper feelings, but another cause,
More subtle and less easily explained,
That almost seems inherent in the creature,
A twofold frame of body and of mind.

(12.118–26)[35]

Following Wordsworth, Martin Price criticizes all the adherents of the picturesque for a "failure of moral sympathy" and for a "dissociation" among the faculties of the perceiving mind.[36] Samuel Monk in *The Sublime* similarly writes of "that total ignoring of the emotive quality of landscape that is characteristic of the picturesque school."[37] Such a failure, he argues, results from the way in which the picturesque "intervened between the individual and the object" by supplying artistic preconceptions inapplicable to the actual scene. His criticism corresponds to Wordsworth's complaint of "barren intermeddling subtleties" that prompt the viewer to judge one scene against another. It also echoes the objections of Brown and Keats to the fashionable predictability in picturesque viewing.

Thus two possible objections to the picturesque emerge, both based on a sort of dissociation: the picturesque attitude blocks an accurate, "objective" view of nature by mental frames and preconceptions; and, even if this problem is overcome, it blocks the perceiver's integrated response to an external but value-engendering nature.

Wordsworth overcomes these dissociations of the picturesque in several ways. Answering the crisis of book 11, he praises the "spots of time" when "feeling comes in aid of feeling" (*Prelude* 12.269–70), when all other senses and emotions check the tyranny of sight and "outward sense." In "Tintern Abbey" he also celebrates "a motion and spirit, that impels / All thinking things, all objects of all thought, / And rolls through all things."[38] Although horizontal in perspective, this motion or spirit, like the hierarchical working up to spirit Raphael describes in *Paradise Lost* (5.468–505), reconciles mind to the external world. Although both solutions overcome dissociation, the first unifies the subjective self to celebrate its dominance over nature; the second celebrates a union between the mind and nature through a motion that inhabits both.

The art historian Heinrich Wolfflin suggests, however, that even the patterns of visual imagery in landscape painting may not be tyrannical but creative. Contrasting the objective scene from which the painter begins to a subjectively perceived movement in the scene, Wolfflin defines that movement as the picturesque effect:

> Over the solid, static body of things there will always play the stimulus of a movement which does not reside in the object, and that also means that the whole only exists as a *picture* for the eye, and that it can never, even in the imaginary sense, be grasped with the hands.[39]

This "movement which does not reside in the object," but which the viewer perceives through compositional arrangement, is repeated and intensified as the picturesque observer of landscape, like Gilpin or West, moves from one station to another. Each scene "composed" through the observer's stance or station possesses that subjective movement described by Wolfflin, and the sequence of such scenes, formed for example by the observer's walking around the lake and pausing at several different stations, creates a second, larger pattern of motion also dependent on the observer's point of view. Both the compositional motion and the motion of the spectator impose not only human order but a human movement on the "solid, static body of things."

Although Martin Price, too, criticizes the dissociative tendencies in the picturesque, he ultimately argues in "The Picturesque Moment" that its formulation of those problems led to the later development of the romantic imagination as a synthetic, reconciling force. His point can be developed in two apparently opposed ways. First, the very dissociations of the scenic picturesque criticized by Wordsworth and modern theorists, reflecting the tyranny of the eye, can become analytical metaphors for these poets' criticisms of Milton, for they are reflected in the dissociating rivalry among the sister arts of painting, sculpture, and poetry mentioned earlier. Second, the synthetic romantic imagination that arises to overcome these dissociations is in Coleridge's definition of a reconciliation of opposites closely related to Schlegel's metaphysical "picturesque" or romantic consciousness. This modern consciousness builds upon the paintinglike visual synthesis of figure, landscape, and perceiver as a model for its broader reconciliations.

"Stationing" as Poetic Technique: Three Lyric Prefaces to Epic

The lesson in stationing that Keats learns from Milton, reinforced by the eighteenth-century convergence of *ut pictura poesis* associations, description, and picturesque focusing of such description, is immediately obvious in the odes written between the two *Hyperion* poems. His "Ode to Psyche," hymning a figure poised between mythic deity and personified abstraction, exemplifies the technique of stationing Keats develops more extensively for his ambiguously divine Titans:

> . . . Surely I dreamt to-day, or did I see
> The winged Psyche with awaken'd eyes?
> I . . .
> . . . .
> Saw two fair creatures, couched side by side
> On deepest grass, beneath the whisp'ring roof
> Of leaves and trembled blossoms, where there ran
> A brooklet, scarce espied. . . .
> They lay calm-breathing on the bedded grass.
>
> (ll. 5–7, 9–13)

In the first two lines, Keats announces a recurrent problem for all the odes, the search for a context in which he may evaluate imagination, vision, or dream—all powers or products of "the winged Psyche." His resolution in this ode, "To build a fane," a "rosy sanctuary . . . in some untrodden region of the mind," clearly echoes and internalizes the "blissful Bower . . . Chos'n by the sovran Planter" in *Paradise Lost* 4.690–92. This mental enclosure may seem a retreat from the "deepest grass" and "whisp'ring roof / Of leaves" in the first stanza, as its subjectivity is a retreat from the objectivity of Saturn's fallen station, "Deep in the shady sadness of a vale," at the opening of *Hyperion*. Nevertheless, its carefully ambiguous portrayal of "the warm Love" that may enter through the "casement ope at night" is a final, liminal stationing that escapes from solipsism. Simultaneously it confirms the two mythic figures glimpsed in the first stanza and admits that if Love is a power beyond the individual mind, neither it nor Psyche need fear that their existence as powers, not deities, is a lesser role.[40] It also looks forward to the complex arguments over the relation of dream to reality in *The Fall of Hyperion* and to the changing locations that symbolize those arguments: from rosy sanctuary to almost deserted fane, to Moneta's mind, and again to Saturn's vale.

Blake could not have known of Keats's marginal comments, nor does he use the word "station" as Keats does. Yet he develops a poetic technique similar to the Miltonic stationing Keats points out and practices: an observer sees a central mythic figure in landscape and attempts to persuade himself, by a kind of topographical metonymy, that the figure is both present and really existent. The most striking and also the most familiar example of this technique appears in his prefatory lyric to *Milton*.[41] So familiar is the confident tone of its conclusion, in fact, that readers tend to overlook the undercurrent of doubt in its apparently rhetorical questions. Both that undercurrent and the situation that causes it strongly resemble those in the "Ode to Psyche":

> And did those feet in ancient time.
> Walk upon Englands mountains green:
> And was the holy Lamb of God,
> On Englands pleasant pastures seen!
>
> And did the Countenance Divine
> Shine forth upon our clouded hills?
> And was Jerusalem builded here,
> Among these dark Satanic Mills?[42]

The elliptical questions that shape the lyric's first two stanzas assume a vision common to singer and audience. Yet as questions, even if only rhetorical ones, they call into doubt the validity of that vision. In their cryptic syntax, the opening lines also give the song a sense of coming after something not fully known or only half remembered. The antecedent for "those feet" is clearly "Jesus our Lord," named at the end of the preceding preface: "those Worlds of Eternity in which we shall live forever: in Jesus our Lord."[43] Yet the prose preface places us in Worlds of Eternity and those worlds in "Jesus our Lord"; the lyric places the divine figure in a temporal landscape.

Although the poet locates the figure and the pastorally idealized "green & pleasant Land" within England, this realism does not dominate the first stanza. Instead, the traditional pastoral images reinforce the singer's stationing of the figure in an indeterminate, mythic "ancient time." The singer's own viewpoint completes the blending of realism and mythic sublimity in his scene, for the figure is incomplete—as if his observer, lower in the landscape, can glimpse only the feet, or as if the figure itself is vast enough to use mountains as stepping-stones.[44] In contrast, the lamb in the third line does not transform the spatial and temporal scale of "Englands . . . pastures"; its very lack of dominance, its passive enclosure within the setting, anticipates the transformed tone of the second stanza.

There, the irony implicit in the "holy Lamb of God," once pastoral but now sacrificial, becomes bitterly evident. The parallel structure of the speaker's questions defines with increasing sureness the divine nature of the appearances he catalogues, yet the landscape in which he attempts to station them is radically changed.[45] That desecrated landscape turns the apparently rhetorical questions of the second stanza to real ones that undermine the idyllic perfection of the first. At a second reading, the questions here seem to become as rhetorical as those in the first stanza, because the obvious and expected answer to their irony is an emphatic "No." Yet the real question cuts between these symmetrical stanzas and their rhetoric of conventional response: what has changed these "mountains green" to "clouded hills," and "Englands pleasant pastures" into mill towns that imitate hell? Blake makes the answer inescapable: the clouded hills are "ours," and it is "here" that "these dark . . . Mills" are built. Through the greater realism and more urgent tone of his description both poet and audience enter the poem's suffocatingly immediate landscapes of experience.

Almost immediately, however, Blake attempts to suggest a redemptive countermovement; he does not return to his opening vision of a divine figure in a natural paradise but turns instead to the more fully human design of the city of God. Both the mills and the new Jerusalem enclose the human societies whose values they express. Further, both depend upon human work for their realization. As it encounters the gritty and actual presence of its traditional antagonist in England's pastures and hills, the new Jerusalem changes from a transcendent but private vision to a project made possible by human relationship and interdependent action. With the lyric, yet ironic, indignation of "And was Jerusalem builded . . . ?" the poet has persuaded us that it should be done, and without wasted time.

As the more abrupt rhythm of the third stanza gives dramatic urgency to these questions, it emphasizes the individual action through which their irony must be dispelled. In a traditional invocation, the poet calls for the gifts to make his vision effective. The personal focus of his demand almost seems to contradict the social awareness and desire for reform shown in the preceding verse. Yet it is precisely the insistent repetition of "Bring me," the passionate intensity of his phrasing, that breaks through the formality of tradition to bring the symbolic gifts for which he asks: "my Bow of burning gold," "my Arrows of desire," "my Chariot of fire." Finally, these imperatives change the earlier questioning of a divine presence in the landscape to a suggestion of affirmation: this assurance is in one sense exactly the gift he needs. The message and the answer become the same: by prophesying, not only does he become a prophet but he may become an even more powerful, more militant version of the Christ he so tentatively stations in the landscape of his stanza.[46]

Powerful and exhilarating as it is, however, the third stanza does not make its claim to godhead absolute. For all the intensity of the speaker's demand, the chariot remains for the moment concealed behind the clouds, as Hyperion's will do in Keats's poem. Yet because this singer does not begin as a sun-god, the uncertainty shows no loss of power but an openness to its presence in the future. And because the clouds have not yet unfolded, because Noah's rainbow has not yet been given him to wield, the singer need not yet confront the crucial problem of belief in the validity of such an appearance or the deification he demands.[47]

Although the fourth stanza places the promise of such resolution clearly in the future, at the same time it affirms the continuity of active effort that will bring it about:

> I will not cease from Mental Fight,
> Nor shall my Sword sleep in my hand:
> Till we have built Jerusalem
> In Englands green & pleasant Land.

In contrast to the passive voice of "was Jerusalem builded here, / Among these dark Satanic Mills?" his building appears as active and actual as Nehemiah's and Ezra's biblical account of the historical rebuilding.[48] The song moves from the poet's dream alone to the common dream and the shared effort. Yet the turn from the "I" in the first line to the "we" in the third, however necessary, is still conditional. In his image of "Mental Fight," the sword is the weapon of the engraver who might persuade his people to build a renewed society. Finally, he makes it explicit in the conditional phrasing of the verse from Numbers that follows the song: "Would to God that all the Lords people were Prophets."

When they become so, the exodus during which Moses makes his declaration will cease to be the type for the divine figures awaited by the poet. Christ's feet will appear again in England, as they do in the visionary moment that completes *Milton:* "Jesus . . . walked forth / From Felphams Vale" (E:143.42.19–20). Jerusalem, too, will appear, though her return from exile in Blake's final poem as a human form more than as a city signals an apocalyptic transformation beyond that of the earlier poem. In this lyric, the arrival of the city of Jerusalem does not annihilate the earth but instead redeems it. Reversing the stationing of his opening stanza, in which mountains and pastures validated the mythic figure, Blake now envisions the city giving renewed color and vitality to the landscape's darkened features. The idealizing adjectives of the first stanza now prophesy for the place as well as for the city to be built there a redemption without irony: "Jerusalem / In Englands green & pleasant Land."

Although Blake's lyric preface to *Milton* resolves its ironies of location, the poem it introduces makes them far more explicit in order to challenge Milton's mistakenly authoritarian universe. Shelley's "Ode to Liberty," written in 1820 and published with *Prometheus Unbound* the same year, praises Milton for witnessing the elusive figure of Liberty, but like Blake it places the origins of his redemptive divine figure in a past culture that Milton attempted and failed to recreate. Even more explicitly than in *Prometheus Unbound*, Shelley's cultural ideal is Periclean Athens. The difficulty of visualizing either this cultural ideal or the presence of Liberty, "the lightning of the nations," can be measured by Shelley's use of "station" in the opening stanza. Lifted by the medium of his song to catch sight of this "contagious fire" in "the sky," the poet's soul "from its station in the heaven of fame" is carried still higher by a "Spirit"; but neither position in a hierarchy of poets (a Miltonic use of "station") nor scenic vantage point (a picturesque one) yields him vision. Instead, a "voice from the deep" tells him of Liberty's intermittent manifestations. Literally from the Mediterranean that lies between Shelley and revolutionary Spain, the voice also speaks from an abyss of creative potentiality like Demogorgon's cave.[49]

In the most striking of these manifestations of Liberty, Shelley's "voice" returns to visual images and to traditional patterns of height as a source of vision. Yet the location only gradually becomes actual. His three successive descriptions of Athens in stanza 5 enact a kind of visionary stationing that validates itself by evoking natural landscape and then transforming it:

> Athens arose: a city such as vision
>   Builds from the purple crags and silver towers
> Of battlemented cloud, as in derision

Of kingliest masonry: the ocean-floors
Pave it; the evening sky pavilions it;
    Its portals are inhabited
    By thunder-zoned winds, each head
Within its cloudy wings with sunfire garlanded,—
    A divine work!

(ll. 61–69)

"Athens arose," Shelley begins, like Thebes built to music, or Milton's
Pandemonium. Does he describe in these first nine lines a visionary city,
or an actual city but one "such as vision builds"? The answer remains
open. Whether the visionary city is literal or the vehicle of a simile,
however, it is built from natural elements that also form a sublimely
expansive location for the vision.

From these natural and external materials for vision, Shelley's second
description of the city (ll. 69–71) begins as an apparently realistic architectural portrayal; realistic stationing of the city in an actual place, however,
is delayed until the third, final description (ll. 72–75):

. . . Athens diviner yet
    Gleamed with its crest of columns, on the will
Of man, as on a mount of diamonds, set;
    For thou wert, and thine all-creative skill
Peopled with forms that mock the eternal dead
    In marble immortality that hill
Which was thine earliest throne and latest oracle.

(ll. 69–75)

Sense and sound suggest that "its crest of columns" will be stationed on a
"hill." Yet that rhyme is delayed—and the city remains stationed in the
mind. Again the simile holds out the promise of a stable spatial location—
"as on a mount"—but playfully replaces an external, topographical stability with a fantastic, jewellike permanence recalling medieval romance.

In his third and final stationing of the city, Shelley finally uses the
expected rhyme "hill" to place Athens in an actual landscape. An earlier
art than his own poetic metonymy, however, completes the building of
the city, for the "all-creative skill" of Liberty "Peopled with forms that
mock the eternal dead / In marble immortality that hill."[50] Only after a
liberated human art has created the city as cultural artifact does it claim
and at the same time transform its own earthbound place, "that hill."
Behind the human forms of the sculptures wrought by a free and freely
creative people, Liberty almost appears as a larger "human form divine"
whose "earliest throne and latest oracle" is the Acropolis.

Yet finally we must infer Liberty's "human form" only from the forms molded by the human sculptors she inspires. Later in the ode Shelley suggests that Milton may have seen her, yet his insight is spiritual, not physical:

. . . not unseen
Before the spirit-sighted countenance
    Of Milton didst thou pass, from the sad scene
    Beyond whose night he saw, with a dejected mien.

(ll. 147–50)

Furthermore, Liberty passes from the "sad scene" of this earth with a poignant untouchability and invisibility like that Milton describes in the sonnet to his "late espoused wife." Although he sees "Beyond the night" of his own physical blindness to glimpse her passing, and although he also sees beyond the night of a "scene" unenlightened by Liberty, we still see his "spirit-sighted countenance" become a "dejected mien." He seems to glimpse her stationed neither in this sad scene nor in some happier realm but as she moves from a physical to a spiritual scene where even his spiritual sight cannot follow her very far. Instead, with Shelley's repeated insistence upon Milton's own "countenance" and "mien," we begin to see him, instead of Liberty, as a sculptural object—but one that, like Keats's Moneta, remains profoundly aware of his loss. Neither Liberty nor Milton, however, appears to us as concretely as Adam "Fair indeed and tall—under a plantane" or Satan "disfigured—on the Assyrian Mount," the examples of Milton's own stationing cited by Keats. Nor are they located as precisely in a specific landscape as are Keats's Psyche or Blake's Christ. If the lines praise Milton's understanding of Liberty, they also leave room in this "sad scene" for a less shadowy, more plastic realization of Liberty's Athenian sculpting.

As each of these lyrics develops versions of Milton's "stationing or statuary," the transcendent figure witnessed by the singer brings the creative energy to build a redeemed architecture and thus to organize landscape into forms of human art. Thinking he may have seen Psyche, Keats's speaker can build a "rosy sanctuary" that rivals Milton's, though in the "wild ridged" mountains of the mind. Convincing himself of the presence of Christ's feet and even laying claim to the "Chariot of fire" wielded by Milton's Christ, Blake's singer will complete the task Milton and his puritans could not, to build "Jerusalem / In Englands green & pleasant Land." In the "Ode to Liberty," Shelley's voice from the deep gives Milton the power to see the presence of Liberty behind her radiant energy, but it suggests that Athens manifested her presence even more fully and that she continues, through her art's inspiration, to do so. This is an argument similar to the one Shelley had just used in *Prometheus Unbound*, in which the Greek Prometheus corrects Milton's magnificent but flawed vision of human capability. In the longer works through which these three poets revise *Paradise Lost*, these images of a redemptive architecture are still present but less central. Instead, each of the longer works develops a more extended confrontation between the picturing witness and the tableau of sculptural mythic figure in natural landscape; and this confrontation becomes the means for examining larger cultural and historical patterns. Milton's Uriel, who witnesses Satan "disfigured— on the Assyrian Mount," suggests a model for this confrontation.

"Angel's ken": Models for Epic Revision

"—and so we see Satan '*disfigured—on the Assyrian Mount.*' " This passage, Keats's concluding example of "stationing or statuary" from his marginal note to *Paradise Lost*, illustrates Milton's own skill at revealing a moment of dissociation between moral and aesthetic values. When "on *Niphates*' top he lights" (*Paradise Lost* 3.742), Satan resembles for a poised moment the statue of a classical god. To ask directions from Uriel, he had changed "his proper shape" to that of "a stripling Cherub," in whose "face / Youth smil'd Celestial, and to every Limb / Suitable grace diffus'd" (3.636–38). Although winged like a Victory, he resembles a young Apollo or Dionysus—or perhaps the Donatello David. Because "Eden . . . now in his view / Lay pleasant" (4.28–29), his stance as per- ceiver, though not his objectively seen figure, resembles that of the biblical patriarchs who gained prophetic mountain visions. When Uriel sees him, however, it becomes clear that Milton has evoked both prophet as perceiving subject and classical god as sculptural object in order himself to "disfigure" Satan on the Assyrian Mount. This complex disfiguring is, first of all, a model for Milton's organization of the larger forms of his own narrative; and, second, it points to the ways Keats, Blake, and Shelley organize their emulations of *Paradise Lost*.

The context of this passage from book 4 shows how thoroughly Keats had its telescopelike perspectives in mind when he defined "stationing or statuary." Satan is on the wing,

> Yet not anough had practis'd to deceive
> *Uriel* once warn'd; whose eye pursu'd him down
> The way he went, and on th' *Assyrian* mount

Saw him disfigur'd, more than could befall
Spirit of happy sort: his gestures fierce
He mark'd and mad demeanor, then alone,
As he suppos'd, all unobserv'd, unseen.

(4.124–30)

Working through the angelic agency of Uriel, Milton "pursues" Satan in still another repetition of his fall. This time the angel's pursuit, like the narrator's, is not physical but visual and psychological. When it ends with the stationing of that once-heroic figure on the mountaintop, Satan betrays to Uriel the discovery he has just made about himself:

Which way I fly is Hell: myself am Hell;
And in the lowest deep a lower deep
Still threat'ning to devour me opens wide,
To which the Hell I suffer seems a Heaven.
O then at last relent: is there no place
Left for Repentance . . . ?

(4.73–80)

No place; mental space, now having built too well a Hell of Heaven, denies any but an ironic validity to his present mountain vision. While momentarily poised on a peak showing him the outward Eden, he is more permanently "disfigur'd" in his own inner vision.

As his emotions break through their cherubic mask and make him "disfigur'd," two other aspects of "statuary" as poetic analogue come into play, both based on the meanings of "figure." First, in a theory that explained how sculpture might have the expressive and narrative content usually attributed to poetry, Leonardo da Vinci argued that the whole figure's external gestures should reveal inward emotion.[51] Like Leonardo, later theorists of the *ut pictura poesis* tradition agreed that verbal personifications, like sculptures, expressed living figures caught at their most self-revelatory moment.[52] In personifications, from the Renaissance on, the self-revelation often emerges through gesture and emblem. In Milton's passage it emerges through gesture and "demeanor," so that Milton's "disfigur'd" refers both to the stance of the whole body and to the demeaned face.[53] He thus adds to the sculptural analogue some characteristics of painting, an art usually thought more capable of revealing facial expression.

Most important, narrator and reader share Uriel's perspective, as the archangel's "eye pursu'd him down" onto the mountaintop. Although Uriel does not move from one viewpoint to another, the height of his position both physically and morally allows him to recognize the incongruities between Satan's physical and moral stance.

In Keats's marginal note Uriel's pursuit also becomes a metaphor to describe Milton's poetic creativity. At the beginning of the note, Keats writes: "Milton in every instance pursues his imagination to the utmost—he is 'sagacious of his Quarry,' he sees Beauty on the wing, pounces upon it and gorges it to the producing his essential verse. . . . But in no instance is this sort of perseverance more exemplified than in what may be called his stationing or statu[a]ry." As Keats, Shelley, and Blake imitate this pursuit of aesthetic value, they more often discover that to gorge upon it would be to "ravin down their proper bane." Instead, their perceivers must analyze, as Uriel does, the conflict between aesthetic values and emotional ones. In his note Keats suggests that Uriel is the perceiving poet or the poet's dramatic representative within *Paradise Lost*. In their own Miltonic poems, however, Keats and the other two poets tend to see Milton or his massive epic as the central, statuesque figure whose "disfiguring" must be recognized and transformed by other pursuers.

To see more clearly how such a Keatsian analysis of Milton's episode acts as a model for these romantic poems, we first must consider it as a structural model for *Paradise Lost* itself. If we look at the narrative structure of Milton's poem in this context, we realize that Milton begins in book 1 with the portrayal of Satan as sculptural object or "statuary" and then encloses the narrative of his fall, as he encloses the figure of Satan himself, within the perspective of multiple witnesses.[54] In this *in medias res* construction he follows earlier epics; but his relation of objective figure to subjective perceiver points toward further romantic revisions of the pattern. As these three poets revise Milton's portrayal of Satan's mythic fall, they use the sculptural and visual analogues of "stationing or statuary" to redefine narrative action.

When the narrative action of *Paradise Lost* begins, Satan lies "vanquished rolling in the fiery Gulf / Confounded." His position parallels that of Aeneas shipwrecked on the shore of Africa and Odysseus marooned and despondent on Calypso's isle. Because this passive, fallen state prompts backward musings in each of these heroes, each of these three poems begins with a perceptual and epistemological focus: "As far as Angel's ken he views / The dismal situation Waste and wild." In all three of these earlier epics the inner narrative that recounts the beginning of action comes well after the heroes again have returned to action and is more often effect than cause of this return. In *Paradise Lost*, for example, Raphael must tell his history precisely because of Satan's continued action.

When Blake, Shelley, and Keats emulate these earlier models, they follow to some extent both the initial image of a static, meditative figure and the infolded structure of an *in medias res* narrative. The relationship between initial static figure and inner narrative, however, is strikingly different in their poems, where the remembering, retelling, and recognizing of the past enables the static figure to explore his own subjective attitude and thus to act. As he confronts his past, a past frequently represented not as a narrative but as another statuesque figure, he becomes a more committed Uriel, including that figure in his own self-conscious awareness. In Schlegel's terms, he has moved from a statuesque to a picturesque or romantic consciousness that contains the statuesque as one pole of its dialectic. This pattern works quite differently in each of these poems; but even the divergences from it often seem conscious revisions and criticisms of the patterns.

The opening image of a figure "stationed" as a momentarily static, objective figure in a defining landscape is clearer in *Hyperion* and *Prometheus Unbound* than in *Milton* and *The Fall of Hyperion*. Keats's first Saturn, sunken "Deep in the shady sadness of a vale," makes that deadened valley where he has just fallen a kind of hell. His stillness and the similes Keats uses to describe it, however, make him far more clearly statuesque and "stationed" than the just-fallen Satan "rolling" in the fiery gulf. In the first act of *Prometheus Unbound*, Shelley's Titan is stationed not by the momentary inertia immediately following a fall but—most apparently—by the nails and "bright chains" with which Jupiter has held him bound for three thousand years. The primary literary model for this opening, of course, is Aeschylus's *Prometheus Bound*, but the preface and a series of allusions in his first speech make clear Prometheus's status as Satanic rebel. Further, he is bound on a "wall of eagle-baffling mountain" in a "Ravine of Icy Rocks." Although not so far down as Saturn's vale or Satan's abyss, he is located in the same symbolic, even archetypal, landscape of the vale.

Although it is less obvious, this initial image of a passive central figure also appears in *Milton* and *The Fall of Hyperion*. In *Milton*, the earlier poet, "sitting at eternal tables," hears the song of a Bard and is inspired "to go into the deep to redeem" his imaginative works "and himself perish." His physical passivity has existed only for the duration of the Bard's song; before that he has restlessly "walked about in Eternity / One hundred years." Yet during those hundred years, even though seeing the works of his imagination held in a kind of underworld bondage, "he obeyed, he murmur'd not, he was silent"; he had been spiritually passive. And this Eternity resembles heil, as he resembles Milton's fallen angels, "Pondering the intricate mazes of Providence / Unhappy though in heaven." Finally, although the brief physical stillness of his "sitting at eternal tables" is scarcely set in a fully developed landscape, Milton himself identifies it with the climactic revelation of hell in the Bard's song, the vast abyss that opens in Satan's bosom.

When Keats recasts the fragmentary *Hyperion* into *The Fall of Hyperion*, he distances the fallen gods by the successive frames of the narrator's visions. Even more explicitly than in *Hyperion*, he treats them as parts of a pictorial composition or sculptural grouping. As they move back both narratively and spatially, the narrator becomes both perceiver and initial static figure: "Methought I stood where trees of every clime. . . ." At first not fallen himself, he undergoes a series of falls that initiate him into new kinds of vision. Although less abruptly than in Blake's *Milton*, he falls into a succession of symbolic settings; these settings, in turn, organize the highly pictorialized narrative. To use the passage from *Paradise Lost*, book 4, as a model, he moves from the role of Uriel to that of Satan and then finally to a figure whose consciousness incorporates both roles—peripheral observer and stationed central figure.

In each of the other poems, such a turn to a more inclusive consciousness also occurs—a turn from a passively stationed, objective central figure to an observer who also comprehends the significance of that figure and his landscape together. And in each of these poems, the turn develops from a revised version of Raphael's inner narrative recalling past events. "Narrative," however, may not be the most accurate term for these romantic poems. As I suggested above, narrative may be compressed into the image of a single typifying figure or group of them, or it may be recounted in response to the dominating presence of such a figure. Both versions of Keats's *Hyperion* poems, for example, make the figure of Mnemosyne one who calls up such figures to educate the poet or poet-god. In *Hyperion* the final vision of "creations and destroyings" that pours into the "wide hollows" of Apollo's brain compresses the impersonal narrative of the Titans' fall and locates it in a valley—the "wide hollows"—which recalls Saturn's station at the poem's opening. In *The Fall*, even more clearly than in the earlier version, this turn back to the Titans' fallen state becomes the central action of the poem. Moneta embodies and then shares her vision, the "things [her] hollow brain / Behind enwombed," though they seem almost inadequate to the response they engender in both memory-figure and poet. Keats frames the scarcely active figures of the Titans first visually in the landscape and then narratively in Moneta's "wan face." She is "disfigured," in a complex way, by the figures contained in her consciousness and expressed by her nearly tragic countenance.

This reflective act of memory appears in the other two poems as well, though represented through a figure other than Mnemosyne herself. Both *Prometheus Unbound* and *Milton* make this turn to confront the past early in the poem and use figures whose symbolic function is similar to Mnemosyne's. In *Milton*, the Bard acts as Mnemosyne, recounting a mythic history analogous to Milton's own past. Milton's recognition that "I in my selfhood am that Satan" acknowledges the success of the Bard's narrative as a whole but also, more particularly, of its climactic image. The vast abyss opening in Satan's bosom is an abyss within Milton's, as well as Satan's, consciousness and one that the poet must explore. With that landscape of the abyss recognized as his own, he becomes observer of Satan as his own selfhood, and he is then ready to move into the landscape prefigured in that momentarily static vision of the Bard's narrative.

In *Prometheus Unbound*, as in *Milton*, the static central figure early in the poem confronts a Mnemosyne-figure whose imaged or incorporated narrative enables him to act and thus to find release. His "Bard" appears in two guises: first that of the maternal Earth, whose account of "the magus Zoroaster" tells Prometheus how to call up shadow-figures from a "world beneath the grave"; and then that of the phantasm of Jupiter, called from that world, who repeats Prometheus's own, original, curse.[55] Like Satan in the Bard's song, the phantasm of Jupiter embodies the mythic past and shows to the watching Prometheus a similar though less literal abyss that he must claim as his own. As he witnesses this "disfiguring," Prometheus becomes like Uriel watching Satan on Mount Niphates. Yet, because the shape speaks his own curse in his own voice, he is like the magus Zoroaster confronting his own image. Like Milton in Blake's poem, he comes to recognize that "I in my selfhood am that Satan." Unlike Milton, however, he does not descend to redeem his emanation; instead, Asia descends to complete his redemption.

As all of these encounters suggest, the protagonists of these poems confront both individual and mythic pasts and thus reassess their present circumstances. Those present circumstances are symbolically represented through the landscapes in which the encounters take place. In the *Hyperion* poems, as I have suggested above, this recognition comes late enough to be the central action of the poems. In *Milton* and *Prometheus Unbound* the major action follows and is partially caused by such a recognition. Moreover, both latter poems include descents into the underworld like those in *The Odyssey* and particularly in *The Aeneid*, which extend this confrontation of the remembered past and convert it to future use. In this more extended confrontation, the past may be place or figure or both.

Finally, these descents lead us to a further generalization: all of these encounters with memory-figures or memory-landscapes lead to a reshaping of the past by bringing it from sculptural stasis into some new life. Seen most literally in Milton's remolding the marble figure of Urizen, this renovation also may lead the protagonist or a surrogate to reenact past events. All of these poems as wholes of course reenact Milton's poems; but the pattern they choose to follow most frequently, the mythic literalism of Satan's fall, changes in the course of these poems from fall to willed descent. Through this conversion, the Saturn- or Satan-figure, made static by his fall, changes into or is replaced by one who deliberately stations himself in the same underworld or earthly vale. Through this conscious stationing he then sees himself as object—or better, sees both subject and object as aspects of himself.

These memory-narratives, summed up in mythic, quasi-human figures that may then be seized, wrestled with, and reshaped, represent in all four of these poems a past that is individual yet more broadly historical. The poets seek a mythic and imaginative version of history that will make their emulative revisions of Milton one instance of such a free reshaping or reencountering of the past. In *Hyperion*, Oceanus's consolation to the Titans—"to envisage circumstance, all calm"—becomes the model of a more actual, less consolatory sovereignty for Apollo. Like Apollo, all of these poets attempt to make the imaginative envisaging of circumstances a means to intellectual and aesthetic, if no longer physical or political, sovereignty. They do this through a visual and sculptural reshaping of landscape and through the embodying of change in cosmological myths that generate history.

In the struggle between Milton and these later poets, I see the later writers as following Schlegel's fundamental optimism in making the "picturesque" or romantic consciousness a vision that incorporates and reinterprets the past instead of one that is haunted by it. Blake and Shelley reinforce this optimism with a radical optimism about the power of imagination to transform nature as well as history. In contrast, Keats's successive versions of *Hyperion* acknowledge his mythological figures' lack of success in controlling either nature or history, and thus this pessimism is, I will argue, a broader anxiety than that posed by Milton or by any poetic predecessor alone. Although Milton does indeed pose problems for these poets, the problems are at least in part those of no-longer-satisfactory answers to the problems of imagination and its realized arts in confronting natural and historical process. "Stationing," "statuary," and their historical analogues give these writers a figurative language and structure to correct the disfigurings named by Shelley's Demogorgon: "Fate, Time, Occasion, Chance, and Change."

Two

❧

Blake's *Milton*

From Marble Landscape to Living Form

Rival Arts

When Blake's character Milton chooses to "go down to self annihilation and eternal death" (E:108.14.22), his most important act in those hells of his own making is to mold the stony Urizen into living form.[1] He must restore that statuelike figure in order simultaneously to make Urizen's desolate landscape and himself fully human. If we interpret Urizen as a strange version of Keats's "statuary," we can see that Milton also must transform the two elements that define Urizen's Keatsian "stationing": the landscape and himself as witness. As he molds "the red clay of Suc-coth . . . and on the bones / Creating new flesh on the Demon cold, and building him . . . a Human form" (E:112.19.10, 12–14), Milton also continues the task Los had begun in the Bard's song: to shape the inchoate Urizen with "Hammer & Tongs." By focusing so much of his illuminated book upon these symbolic struggles of the sculptor to reshape his medium and his world, Blake draws even more attention to his own arts and their different media than he does in his other illuminated books. His own presence as character within the work, of course, increases this positive self-consciousness. As character, he witnesses more than he acts or actively creates; as artist, he gives critical shape to Milton's renovation of his own art. Yet as he transforms Milton from speaker and witness to sculptor, Blake does not merely illustrate concretely his predecessor's new imaginative understanding of himself and his world. Beyond this, he reevaluates the verbal and visual elements functioning both directly and symbolically in Milton's work and, more obviously, in his own. The

29

illuminated book *Milton* becomes then a way to free the earlier poet from the rigid legalism of Old Testament Puritanism and Newtonian natural religion—a legalism embodied in Urizen. It also frees him from the misguided artistic claims of the merely pictorial or the merely visualizable, whether in painting or in pictorializing poetry. First asserting his own verbal power to evoke and then transcend the pictorial, Blake can return as artist to a pictorialism redefined, through the plastic, tactile aspects of sculpture, as a renovated corporeality.

This complex, purgatorial evaluation of all three sister arts is particularly appropriate in a poem that confronts and redeems Milton to confront and redeem Blake's own self-doubts. In this poem Blake must evaluate his capacity not only to correct Milton's errors—both his own and those added by his eighteenth-century readers—but to emulate his prophetic greatness of vision.[2] Blake alludes to Milton's physical blindness only indirectly, through his choice of the tactile art of sculpture as means to Milton's redemption.[3] Even without that allusion, however, the nature of Milton's prophetic "vision" in the context of eighteenth-century *ut pictura poesis* controversy becomes a richly ironic one for Blake and for his contemporaries. In his obvious yet puzzlingly individual greatness as modern epic poet, Milton had become the focus for continued debate over the extent to which his poetry was a series of "speaking pictures." On the one hand, Jonathan Richardson blithely asserted that almost every paragraph of *Paradise Lost* constituted a picturesque landscape or a grouping of sculpturesque figures paintable in the grand style. On the other, Edmund Burke praised Milton's figure of Death for its obscure and terrifying sublimity.[4] In his attempts to sustain and correct Milton's prophetic, visionary insight while freeing it from a naturalistic pictorialism, Blake avoids a Burkean indefiniteness both in his illuminations and in his poetry. Instead, his poetry develops a version of Keatsian stationing that carries Richardson's picturesque tableaux to radical, sometimes grotesque, extremes; and this antiscenic verbal technique makes us question the pictorialism of the illuminations as well.

Although Blake does not use the words "statue" or "statuary," he compares Milton to a "sculptor silent stand[ing] before / His forming image" as he is "forming bright Urizen" (E:114.20.8–10). Keats's analogue of "statuary" clearly describes the way Blake portrays his mythic figures both in his illuminations and, as the sculpting Urizen shows, in his text. Influenced by Michelangelo and the grand style of history painting that based its heroic universality upon classical sculpture, Blake uses a linear, yet sculptural, human figure as the primary visual image in both his arts. Anne Mellor has argued that this corporeal image raises problems for an artist who would illustrate the "human form divine": is the image we see a corporeal limit or a renewed, human transcendence of that limit?[5] Our very familiarity with this symbolic visual image, however, may have obscured a complex change in the way Blake's verbal text defines sculpture and thus redefines the visual image of a sculptural human form. By investigating attitudes toward sculpture as a separate art, the last section of this chapter will explore that change in Blake's poem.

The need for sculpture as a redeemed and redeeming medium in *Milton* emerges from what we might describe as a persistent stationing in Blake's poetic and in his pictorial media. Blake develops these versions of stationing to make definite those aspects of Milton's vision that have held his imaginative insight captive, like his wives and daughters, in rigid theological and natural perspectives. Not surprisingly, he begins by revising, in his own poetic medium, two of the most spatial elements in Milton's poetry: the large planes of symbolic landscape developed most fully in *Paradise Lost,* and his use of the term "station" as spatial metaphor. Milton's hierarchical sense of "station" to compare fallen to unfallen figures in *Paradise Lost* appears four times in Blake's poem: at crucial moments we hear that Satan or Los "is fallen from his station." With this Miltonic verbal echo, the Bard who sings to Milton begins to transform a hierarchy that almost totally defines the person placed in its ranks or "stations" into a scheme of "States" through which the person can pass. Because these hierarchical landscapes and the "stations" of mythic figures in them form a basis for Blake's radical revision of Milton's spatially organized narrative, their analysis comes early in this chapter as well.

Like this limited and yet thematically important use of the term "station," a version of the Miltonic technique of stationing becomes another starting point for Blake's transformation of Milton's landscape and hence of the orthodox external world. In contrast to Milton, Keats, and Shelley, Blake has two possible starting points for this transformation: his poetry and his illuminations. Yet as Robert Rosenblum has shown, the illuminations very quickly begin to question conventional Renaissance perspectival space. Blake's artistic practice of the new "international style" or "romantic classicism," with its linearity drawn in part from Greek vase painting, is anti-illusionistic. His repudiation of three-dimensional, homologous space is of course consistent with the repudiation of that and other Newtonian concepts of his poetry. Even though this style has many affinities with sculpture, it tends to flatten such sculptural representations to the pictorial frame.[6] In discussing Blake's pictorial style, W. J. T. Mitchell extends Rosenblum's category by describing Blake's style as "one in which the human figures of classical, Renaissance history . . . painting are placed in a Gothic (i.e., prophetic or apocalyptic) spatial setting."[7] He also describes how the illustrative framing of figures in landscape, exuberant in *Thel* and *The Songs of Innocence*, more threatening either in their confusion or their greater architectural rigidity in other early works, gives way in the Lambeth prophecies to a more chaotic representation in which the figures fall without even the refuge of a consistent ground plane. This visual representation corresponds to the similar falls but more radical metamorphoses of the external shapes of landscape and figure in the verbal narrative of *The Four Zoas*. The major sequences of illustrations to others' visions, to those of Milton, Dante, and the Book of Job, show a renewed interest in landscape.[8]

Milton, born out of Blake's struggles in rural Felpham, stands at a turning point. As Mitchell argues, its return to a grounded setting and to an interest in landscape, though not as fully developed as in the later illustrative sequences, seems to correspond to Blake's own reaffirmed sense of his prophetic stance, a sense he gains as character and as artist through the narrative events of *Milton* itself.[9] The illuminations in this poem even include some landscapes, though very schematic ones.

Similarly, the descriptive poetry of Blake's prophetic books seems to jolt the reader from one perspective or level of existence to another. Josephine Miles concludes from her study of Blake's vocabulary and phrasing, however, that his poetry "is an extremist structure, heightening the eighteenth century locational terminology, intensifying the spatial," in the tradition of the Bible, Spenser, Milton, and James Thomson.[10] These two assessments of his descriptive poetry are not necessarily in conflict, inasmuch as Miles analyzes smaller subscenes and the reader still may experience jolting transitions from one of these to another. And in fact this is the very point I want to make. In this poem set on redeeming Milton's world, I would argue, Blake returns momemtarily both in his illuminations and in his poetry to a more conventional way of locating figures in space—and at such moments both his arts tend to "illustrate" the same scene or episode. These moments in which visual and verbal arts converge create a kind of Keatsian stationing, in part through their evocation of spatial settings—though far less naturalistically than in Milton or Keats—and in part through the multiple viewpoints resulting from Blake's different but temporarily similar arts. Almost immediately, however, this momentary fidelity of the two arts to each other and to naturalistic representation breaks apart. As the verbal text very economically and yet radically redefines ordinary landscape perspectives, it relates objective focal figure, surrounding landscape, and subjective perceiver in ways that challenge the concentric horizons assumed by Milton: the objective figure, for example, suddenly may grow to contain its subjective perceiver within its own vast regions.

Viewed without consideration of their verbal context, the illuminations are in some ways more conservative than that context: the figures of Milton, Blake, Los, or Urizen are consistent with one another in scale, as they are with the occasional tree, cottage, set of steps, or trilithon. Thus the radical changes of scale and of planes of action in the verbal context transform the ambiguous images of the figures in these illuminations, changing them from corporeal to fully human forms that can dominate and reshape landscape. Only from the verbal text can we know that Urizen and Albion must be awakened from the stone that has made them part of the scenery, in order for us to understand correctly their human figures in the illuminations. That awakening cannot take place until Blake's prophets—Los, Milton, and Blake himself—have acted out a mutual, repeatedly surprising stationing of each other and of landscape.

Although the scale of the figures and schematic setting in the illuminations is somewhat conventional, Blake's treatment of the Renaissance conventions of three-dimensional pictorial space is not—and this difference suggests another way of analyzing Blake's challenges to *ut pictura poesis* theory. In each illumination, a window of space opening out before us seems to offer a potential three-dimensional space.[11] In it we, as active viewers, amplify the details of our more conventional perspectives as we try to sense the circumstances and settings that prompt the momentarily frozen gestures and stances of the figures. Our process of continued creation, however, recalls us to the primary creative process of the artist, and the flatness of page and composition reasserts the artist's "bounding line" as the most dynamic element in the composition. If the dynamism of a picturesque landscape lies uncertainly between the perceiver or painter and the "objective" scene itself, the dynamism in Blake's pictorial art begins to locate itself far more explicitly in the artist. Marshall McLuhan's analysis in *The Gutenberg Galaxy* is indeed, as Mitchell says, "very close to the mark: . . . Blake's 'bounding line of sculptural form' produces an 'interplay among experiences,' a kind of 'tactility' or 'synaesthesia.' "[12]

Because the protagonists of *Milton* are a cluster of poets and poet-artists struggling to practice their arts, it would be tempting to look for the equivalent of this pictorial "bounding line," with its self-referential quality, in the poem as well as in its illustrations. Thus we would have a kind of *ut pictura poesis* in which both elements of the composition would share an antipicturesque, antinaturalistic bias, in paradoxical distinction to the naturalistic bias Jean Hagstrum traces in the tradition that the eighteenth century inherits. We might say that Blake's figures or compositional unit possesses not *enargeia*, but *energeia*, not detailed mimetic faithfulness to an absolute external world, but expressive energy.[13] This equation would resemble a Longinian version of *ut pictura poesis* instead of a Horatian, mimetic one. As Blake tests the perception of landscape in *Milton*, however, he encourages both the poet-protagonists and the reader not to abandon but to reevaluate the significance of landscape as a conventional way of representing the natural world. In order to challenge that conventionality and to redeem that world, he begins by evoking it.

In the passage from *The Gutenberg Galaxy* quoted above, McLuhan goes on to remark that "The Romantic poets fell far short of Blake's mythical or simultaneous vision. They were faithful to Newton's single vision and perfected the picturesque outer landscape as a means of isolating single states of the inner life."[14] Blake, I would argue, uses momentary, simultaneous evocations of the picturesque outer landscape both in his illuminations and in his poetry as "stations" or visual vantage points from which to criticize Newton's and Milton's consolidation of single vision. His final means of criticism, the art of sculpture practiced by Los, Milton, and finally Blake himself, defines—in the molding Blake describes verbally and in the driving, energetic lines he creates visually—a more tactile, felt unity of vision.

Because Blake repeatedly adapts ideas and images he disapproves of in order to transform them, it is not surprising that he would develop a version of picturesque "stationing" to criticize naturalistic styles of representing landscape. His most explicit references to the picturesque mode in landscape painting are associated directly or indirectly with his stay at Felpham and his work on *Milton*. In a letter to Thomas Butts written from Felpham (22 November 1802), Blake energetically discusses William Gilpin's *Three Essays: On Picturesque Beauty; On Picturesque Travel; and On Sketching Landscape*.[15] This work may have interested Blake more than did Gilpin's specific guidebooks because in it Gilpin debates Sir Joshua Reynolds over the relative merits of the picturesque style of painting, with its chiaroscuro and detailed natural perspectives, and the sculpturesque grand style advocated by Reynolds.[16] Gilpin includes, in order to refute it, a letter Reynolds had written him which suggests that the picturesque characterizes inferior schools of painting and poetry. In *his* letter Blake approvingly quotes Reynolds's letter from Gilpin and denies Gilpin's refutation: " 'Perhaps Picturesque is somewhat synonymous to the word Taste, which we should think improperly applied to Homer or Milton, but very well to Prior or Pope.' " Reynolds agrees with Gilpin that " 'variety of Tints & Forms is picturesque; but it must be remember'd . . . that . . . (*uniformity of Colour & a long continuation of lines*) produces Grandeur.' " Although opposed to the naturalistic, generalizing

basis of Reynolds's "Grandeur" as described in his *Discourses*, Blake
opposes even more strongly Gilpin's insistence upon landscape values and
upon sketching techniques. With gusto, he concludes, "So says Sir
Joshua, and so say I." Blake agrees with Reynolds, not Gilpin, on the
limited merits of the picturesque; yet he may well have found in Gilpin
and other writers on the subject a method for revising naturalistic pictorialism that would in some ways challenge Reynolds's "general nature" as
well. Although Gilpin does not use the term "station" in these *Essays*, as he
does in his series of *Observations on Picturesque Beauty*, he does emphasize
repeatedly the importance of the individual perceiver's point of view as
active shaper of his perspective.[17]

In two prose statements written as Blake may have been completing
Milton, he also shows his familiarity with the practice of the picturesque.
His *Descriptive Catalogue* mentions an experimental subject "varied from
the literal fact, for the sake of the picturesque scenery" (E:546), and the
scenery is a nice joke on the picturesque: goats are just stripping some
"vine leaves" off a group of "savage girls" visiting a missionary ship.[18] Here
the girls' natural surroundings rapidly are redefined not by the onlook-
ers—the missionaries—but by the unintentionally creative goats. In
Blake's 1809 and 1810 draft of a "Public Address," an attack on the
engravers Woolett and Strange for their weakness in drawing correctly
even a "single leaf," he also attacks their typically picturesque subjects:
"Cottagers & Jocund Peasants the Views in Kew Gardens" (E:574).[19]
Embedded in his attacks on these engravers is his announcement of "a
Poem concerning my Three years [Herculean] Labours at Felpham which
I will soon publish" (E:572), a poem usually taken to be *Milton* (see E:882).
His attack on the engravers of picturesque landscape shares with *Milton* a
double criticism: first, that their imitation of nature is defective in its
execution, and, second, that it is misguided in its conception (E:575ff.).[20]

In *Milton*, this two-stage criticism begins with the revised form of
stationing I have been describing. Such a revised stationing, in which
Blake's two arts converge for a moment of relatively naturalistic representation only to test the limits of that representation, occurs at a number of
points in his poem. For example, the Bard's announcement that "Satan is
fallen from his station" and that a vast abyss has appeared in his bosom
treats inner and outer space, figures, and their observers quite differently
from the related illumination that shows two male figures watching a
third, on a pedestal, bursting into flame.[21] In another example, Blake's
geographical and physical low point, "Felphams Vale," ironically becomes the location—shown in illumination and in text—for the poem's
final recognitions (E:137ff., plates 36–39, and *IB* 42A).[22] Both of these
moments revise Milton's own patterns of fall or descent and final station-

ing in *Paradise Lost*. Two other momentary clusters of motifs that also
revise Milton's patterns of fallen and stationed figures are far more
important and will be considered more fully later in this chapter. In the
first of these clusters, Milton descends through the vortex, appearing to
Blake like a falling star; in the second, Blake repeatedly stations feet, as in
the prefatory lyric, in the poem's landscapes. The figures who experience
these unconventional journeys and walk through this poem's places challenge ordinary visual assumptions, assumptions evoked in part through
the illuminations and in part through the poetry's assertive spatial language. Even as pictorial and poetic expression approach each other with
unusual closeness, Blake's aim is to use this closeness only as a step toward
a poetic level beyond the visual. At the beginning of book 2, the voices of
Beulah, Blake's version of an earthly paradise, demand "a habitation & a
place," a "Temporal Habitation" in which to find temporary refuge from
the "fury of Poetic Inspiration . . . build[ing] the Universe stupendous"
(E:129–30.30.24, 29, 19–20). For the reader and the poem's earthly
characters, the "local habitation" is only a way of approaching and
understanding the less visualizable "fury of Poetic Inspiration." Finally, as
Blake has Milton remold the landscape itself into a fully human figure, a
revised, living "statuary," the art of sculpture proves a way of reconciling
these opposed arts and thus answering the challenge of Milton.

Epic Topography

In the poetry of *Milton*, Blake organizes these "local habitations" into
larger perspectives that remind us of the hierarchical planes of action in
Paradise Lost but only in order to redefine them. Northrop Frye and others
have suggested that the primary structural model Blake borrows from
Milton to organize his own *Milton* may be *Paradise Regained*, the "brief
epic" as individual encounter or dialogue modeled on the Book of Job.[23]
Such a parallel becomes particularly striking in the context of this
discussion of stationing: at the moment of theophany in *Paradise Regained*,
Christ remains fast on the "uneasy station" of his pinnacle while Satan
falls (4.584). Not only does Blake analyze this moment in his illustration to
Paradise Regained, but he echoes it in his own Bard's announcement that
"Satan is fallen from his station."[24] Many critics have argued that the
moment of ephiphany in *Milton* is far stronger even than in *Paradise
Regained*, so that all events of Blake's poem occur simultaneously in the
renovated moment of a last judgment "that Satan cannot find."[25] I would
argue, however, that the complex sequences of journeys in *Milton* from
one vast topographical realm to another are clearly drawn not from

Paradise Regained but *Paradise Lost*. They raise epic expectations of temporal and topographical sequence and thus give Blake a framework for his revisions. Although the various "descents from heaven"[26] eventually may reveal themselves as simultaneous, occurring in an instant before the final moment of the last judgment is hammered into shape,[27] I think Blake intends us to experience them first as sequential, then as integrated into a more simultaneous event.

Revising the temporal sequence of narrative, he then can free Milton from the analogous temporal sequence of history. In the process of reading we must transform time as a rigid sequence of past, determined moments—a definition Milton would claim was caused by the irreversible fall he describes in *Paradise Lost*—into prophetic moments. In these "pulsations of an artery" epiphanies or theophanies can occur. Although this freed, expansive time would seem a spatialization of temporal sequence, it must be a spatialization defined by its freedom from the ordinary space we tend to think of as objective and nonmental. Blake transforms temporal flow into the simultaneity of a "moment," but at the same time he denies the adequacy of "merely" pictorial space through an almost forced return to a verbal narrative sequence in which the events scarcely seem visualizable. In a rather comic demonstration of this process, each section of "linear" journey ends as the traveler is absorbed or integrated physically into the figure who defines the next level of his journey. He is stationed, then, not in landscape but suddenly in figure. In this process, the narrative of *Milton* transforms and integrates its own sequences into a higher order of meaning.[28]

Through ironic relocation, Blake uses Milton's own symbolic topographical planes, defined as Milton's are through the perspectives of journeying figures, to criticize his predecessor's values. It will be helpful, then, to review from what we might call a "naively realistic" perspective Blake's broadly sketched parallels to the topographic structure of *Paradise Lost*. Milton's epic begins in hell, moves to heaven, then remains on earth, though Raphael's myth of origins describes a prior existence in heaven. Using levels of spiritual topography similar enough to evoke Milton's, Blake simplifies his predecessor's infolded *in medias res* construction by moving the Bard's song, his incomplete equivalent both of Raphael's myth of origins and of Milton's whole epic, almost to the beginning of the poem. In fact, he begins neither *in medias res* nor *ab ovo* but *post obit*, after Milton's death, in defiance of the idea that "Eternal Death" must be an end. Before the Bard begins his song, his audience is described as in "Eternity" or "heaven," though Milton's restlessness as he "ponders the intricate mazes of providence" recalls that of his own fallen angels, who "reasoned high / of Providence, Foreknowledge, Will, and Fate . . . And found no end, in wandering mazes lost" (2.558–59, 561–62).[29] The Bard's mythic narrative plays down the causes for Albion's fall in order to emphasize the ambiguous process of this world's creation, a process that is ground not only for a Satanic rebellion but also for human salvation. Though beginning as unlocalized, this process builds its own place that extends downward to "the Starry Mills of Satan . . . built beneath the Earth & Waters of the Mundane Shell" (E:97.4.2–3). Furthermore, the events of the Bard's myth clearly correspond to the rebellion and fall of Satan in that Homeric, though heavenly, early-epic world of *Paradise Lost*, books 5 and 6.

Like the heaven where the Bard sings to Milton, which resembles a private version of Milton's epic hell, and like the earth of Los, which is a troubled version of his epic heaven, the next major plane of action is also ambiguous. It draws upon imagistic and thematic parallels from *Paradise Lost* and other major epics to establish its identity as a landscape of "Hells" and "Furnaces," an underworld of "Eternal Death." There Milton willingly descends to redeem the imaginative works whose distortions and potentialities alike he has recognized through the Bard's song. Yet as his journey makes clear, that hell contains "our" world of generation, the world where Blake as ordinary man, our surrogate perceiver in the poem, sees Milton "in the Zenith as a falling star, / Descending perpendicular" as he falls into the sea of space and time (E:110.15.47–48). For most of book 1 following the Bard's song and recurrently in book 2, as Milton confronts the Satanic selfhood of his earlier vision, this landscape seems hellish. Yet because he chooses to descend, his journey becomes a redemptive underworld quest like those of Gilgamesh, Aeneas, Christ in the accounts of the harrowing of hell, and Milton himself in his inductions to *Paradise Lost*. In this redemption, the hellish scenes give way to more positive ways of seeing this world.[30]

In book 2, Blake alludes in two ways to the natural beauty of a Miltonic Eden or a natural, earthly paradise: as Blake's mythic Beulah and as his "actual" garden in Felpham. As in *Paradise Lost*, then, the action converges from the more extreme locations, whether heaven or hell, into landscapes that seem familiar and desirable. Yet, because Beulah and Felpham are so topographically similar we must continually reevaluate our interpretations of their significance. The visions of Beulah confirm our need to rely on "temporal habitation" and yet also point toward the hellish vision that results if we accept such habitations either as Edenic or as an immediate and consistent analogue of Eden. Thus as Ololon moves from Eden through Beulah toward Blake's Felpham garden, she pursues "A long journey & dark thro Chaos in the track of Miltons course" (E:134.34.22), a track that leads to "the Ulro: a vast Polypus / Of living fibres down into the Sea of Time and Space growing" (E:134.34.24) and thus to Felpham within that encircling chaos.

"The track of Miltons course" is in a larger sense his own model of *Paradise Lost*, followed in precise, if transformed, detail in order ultimately to free travelers and readers alike from the tyranny of an absolute space and an irreversible time. As Ololon makes clear, that tyranny is internally caused:

> . . . How are the Wars of Man which in Great Eternity
> Appear around, in the External Spheres of Visionary Life
> Here renderd Deadly within the Life & Interior Vision
> How are the Beasts & Birds & Fishes, & Plants & Minerals
> Here fixd into a frozen bulk subject to decay & death [?]
>
> (E:134–35.34.50–54)

Paradoxically, then, "Visionary Life" can extend its energies "around, in . . . External Spheres," while what we conventionally call the external or objective world is in its "frozen bulk" the result of too rigid and enclosed a way of viewing the constitution of the universe. The garden at Felpham, then, is "firm ground" at the end of all the shadowy ground the reader is forced to tread or even fall through, and it is a location in which such firmness comes all too close to becoming a "frozen bulk subject to decay & death." Because Felpham is the actual Blake's actual garden, his presence there makes us feel that we, too, may experience the descents of visionary figures into our ordinary garden plots, just as Keats's examples of Miltonic stationing place such figures "under a plantane" or "on the Assyrian Mount." As those figures descend, finally, we must ask whether Felpham will be transformed into the Eden in which Adam once saw God "under this Tree" or "at this Fountain."

Station, Class, and State: "Mark well my words!"

Blake does not begin his poem with this aspect of Keatsian stationing, with the perceiver's organization of mythic central figures in the specific landscape of Felpham, but with its opposite: the appeal to "stations" as places within a preordained hierarchy. Appearing three times in the Bard's song at the beginning of the poem, this direct Miltonic use of the term "station" describes Satan's rebellion: "Satan: with incomparable mildness . . . soft intreated Los to give to him [his brother's] station" (E:100.7.4, 6). Los finally lets him use the harrow, but, after seeing how Satan has thrown the work into chaos, he forgets that he has given permission and lectures his innocent son: "Henceforth Palamabron, let each his own station / Keep" (E:101.7.41–42). Once Satan's true tyranny appears, so that he can no longer work harmoniously either at his own task or in another's place, one of the Eternals in a "Great Solemn Assembly" announces that "Satan is fall'n from his station & never can be redeem'd" (E:105.11.19). In contrast, Los later can announce to a Blake newly confident as Milton's rehabilitation begins, "I am that Shadowy Prophet who Six Thousand Years ago / Fell from my station in the Eternal bosom. Six Thousand Years / Are finishd. I return!" (E:117.22.15–17). Blake uses this conservative term "station" not only to describe Milton's militant and rigid hierarchy but also to show how even the most conservative structures become redemptive as they define error so that it can be recognized and worked out of the structure.[31]

Los sees these stations, which he attempts to maintain, as the patterns of an eternal order marred in Albion's fall. In the fallen world each of Los's three sons directs a crew of mythic agricultural workers who ready humanity for a final harvest. At the same time their tasks or "stations" of plow, harrow, and mill transform the landscape and thus transform Urizen, the god or zoa who claims that there is a single, external horizon. Ironically, Los tends to see the stations as spatial metaphors for absolute tasks, even if those tasks are performed to challenge Urizen's dogmatic attitudes toward space.

But the disastrous exchange of functions into which Satan forces Palamabron "with incomparable mildness" makes clear that Satan's task, even though part of the same complex harvesting for the last judgment, differs from those of the other two. To begin with, Satan himself differs from his brothers: he is "brought forth . . . Refusing Form" (E:97.3.41). Next, though it is almost as dangerous for a critic to assert a sequential narrative order for *Milton* as it is for Satan to claim Palamabron's harrow, the poem strongly suggests on plate 7 that Satan initiates the exchange of tasks:

> Of the first class [the Elect] was Satan: with incomparable mildness;
> His primitive tyrannical attempts on Los: with most endearing love
> He soft intreated Los to give to him Palamabrons station. . . .
>   (E:100.7.4–6)

Responding to this request, on plate 4 Los praises the importance of Satan's task as a way of reconciling him to it: "art thou not Prince of the Starry Hosts / And of the Wheels of Heaven, to turn the Mills day & night? / Art thou not Newtons Pantocrator weaving the Woof of Locke / To Mortals thy Mills seem every thing . . . / Get to thy Labours at the

Mills." Yet as "Satan was going to reply," Los breaks out in a more negative interpretation: "thou canst not drive the Harrow. . . . Thy work is Eternal Death, with Mills & Ovens & Cauldrons. / Trouble me no more. thou canst not have Eternal Life" (E:98.4.9ff.). The sonorous permanence of the phrases "Eternal Life" and "Eternal Death" implies an absolute difference not only between Satan's task and those of the rest of the family, but between himself as rejected youngest son and the other members of the family.

What, then, is the relationship between "station" and self? Even if Blake's myth analyzes the forces shaping our phenomenal world as they ready it for redemption, its portrayal of family conflicts prompts us to analyze these figures as human characters. It is easy enough, for example, to understand Satan's desire to drive Palamabron's harrow: his father has told him he is not able to. Within the same family model, it is also easy enough to see a critical parallel to the rebellion of Milton's Satan. Nor is it difficult, with the help of biographical information, to read into the controversy William Hayley's (Satan's) usurpation of Blake's (Palamabron's) poetic vision. Finally, the episode surely expresses a more universal fear that the prophet's (Rintrah's) more radical vision, shaped by the poet for ordinary human understanding, will be further shaped by the grinding reduction of Satan's mills.[32]

Yet the lines between Los's blustering refusal of Satan's request on plate 4 and the passage on plate 7 that describes both the earlier request and Los's eventual succumbing to Satan's "incomparable mildness" portray neither family drama nor poetic vocation. Instead, they show the work of separating "Mortal Men" into the "Three Classes" that will prepare them for judgment: "The first, The Elect from before the foundation of the World: / The second, The Redeem'd. The Third, The Reprobate & form'd / To destruction from the mothers womb" (E:100.7.1–3). Blake borrows these classes from orthodox Calvinism, but as they are "regulated by Los's Hammer," he reverses the extreme categories. Thus the class of the Elect, the most desirable in Puritan theology, becomes in Blake's critical revisions the "Reasoning Negative," the category for irredeemable discards; and the Reprobate becomes not only the most desirable in itself but also the class capable of saving those in the other two. The Redeemed can find this salvation through the persuasive prophetic example of the Reprobate; the Elect can be recreated through the self-sacrifice of the Reprobate.[33] Although Blake draws these categories from a starker Calvinism than Milton's in *Paradise Lost*, he clearly intends to criticize a similar tendency in Milton's theology.

So far, then, Blake has established two analytical frameworks for examining and challenging Milton's values. The "stations" of Los and his three sons adopted from the hierarchical vision of *Paradise Lost* organize the redemptive tasks of those mythic figures; and the "classes" borrowed from the Gospel of Mark and from Calvinist theology organize the harvest of mortal humanity. Complicating this pattern, however, is the Bard's attempt to apply the framework of classes to Satan. On plate 7 he announces, "Of the first class [the Elect] was Satan"; but is he subject to that class by virtue of his original "station" at the mills or by his rebellion from that task? In what sense is Satan an individual independent of his "station," that is, his function? Los insists very early that he bases his assignments on the individual talents of his sons: "Every Mans Wisdom is peculiar to his own Individ[u]ality / O Satan my youngest born, art thou not Prince of the Starry Hosts / . . . to turn the Mills day & night?" (E:98.4.8–10). Yet Satan challenges his father's assignment, one conjectures, because presiding over the mills of "Eternal Death" as his "station" would not necessarily be objectionable, but being a member of the class that must go to death without redemption would be less desirable. Paradoxically, as he leaves his own "station" to see whether Palamabron's task is more life giving, he confirms that the "Individuality" he carries with him remains a rigid self-righteousness that is a kind of Eternal Death. Palamabron's supervision of the mills, on the other hand, has released their mechanical repetition into a joyous country holiday. Thus Los is right: Satan's personality, echoed in his task at the mills, is shown more clearly when he leaves his "station." It is a disposition independent of station although consistent with it.

Yet as the difficulty of showing this distinction between Satan's character and his station suggests, Los's terminology needs refining. A careful look at the uses of "station" and "class" in the Bard's song shows how Blake works from Los's unexamined assumptions about "stations" to the Bard's—and his fellow Eternals'—more self-conscious and analytical use of "classes." Thus Los analyzes his world by "stations," using "task" or "place" as interchangeable synonyms. When the Bard reports the arguments of Los's sons in indirect discourse (as on E:100.7.5), he also occasionally uses this pattern. The Bard himself begins his song with the assertion that "Three Classes are Created by the Hammer of Los, & Woven / By Enitharmons Looms" (E:96.2.26; 3.1). He applies these categories to men on E:97.4.4–5, expands his mythic account of their development by the Daughters of Albion on plate 5, and briefly mentions them again on the top of 7. As noted above, he returns to Satan early on plate 7, announcing that Satan is "Of the first class"—the Elect. These are all narrative comments, however. Blake's characters first apply this scheme of characters within his narrative in the Great Solemn Assembly called by Palamabron on plate 9. As the Eternals see Rintrah's wrath flame up in Satan, their assessment of this situation "became a proverb in Eden. Satan is among the Reprobate." This conversion of a momentary outburst into a proverb is particularly ironic, for Satan's wrathful self-revelation in fact shows a self-righteous absolutism, characteristic of the Elect. The Eternals are correct in rejecting him, but they do not fully condemn the more characteristic "Moral laws and cruel punishments" as aspects of Satan's Elect nature until plate 11. Their judgment on plate 9 condemns the aspect of Satan that is wrath, or Rintrah, but without really separating wrath from Satan. That is, they fail to recognize that his momentary wrath is less essential to his character than is his dogmatism; they also fail to recognize that the wrath has done them a service by revealing the dogmatism. On plate 11 the solitary Eternal acknowledges Rintrah's innocence. He also explains Rintrah's sacrifice both to redeem Palamabron from "Satan's Law" and to recreate Satan, because he "is fall'n from his station & never can be redeem'd."

The change in the status of Rintrah through this section of the Bard's song is particularly confusing, because he changes from separate and equal son of Los to an aspect, if a temporary one, of Satan's personality. The doctrine of classes develops out of this problem to clarify it, for the classes are not only larger categories into which individuals may be sorted, but subcategories of the individual psyche whose relative dominance determines the individual's capacity for salvation. The doctrine of the Three Classes, then, can explain how wrath may be self-destructive not as a selfish way to damnation but as a self-sacrificing way to allow new creation of the spiritually empty or negating Elect—whether these classes are groups of people or aspects of a single psyche.

Yet the Eternals do not develop this dynamic use of the Three Classes until they face the perplexing problem of a Satan who rebels wrathfully against the mills of reason that grind toward Eternal Death. As central figure in a test case, Satan in the Bard's song is extremely vexing, and part of this vexation surely reflects Blake's ambiguous attitude toward Milton's Satan. The Bard's Satan is admirable because he forces the Eternals to develop a distinction between cosmic "station," or task, and individual self, and thus to allow tasks to be chosen, not predestined. On the other hand, because his very rebellion seems based on a claim that any individual can do any task, it supports an atomistic reductiveness characteristic of the mills he tries to abandon. Satan's fall, then, is a further fall from Albion's original wholeness into self-consciousness about the relationship of personality to place. As his moment of rebellion leads to his recognition as Urizen, it also leads to the creation of space. Yet, although its definite form appears at first to be absolute, Urizenic, and Newtonian, Blake and his prophets later transform it to a more individual space in which a person's station or perspectival viewpoint, shapes a world.

Even these classes, revisions both of Miltonic hierarchical "stations" and of Calvinistic categories of salvation, seem to be transitional groupings. Later in the poem, Blake replaces them with the idea of "States," which develop further the classes' definition of spiritual conditions. Specifically and spatially defined as separable from the individual, they also answer more completely than do the classes the challenge to spatial identification that Satan raised. Lucifer, one of Blake's seven Angels of the Presence, though not connected with the Satan of the Bard's song, answers him on plate 32 (E:132.32.22–24), as if he recalls an unfallen Satan, Prince of Light:

> Distinguish therefore States from Individuals in those States.
> States Change: but Individual Identities never change nor cease:
> You cannot go to Eternal Death in that which can never Die.

Milton, he explains, is "a State about to be Created / Called Eternal Annihilation"; that state is a temporary stage of Milton's experience created to allow his self-sacrificing descent. By its capacity to be created, it analyzes and transforms Eternal Death:

> Judge then of thy Own Self: thy Eternal Lineaments explore
> What is Eternal & What Changeable? & what Annihilable!

> The Imagination is not a State: it is the Human Existence itself
> Affection or Love becomes a State, when divided from Imagination
> The Memory is a State always, & the Reason is a State
> Created to be Annihilated.
>
> (E:132.32.22–24, 30–35)

Even more malleable than "Classes," "States" move further from predestined categories of salvation toward self-shaped revisions of self. Donald Ault explains that "the doctrine of States redeems individuals because it allows the particular human to retain his integral identity even though he may participate in the state of Evil";[34] but in the passage above, it is the disintegration of the individual that is turned to a creative process.

Further, because of Milton's journey, the meaning of Eternal Annihilation here takes on a meaning almost opposite to that involved in Satan's "work" of "Eternal Death" in the Bard's song. Because it is a "State" or stage through which many individuals may pass, not an ultimate spiritual situation or condition for a specific individual, the process by which the living dare to enter it in search of redemption also makes less final the Reprobates' sacrificial atonement for the Elect proposed by the Bard's Eternal on plate 11. The living are not dying totally; they are not making a total sacrifice of the self but a partial sacrifice of aspects of the self, thus pursuing through their entry into Eternal Annihilation their own route to redemption. In this scheme Satan can be either a mythic "individual" or a phase or state in which they may indeed participate; but he is not a category that can reduce all individuals to itself, as either a "station" or a class condemned to Eternal Death would do.[35]

Warning against conflating definitions of the same term as it appears in several works, Susan Fox points to the changing definitions of "state" in *Milton, Jerusalem,* and *The Vision of the Last Judgment* as crucial evidence of the problem.[36] The more developed spatial metaphors Blake uses in *Jerusalem* (E:299; *Jerusalem,* plate 73, lines 44–45) and *Vision of the Last Judgment* (E:556) do in fact lead to problems, as they naively if momentarily assume the permanence of the external landscape and devalue the capacity of the traveler to transform it. In *Milton,* such an attitude toward landscape already has been challenged thoroughly by the time the reader reaches plate 32, when Lucifer offers his explanation of states; and in fact the analysis of landscape first forced upon the Eternals and the readers alike by the "vast Abyss" opening in Satan's bosom leads toward *Milton's* creative doctrine of states.

"Everything has its / Own Vortex"

Like his transforming of those epic, hierarchical planes of Miltonic landscape, Blake represents his transforming of Milton's "stations" in his predecessor's own medium of words. In his second medium, his illuminations, Blake seldom makes his spatial settings detailed enough to show a heaven, a hell, or an earthly paradise. Similarly, the human figures may belong to the world of generation or may be "human forms divine." Because of this visual ambiguity, the verbal text usually interprets for us the specific identity of the ground planes in the illuminations and the figures who confront one another or themselves on those universalized surfaces.[37] As I suggested earlier, however, in *Milton* Blake develops a deliberate interplay between his two arts, representing the same episode or motif both in written text and in illumination. Two of these are particularly striking because they explore modes of travel between one plane and another. Both also focus upon variants of a fall and the stationing of fallen figures. Because this spatial metaphor of the fall defines a directional motion, that dynamic and temporal process shapes the larger

structural patterns of the poem. The various representations of an episode
or motif, however, seldom appear together or even sequentially in Blake's
organization of the plates for *Milton*. Instead, they are more wide-ranging
and, to use Northrop Frye's musical term, syncopated.[38]

Like the Shadow, the vortex is a means of descent; but it also links
subjective perception and "objective" landscape in this world in a way that
is not destructively hermaphroditic. Milton's entrance into the Shadow
(E:108.14.36–41; 15.1–4) dramatizes the subject's perception of other
aspects of himself, particularly the descending self looking back up at the
eternal self as model. The vortex, on the other hand, points forward to
examine the objects of perception familiar to us on earth. Its most
important function is to show how "place" and other people are functions
of the perceiver's mind as his viewpoint or "station" changes:

> The nature of infinity is this: That every thing has its
> Own Vortex; and when once a traveller thro Eternity
> Has passd that Vortex, he percieves it roll backward behind
> His path, into a globe itself infolding; like a sun:
> Or like a moon, or like a universe of starry majesty,
> While he keeps onwards in his wondrous journey on the earth
> Or like a human form, a friend with whom he livd benevolent.
>
> . . . .
>
> Thus is the heaven a vortex passd already, and the earth
> A vortex not yet pass'd by the traveller thro' Eternity.
>
> (E:109.15.21–27, 34–35)

Because of their initial difficulty and because of the hope that, once
explained, they will offer a coherent model for the narrative method of the
various journeys, these lines have fascinated critics. Although my reading
does not claim this figure as the key to the poem, it does see the vortex as a
positive mode of vision. Clearly, Blake uses the vortex to analyze how
time, both instantaneous and historical, functions in the individual's
perception of landscape. In contrast to such vast historical schemes as
Giovanni Battista Vico's, Shelley's, or Yeats's, however, the vortex does
not offer a conceptual scheme for the whole poem. On the contrary, it
urges us to replace rigid conceptual models of landscape with more
experiential and imaginative ones. Its explanation of "the nature of
infinity," the "Eternity" through which the traveler moves, suggests an
expansion and transformation of our earthly perspectives; its position in
the midst of a neo-Miltonic pattern of descent redefines the stratified levels
of Eden, Beulah, Generation, and Ulro as functions of the understanding
mind instead of absolutely existing places "out there" somewhere.

This flexibility emerges as soon as one tries to diagram the vortex. Although Mitchell has shown Blake's recurrent visual experiments with a vortical or spiraling line, these poetic lines on the vortex surely tease us out of ordinary sight.[39] Not only does Blake avoid describing the vortex precisely as a mathematical or physical figure, but definition of the mathematical or physical figure itself is surprisingly flexible. Its most common definition is that of a pattern traced by a particle moving in a whirlpool, whether spiraling down and inward or up and outward as in a tornado. Yet the vortex also may be a helical or cylindrical pattern in which the particle remains equidistant from its central axis as it spirals in one direction or the other.[40] Common to these definitions is a figure traced by a particle or object moving through a three-dimensional field in a spiraling, directional pattern that is a function of time.

Ironically, one cause of this obscurity is its origin as a crucial and relatively precise concept in Cartesian physics. In Descartes's scheme, the vortex allows the motion of bodies—particles or planets—by suggesting that they whirl inward and downward toward their "center of motion."[41] When Newton refuted this theory with his own explanation of motion in a void, the vortex became scientifically unnecessary but, because so much more concrete than Newton's forces acting at a distance, continued to seize the imagination of scientist and layman alike. Even when it eventually lost all credit as scientific hypothesis, the theory remained as a monument to, and eventually a catchword for, the effect of false or wildly "visionary" theories.[42] From this beginning the word "vortex" has lived a rich metaphorical life, one that has tended to broaden, instead of making more precise its range of meaning, and to preserve a powerful yet inexplicit visual image.

To challenge Newton, Blake turns to these associations of the vortex with what later scientists condemned as merely "visionary" theory.[43] He also adapts a more serious use of the vortex, however, from more recent optical theory. Blake's description of the "eye of man" that "views both the east & west encompassing / Its vortex" (E:109.15.28–29) draws upon eighteenth-century theories of the field of vision as cone-shaped. Yet some theories saw the vertex of the cone as in the eye and some saw it as in the object; and the optical vortex as a cone expanding away from the eye toward objects also seems opposite to the Cartesian, mechanical vortex spiraling downward and inward.[44] If we assume that the vortex is conical, does Milton enter the larger end as one might enter a funnel, pass through the apex or vertex, then find himself emerging into a widening funnel "on the other side," so that looking back from a Newtonian point of view he sees the passed cone point-on, appearing as a globe? This is apparently

Frye's interpretation.[45] Does Milton follow the path of a particle in a vortex, spiraling downward as Dante does through the Inferno, until—like Dante passing the frozen Satan—he passes a central point and "what was beneath soon seemed above"? How does the cone of vision, with its apex in the lens of the eye, relate to such a physical journey? Although these questions may reflect only my own inability to pursue a specific image far enough, because others share my difficulty I suspect that Blake teases us, drawing us with an apparently visualizable image to the point where we must abandon our now almost-intuitive Giottoesque or Newtonian demands for spatial consistency.[46]

Several points are clear, however, in Blake's use of the vortex. Once more he explores the limits of corporeal vision. His illuminations do not illustrate this passage but moments including and following it. In the full-plate illumination 16A, Milton discards his robe of the promise and steps forward to begin his journey. In the interlinear drawing on 17A, between lines 46 and 47 of the verbal text, he enters our world as a star about to fall on Blake's foot—thus illustrating lines 47–49. His verbal art first imitates a visual mode and then shows how its own more temporal mode extends from seeing into vision. The traveler's perceptions of other things—from friends to solar systems—do not remain distanced, in an objective relationship "out there," but transform those things as he experiences them during a time rendered as vortical distance. This three-dimensional journey through the center of the perceived object, moreover, we can read as Blake's extreme version of the perspectival vanishing point in orthodox, orthogonal pictorial space from the Renaissance on. If his own illuminations assert an infinite frontal, vertical plane, his concept of the vortex suggests an infinite horizontal plane perpetually converted into curved objects as the traveler passes through their central points. As he moves like Alice further into the framed space behind the frontal pictorial plane, the known world is created behind the traveler.

Although both Ault and Thomas Frosch interpret this transformation as an entirely negative one, in which the perceiver is sucked into the Newtonian void and its discrete objects as into a vacuum,[47] I think that Blake uses the vortex in *Milton* as a positive image, though its positive function shows at this point, like Milton's fragmentation in order to travel as Shadow, a negative aspect. It is both a means of descent into our Newtonian and Urizenic world and, if we and Milton can understand it, an assurance of this world's dependence upon our own visions, shaped by temporal experience and spatial standpoint. Even Urizen's use of vortices in *The Four Zoas* is, as Martin Nurmi suggests, an attempt—though an ineffective one—to organize chaos instead of being swallowed by it.[48]

Thus the vortex is not "merely" visionary, as the eighteenth-century scientists thought—but can become positively so.

Milton's descent into the vortex leads him into a temporary commitment both to Newtonian space and to the ordinary time of his own past modes of seeing. His ability to return, however, itself denies linear, nonrepetitive time; his descent reverses his past by reseeing that process in visual terms, though terms strained beyond any ordinary visualization. Because Milton descends in part into his own past consciousness of time and space, the vortex reminds us that the ordinary world of space and time that Milton approaches through the vortex is not the only one but is a function of the individual perceiver's experience in time, the product of a certain phase or even state of vision. Objects seen as separate from oneself, cut off "out there" or "up there," become functions of an overdetached memory. The ambiguous double meaning of "heaven" in this passage is particularly suggestive here: "Thus is the heaven a vortex passd already, and the earth / A vortex not yet pass'd by the traveller thro' Eternity" (E:109.15.34–35). Even if the earth threatens to turn into a Newtonian or Miltonic heaven as the perceptual vortices approach and swallow it up, rolling it up into a ball, these heavens can be left behind. For the traveler in Eternity, if not for the "weak traveller beneath the moony shade," the infinite plane always will lie ahead. Although in his descent through Albion Milton must become such a "weak traveller," in another sense he is placing his Newtonian Heaven of the Elect behind him and committing himself eventually to an earth that will seem, as it does to the intuitive observer and not to the scientist, an "infinite plane." The full-plate image of Milton stepping across the curved horizon of the earth as he takes off his robe of the promise (*IB* 16A) points toward such an interpretation; the curved horizon is still partially Newtonian but becoming an infinite plane.

The vortex that formed part of Urizen's desperate attempt to establish spatial direction in *The Four Zoas* represents in *Milton*, then, first a directional model for Milton's self-sacrificial descent into a Newtonian world: he leaves heaven and enters the hellish Ulro that is our world as defined by science and a Mosaic natural, legalistic religion. Second and ultimately more important, however, the vortex redefines "up" and "down" and their traditional moral evaluations, not back into the chaos Urizen feared in *The Four Zoas*, but into terms dependent upon the traveler who must reevaluate his moral, personal, and imaginative commitments. The vortex becomes the link between an Eternity that transcends ordinary spatial needs and "Albion's World," which is defined within them. In *Milton* the vortex is not itself a Satanic mode of perception, nor even a Satanic mode used for redemptive purposes, but a relational mode between Eternal and Satanic ones. Finally, its relational mode seems more than a freely experimental way of playing with new perspectives: it becomes almost a Keatsian "greeting of the spirit," though the palpable form of such a greeting appears more fully in Milton's remolding of Urizen.

Because it emphasizes such a radical interdependence between the viewpoint of the perceiver in time and the configuration of the landscape or cosmos or even other person seen, we may interpret the vortex finally as an example of Keatsian stationing pushed almost to absurdity. One's perspective changes much too fast. As Frosch suggests, "every viewpoint is lost as soon as it is taken; even though he may choose it, the observer immediately loses control of his cognitive position. To assume a viewpoint is necessarily to glide through the cone into a radically altered field of objects."[49] I am deliberately quoting Frosch out of the context of his generally negative discussion of the vortex, but his statements here surely suggest that precisely what Milton needs in his reeducation, in his descent from an Eternity that is for him only a Miltonic heaven, is "a radically altered field of objects." The problem is to catch and halt it before the newly altered pattern itself recedes into a doctrinaire universe as rigid as the one shaped by "Newtons Pantocrator." Shortly after this passage describing the vortex, Blake's own journey moves forward under Milton's impetus to a provisional glimpse of a universe not structured by Satanic or Urizenic sight, but by Los's hammer and Milton's touch. As the dominant verbal image for Milton's entry into the world of space and time, the vortex also frees Blake's illuminations from Satanic sight.

"*To walk forward thro' Eternity*"

Just as the illuminations surrounding Blake's lines on the vortex and its verbal description represent Milton's descent in quite different ways, another group of illuminations and verbal descriptions focuses in very different ways upon a common motif: the feet of the poem's characters. This motif shows with dramatic effectiveness how Blake uses stationing in his sister arts as a starting point for approaching the fury of "Poetic Inspiration."[50] One of the most famous visual motifs of "the burden of the past" for the romantic period, the colossal feet suggested in several of these episodes also show affinities with a romantic classicism that denies Newtonian spatiality. When examples of this style did evoke landscape or architecture as background, they frequently denied its objective validity by distorting its perspectives or altering normal expectations of scale.[51] In its enormous disproportion of scale Henry Fuseli's sketch, *The Artist in despair over the magnitude of antique fragments*, illustrates this romantic variation upon the classical. Its gigantic but disembodied marble foot and hand, apparently from the colossus of Constantine, overwhelm the crouched, living human figure. Furthermore, they almost deny a rational perspective—far more so than do those in Giovanni Battista Piranesi's frontispiece to *Antichita di Roma*, possibly one of Fuseli's sources.[52] Leslie Brisman suggests that in contrast to Fuseli's despairing figure, "we might imaginatively place the figure of the romantic poet putting one foot forward into eternity in defiance of the weeping figures of the past. In Blake's *Milton* . . . Milton descends to enter Blake's foot."[53] As Blake verbally makes himself a giant form, however, he uses and extends Fuseli's own visual method: his perspectives challenge classical and neo-classical expectations and thus already form a subtle counterargument to despair. Fuseli's drawing makes us uneasy not only in its lament for an energetic classical past but also in its romantic revision of perspective: excluding the trees and vines of Piranesi's engraving, he places the living figure below instead of above the marble fragments and sets it among blocks of stone ambiguous in their scale. In the verbal stationing of *Milton*, Blake also revises Piranesi's natural landscape, as both Albion's and Blake's bodies become the scenes—vegetal worlds—for Milton's journey. Ultimately, too, he not only reverses scale but remolds fragmented, rigid statuary into Urizen's living form.

Even though Blake abandoned the famous "Jerusalem" stanzas from the preface in the two later of *Milton*'s four extant copies, their passionate opening question echoes through the expanded poem: "and did those feet in ancient time. / Walk upon Englands mountains green[?]" In the preface, "those feet" are Christ's; in the poem, the feet are those of all the figures, human and superhuman, who locate themselves in its sometimes ordinary, sometimes visionary realms. The most central of these figures is Blake himself; as he becomes actor in his own poem, his empirical reality as ordinary human being like us gives greater urgency to the way he finds his footing across the weird landscapes of his poem. The perilous path of that footing soon leads us beyond the ordinary modes of the visual.

Many of the illuminations in the poem show a figure striding forward or else pulling back along a clearly defined ground plane, in each case with a foot outstretched.[54] Several of these illuminations cluster around the passage describing Milton's descent through the vortex, into the "Sea of Time & Space," and his confrontation with Blake. Their transitional nature is important: the forms appear as almost sculptural models of the "human form divine," caught momentarily in a revealing and vulnerable commitment to, or withdrawal from, a new stance. That stance, Harold Bloom suggests, frequently signals a new psychological attitude (E:915).

These illuminations employ a directional symbolism characteristic, according to Rosenblum, of the romantic classicism Blake shares with Fuseli and John Flaxman, but in this case probably drawn from traditional representations of the last judgment: the left foot indicates an earthly commitment, the right a spiritual one.[55] Blake also uses this directional symbolism on the verbal level of his narrative.

The narrative moment in which Blake first confronts the descending Milton is illuminated as well as described verbally. Both arts use a radical change of scale even more startling than the Bard's revelation of the "vast . . . Abyss" in Satan's bosom (E:103.9.30–35). Here the pictorial transformation appears less striking than the verbal one, because although the character Blake is also a viewer like us and acts as proportional norm for the scene in both media, Milton appears not in human form but as a falling star

> Descending perpendicular, swift as the swallow or swift;
> And on my left foot falling on the tarsus, enterd there;
> But from my left foot a black cloud redounding spread
> over Europe.
>   (E:110.15.48–50)

Because Milton appears like a star as small as those we see in the sky, the illumination for this episode, which illustrates the moment exactly before the star enters Blake's foot, coincides at least superficially with the narrative: a baseball-sized star hurtles toward Blake's outstretched foot (*IB* 17A; E:110.15). But as Blake a few plates later continues his narrative of Milton's encounter with him, he moves beyond this momentary alignment. His verbal descriptions of landscape only show us why Blake does not illustrate this passage:

> But Milton entering my Foot; I saw in the nether
> Regions of the Imagination; also all men on Earth,
> And all in Heaven, saw in the nether regions of the Imagination
> . . . the vast breach of Miltons descent.
> But I knew not that it was Milton, for man cannot know
> What passes in his members till periods of Space & Time
> Reveal the secrets of Eternity: for more extensive
> Than any other earthly things, are Mans earthly lineaments.
>   (E:115.21.4–11)

As the muse inspires him through left foot instead of the conventional right hand mentioned in plate 2, Blake absorbs the figure of Milton into his foot. At the same time, seemingly the whole universe, that vast cosmos which parallels Milton's in *Paradise Lost*, has become his body. Milton is stationed in a landscape shaped by Blake as perceiver—shaped so thoroughly, in fact, that it has become "Regions of the Imagination." This passage vividly represents Frye's definition of romanticism as an epic journey redefined downward and into the self.[56] Blake's imagined absorption of Milton has made him somehow a giant form, here as vast as his ultimate giant form Albion. As Blake's earthly lineaments expand to contain the universe, his left foot remains the link which signals that the earthly or generative world that absorbed so much of Milton's poetry will not simply be abandoned as Milton is regenerated.

As Milton enters Blake's foot, Blake takes on enough of that poet's radical imaginative power to walk not in his footsteps but almost with his feet. He will use Milton's earthly garden, fallen and vegetal though it is, to redeem himself and Milton:

> And all this Vegetable World appeard on my left Foot,
> As a bright sandal formd immortal of precious stones & gold:
> I stooped down & bound it on to walk forward thro' Eternity.
>
> (E:115.21.12–15)

Although the vegetal world in this passage and the "nether regions of the Imagination" in the earlier passage are not precisely the same, their provisional equation through landscape makes Blake more vast, as well as more powerful, than before. The next step in the narrative confirms Blake's redemptive and radical stationing of foot on world:

> . . . what time I bound my sandals
> On; to walk forward thro' Eternity, Los descended to me:
> And Los behind me stood; a terrible flaming Sun: just close
> Behind my back; I turned round in terror, and behold.
> Los stood in that fierce glowing fire; & he also stoop'd down
> And bound my sandals on . . .
> . . . .
> . . . I arose in fury & strength.
>
> (E:116–17.22.4–9, 14)

With this passage, his transformation of the relationship between figure and landscape leads to the encounter between Blake and Los as equals in scale and strength. Accordingly, Blake illustrates the passage in a full-plate illumination (*IB* 47A).[57] In this return to the unity of his two arts, he shows the sandal simply as a sandal, though it retains its verbally achieved richness of significance. This compression returns us to the similar moment in which we see Milton, as star both in illumination and in text, entering Blake's foot. Yet the return is not complete, for through these dramatic verbal acts of stationing Blake has gained a blessing from his Prophet of Eternity and thus can be assured of his own prophetic stance. As a result, each time his words rise out of and return to the visual mode, they carry greater assurance of "Poetic Inspiration" for himself and, by the end of the poem, for Milton as well.

Seen as a whole, this motif shows a "composite art" in which the relationship of Blake's two arts changes as a function of his own strides forward into vision. In the precisely located but temporary moments of stationing, his visual and verbal arts come closest to each other and thus assert a version of the *ut pictura poesis* tradition. The more Blake develops extreme forms of verbal stationing, however, the more he asserts a verbal independence that creates a new context of meaning for each pictorial moment. This consistent reevaluation of pictorial representation, whether that representation appears as illumination or in the poetry, does not discard but redeems a fallen sister.

"His forming image": Sculpture as Redemptive Metaphor

As I suggested at the beginning of this chapter, the episode in which Blake's Milton confronts and remolds Urizen proposes another, more complex model for the relationship between verbal and visual arts. Because these two arts treat this episode in much the same way, Milton's sculpting seems at first to assert an *ut pictura poesis* hypothesis more strongly than do the instances of "stationing," by adding another sister art—sculpture. Yet, as Blake's use of sculpture in this poem shows, he again asserts a parallel in order to work out a distinction. His "statuary," to use Keats's second analogue, leads Milton to recognize his own art and thus to sacrifice the "marble" aspects of that art.

Because Blake is intensely conscious of his own artistic processes and is always ready to use them as symbolic acts, we might well examine the significance of sculpting in this episode for Blake himself. Are sculpture and poetry simply to be equated, as a further extension of *ut pictura poesis* theory? Does the sculpting extend the significance of "sculpsit," the declaration of an engraver's work, as David Erdman suggests?[58] Does Blake imply that Milton's poetry must be completed by a composite art like his own, that Milton must become plastic or visual artist as well as a verbal one, in order to complete his regeneration and serve as adequate model for Blake, himself both poet and painter? Or should we see this emphasis upon sculpture in the creation of human form as a deliberate distinction from painting as well as poetry, a distinction that carries its own symbolic significance?

Although the obvious way to answer these questions is to look at Blake's own work as context for his *Milton*, the references to sculpture in his own work are symbolically rich but also infrequent and ambiguous. To interpret sculptural metaphor in *Milton*, these references need a larger context: the arguments over defining sculpture as a separate art that emerged in the aspirations of Renaissance artists and gained complexity during the second half of the eighteenth century and the beginning of the nineteenth. Although many of these discussions began by defining the appeal of ancient sculpture and of the Laocoon group as its paradigm, they went on to consider ancient and modern rivalry, the spatial and temporal dimensions of these arts, their perceptual and emotional bases, and their relationships to landscapes and thus to the external natural world. First examining Blake's own references to sculpture and then his own aware-ness of this larger historical context, we can recognize the significance of his Milton as sculptor.

The single work of his that bears most obviously on the topic, the Laocoon engraving, is as provocatively enigmatic as Milton's sculpting of Urizen, but treats sculpture in a sharply contrasting way.[59] Blake's Milton molds with his hands, then walks around his "forming image" like a sculptor. The unusually finished, almost three-dimensional engraving of Laocoon and his sons indeed appears solid enough to touch or even walk around—but the writing that encircles the figures forces us, instead, to turn the page again and again, denying the figures their space as we assert the control of word over image, or flat pictorial surface over sculptural form. In spite of this interplay among sculpture, painting or drawing, and words, however, neither *Milton* nor the engraving makes any systematic statement about sculpture as a separate art.

In *Milton*'s other references to sculpture, in the Laocoon inscriptions, and in the *Descriptive Catalogue*, Blake shows a clear sense of this dramatic, even competitive, interplay among the various arts. Yet no clear system or hierarchy of arts emerges. In the prose preface, omitted from the later and longer copies C and D of *Milton*, Blake exhorts "Painters! . . . Sculptors! Architects!" as well as poets to abandon "Greek or Roman Models" for "our own Imaginations."[60] Within the poem, the task of molding natural forms undertaken by Los and his sons toward the end of book 1 is clearly sculptural;[61] yet the omission of sculpture from the "eternal" arts listed as models for redemptive process—"Poetry, Painting, Music, and Architec-ture"—leaves us wondering whether sculpture is the most generic or elemental of these arts, a lesser subdivision of one of these, or a form so fallen that it cannot be spoken of as eternal. Even more startling is the repetition of the same list, again excluding sculpture, in the inscriptions around the Laocoon engraving, where these arts are once more agents of redemption from the natural world. These inscriptions do not argue against sculpture itself, however, but against the priority of Greek and Roman models, claiming that those derive from still earlier sculptural models. Again, sculpture seems a basis for the other arts, but this relationship is not made explicit. In the *Descriptive Catalogue*, Blake cites visionary models, or "wonderful originals," for his paintings, some of which were painted, some "carved as basso relievos, and some as groupes of statues" (E:531). The classical statues his own era accepted as standards for all beauty, "Hercules, Farnese, Venus of Medicis, Apollo Belvidere, and all the grand works of ancient art" (E:531), he catalogues as mere copies of these originals. Although these passages do not exhaust Blake's references to sculpture or statuary, they are representative enough to show his interest in sculpture as well as the need for a larger historical context in which to evaluate that interest.[62] They also begin to suggest motifs that a more precise definition of sculpture will yield: a focus for the continuing debate between ancients and moderns, and a role for sculpture as an art reconciling the sometimes divergent arts of Blake's own composite work.

Both the Bard's song of *Milton* itself and the biographical context of the poem's origin and execution show Blake's need to reevaluate his own sister arts of poetry and painting. During this time almost all of his most valued friends and patrons were urging him to relinquish poetry, painting, and even the design of engravings in order to build a more solid professional career as engraver of others' works.[63] To interpret Milton's sculpting of Urizen as engraving alone, then, would condemn Milton to Blake's own commercial servitude. Yet Blake's consciousness of Milton's achievement under much more savage pressure, both political and physical, must have driven him to consider through what art or medium to emulate Milton: Should it be in the poet's own verbal mode? Should it be in a pictorial mode that many eighteenth-century readers and painters thought implicit in Milton's words and that others, with equal vigor, denied? Or should it be in some composite form that would use these arts critically and symbolically? This narrow but painfully immediate controversy over his artistic vocation points toward the larger controversies over the relationship of poetry not only to painting but also to sculpture as a separate art. Because I have analyzed these complex arguments elsewhere in detail, I will only review here their conclusions and implications for Blake's use of sculpture in Milton.[64]

Of the broader Renaissance and eighteenth-century discussions about sculpture as a separate art, the Renaissance one is less directly important for Blake but still significant. As artists during the Italian Renaissance struggled to raise painting and sculpture from the level of mere crafts to the status of intellectual art already accorded poetry, that struggle generated a series of formal debates, called *paragone*, over the merits of the various arts and the qualities demanded of the artist.[65] Leonardo, for example, claims wittily that painting is superior to sculpture because its practice is less sweaty.[66] It is also superior, he argues, to music and poetry;[67] here, of course, he challenges the domain of the more traditionally accepted liberal arts.[68] Although Blake probably did not know the Italian Renaissance *paragone* directly, he had had some opportunity to learn about them through Flaxman's and Fuseli's Roman visits and through English Renaissance versions.[69]

In the eighteenth century, sculpture—and particularly the Laocoon group as paradigm of Greek classical sculpture—stood almost unrecognized at the center of *ut pictura poesis* debates. Claiming Milton as witness on both sides of the argument, those debates entered a new, active phase with the publication of Johann Joachim Winckelmann's *Reflections on the Painting and Sculpture of the Greeks* (1755, translated by Fuseli in 1765) and Gotthold Ephraim Lessing's combative response in *Laocoon: An Essay Upon the Limits of Painting and Poetry* (1766). From this dramatic reopening of an enduring debate over the sister arts of painting and poetry, we can trace three major stages in the arguments for sculpture as a separate sister art. Although often entwined within the arguments for and against *ut pictura poesis*, they are not identical to those arguments and demand fresh consideration of the sources. By choosing the Laocoon as the focus of his engraving, Blake chose to call up and challenge a view of classical sculpture that the Laocoon group epitomized for neoclassical theorists.[70] For the first group—Winckelmann, Lessing, Reynolds, Flaxman, and to some extent Cumberland—a Greek statue is an ideal image of general nature, a figure of "noble simplicity and sedate grandeur" so distanced from the minute particulars of human experience that it becomes almost a rational abstraction. A second stage, which in effect if not always in intention challenges the first, proposes that sculpture is an art of feeling—of touch for Herder and Cumberland, and of emotional feeling for Hayley and Fuseli. Still a third stage in this historical development is itself a theory of historical development. Coleridge builds his famous, though borrowed, distinction between classical and modern literature upon the analogy of classical literature as sculpturesque, modern as picturesque.

We can begin to see why Blake responds ambiguously to the idealists' view of classical sculpture if we recognize distinctions within this first group. John Flaxman's ideal forms that transcend space and time obviously differ from Reynolds's images of a general nature built up from observed detail.[71] Advocating outline, Blake nevertheless opposes abstraction or generalization.[72] Advocating a Winckelmann-like greatness of soul and even a "noble simplicity," he nevertheless must have been troubled by Winckelmann's "sedate grandeur" and even more by Lessing's limitations upon the visual arts as capable only of a formal beauty, spatial and superficial.[73] His acquaintance with these ideas is broad, though, as it ranges from actual reading to probable discussion. He knew Winckelmann's *Reflections* in Fuseli's 1765 translation. Fuseli also translated sections of Winckelmann's 1765 *History of Ancient Art*, which both Flaxman and Hayley knew well.[74] Although Blake's annotations to Reynolds stop after Discourse 8, he probably heard Discourse 10 as a student at Royal Academy schools in 1780; in 1802, moreover, he evidently read all the *Discourses*.[75] As Blake began to write *Milton*, then, he shared with his fellow artists a renewed awareness of the idealists' attitude toward sculpture.

Although more difficult to establish, the connection between Lessing's *Laocoon* and Blake is significant, for it may well lead to the spatial and temporal transformations Blake brings about in the *Laocoon* engraving and in *Milton*. Although Johann Kaspar Lavater asked Fuseli to translate the essay in 1767, Fuseli refused; in fact, no translation in English appeared until Thomas De Quincey's 1826 excerpts in *Blackwood's*.[76] By 1794, however, Fuseli mentioned in a review Lessing's primary distinction between poetry as a temporal and painting as a spatial art.[77] In 1801 Fuseli made his first three Royal Academy lectures on painting the occasion for a further discussion of Lessing's arguments in his *Laocoon*, and Blake engraved the frontispiece for the published lectures. Lessing's influence seems not to focus directly on sculpture itself, but to increase awareness of the different physical limits inherent in artistic representation: in a sense, to dramatize the *ut pictura poesis* problem. Los and Enitharmon, temporal and spatial aspects of the fallen but redemptive imagination, appear in Blake's art soon after Lessing first appears in Fuseli's criticism, and they develop their characters most fully in *Milton*, a work conceived during the time Fuseli was lecturing to the Royal Academy.[78]

Although he shares much with my first group, the idealists whose ideas he transmits, Fuseli himself belongs more properly in the second.[79] The members of this second group share a sense that sculpture yields certain nonrational, nonobjective "felt" experiences. Blake may have learned of Johann Gottfried Herder, the earliest of this second group, through Fuseli's translations and reviews.[80] Working from James Harris's identification of painting with sight, and of poetry and music with hearing, Herder extends this sensuous basis of the arts to include sculpture as an art of touch.[81] Herder "assigns to the touching person, blind or seeing, a special plastic experience of space and shape," according to Clark.[82] Such a discussion, of course, would fascinate those who speculated about Milton's special poetic abilities.

In *Thoughts on Outline*, George Cumberland proposes a similar assignment of sculpture to "touch, the test of truth."[83] Further, he makes sculpture, instead of poetry, the art that embraces "the united excellencies" of the other arts and combines the "enjoyments of all the other senses . . . affected by the other arts." By defining the "sculptor's art" as "not . . . merely finishing his compositions in marble, but forming, with correctness, figures in any material," even clay models, he slides between tactile molding and the more visual, idealist designing suggested by his emphasis on outline. Blake, as the engraver of Cumberland's designs for *Thoughts on Outline*, receives high praise within the volume itself for the accuracy and continuity of his outlines. Although he continues to share with Cumberland through 1800 an excitement over Greek models as ideal forms, his praise of outline outlives his direct classical enthusiasm.[84] In *Milton*, Cumberland's idea that sculpture is an art of touch appears both in the tactile molding of red clay, not the nearby marble, to generate a new form for Urizen, and, as we shall see, in the importance of Milton's relationship to the figure Ololon. As the form of his redeemed imagination, she shows a way to salvation through touch as sexual encounter.

Two other engraving commissions, one for Hayley's *Essay on Sculpture* in 1800 and the one for Fuseli's first three lectures on painting in 1801, may well have led Blake to emphasize the element not of tactile but of emotional feeling in sculpture. Although this emphasis does not distinguish sculpture from painting as does the preceding emphasis upon feeling as touch, it redefines the way both arts—and particularly the cool, white, abstracted figures of classical sculpture—might be experienced. By making sculpture "a mighty Poet's intellectual child," Hayley's *Essay on Sculpture*, written between 1794 and 1800, points to a Longinian energy underlying formal differences between the arts.[85] Like Hayley, Fuseli makes sculpture an expression of the Longinian sublime in which grandeur of conception and emotion outweighs formal differences between the arts.[86] His third lecture, on invention, explicitly confronts Lessing's attack on *ut pictura poesis* in the Laocoon essay. Although he agrees with Lessing that the pictorial or plastic arts, because spatial, can represent only a single, pregnant moment, he characterizes that moment not as Lessing's snapshot of suspended physical action but as a portrait of inner character through passionate emotional expression. Thus it expresses a meaning as profound as that of poetry.[87]

Fuseli's concept of the moment is not, of course, the only one that leads to the redemptive moment in *Milton*. As Donald Ault shows, Blake defines it in ways consistent with Newtonian physics in order to challenge

the Urizenic rational framework.[88] In *Milton*, the moment is not emotionally expressive alone but also seeks to humanize reason in the creative
restructuring of our limited world of space and time. In Los's sculpture
halls at the end of book 1, Blake as actor in the poem sees how that
restructuring is hammered out; and in a specific narrative moment that
reveals this deeper renovation of expressed identity, a "Moment . . . that
Satan cannot find" (E: 136.35.42), Ololon as Milton's alienated imagination descends in an impulse analogous to that of divine grace descending to
one suddenly ready for it. In that moment she arrives to witness his
sculpting of Urizen and to make possible its incorporation both of the
expressive and of the constitutive moment. The first of these is Fuseli's;
the second is Blake's transformation of Lessing's categories.

Unlike the writers of my second group, who use feeling to humanize the
marble figures of classical sculpture, a third group of writers on sculpture
sees those marble figures as characteristic of a now-distant classical
culture, in contrast to a paintinglike or "picturesque" modern culture.
Because this pattern of historical development through analogy to sculpture and painting is far more important for Keats and Shelley than for
Blake, as suggested in Chapter 1, the next chapter will consider it in more
detail. Its importance for Blake lies in its further evidence of contemporary interest in distinguishing sculpture from painting and in using these
arts as analogies or metaphors for other arts. Although John Black's
translation of Schlegel's lectures did not appear until 1815, and Coleridge's adoption of their ideas in his own lectures did not begin until
December 1811, Blake may have learned of them through Fuseli or
through Coleridge's earlier conversations.[89] Although Coleridge already
was differentiating casually between "statuesque" and "picturesque" as
early as 1799, his visit to Richard Payne Knight during the spring of 1804
must have directed his thinking to a more systematic opposition between
the two adjectives and the arts from which they are drawn.[90] In his
Analytical Inquiry into the Principles of Taste, published in 1805, Knight
returns again and again to the relationship of these two arts. He is
prompted by interest not only in sculpture but also in the associative effect
of painting, an interest developed during his writings on the picturesque
in landscape a decade earlier.[91] Close to the time he visited Knight,
Coleridge dominated a "very metaphysical conversation" at Sir George
Beaumont's, exploring the "differing powers required . . . for painting
and Sculpture." Fuseli, though apparently not at the Beaumonts', discusses the conversation with Joseph Farington the following day and
remarks that he has met Coleridge at Joseph Johnson's some time earlier.[92]

As I suggested earlier, Blake's Laocoon engraving sets out a three-dimensional sculpted image and then irons it out with a space-denying page

of inscription. In both the Laocoon and *Milton*, he plays with these spatial perspectives to participate in the energetic debate over the relationship between painting, poetry, and sculpture begun for his era with Winckelmann's and Lessing's argument over the Laocoon. Moreover, as Blake recommends for the modern artists a preclassical inspiration, he challenges the dominance of classical sculpture as do Coleridge and his German predecessors who develop the opposition between sculpturesque and picturesque eras of culture. Both the Laocoon engraving and *Milton* enrich Milton's own rejection of classical for biblical models. Both engraving and book redeem those arts and thus our world by transforming sculptural images from classical marble into living form. In the Laocoon engraving the living form is a whirl of words that makes the statue not monumental but pictorial, contained in an imaginative verbal frame. In *Milton* the monumental Urizen of plate 18A gains a less rigid and more living form on plate 45 through the verbal account of Milton's molding with red clay. Here, however, Blake does not subordinate it to pictorial and then verbal art but makes it an image for Milton's self and for his own composite, often competing arts.[93]

Two other treatments of such sculpting in the poem provide a context for understanding this episode. Although neither of these receives direct visual treatment, each tells of the struggle of Los to reshape the forms of this visible, natural world. The first of these, in the Bard's song at the beginning of the poem, shows Los's attempt to reshape Urizen and his almost complete failure. The second, at the end of book 1, shows his gradual success in shaping definite spiritual form for all living things: he thus makes possible an apocalyptic end to their existence as natural things. Because Blake as character in his own poem witnesses "the bright Sculptures of / Los's Halls," to use the more explicit phrase from *Jerusalem* (E:161.16.61–62), all three of the poet-prophets, whose relationship to one another the poem explores, see this crucial task as an act or metaphor to define their own art.

In the first example of this statue making, Los fails to shape a fully human form out of the nonlandscape that contains the fallen Urizen:

> Urizen lay in darkness & solitude, in chains of the mind lock'd up
> Los siezd his Hammer & Tongs; he labourd at his resolute Anvil
> Among indefinite Druid rocks & snows of doubt & reasoning.
>
> Refusing all Definite Form, the Abstract Horror roofd. stony hard.
> (E:96–97.3.6–9)

This abrupt beginning leaves uncertain the location, the temporal sequence of events, and the status of Urizen: it mirrors Los's need to give

Urizen definite form. Yet Los's task is ambiguous. From this landscape of darkness and solitude resembling the chaos or *tehom* of Genesis, he must hammer out a "Human form." Yet as he does so, repeating his attempts in *The Book of Urizen*, *The Book of Los*, and *The Four Zoas*, the figure he creates may come to resemble those heroic figures whose statuelike passivity marks the *in medias res* beginnings of classical epic. Urizen thus threatens to bind Los's and Blake's creativity to the "creeds outworn" of those epic heroes and their gods; his definite form then would become only a static, limiting image.

As Los works with hammer, anvil, and tongs, seven ages pass over Urizen. Although in the first the "Abstract Horror" "Refus[ed] all Definite Form," in the second a placentalike globe of blood sinks "Deep down into the Abyss," and in each of the five following ages one of the five senses develops, ending finally with touch. Ironically paralleling the seven traditional days of creation, the passage makes epic deity internal, but the process goes berserk. Each sense is limited as it develops: "Two Ears in close volutions / Shot spiring out in the deep darkness & petrified as they grew" (E:97.3.9, 12, 17–18). Not only does each sense grow grotesquely out into the abyss to locate itself, but the apparent creator, Los, exerts only minimal control. Although he seems at first to create—or let happen—an image of a mind based on the limitations of the five senses, the final sense—that of touch—appears in the passage as a full if not fully visualized figure pushing against his limits. At this point neither the reader nor Los can tell whether touch offers an escape from solipsism or simply a venture into epic statuary.

The fully developed figure of Urizen never actually appears in the Bard's song. Because Los sets his anvil "Among indefinite Druid rocks & snows of doubt & reasoning" (E:97.3.8), because Los now shares too much of the fallen Urizen's limited perspective, it is as if Urizen himself dissolves from statue back into the landscape perceived by the five senses alone. A crucial problem both for Los and for us, then, is to distinguish between a definiteness of outline or sculpted shape that is merely a naturalistic limit and one that images a fully human and spiritual form. Because the physical human body is in visual terms an ambiguous image for Blake, because it must represent both physical and spiritual humanity, much depends on gesture or stance.[94] For our argument, much also depends upon defining the act of sculpting as one that can acknowledge this difficulty.

The second episode of sculpting in Blake's *Milton* (E:121.24.68ff.) in part continues the first: Los is still master sculptor. His creation is less ambiguous in his own halls than among the Druid rocks of the Bard's song, however. The objects he and his sons build in their workshops or sculpture halls for the universe are all the living creatures of the natural world, all given definition as if they are crops brought to harvest out of Urizen's stony soil (E:126.28.13–17). Within this account of communal sculpting that explains the objective, communally perceived natural world, however, is an account of individual perception as vision so radical that it too constitutes creation. In this new perception Los reshapes both space and time. Through this reshaping, moreover, Blake revises the idea of the "moment" that is central both to *ut pictura poesis* arguments and to Lessing's counterarguments in his *Laocoon*.

To recognize that all living things in the natural world are artifacts of Los and his sons is to understand, Blake says, that all natural objects have spiritual causes (E:124.26.39–46) and that the forms or shapes of those natural beings are not merely temporary manifestations of a world of generative flux but eternal forms that those mythic artists have made actual. Furthermore, as this underlying aesthetic permanence manifests itself in the natural world, that world gradually moves toward apocalypse. The flux of history, too, can take on sculptural or architectural form: "others of the Sons of Los build Moments & Minutes & Hours / And Days & Months & Years & Ages & Periods; wondrous buildings" (E:126.28.44–45) stationed in an artist's created cityscape. Thus the statue making in Los's sculpture gallery does not exclude energy or motion but redirects it to make a cosmic, eternal whole. Vincent De Luca characterizes this process as one of those iconic moments in Blake's poetry when the narrative flow of the poem halts in a meditative act for poetry, characters, and audience.[95]

Yet though the passage is about the making of icons, it is in fact difficult to visualize. Moreover, Blake illuminates it only with a series of tiny marginal and interlinear figures. This technique allows him to show how Los's work creates and sustains in their individuality even the smallest, most minute particulars of the natural world. Another reason emerges, however, as the passage explores the relationship of the individual, earthly perceiver—Blake or one of us—to this cosmic statue making.

We are all potentially Los's sons, Blake suggests, and can remake that "objective" world even more radically through our subjective, phenomenal experience of space and time:

> . . . every Space that a Man views around his dwelling-place:
> Standing on his own roof, or in his garden on a mount
> Of twenty-five cubits in height, such space is his Universe;
> And on its verge the Sun rises & sets. . . .
>
> .   .   .   .
> The Starry heavens reach no further but here bend and set . . .
>
> .   .   .   .

As to that false appearance which appears to the reasoner,
As of a Globe rolling thro Voidness, it is a delusion of Ulro
. . . .
For every Space larger than a red Globule of Mans blood.
Is visionary: and is created by the Hammer of Los
And every Space smaller than a Globule of Mans blood. opens
Into Eternity.

(E:127.29.5–8, 10, 15–16, 19–22)

Although this reworking at first emphasizes a commonsense phenomenal perception of space, that perception depends upon the subjective observers who shape their world from their own "stations." Every space is Los's artifact and our individual, subjective perception—thus our artifact. With that recognition, narrator and reader can reshape Urizen as rational, Newtonian horizon, if not yet as dramatic figure.

Los's hammer also transforms time; in showing this, Blake as poet transforms the eighteenth-century idea of the pictorial moment. *Ut pictura poesis* theorists celebrated both poetry and painting for revealing character through gestures caught in one significant moment that reveals its place in an ongoing sequence or process. That process becomes ordered and meaningful through the assumed identity of natural and moral order. In contrast, Blake saw natural process as potentially dehumanizing. By making the perceiver's or artist's individual pulse a measure of prophetic time, he transforms biological process into visionary moments capable of including all of time:

Every Time less than a pulsation of the artery
Is equal in its period & value to Six Thousand Years.
For in this Period the Poets Work is Done: and all the Great
Events of Time start forth & are concievd in such a Period
Within a Moment: A Pulsation of the Artery.

(E:127.28.62–63; 29.1–3)

If each moment less than a pulsation of the artery equals the traditional time between creation and apocalypse, then the last judgment—in which Los's work of sculpting becomes complete—can come within such a moment of imaginative renovation. Time is both enormously expanded and enormously compressed; with an imaginative leap we are not comprehended within it but comprehend it. In method and subject, these passages describing Los's sculpting defy ordinary narrative sequence and ordinary pictorialization. As they do so, they free each of the sister arts of poetry and painting to follow its own redefinition of such ordinary limits.

Yet these passages also suggest a new integration of time and space, an integration worked out by Los's sculpting of every minute particular larger than pulsation or corpuscle. After his failure in the Bard's song to remold Urizen into definite form, Los becomes self-divided: in this further fall, he represents time and his female emanation Enitharmon represents space. Their split acknowledges their inability to give the fallen world definite shape. Yet because these two figures are aspects of a divided self that if redeemed can again become one, Blake overcomes the rigid division between spatial and temporal, plastic or visual and verbal arts, that Lessing proposes; he accepts this separation only as a provisional, fallen aspect of art.[96] When Los and his sons complete their sculpting, these figures will merge not only with one another but with the other zoas and emanations to create the fully humanized, whole figure of Albion.

The third and most important example of statuary in the poem, Milton's wrestling with Urizen in order to mold him a "Human form," reworks the solitary struggle of Los with Urizen at the beginning of the poem, but it succeeds far better. Although that disastrous attempt at definition led to Los's separation from Enitharmon, here Milton's emanation Ololon joins him. Because he now accepts his sensual as well as intellectual self, his sculpting—an art of touch—and the descent of Ololon become interdependent, mutually defining actions. Blake's method of representing this process, however, at first seems simply to reaffirm *ut pictura poesis*. Milton's solitary struggle is far more sharply defined than was Los's; Blake's more specific, more visual manner of representation both in poem and in illuminations seems to correspond to Milton's ultimate act of reshaping Urizen. Two full-page illuminations at widely separated points of the poem illustrate slightly differing stages of this episode. Two verbal passages also describe the episode in pictorial terms:

> . . . Milton took of the red clay of Succoth, moulding it with care
> Between his palms; and filling up the furrows of many years
> Beginning at the feet of Urizen, and on the bones
> Creating new flesh on the Demon cold, and building him,
> As with new clay a Human form.
>
> (E:112.19.10–14)

> . . . Silent Milton stood before
> The darkend Urizen: as the sculptor silent stands before
> His forming image.
>
> (E:114.20.7–9)

Blake's handling of this episode seems, then, to define prophetic verbal art as a pictorial mode. Because Urizen represents precisely the views of space and time that have just been condemned as "delusions," however, Milton's work of remolding him marks the attempt of a mortal poet to take up the work of Los, immortal prophet. If Milton's art is at first ambiguous, it reflects his own condition as mortal, a condition Milton has accepted willingly in search of a redeemed imagination.

The Bard's song already has linked Urizen, as has Blake's earlier poetry, to the sort of Old Testament God whose tyranny Milton so well, though so unwittingly, portrayed in *Paradise Lost*. Milton, then, wrestles with and struggles to reform that God. At the same time, he wrestles with the aspect of himself that worshiped law, order, reason, and "objective" external nature until those qualities became that white-bearded figure supported by the tablets of the decalogue that we see in plate 18A (*IB*). The rigid, central, and monumental visual image of plate 18A, however, forms a marked contrast to the second full-plate illumination of this motif, plate 45A. In this one, Urizen "faints in terror striving . . . with Miltons Spirit" (E:141.39.53–54) and appears as a figure so limp that Milton barely can hold him up.[97] The product of the sculptor's art, normally the static representation of the expressive, significant moment of the *ut pictura poesis* theorists, proves in this case more flexible. While Urizen freezes "dark rocks between / The footsteps, and infixing deep the feet in marble beds" so that Milton's "feet bled sore / Upon the clay now chang'd to marble," Milton reverses the process and undoes Urizen's malign "stationing or statuary" of the poet. "Milton took of the red clay . . . building him, / As with new clay a Human form" (E:112.19.1–4, 10, 13–14). "Infixing deep [Milton's] . . . feet in marble beds," Urizen has attempted to cast into rigid form the acceptance of mortal connection, of stance in the landscape, which Milton had risked in his descent into the vegetal world and into Blake's left foot. As Urizen attempts to freeze this commitment to earth into a hellish marble fixity, Milton counters with his sculpting, an art that redefines touch from a merely generative link to a redemptive shaping. As Hazard Adams notes, the foot in Blake frequently signifies Tharmas, the zoa of corporeal organization; here also its frequent Freudian significance as phallic symbol reinforces the ambiguity of sexuality for Blake as either generative trap or as the sensual enjoyment that will lead to regeneration.[98] Milton's sculpting, however, converts this ambiguity to a rite of passage, just as "stationing" of figure in landscape became a stage for redefining the visual. Sculpting in red clay, then, has released both antagonists from the statuelike immobility of marble. Milton's work of art assumes the form of sculpture as a means of achieving release from it, just as Milton as redeemer of his imaginative vision must reassume the burden of red clay, of mortal flesh, to find that vision and free himself from rigidity.

Appropriately, Ololon's point of view frames the final vision of this process of sculpting. She represents Milton's capacity for redemption through touch, both as sexuality and as his shaping imagination. This commitment to mortal flesh also links her with the redemptive, self-sacrificing descent of Christ into mortal shape:

> . . . I heard Ololon say to Milton

> I see thee strive upon the Brooks of Arnon. there a dread
> And awful Man I see, oercoverd with the mantle of years.
> I behold Los & Urizen. I behold Orc & Tharmas;
> The Four Zoa's of Albion & thy Spirit with them striving
> In Self annihilation giving thy life to thy enemies.

> (E:141.40.3–8)

Not only does Ololon see more than the illumination and the earlier verbal versions of the scene have shown, but she recognizes for the first time Milton's self-annihilation. The aesthetic act of "stationing or statuary" gains spiritual dimensions as it provokes self-recognition. "Stationed" in Blake's cottage garden, Ololon describes for Milton his own struggle to become whole. As Ololon sees Milton's task of sculpting made greater to include all four zoas or living forces of universal man, she points toward the integration of all those faculties in Milton, in Blake, and in Los—and thus toward the awakening of Albion, the universal man, at the end of Blake's final illuminated work, *Jerusalem*.[99]

Yet the tableau she describes here seems with its participial forms to suspend that action, so that the struggle continues. Although the "moment" in which the poet's work is done is the moment in which Ololon has found Milton and has recognized his self-achieved redemption, her verbal and yet visualizable scene returns to the less radical suspended moment of the *ut pictura poesis* theorists, as if to remind us that all poets must continue to wrestle with the phenomena of this natural world until all of us become capable of reworking Urizen. As we do so, we will use touch to renovate sight; sculpting moves through the most immediate of senses, touch, to create an image for a renewed sight, once the most intellectual and Urizenic. As sculpture, represented in Blake's pictorial and poetic arts, leads from indefinite chaos through the rigidity of marble to the living forms of a sacrificial and redeemed red clay, his composite art too can take on new life.

Three

🦚

Keats's *Hyperion*

"shap'd and palpable Gods"

Plastic to Picturesque

In obvious contrast to Blake's illuminated *Milton*, Keats's two attempts at Miltonic epic must confront *Paradise Lost* more directly in its single, verbal medium. Although the "stationing or statuary" Keats finds in *Paradise Lost* draws upon the *ut pictura poesis* tradition, Keats's *Hyperion* poems appear to use that technique without the complex, self-consciously evaluative and ultimately symbolic rivalry between the arts developed by Blake. Assimilating plastic, pictorial, and verbal arts to one another, Keats's statuelike figures also silence for the moment our questions about the relationship of myth, imagination, and the natural world. Milton's "Satan . . . on th' *Assyrian* mount" or Keats's own Saturn "Deep in the shady sadness of a vale" is each the quasi-human focus of an apparently objective tableau. Their validity as natural yet transcendent figures is born both from their statuelike immobility and from their placement in natural landscapes we accept as actual. Yet this union of art with art, and the suggested union of the visionary with the natural, are fragile and momentary. Christopher Ricks and John Jones argue that Keats abandons his true gifts of snail-horn perception for the coldly statuesque manner of his *Hyperion* poems; I would argue instead that he posits such a manner in these poems, planning to make them more "naked and Grecian" than his lush *Endymion*, and then finds that he must challenge it.[1] In the course of the two poems, particularly in *Hyperion*, "stationing or statuary" and the aesthetic analogue among the arts on which Keats bases his phrase changes from a poetic technique into a central theme. This discovery emerges most dramatically in *Hyperion*, yet its implications continue to unfold in *The Fall of Hyperion*.

One of the major difficulties Keats finds as he emulates Miltonic epic emerges from his decision to make vast impersonal processes of change the motivating forces in these poems. As a result his protagonists, even the Apollo of *Hyperion* and the narrator of *The Fall of Hyperion*, become witnesses able only to embrace the "knowledge enormous" of their own inability to shape that action. From the beginning of *Hyperion*, we see these figures as statuelike, rigid if beautiful memorials to the loss of transcendent power or the loss of belief in such transcendent power. The personal actions involved in these two poems, moreover, seem only a process of envisaging this stasis: in the course of the first poem, and from the beginning of the second, a framing mind provides a local habitation for these statuesque figures that the course of an impersonal history has cast off.

Many critics, among them Douglas Bush, W. J. Bate, and Ian Jack, have pointed out the pervasive influence of sculpture and painting upon the specific details of Keats's poetry but have argued that such description halts the narrative action of these long poems.[2] Bate and others, most notably Harold Bloom, also have explored Keats's theories of historical progress in *Hyperion* and in his letters as developments of his individual search for a place in more recent poetic history, particularly in the history of writing successful epic.[3] John Middleton Murry, for example, considers "whether . . . Keats, when he attempted his epic, did not find himself inevitably caught between the Miltonic objectivity and the Wordsworthian subjectivity" he describes in the 3 May 1818 letter to Reynolds.[4] Wordsworth's ability to explore the "dark Passages" of the "human heart" may indeed share in "the general and gregarious advance of the intellect" since Milton's time, but those passages may lack Milton's epic grandeur. Yet because the movement from statuesque object to picturing subject within *Hyperion*, and a similar movement between *Hyperion* and *The Fall of Hyperion*, correspond to developmental theories of aesthetic history current in Keats's time, considering these two critical problems together leads to a solution.

Two recent analyses of the *Hyperion* fragments point toward this solution. Although Dorothy Van Ghent's recently published reading of *Hyperion* argues that Keats's theories of progress in the poem only interfere with a more profound pattern of rebirth, she links the poem's sculptural metaphors to this rebirth through an implicit scheme of history—if a cyclic instead of a progressive one. The unfallen sculptural serenity of the Titans, she suggests, is in Nietzsche's terms Apollonian, and this is the godlike state toward which the Dionysian Apollo struggles.[5] More explicitly making use of patterns of cultural history, Tilottama Rajan interprets

Hyperion as a similar longing for a serene Greek idealism. Schiller's 1800 comparison of Greek consciousness to objective, serene sculpture and modern, romantic consciousness to a subjective, restless music becomes the basis for a series of nineteenth-century interpretations of cultural development, including Arthur Schopenhauer's in 1819 and Nietzsche's in 1879. Rajan uses the two latter thinkers to revise Schiller's division between the "naive" Greek culture and the "sentimental" modern culture. Because even the supposedly calm Greeks wrote tragedy, she suggests that a more accurate pattern within any culture and particularly within romanticism is a development from the sentimental longing for ideal serenity as if it once existed, through the ironic, to the tragic. *Hyperion*, she argues, is sentimental because the poem "commits [itself] to the myth of a recoverable perfection"; *The Fall of Hyperion* is an ironic poem moving toward sublimity and tragedy.[6] Like Van Ghent's archetypal reading of *Hyperion*, Rajan's complex, partially deconstructive reading sees the development of Apollo as an incomplete return to a sculptural idea. Unlike Van Ghent's, her interpretation is more concerned with the conflict between ideal and real in the poems than with a close reading of their aesthetic metaphors.

Yet by following even more closely than Van Ghent does the poem's analogues of figures to sculptural objects, and by following, as well, its development of painting as a second analogue, we can interpret the end of *Hyperion* somewhat differently[7]—for that movement from statuesque object to picturing subject within *Hyperion*, and the similar movement between *Hyperion* and *The Fall of Hyperion*, correspond closely to the developmental aesthetic theory of A. W. Schlegel.[8] Like Schiller, whose theory he modifies, Schlegel proposes Greek sculpture as the model for classical culture. In contrast to Schiller—and also to the later Schopenhauer and Nietzsche—he makes painting or the "picturesque" the model for romantic or modern culture. Although Schlegel's theory of development from sculpturesque to picturesque models of consciousness has some of the same difficulties Rajan points out in Schiller's theory, those difficulties did not prevent it from appealing to English critics; and it is his version of the developmental theory that became better known in England.[9] In his lectures on literature from 1811 through 1818, Coleridge frequently drew upon the attempts of Schiller and Friedrich von Schelling but most extensively upon Schlegel to define the relationship of ancient to modern culture through analogy to the plastic and visual arts. "The spirit of ancient art and poetry is *plastic*, and that of the moderns *picturesque*," Schlegel declared in his lectures, first given in Vienna in 1810 and given here in John Black's 1815 English translation.[10] In an 1811 lecture on Shakespeare, Coleridge followed Schlegel closely: "The Shakespearean [or modern] drama and the Greek drama may be compared to statuary and painting. In statuary, as in the Greek drama, the characters must be few, because the very essence of statuary is of a high degree of abstraction, which prevents a very great many figures being combined in the same effect. . . . Compare this small group with a picture by Raphael or Titian. . . . an effect is reproduced equally harmonious to the mind, more true to nature with its varied colours, and, in [almost] . . . all respects, superior to statuary."[11] Schlegel's conception of this "picturesque," envisaging consciousness is a complex one that can help us to understand both Apollo's new "knowledge enormous" in *Hyperion* and the poet's and Moneta's similar vision in *The Fall.* Through it we can define more precisely than we can through other cultural models the relationship between static protagonists and active historical process in both *Hyperion* poems. Schlegel's contrast between ancient and modern, plastic and picturesque consciousness corresponds closely to Keats's apparently central contrast between statuelike Titans and the more pictorially defined Apollo in *Hyperion.* Coleridge's and Schlegel's terms also can explain, if not fully resolve, the apparent contradiction between Oceanus's scheme of cosmic historical development from Titan, to Olympian, to "some fresh perfection" beyond them, and the actual, more complex development within each god, whether Titan or Olympian, from beginning to end of the poem. Moreover, the same development from "plastic" to "picturesque" seems to shape Keats's own development as poet from the "naked and Grecian Manner" of his Miltonic epic, *Hyperion,* to the subjective dream vision of *The Fall of Hyperion.*

Finally, to analyze this development, we can extend the significance of Keats's own analogues from the plastic and visual arts: Milton's "stationing or statuary" in *Paradise Lost.* If, as Murry suggests, Keats struggles with the Satanic objectivity of Milton and then redefines himself as a more subjective and modern poet, Uriel's eye framing Satan "disfigured—on the Assyrian Mount" is not only an example of stationing but an image for that subjective consciousness. In contrast, Satan as "statuary" for a moment becomes an image for a debased form of sculpturesque, objective consciousness—or for a consciousness limited from the beginning by its sculptural characteristics.

Even as he uses the relationship between those analogues of sculpture and painting to describe and question an evolution of consciousness, Keats also tests the significance of each art—of sculpture, and then of painting— as models for validating the poet's imaginative vision. Each, in turn, proves inadequate and troubling; yet painting, in its oxymoronic representation of contraries and in its acceptance of natural and human mortality, becomes a truer and more valid analogue than the static and immortal beauty of sculpture. This recognition emerges in each of the *Hyperion* fragments and especially in the relationship between them. Because the argument of an aesthetic development in history is central to *Hyperion*, even if apparently contradictory in its applications, this chapter will first discuss Schlegel's historical model of the development from "plastic" to "picturesque" as a framework for an analysis of *Hyperion*. As each of his two concepts is defined, it will be tested within the structure of the poem.

Schlegel: The Sculptural Analogue

Schlegel's idea of "contrariety" gives energy to his historical categories. Beginning his defense of modern art in the first lecture, he explains, "The whole play of living motion hinges on harmony and contrast. Why then should not this phenomenon be repeated in the history of man?" Although he goes on to add, "Those who adopted [this contrast] . . . gave to the peculiar spirit of *modern* art . . . the name of *romantic*" (1:8), his fundamental contrast between ancient and modern, plastic and picturesque, is itself a romantic formulation—more a dialectic of opposites than a continuing evolution from one form to another to still a third. Winckelmann's *History of Art* had argued that Christianity and the inhospitable northern climate prevented the north from imitating Greek achievement in the arts;[12] Schlegel accepts the description but challenges Winckelmann's evaluation. The "refined and ennobled sensuality" of the Greeks led to a "deification of the powers of nature and of the earthly life" (1:12) and in human life to a "perfect concord and proportion between all the powers—a natural harmony" (1:16). "The stern nature of the north," however, "drives man back within himself" and makes him aware of "internal discord" as he yearns for something beyond his external limits (1:13, 16). Thus Schlegel's category of the "picturesque" modern, though beginning with a visual analogue, is clearly more than a visual one.[13]

Schlegel's definition of the "plastic" qualities of ancient drama emphasizes at first glance the visual appearance of sculpture: "These models of the human form require no interpretation," as does literature, because no one will be "insensible to genuine corporeal beauty" (1:45–46). The study of such forms is appropriate, Schlegel writes, because "Their religion," deifying "the powers of nature and of the earthly life," developed "idols" that "became models of ideal beauty" (1:12). To understand the "dignity" and "theatrical animation" of "their idea of the tragic," we need "to have always present to our fancy the forms of their gods and heroes"; "we can only become properly acquainted with the tragedies of Sophocles, before the groupes of Niobe or Laocoon" (1:46–47).

Yet as he develops this analogy of sculptural group to tragedy, he suggests an almost Platonic idea of beauty well beyond the "refined and ennobled sensuality" to which he earlier limits Greek art:

> in the distinctly-formed groupe, as in tragedy, sculpture and poetry bring before our eyes an independent and definite whole. To separate it from natural reality, the former places it on a base, as on an ideal ground. . . . the eye . . . rest[s] on the essential object, the figures themselves. These figures are wrought into the most complete rounding, yet they refuse the illusion of colours, and announce by the purity and uniformity of the mass . . . a creation not endowed with perishable life, but of a higher and more elevated character.
>
> (1:87; Lecture 3)

In its unity, sculpture affirms its objectivity and begins to move beyond direct and realistic visual representation.[14]

In such a cool, Flaxman-like distancing, however, the "higher and more elevated character" of sculpture seems to move away from the representation of human suffering in Greek tragedy. To reunite these on a level beyond yet still including the corporeal, Schlegel turns to Winckelmann's controversial analysis of the Laocoon in his *Reflections*. More surprisingly, however, he also draws—though tacitly—upon Winckelmann's antagonist Lessing. Incorporating some of Lessing's objections to Winckelmann, he redefines the representation of action in art and suggests a way to analyze Keats's handling of narrative action in *Hyperion*.

As Schlegel develops his argument for the sculptural, plastic nature of Greek culture, he concedes to Lessing the formal aesthetic point that "Beauty is the object of sculpture, and repose is most advantageous for the display of beauty. Repose alone, therefore, is suitable to the figure" (1:87). He goes on to argue:

> a number of figures can only be connected together and grouped by one action. The groupe represents beauty in motion. . . . This can only be effected when the artist finds means . . . to moderate [anguish] by manly resistance, calm grandeur, or inherent sweetness, in such a manner that . . . the features of beauty shall yet in nowise be disfigured. . . . conflicting sufferings and anguish of the body, and the resistance of the soul, are balanced with the most wonderful equilibrium.
>
> (1:87–88)

Finally, "The sight of these groupes [leads to a] . . . composed contemplation" in the perceiver as well as in the central figures (1:89). Thus his distinction between static single figure and active group allows him to

incorporate a Winckelmannian "composed contemplation" into the configuration of central figures, subordinate figures, and living observer. In fact,
the "action" of the group that Schlegel describes as "beauty in motion" is a
type of post-Coleridgean, formalist "tension." Although we do not see the
figures move in a temporal sequence of acts, we do see a dramatic conflict
held momentarily in tension, as several figures respond to the same
stimulus or situation. Schlegel never explicitly says that he seeks to
challenge Lessing's split between the spatial and temporal, static and
progressive arts, yet it seems apparent that his redefinitions of "action"
and "motion" do just that.

He develops several other ways to relate sculpture and tragedy through
a common relationship to "action" or "motion," and all of these influence
Keats's sculptural analogues in *Hyperion*. One of the broadest of these,
noted by Roy Park, includes the plastic and the picturesque as eras in a
temporal progression.[15] Even if individual sculptures and paintings are
simply static representations of single moments, a view that Schlegel only
partially accepts, those representations are themselves caught up in a
stream of time, a pattern of half-natural, half-cultural necessity. This
determinism is external and yet internally compelling for each artist in his
or her historical cultural milieu.

The internal structure of a tragedy, whether ancient or modern,
displays for Schlegel a similar pattern of necessity revealing itself in
temporal sequence. Unity of action, he argues, cannot be simply a linear
sequence of cause and effect, as Aristotle claims, for there is no artistic or
psychological sense of a whole in such an unlimited, continuous series. To
this limited, somewhat mechanical assessment of Aristotelian causality he
opposes the recognition of fate as the shaping action of tragedy. As fate
gives an external shape, the characters' recognition of that external shape
provides an internal action converging toward the external one (1:333;
Lecture 9). Because in this lecture Schlegel seeks a common ground for
unity of action in all tragedy, ancient and modern, he does not apply his
antithesis between plastic and picturesque. Yet as critical readers we can
use it to see each tragedy as a development from classical self-sufficiency
to romantic recognition of human smallness in a vast and impersonal
universe, or from a statuesque focus upon a heroically scaled figure or
group to a picturesque recognition of figures within a context of biological
and historical process.

Yet that recognition shows the perceiver's contribution to a unified
whole. First the dramatist's and then the audience's recognition creates
this unity: "The idea of *one* and of *whole* . . . arises out of the original
free-activity of our mind." Just as "the organical unity of a plant and an
animal . . . is brought by us to the individual living object, otherwise we

could not obtain it through that object," so "the separate parts of a work of art, and consequently . . . of a tragedy, must not be received by the eye and ear alone, but be taken in by the understanding. . . . The unity consists . . . in a higher sphere, in the feeling or in the reference to ideas" (1:336–37). Not only does this neo-Kantian definition move well beyond the isolation of the arts proposed by Lessing, but it also moves from the objective, universally valid and visual criterion of plastic corporeal beauty (the stone with which Lessing beats Winckelmann) to the highly subjective realm of "feeling," though a feeling qualified by its reference to "ideas." Even within the realm of the classical, plastic spirit, then, Schlegel discovers a development from objective sculptural group to subjective apprehension of an organic unity of action, a pattern like the larger development from plastic to picturesque.

English Sources for Sculpture as Analogue

Much of Keats's awareness of aesthetic theory about sculpture would have come from his friend Benjamin Robert Haydon, whose long campaign for recognizing the Elgin marbles as more classically Greek than the Hellenistic Laocoon and the Belvedere Apollo finally prevailed in 1816.[16] At issue in this controversy were the criteria for identifying an ideal "Greek" style and for judging sculpture more generally. Because the manifest energy of the Elgin marbles challenged the Winckelmannian rhetoric of repose accepted by the Royal Academy, Haydon enlisted Schlegel's romantic qualification of Winckelmann in their support: "Schlegel, speaking of the Greek Drama, also lays open their principles without ever having seen them. 'The Greeks,' says he, 'succeeded in combining in the most perfect manner in their Art, *ideality* with *reality*, or dropping school terms, an *elevation more than human with all the truth of life and all the energy of bodily qualities*.' It is on these incontrovertible principles, by which the Apollo can be proved so inferior to the Elgin Marbles." In this journal entry on 28 May 1817, Haydon quotes directly from Black's translation, adding his own italics; he thus apparently had a copy at hand.[17] When he had taken Keats to see the Elgin exhibit two months earlier, the visit prompted Keats's two sonnets on the marbles and may well have prompted a discussion of Schlegel.[18]

Although Keats makes no explicit references to Schlegel in his letters or other writings, Haydon was not the only one of his friends or acquaintances to draw upon Schlegel's *Lectures*. Coleridge's debt to Schlegel, extensive from 1811 on, was compounded in his lectures of early 1818 that defined as their scope the romantic or picturesque modern writers, in contrast to the sculpturesque ancients. Although Keats himself did not attend these lectures, going instead to William Hazlitt's almost simultaneous series, they surely led to discussion of Schlegel's paradigm among Keats's circle of friends.[19] From Hazlitt, moreover, Keats drew a series of ideas about sculpture as well as quite probably some acquaintance with Schlegel's use of the plastic as model for Greek culture.

In fact, we might trace some of Hazlitt's ideas about Milton and epic in those 1818 lectures back to his review of Black's 1815 translation of Schlegel, an essay published in the *Edinburgh Review* of February 1816. In the review he describes Schlegel's interpretation of the Greek and modern spirits in terms that sound remarkably close both to Keats's techniques and to his themes in *Hyperion:*

> The Pagan system reduced the Gods to the human form. . . . Statues carved out of the finest marble, represented the objects of their religious worship in airy porticos, in solemn temples and consecrated groves. Mercury was seen "new-lighted on some heaven-kissing hill"; and the Naiad or Dryad came gracefully forth. . . . In the Heathen mythology, form is everywhere predominant; in the Christian, we find only unlimited, undefined power. The imagination alone "broods over the immense abyss, and makes it pregnant."[20]

As Hazlitt quotes Milton to illustrate the godlike power of the "modern" imagination, he poses for Keats just the problem of historical anxiety over precursors with which his own epic poems must wrestle.[21] Keats may well have asked himself to what extent Milton's epic was classical or "plastic" and to what extent modern or picturesque. His characters in *Hyperion*, both Titan and Olympian, do indeed ask how their godlike forms are related to the "unlimited, undefined power" that disposes of them so mysteriously.[22]

As Judy Little has shown, Hazlitt's discussions of *Paradise Lost* in his 1818 *Lectures on the English Poets* and in his earlier *Round Table* essays, republished in 1817, clearly point toward Keats's use of sculptural models in his *Hyperion* poems.[23] In these discussions Hazlitt does not, in general, use Schlegel's method of defining whole cultural eras by a single paradigmatic art. Instead, he initially distinguishes quite sharply the progressive development of the arts from the sciences ("Why the Arts are Not Progressive?—A Fragment," *Round Table* 4:160–64; *Lectures on the English Poets*, 1818 series, Lecture 1: "On Poetry in General," 5:9; Lecture 3: "On Shakespeare and Milton," 5:45); verbal from pictorial or plastic arts ("On Poetry in General," 5:10); and epic from tragedy ("On Shakespeare and Milton," 5:51–53). Furthermore, his recurrent use of the terms "plastic" and "picturesque" in these essays is not fully consistent with Schlegel's, as

Black translates him.[24] Nevertheless, all his discussions of the English poets in the 1818 lectures use analogies to the visual and plastic arts as a method of distinguishing these poets from one another; and his discussions of Milton in particular challenge the assertion—current at least from William Gilpin's era and soon to be echoed by Coleridge—that Milton was fundamentally a "musical," not a "picturesque," poet ("On Milton's Versification," *Round Table* 4:38).[25]

Although Hazlitt attacks Greek sculpture itself at the beginning of his 1818 lectures, sculpture set in a visual field becomes both a dominant and a praiseworthy characteristic of Milton. "Greek statues," although "deified by their beauty," have no "resting place for the imagination" and are thus "specious forms. They are marble to the touch and to the heart. They have not an informing principle within them" ("On Poetry in General," *Lectures on the English Poets* 5:11). Yet Hazlitt praises Milton's poetry for precisely this sculptural distance. A visual clarity and a "palpableness and solidity" characterize Milton's poetry both before and after his blindness; and "the persons of Adam and Eve, of Satan, etc. . . . are always accompanied, in our imagination, with the grandeur of the naked figure; they convey to us the ideas of sculpture. . . . The figures . . . have all the elegance and precision of a Greek statue" ("On Milton's Versification," *Round Table* 4:38–39). Moreover, this appeal to touch and sight is not a weakness amid the musical, imaginative strength of "the variable and indefinite associations of ideas conveyed by words" (4:38). Instead, Hazlitt goes on to develop his idea of these statuesque figures as "epic objects":

> The interest of epic poetry arises from the contemplation of certain objects in themselves grand and beautiful. . . . The Pyramids of Egypt are epic objects . . . Now, a poem might be constructed almost entirely of such images, of the highest intellectual passion, with little dramatic interest: and it is in this way that Milton has in a great measure constructed his poem. That is not its fault, but its excellence.
> ("On the Character of Milton's Eve," *Round Table* 4:110)

Unlike Shakespeare's characters, Adam and Eve prompt in us not immediate sympathy but admiration and contemplation.

In his 1818 lecture on Shakespeare and Milton, Hazlitt includes Gothic ruins and even Roman camps as "objects of epic poetry." They "affect us through the medium of the imagination, by magnitude and distance, by their permanence and universality . . . a sense of power and sublimity coming over the mind" (5:52). As he discusses these objects a second time Hazlitt no longer focuses upon the definite, objective "form" of Greek statuary but upon the indefinite Burkean "power" of the romantic imagination. Although prompted by the visual focus of state or ruin, this perspective also includes an affective, associative awareness of vast visual and temporal distances and of a mutable natural context. Significantly, when he repeats his *Round Table* analogy of Milton's figures to sculpture in the 1818 lecture on Shakespeare and Milton, Hazlitt adds a final phrase that places the central form of the statuesque figures in an atmosphere of mutable light and light-prompted music: "The figures . . . have all the elegance and precision of a Greek statue; glossy and impurpled, tinged with golden light, and musical as the strings of Memnon's harp" (5:60). As the added phrases imply, Hazlitt does not identify Milton with the statuesque alone but includes those statuelike figures, as he does other "epic objects," in a picturesque context characterized, as in Schlegel, by a more indefinite, unlimited evocation of paintinglike color and spatial perspective, of the passage of time, and of music.

Little argues that in *Hyperion* Keats succumbs too far to Hazlitt's enthusiasm for this Miltonic statuary and fails to heed Hazlitt's 1818 plea for dramatic action as well as monumental epic stasis.[26] Yet we can see in Hazlitt's addition to his earlier comments an "action" that is dependent upon the perceivers of that statuary, perceivers both within and beyond the poem. This action, moreover, is "dramatic" not in the traditional terms of objective physical conflict but in Schlegel's terms of the subjective recognition of tension, particularly the tension between the individual and his or her place in an apparently infinite, indifferent natural world. Precisely this development takes place in *Hyperion*.

Oceanus and the Sculptural Ideal

If the poem seems to abandon objective mythic action for the more subjective contemplation of "epic objects," that abandonment forms a part of the larger historical myth Keats employs. As Saturn's questions— "Who has power?" and "Cannot I create?"—force us and Keats's characters to consider, the burden of physical external action has moved to historical necessity or "Nature's law." When Keats read Wordsworth's *Excursion,* Stuart Sperry proposes, he found characters who accepted such an indifferent historical process with a stoicism that led only to a stony paralysis. His *Hyperion* poems are thus attempts to define a more graceful, more creative mode of acceptance than Wordsworth shows.[27] Identifying the Titans not solely with Milton, an identification Hazlitt's analogies suggest, nor with Wordsworth, I would propose a less specific reading for *Hyperion:* the sculptural model is a starting point for a narrative in which characters and readers come to station both "epic objects" and epic narrative in a "world of Circumstances."

From the opening lines of *Hyperion* the sculptural images illustrate what Bate calls the massive centering of a single image: the fallen Saturn is "quiet as a stone," his companion Thea like a "Memphian sphinx, / Pedestal'd," and the two are "postured motionless, / Like natural sculpture."[28] Yet these images, like Saturn's state, are ambiguous; and that ambiguity is thematically central to the poem. The weight and palpability suggested in these similes validate the presence of the Titans for us directly as well as by association with the statues of classical gods. Keats specifically suggests Egyptian or what we would now describe as archaic Greek models for their massiveness and compositional stasis. Yet as we continue to read, we realize that Keats does not develop the contrast between Titans and Olympians in terms of a contrast between archaic and golden-age sculpture. Instead, because the Olympian Apollo is presented through analogues of painting, not sculpture, the Titans become associated with all of Greek sculpture as an art, not with a particular stage of it.[29]

The sky-god Coelus, representative of an earlier generation, defines the Titans' divinity precisely as sculptural form. As he tells Hyperion of the Titans' origins, he praises the Titans as "shapes . . . Distinct, and visible; symbols divine" and as "Manifestations . . . new-form'd" (1.315–17, 319). In contrast to Coelus's own impalpable, unshaped existence, they are, as Saturn later suggests, "first-born of all shap'd and palpable Gods" (2.153). Further, Coelus's description of divine psychology—the Titans should be "solemn, undisturb'd, / Unruffled, like high Gods"—draws not only on Aristotle's idea of an unmoved mover but upon Winckelmann's almost concrete identification of sculpture and divinity, or at the very least of sculpture and nobility of soul. Coelus does not make clear whether such perfect form and such impassiveness have developed together from generation to generation, or whether he and the even less-formed generations before him have also been "solemn" and "Unruffled, like high Gods." Because of the associations built up by writers such as Winckelmann, Reynolds, and Flaxman, we tend to assume the former; yet, as we see in Oceanus's speech, evolution and eternal perfection are at odds.

Like Coelus, Oceanus defines divinity largely in terms of a physical beauty sculpturally shaped. Just as the Titans have developed beyond Coelus's self-definition as "but a voice; / My life . . . but the life of winds and tides," so the Olympians are more beautiful and thus more appropriate, more powerful, rulers of the universe:

> . . . as we show beyond that Heaven and Earth
> In form and shape compact and beautiful,
>
> .   .   .   .
>
> So on our heels a fresh perfection treads,
>
> .   .   .   .

. . . fated to excel us, as we pass
In glory that old Darkness: nor are we
Thereby more conquer'd, than by us the rule
Of shapeless Chaos.

(2.208ff.)

Following both Winckelmann's and Schlegel's views of sculpture, Oceanus includes in this account of an evolutionary natural aesthetics a moral beauty imaged through the physical: "will, . . . action free, companionship, / And thousand other signs of purer life." Winckelmann's beauty, however, is a Platonic, eternal perfection; and as Winckelmann and Lessing both argue, though for quite different reasons, only stasis leads to such perfection. Furthermore, the stasis in a sculpted image of a god is not only formal but temporal; the sculptural medium of marble or granite leads to a permanence that, while it may well suggest an eternal divinity, yet seems alien to "will," "might," and "action free"—and to Oceanus's ideal of development in time toward even greater perfection.

Although this conflict between evolutionary development and static perfection becomes acute in Oceanus's speech, it has existed from the beginning of the poem. Saturn's sculptural stasis delays our comprehension of the problem precisely because we do not know whether he is like "might half slumb'ring on its own right arm," all the more powerful because his energy is potential, or whether he is forever frozen in powerlessness.[30] Literary analogues reinforce the ambiguity of the sculptural and pictorial ones, as his static pose recalls those of Odysseus, Aeneas, and Satan—all halted as their narratives begin, all reviving to show near-Titanic power. Verbally and historically closest, the Satanic parallel evokes the myth of a fall from divinity, and this myth controls the first part of the poem: in terms of the emerging plot, as readers and Titans learn of it, Saturn's physical stasis and that of all the Titans appear to result from their fall from divinity and their inability to control the forces of the natural world. Moreover, the emotional turmoil that accompanies Saturn's physical stasis gives further evidence, admonishes the sky-god Coelus, for the Titans' loss of divinity. Although once "unruffled, like high Gods," they "lived and ruled," Coelus tells Hyperion; "Now I behold in you fear, hope, and wrath; / Actions of rage and passion; even as / I see them, on the mortal world beneath, / In men who die" (1.328ff.). As the Titans in their fallen torpor grow more like sculptures of gods, the narrator and the Titans themselves discover that their emotions make of sculpture not an analogue of immortality but a trap for their anguish. This almost Ovidian yet somber entrapment in stone appears most vividly in the lot of those Titans who were "brawniest in the assault" and therefore more punished. They "Were pent in regions of laborious breath . . . and all their limbs / Lock'd up like veins of metal, crampt and screw'd; / Without a motion, save of their big hearts / Heaving in pain, and horribly convuls'd / With sanguine feverous boiling gurge of pulse" (2.22ff.).[31] Although the grotesque last line probably points to a mythic etiology for volcanoes, the tension between rigid form and explosive force exemplifies the ironic redefinition of sculpture in the poem and measures the Titans' fall from either Coelus's or Winckelmann's serene divinity. Reserving the grotesque for these peripheral figures, however, Keats still uses primary images of massive and static serenity for his central figures even as he explores the problems of such images.

As in so many romantic poems, the descent of Saturn and Hyperion is in fact a fortunate fall, a descent into a humanity that gains godlike stature in its very capacity for suffering and self-knowledge.[32] Yet these gods must free themselves from sculptural impassivity as an ideal before achieving a new, more romantic kind of serenity and dignity. As the poem moves from Oceanus's Raphael-like speech of origins through Hyperion's voluntary descent, it shapes our interpretation of the deifying of Apollo, the new Olympian. Keats transforms deity from a "human form divine" that is external, physical, and sculptural in its representation to a "human feeling divine" that envisages and responds to the circumstances of mortality. As Coleridge's and Schlegel's lectures suggest, this transformation is indeed a radical evolutionary change in the course of both cosmic and individual history, from sculpturesque to picturesque, or from objective and other-regarding attitudes to subjective and self-conscious ones. Yet if the conflict between Titan and Olympian represents this change most broadly, in fact subjective consciousness and self-consciousness deepen in all the characters in the course of the poem and particularly in the three main ones. Hyperion's awareness is more acute than Saturn's, and Apollo's more than his; but Apollo is only the final envisaging and feeling character in this progression.[33]

In effect, the progressively more subjective development of the characters alters the significance of the objective myth. Apparently a spokesman for the "objective," classical scheme by which a new, more sculpturally beautiful generation of gods will succeed his own, Oceanus without realizing it urges his own generation of Titans to become "romantic" in a way that anticipates the development of Apollo into a romantic or modern godhead. He first argues that feeling pain at their overthrow is folly, "for to bear all naked truths, / And to envisage circumstance, all calm, / That is the top of sovereignty" (2.203–205). Here he echoes Winckelmann's discussion of the Laocoon, in which the central figure of the sculptural group overcomes his own suffering and the knowledge of his son's imminent death with a serene and stoic triumph over such awareness. Yet this equilibrium attained through struggle, like Schlegel's use of it to define "beauty in action" as the basis of this analogue between sculptural group and tragedy, redefines classical repose as romantic tension. Before the Titans' fall, Oceanus's advice would have reinforced the idea of deity as unmoved mover. Now it becomes the basis of a tragic action; as in Schlegel, actor and audience together recognize a pattern of necessity. Although this model is still the sculptural figure, he makes not its outward beauty but the romantic, subjective elements of inward comprehension his criterion. With that change, we seem to be inside, looking out at the truth of circumstances that makes us not marble but vulnerable. This new sovereignty that comprehends and surpasses pain may well seem both more admirable and more necessary to most humans than the "might" achieved by beauty.

To analyze more fully this undercurrent of transformation in Oceanus's speech, we must examine another aspect of Keats's analogies to sculpture and painting in the poem. Before Oceanus's speech, both the narrator and the characters compare the Titans most frequently to stationed sculptural objects, not—as Blake so emphatically does in his *Milton*—to sculptors or painters. Even as Saturn attempts to restate the crisis for Oceanus in book 2 just before the latter speaks, he asks "why ye, Divinities, / The first-born of all shap'd and palpable Gods, / Should cower beneath what, in comparison, / Is untremendous might" (2.152–55). Their might seems contained in their force as aesthetic objects—indeed, ironically, in "might half slumb'ring," stationed so as to reveal its statuelike beauty. This is the premise Oceanus goes on most overtly to develop. Yet an earlier question of Saturn's, not answered explicitly but perhaps answered by an ineffectual act of the still unfallen Hyperion, explores the "might" of creating instead of being created objects and thus forces us to consider what power "creates" or shapes the mythic history Oceanus describes.

In his opening speech to Thea, Saturn cries out in protest, "But cannot I create? / Cannot I form? Cannot I fashion forth / Another world, another universe, / To overbear and crumble this to nought? / Where is another Chaos? Where?" (1.141–45).[34] Although his creative impulse is anything but disinterested and would seem to rely on a physical, not aesthetic, power, his impulse to give form to chaos is a striking sculptural metaphor. Even more striking, his repetition of "cannot" implies, as does his failure to act and to create such a world, a negative answer—now, evidently, he cannot create. At what point does the impersonal law described in Oceanus's speech develop? Was Saturn's role ever that of creator? Because the earlier part of this speech is not clear, we are left to wonder whether his ideas not only of a rival creation but of a willed creation have sprung from his fallen state. Before returning to Oceanus's speech to test his idea, we should examine the episodes in which Hyperion appears, as Keats's allusive, symbolic imagery shows how physical creation of a new universe is thwarted.

In the first of these episodes, it is clear that Hyperion had never before tried to reshape natural law; this attempt constitutes his act of creation-while-falling. The action Hyperion takes is not directly sculptural. In fact, the dominant analogue for much of the scene is a careful if flamboyant Miltonic sort of painting.[35] The colors suggest a world in startling contrast to the gray, half-sculpted masses of the opening scene and to the glacial cirque of Druid stones in the one that follows; its colors are far richer than anything in the poem until the emergence of Apollo. They both announce Hyperion's unfallen state and anticipate Apollo's deification. Hyperion's colors are those of sunset, though, as Apollo's are those of dawn; and when Hyperion tries to bring dawn at midnight, he discovers that the sun's nature is not and may never have been his to control:

> . . . full six dewy hours
> Before the dawn in season due should blush,
> He breath'd fierce breath against the sleepy portals,
>
> . . . .
>
> [Yet] . . . still the dazzling globe maintain'd eclipse,
> Awaiting for Hyperion's command.
> Fain would he have commanded, fain took throne
> And bid the day begin, if but for change.
> He might not:—No, though a primeval God:
> The sacred seasons might not be disturb'd.
>
> (1.264–66, 288–93)

Although the passage suggests that "nature's law" and not a willing god orders the seasons, it also implies that Hyperion has failed to believe in his own, independent power to reorder that world and thus has failed to command. Furthermore—and most important—this appears to be the first time he has tested such a power.

This newly discovered and yet immediately suspended potentiality of independent willing grows even more significant when we realize that Keats echoes Milton's most central images of creation: light, Ezekiel's chariot or *merkabah*, and the Logos, all of which work together in *Paradise Lost*, book 7, as Christ rides out over chaos to create.[36] In contrast to Milton's "King of Glory in his powerful Word / And Spirit coming to create new worlds," Hyperion cannot command or bid; he cannot say the word. Hyperion's orb (1.272–77), similar in its animate self-containment to the visionary chariot of God witnessed by Ezekiel and echoed by Milton, will not stir. In consequence, not only Hyperion and his fellow Titans but also his successor Apollo, as they become more human, must achieve a more subjective power with words. Hyperion's fall, begun with this separation of will and function, leads to the particular poetic nature of Apollo's apotheosis. Keats's metaphor for this change, however, is pictorial. As the sun-god arrives on that granite peak, Keats suggests more and more strongly that sculptural and pictorial composition are creative, if very different from the world creation suggested and then denied earlier in the poem.

Keats describes Hyperion's descent to the bleak, almost infernal valley where the already fallen Titans have gathered in council as a change both in the natural light and in their own enlightenment:

> It was Hyperion:—a granite peak
> His bright feet touch'd, and there he stay'd to view
> The misery his brilliance had betray'd
> To the most hateful seeing of itself. . . .
> . . . .
> Regal his shape majestic, a vast shade
> In midst of his own brightness, like the bulk
> Of Memnon's image at the set of sun
> To one who travels from the dusking east.
>
> (2.367–70, 372–75)

Hyperion himself is first stationed as an object, a statue on the granite peak.[37] He then becomes a subjective perceiver whose individual viewpoint or "station" allows him to see the Titans as objects. In turn, his light betrays their misery to themselves. "Like a dismal cirque of Druid stones," they see themselves as immobile, passive statues and as feeling subjects tragically conscious of their immobility. Finally, we and the Titans see Hyperion again as statue. For that "vast shade . . . like the bulk / Of Memnon's image" is a statue made lifeless because we see it at sunset, not at the sunrise that, according to legend, would make it sing.[38] As we return to see him as statue, then, we are forced to acknowledge the deathlike stasis inherent in the sculptural simile, and thus the other Titans see—or foresee—the fall of Hyperion into a state like their own. In him, their state discovers a "seeing of itself." Their perception of him as sculptural object now framed in their own temporal consciousness of loss, however, points toward a transformation from sculptural to pictorial analogues for consciousness. It is their revelation, not any physical conflict between the generations of gods, that is surely the symbolic and subjective action of *Hyperion*.

As Hyperion's "own brightness," once natural, becomes more symbolic, it anticipates the symbolic significance of Apollo not as natural force but as the musician, poet, and healer who becomes muse and patron of poets. This anticipation defines Hyperion's own evolution, if an incomplete one, toward contemplative perceiver and mythmaker: he moves unwittingly from the "naked and grecian Manner" of the plastic and sculpturesque to the "naked truths" of a romantic perspective. In this change, Keats moves beyond both his classical and his contemporary sources, which describe Hyperion, in contrast to Apollo, as sun-god alone.[39] Instead, he applies the developmental pattern of these sources not only to the broad contrast between Hyperion's earlier sculpturesque state and Apollo's final picturesque one, a contrast using the traditional metaphor of successive generations, but also to Hyperion's own change.

Though arguing that the Titans must accept the "naked truth" of successive generations of gods ever more powerful in their statuesque corporeal beauty, Oceanus uses his key explanatory terms "power" and "sovereignty" ambiguously. "Power" or "sovereignty" may refer to physical control over the natural forces of the universe; to psychological control over that universe by the aesthetic, visual persuasion of physical corporeal beauty; or finally, to the self-sovereignty of bearing "all naked truths" about the loss of these powers, yet envisaging "circumstances" "all calm." Although the first two of these kinds of power once characterized the Titans, Oceanus suggests that only the second will characterize the Olympians. For the supreme power active in the universe, the one that determines the evolution of these generations of gods toward beauty, is an impersonal natural process: "We fall by course of Nature's law, not force / Of thunder, or of Jove" (2.181–82).

The natural law he describes is an organic one, a "sullen ferment" and "intestine broil" that leads to a spontaneous generation and regeneration more biochemical than personal. Although the images of "engendering," "Our parentage," "born of us," and "we have bred forth" preserve the anthropomorphic shapes of traditional myth, they preserve no more than a framework for an indifferent, demythologizing historical process. So loveless and individually powerless do the participants in this scheme appear that Keats seems to describe an evolutionary version of his vision of the sea in the "Epistle to Reynolds" several months earlier. Then he saw

Too far into the sea; where every maw
The greater on the less feeds evermore:—
But I saw too distinct into the core
Of an eternal fierce destruction.

(94–97)

Surely, in view of this oceanic "fierce destruction," Keats's choice of Oceanus as spokesman is significant.[40] Granted, the chain of evolutionary succession by which one generation of gods succeeds another is not as thoroughly destructive for the cast-off generation of gods as it is for the lower animals on the food chain Keats describes to Reynolds: "Still do I that most fierce destruction see, / The shark at savage prey—the hawk at pounce, / The gentle robin, like a pard or ounce, / Ravening a worm" (102–05). Yet his metaphors of ordered succession draw upon many of the images of the food chain in the verse letter:

> . . . Say, doth the dull soil
> Quarrel with the proud forests it hath fed,
> And feedeth still, more comely than itself?
> Can it deny the chiefdom of green groves?
> Or shall the tree be envious of the dove
> Because it cooeth, and hath snowy wings
> To wander wherewithal and find its joys?
> We are such forest-trees, and our fair boughs
> Have bred forth, not pale solitary doves,
> But eagles golden-feather'd, who do tower
> Above us in their beauty, and must reign
> In right thereof; for 'tis the eternal law
> That first in beauty should be first in might.

> (2.217–29)

Not only does the soil feed the "proud forests," but in his culminating figure Oceanus shifts from dove to eagle, a bird more often than not "at savage prey." His examples increasingly suggest a beauty born of power, not a power born of beauty.

As Oceanus follows with the eye of imagination the "metamorphoses" of the power of beauty from dull soil to forest trees to doves and eagles, that movement of the eye upward is a powerful rhetorical device. It also recalls Keats's description of "stationing" in *Paradise Lost:* "Milton in every instance pursues his imagination to the utmost—he is 'sagacious of his Quarry,' he sees Beauty on the wing, pounces upon it and gorges it to the producing his essential verse, 'So from the root springs lighter the green stalk,' &c. But in no instance is this sort of perseverance more exemplified than in . . . his stationing,—thus, here we see not only how the Birds *'with clang despised the ground,'* but we see them *'under a cloud in prospect.'* " Here the metaphors of nourishing and gorging in the letter to Reynolds and in Oceanus's speech are related explicitly to Raphael's analogy of physical and spiritual subsistence. Milton's imagination, like the Olympian beauty Oceanus describes, is eagle- or hawklike in its pursuit and absorption of the materials that it needs, especially those from the natural world. But the eaglelike imagination both in the marginal note and in Oceanus's speech also perceives: the poet stations the birds "under a cloud in prospect," and Oceanus's "eagles golden-feather'd . . . tower / Above us," we might conjecture, not only because they are more beautiful but because they have a better view. The most important relationship of the marginal note to Oceanus's speech, however, is its suggestion that Oceanus is stationing Olympians, Titans, and even earlier generations in a natural landscape. Although he apparently relies on natural causality, he in fact argues from aesthetic perception of a scene as an interdependent whole. Keats's marginal interpretation of Raphael's symbolic plant already has transformed Milton's holy spirit into a more exclusively human, yet powerful, imagination. No longer subliming material nourishment upward into new forms, it places all forms in the natural world that makes us, fallen and natural as well, capable of envisaging them. Oceanus has done the same; his forest with its soil and birds is not a hierarchical, angelic image of order but a pictorial perspective of temporal process, yet a perspective that promises a certain limited aesthetic control.

Thus, if we see in Apollo a new incarnation of what Coleridge calls "the wandering spirit of poetry,"[41] did the Titans once have the spirit and then lose it to the new Olympians? Or if their loss of objective physical power to rule the natural universe makes them conscious of the desire to create universes and of the sovereignty of envisaging circumstances as painting or tragedy, then have they gained access to that wandering poetic spirit as much as, or even more than, Apollo? The more Oceanus advises the Titans to find a new sovereignty in reconciling themselves to natural process and the admiration of what he thinks is a new but sculptural beauty, the more he anticipates precisely the new subjective, picturesque beauty Apollo discovers in himself. Oceanus's advice "to envisage circumstance, all calm" would have seemed before the Titans' fall merely a reiteration of Coelus's view that they are to be unmoved movers. Now he urges them to take on a human grandeur in which sculptural serenity is achieved through a "picturesque" struggle of contraries. To define this struggle further, we must clarify further Schlegel's definition of the "picturesque" modern spirit.

Schlegel's Picturesque: "all contrarieties"

As the introduction has sho.vn earlier, lively controversy over the definition of the "picturesque" preceded the arrival of Schlegel's analogy in England, providing a background for its acceptance and possibly for Keats's adoption of it. Although both Wordsworth and Keats, we recall, objected to the mechanical quality of a "picturesque" aesthetic that ignored other senses and other, particularly moral, values, Wordsworth's attempts to meet these objections in fact lead toward Schlegel's redefinition of the picturesque and thus toward Keats's structural use of it in *Hyperion*. Repeatedly in his poetry Wordsworth places spatial landscape within the temporal context of personal memory; he frequently places inspiration not on a mountain point of vision but in an abyss or vapor that denies sight; and he places visual perception within the larger context of "feeling" drawn from all the senses.[42] Schlegel's pattern of historical development provides a temporal milieu larger than Wordsworth's individual memory but similar to it; and his visual landscape, like Wordsworth's, frequently turns away from sharp detail toward endlessly expanded perspectives. His definition of "action" in both sculpture and drama as the tension among figures integrates the senses of sight and hearing with the emotions; and his discussion of "unity of action" in both ancient and modern, plastic and picturesque drama allows the perceiver's feelings to determine that unity. Finally, his analysis of the picturesque or romantic mode as an interplay of contrasts points toward the possibility of incorporating other arts or means of perception into his main analogue of painting through the harmony of oppositions. Such a theory would oppose not only the tyranny of visual perception feared by Wordsworth and Keats but also the tyranny of a superficial assertion of *ut pictura poesis* feared by Lessing and his English predecessor Burke.

Schlegel's emphasis upon expanded, nearly infinite visual perspectives in painting becomes symbolic, in his definition of the "picturesque" or romantic modern spirit, of vast temporal as well as spatial contexts, especially as he compares the classical dramatic unities of place and time with modern freedom from those limits:

> Why are the Greek and romantic poets so different in their practice with respect to place and time? . . . The principal cause of the difference is the plastic spirit of the antique, and the picturesque spirit of the romantic poetry. Sculpture directs our attention exclusively to the groupe exhibited to us, it disentangles it as far as possible from all external accompaniments. . . . Painting, on the other hand, delights in exhibiting, . . . along with the principal figures, the surrounding locality and all the secondary objects, and to open to us in the back ground a prospect into a boundless distance.
>
> (1:347–48; Lecture 9)

Later he speaks of the way "such a picture must be bounded in a less perfect manner than the group [a sculptural group such as the Laocoon or the Niobe]; for it is like a fragment cut out of the optic scene of the world" (2:100; Lecture 12). Yet in spite of this visual emphasis, Schlegel's definition of the "picturesque" includes much of the transcendent, antivisual Burkean sublime: "the principle of the antique poetry is ideal, that of the romantic mystical: the former subjects space and time to the internal free-activity of the mind; the latter adores these inconceivable essences as supernatural powers, in whom something of the divinity has abode" (1:349). As Hazlitt reviews Black's translation, he intensifies this sense of subjective indefiniteness of both spatial and temporal perspective. In fact, he transforms it almost into a sublime denial of the pictorial: "History, as well as religion, has contributed to enlarge the bounds of imagination; and both together, by showing past and future objects at interminable distance, have accustomed the mind to contemplate and take an interest in the obscure and shadowy."[43]

Although Blake also challenges pictorial limits, we should notice how different his challenge is from Schlegel's and Hazlitt's. Their admiration of the "obscure and shadowy" Burkean indefiniteness and their worship of a transcendent space and time Blake characterizes in the Fallen Urizen, "refusing all Definite Form." His reshaping frees us from the belief that space and time transcend the human imagination.

As Schlegel and Hazlitt recognize the impersonal and apparently infinite forces of space and time, forces that replace the gods of earlier mythologies, they point toward Oceanus's explanation of "Nature's law." As Hazlitt paraphrases Schlegel, however, he fuses human cosmic creative activity in the "romantic spirit": "in the Christian [mythology], we find only unlimited, undefined power. The imagination alone 'broods over the immense abyss, and makes it pregnant.' "[44] Both Schlegel and Hazlitt have uncreated the visual landscape: they celebrate an imaginative power that retreats, like Wordsworth's, to the abyss that annihilates specific images in order to recreate them. Here, as for Shelley's Demogorgon, "the deep truth is imageless," and the picturesque spirit at its most extreme has become antipictorial. For Keats, as we shall see, no "unlimited, undefined power" dissolves the external, visualizable landscape. Instead, the power of imagination lies in its ability to place sculptural form in a world of natural process that seems to continue infinitely both in spatial and in temporal distance. The Miltonic imagination, both divinely and humanly creative, is replaced by a Miltonic "stationing" in the immediate, concrete landscapes of this world, yet landscapes subject to those almost infinite forces.

In addition to the description of a scenic landscape that evokes and then pushes beyond the visual, Schlegel also includes in his redefined "picturesque" a portraitlike focus upon facial expression, a focus that emphasizes feeling and the constructive power of the perceiving mind. He clearly draws this aspect of the "picturesque" or romantic spirit from his broader analogy to painting, not the narrower definition of picturesque composition in landscape. In contrast to sculpture "painting . . . communicates more life to its imitations, by colours which are made to express the finest gradations of mental expression in the countenance. The look which can be given only in a very imperfect manner by sculpture enables us in painting to read much deeper in the mind, and to perceive its lightest movements" (2:100).[45] As noted by several critics, Keats focuses repeatedly on facial expression in the *Hyperion* poems.[46] His most concentrated use of this paintinglike technique comes toward the end of *Hyperion*, as Apollo confronts Mnemosyne, and at the center of *The Fall*, as the narrator confronts Moneta. In both of these visual but intensely emotional confrontations, the perceiver "can read . . . deeper in the mind," though perceiving its heaviest, not lightest, movements.

Furthermore, as Keats focuses upon faces and then minds to frame or stage narrative histories, he includes both Schlegel's emphasis upon vast temporal and spatial perspectives—the picturesque of landscape—and his most central characteristic of the romantic sensibility: "The romantic delights in indissoluble mixture; all contrarieties: nature and art, poetry and prose, seriousness and mirth, recollection and anticipation, spirituality and sensuality, terrestrial and celestial, life and death, are blended together . . . in the most intimate manner" (2:98–99). Such oxymoronic oppositions, as they hold contraries in suspension with one another, draw upon the sharp contrasts of light and dark, foreground and depth, valued in picturesque landscape, and yet move beyond the visual, spatial logic of the mutually exclusive.

Creations and Destroyings: Apollo and the Picturesque Imagination

In *Hyperion*, the transformation from natural force to perceiving witness, and from plastic to picturesque, begins, as we have seen, with Hyperion's change from sun-god to anguished witness of natural process. Continuing this change, his successor Apollo appears not as sun-god but as a poet and musician whose music responds to natural power instead of embodying or wielding it.[47] Through the "new blissful golden melody" overheard by one of the Titans in book 2 as a prelude to Apollo's appearance in book 3, Keats further defines the subjective and emotional quality of the new order of gods. To define further the "contrarieties" of romantic subjective perception culminating in Apollo's transformation, he turns in book 3 from music to painting: to color, details of a lush spring landscape, and the painter's framing, enclosing composition of scenes. Beginning with that music in book 2, these contrarieties build up from their presentation as separate, opposing contraries toward a more intense, more complex fusion within a single consciousness: from Clymene's hearing, to Apollo's seeing Mnemosyne, to Apollo's own "dying into life."

Apollo's growing understanding of process differs from Hyperion's because just as the natural processes that go on around Apollo point toward a new birth for nature, his awareness of these processes and of larger historical processes of change point toward a new birth for him as their perceiver. As Judy Little points out, the setting of book 3 carefully parallels that of book 1 in order to contrast a wintry stasis to a spring rebirth of the gods and of the landscape.[48] As Keats uses analogies drawn from painting, however, he also develops Schlegel's concept of a pictur-esque consciousness that achieves its regenerative energy by acknowledg-ing and including its opposite—in this case a sculptural stasis that once meant immortality but has come to suggest a wintry mortality.

A landscape of luxuriant, not threatening, process precedes and an-nounces Apollo's direct entrance into the poem. In the first of these annunciations, the Titan Clymene in book 2 describes "a sweet clime . . . breathed from a land / Of fragrance, quietness, and trees, and flowers"; with the same "shifting wind" she hears Apollo's music (2.263ff.). In the second, the narrator of the poem ends his silence about himself to call upon a conventional muse, demanding that the whole universe "flush," "vermilion turn," and "blush," as he names Apollo the new subject of his song. He completes the rich coloring and pictorial massing of light and shadow in this almost Titian-like landscape, ready for the "golden theme" of Apollo, by describing "Delos, with thine olives green, / And poplars, and lawn-shading palms, and beech, . . . And hazels thick, dark-stemm'd beneath the shade" (3.24–25, 27). Strikingly, this landscape is imagined and created at the narrator's command. Unlike Hyperion, he has com-manded a new dawn and thus "bid the day begin." Also unlike Hyperion, however, both he and the muse stand beyond the narrative, and their painterly control of its natural landscapes points toward a radical differ-ence in the role of Apollo: from the making of dawns to the making of dreams or fictions.

As if to emphasize this more subjective perspective, Apollo emerges from an *Endymion*-like "bower," on an island full of "many a green recess," to stand "Full ankle-deep in lilies of the vale." The lushness of his station

recalls Endymion's pursuit of a dream, a parallel confirmed as Mnemosyne acknowledges, "Thou hast dream'd of me" (3.62). Mnemosyne,
however, is no Cynthia, even if her successor Moneta takes on the dark
side of the moon's iconology, and the dreams she calls up are more somber
than those of *Endymion*. In consequence, when Keats stations her in Delos,
he deliberately contrasts her immediate natural setting to Apollo's appren-
tice-visionary lushness, which the Olympian must cast off by seeing her:
"from beneath some cumbruous boughs hard by / With solemn step an
awful Goddess came." The momentary return of his Titanic style shows
Keats using the tonalities of his landscape with great care to station this
meditative, rather than militant, encounter of Titan and Olympian.

This painterly or picturesque emphasis upon a landscape of color and
process culminates in a return to a "human form divine" at the end of the
fragment, a figure transformed by its setting and its perception of setting.
The dawn of the natural world evoked by the narrator takes place within
the figure of Apollo as he incorporates the visions and histories of
Mnemosyne:

> Soon wild commotions shook him, and made flush
> All the immortal fairness of his limbs;
> Most like the struggle at the gate of death;
> Or liker still to one who should take leave
> Of pale immortal death, and with a pang
> As hot as death's is chill, with fierce convulse
> Die into life.
>
> (3.124–30)

The dawn denied to Hyperion in book 1 and demanded of the universe by
the narrator at the beginning of book 3, this "flush" humanizes the
"immortal fairness" of the marble once seen as godlike. Because the colors
of the landscape and of Apollo himself signal a new birth and because the
details of this landscape show profusion instead of isolation, this book
shows far more clearly a continuing natural process. In books 1 and 2, that
process was slowed or suspended, as if petrified to match the statuelike
figures of the Titans, sculpture no longer the image of divine transcendence but of the end of such power. As Apollo flushes, he absorbs into
himself all the vitality of the springlike landscape of Delos—but that
apotheosis, as Keats carefully indicates, is into an ambiguous godhead that
accedes both to the mortality of man's natural existence and to the art that
arises from envisaging that fact.[49]

Keats transforms sculptural figure into living form, not only through
the paintinglike elements of landscape and color, but also through the
portraitlike elements of emotional facial expressions—more intense than

the expressive gesture or stance of a statue.[50] As the Titans become less serene, calm, and sculptural, Saturn gazes at Oceanus, for "in thy face / I see, astonied, that severe content / Which comes of thought and musing" (2.164–66), and his noun "content" is both message and mood.[51] At the end of his own speech, Oceanus acknowledges the "glow of beauty" in the eyes of his "dispossessor." Enceladus, after Oceanus's speech, urges rebellion under Hyperion's "undisgraced" leadership, and then his audience sees reflected on his face "a pallid gleam" that announces Hyperion's arrival and "the misery his brilliance had betray'd / To the most hateful seeing of itself"; this is the dawn of self-consciousness in the most active and outward-directed of Titans.

The most intense focus upon faces and thus upon an inward vision framed in that face comes in Apollo's confrontation with Mnemosyne. Although the narrator describes her as "supreme shape," it is the "purport in her looks" (3.47), "those eyes . . . / And their eternal calm," that perplexes and fascinates Apollo. Although he recognizes, like Socrates' Meno, that he already has dreamed of her and of her knowledge, he now reads "a wondrous lesson in . . . [her] silent face: / Knowledge enormous makes a God of me." And as he reads that lesson in her expression, his own mind becomes the framing landscape for its drama:

> Names, deeds, gray legends, dire events, rebellions,
> Majesties, sovran voices, agonies,
> Creations and destroyings, all at once
> Pour into the wide hollows of my brain,
> And deify me.
>
>   (3.114–18)

His questions, too, echo Saturn's: "Where is power?" And the answer he receives as he reads Mnemosyne's face is similar: if natural law brings about change, he can achieve a limited power in response if he is able to "frame" and "envisage circumstance." He sees in Mnemosyne's face and mind, and takes into the "wide hollows" of his own brain, as if into the "shady sadness" of the vale at the poem's opening, histories of "creations and destroyings" that are very like the Titans' fall from power as forces ruling nature. At the same time he sees that Titan and Olympian alike are no longer shaped embodiments of natural process but humanlike figures set within and controlled by those natural forces. In this focusing the observed face and then the brain's wide hollows become a stage scene that frames the outer perspectives, "envisaging" the world, not to reconstitute it physically as Blake's characters do, but to comprehend it as a unified, significant whole.

These visual methods used as symbolic metaphors are only a part, though a basic part, of the poem's picturesque final movement.[52] Like the pictorial evocations of landscape, the oxymoronic evocation of emotional contraries becomes more central as the fragment moves toward its final image of Apollo. Although Mnemosyne tells Apollo that "the whole universe / Listen'd in pain and pleasure," as did Clymene in 2.265ff., she herself apparently feels no pain before hearing of his: "Tell me, youth, / What sorrow thou canst feel; for I am sad / When thou dost shed a tear: explain thy griefs." If her sadness only mirrors his, she is surely less sensitive than the overwrought Clymene, "sick / Of joy and grief at once": Mnemosyne seems emotionally to have deserted the Titans' "old and sacred thrones." Yet as we have already seen, she carries with her the knowledge that can teach Apollo. When he reads or sees that "Knowledge enormous," he not only feels the emotional stress between its "creations and destroyings," but he embodies the ultimate objective, physical consequences of this mixing of pleasure and pain, creation and destroying, as he dies into life.

Mnemosyne's lack of explicit awareness about the knowledge that she carries might be accounted for by her desertion of the other Titans and thus by her failure to submit to their humanizing and ennobling release, through suffering, from rigid statuary. Yet such an explanation, though adequate on the narrative level, fails to account for her symbolic definition as the mythic personification of memory. Through the narrator's invocation of his muse, narrative method has begun to question itself, and Mnemosyne accelerates and completes that process. Not a natural but a mental power, she completes the inward and symbolic turn of the narrative as she leads toward Apollo's completion of a new vision of time. This new temporal consciousness finally provides a context, if a problematical one, for the mythic history of the Titans' fall into history.

As muse, narrator, and finally Mnemosyne enter the poem, they bring to it a temporal as much as a spatial frame, a historical consciousness that for Schlegel and partially for Hazlitt characterizes the romantic or metaphysically "picturesque" spirit. At the opening of the poem no muse or temporally defined narrator placed the Titans' story in time, as Milton does so fully in *Paradise Lost;* interpretation as well as natural process seemed suspended. As in *Paradise Lost,* however, fallenness immerses one in directional time.[53] As he invokes the muse in 3.13, Keats as narrator explains, "For lo! 'tis for the Father of all verse." This conventional phrase jars with the images of a youthful, energetic new generation that both precede and follow it: Apollo suddenly appears as progenitor of "all verse" from its distant beginnings to the present time of both writer and reader. The Titans gain this sense of directionality from Oceanus's speech that describes "nature's law" of successively more perfect or beautiful forms. As they become envisagers of their circumstances, then, they stand aside from the sculptural, focal center that Oceanus conjecturally describes. And as they do so, they become not only witnesses of Olympian beauty but also witnesses of their own new role as part of the picturesque milieu of temporal process. Yet as Mnemosyne tutors Apollo, that sculptural focal center becomes itself romantic or picturesque as it embodies temporal process.

If Apollo is "Father of all verse," Mnemosyne is conventionally mother of the muses. This parentage Keats largely ignores; even as she tutors Apollo in vision, her isolation from all familial relations makes her knowledge all the more eerie. Yet although Keats subordinates the sense of past time implicit in this role as mother of the muses, her capacity as Memory makes her the hoarder of all our fragmented knowledge of the past. That inner visionary knowledge which she cannot herself comprehend includes both the narrative of the Titans and now also, with the more explicit definition of Mnemosyne and muse, our own past. It becomes a collective consciousness not only of repeated archetypes but of specific events: "Names, deeds," and "dire events," as well as "gray legends." Thus from Apollo's point of view she knows and conveys both past and future knowledge, upholding "her arms as one who prophesied." Moreover, his full understanding of the Titans would seem to include their roles first as mythic natural forces, next as statues poised between power and stasis in "might half slumb'ring," and finally as witnesses who frame and envisage this transformation from power to stasis. Just as the Apollinian music fused Clymene's pain with Delos as a *locus amoenus* of pleasure, so Apollo seems to incorporate this Titanic and tragic framing with his own exultant consciousness of poetic power. And just as the vastness and vitality of the landscape's natural processes are absorbed into the "flushing" of Apollo's dawning deification, so this process of "dying into life" absorbs and concentrates the temporal processes and sequences of history into an almost oxymoronic moment of tension. The statuesque central figure thus embodies and is transformed by his picturesque context, in an accelerating progress that demonstrates romantic, picturesque contraries.

Yet image and consciousness are at odds; and the mortality faced by the Titans has more power, more poignancy, and in some ways more of Coleridge's "wandering poetic spirit" than this rejoicing over "agonies" that taste to Apollo like "some blithe wine." As they become immortal, these oxymora have become immoral; and this metaphysical version of the picturesque risks the same detachment that Wordsworth sensed in the scenic picturesque.

Four

🔊

Keats's *The Fall of Hyperion* ·
"Like sculpture builded up upon the grave
Of . . . power"

"An eagle's watch": Epic to Dream Vision

In *The Fall of Hyperion*, Saturn and his Titans have been cast aside not only by "Nature's law," as Oceanus argues in *Hyperion*, but also by a great majority of critics. Most argue, like David Perkins, that Keats fails to integrate the "objective" and Miltonic narrative drawn from *Hyperion* with the new, more subjective dream vision that "turns frankly and powerfully on the nature and uses of the imagination [and] . . . of the self."[1] Because the new beginning of the poem develops an intense dramatic conflict over these issues, it displaces the already static plot of the original Titanic narrative toward which it leads. Or, to use the terms developed in the preceding chapter, the new "picturesque" or romantic dream vision makes the original sculpturesque narrative seem not only more static and stony than *Hyperion*, but a poetic dead end. Even if one challenges the validity of Oceanus's myth of progress in *Hyperion*, that broad framework reinforces both the superficial development from sculpturesque Titan to picturesque Olympian and the more profound development from sculpturesque to picturesque consciousness in all the characters. *The Fall of Hyperion*, on the other hand, seems to revise itself backward as we read the poem. When Moneta begins the original narrative of Saturn's fall, she turns from her restless debate over the significance of poetry in a "world of Circumstances," to describe a god only at the beginning of his confrontation with that indifferent world. Because the fragment ends before Hyperion descends, Saturn's sculpturesque images and consciousness dominate its de facto conclusion; and because the style of the earlier fragment remains largely unchanged, its Miltonic massiveness reinforces this sculptural effect.

Yet it is surely worth examining the consequences of the changed viewpoint from which we see that Titanic narrative: for Moneta and the narrator both struggle to define their stances toward her vision. In a thorough and thoughtful discussion of the later fragment, Brian Wicker suggests that the terms "dream" and "Poesy," from the narrator's induction and Moneta's contentious debate with him, find dramatic form in the attitudes of Titans and Olympians. The

> opposition of poet and dreamer is the same as the opposition of Olympians and Titans, Apollo and Saturn. Apollo . . . is the constant symbol of the true poetic nature. Saturn (and Hyperion as well) are representatives of the world of dreamers. It is a dreamworld which Saturn lives in, and which he threatens with futile oratory to create. . . . [Yet] just as the destruction of the Titans is but the prelude to the rise of Apollo and his fellows, so the extinction of the poetic illusion, the dreamer's world, is but the prelude to the rise of the poet's.[2]

Because it integrates the Titanic narrative with the frame of dream vision, and because it makes the original narrative illustrate the thematic arguments over dream, this argument is persuasive. It also appears to extend my own interpretation of *Hyperion*. Wicker's definition of the Titans' dreamworld resembles Schlegel's most ecstatic descriptions of the "sculptural" or classical consciousness; and his definition of an oxymoronic Apollinian Poesy seems close to Schlegel's description of the romantic or "picturesque" development beyond the classical.

Yet Wicker's equation of generational conflict among the gods with the stages of an escapist and a more realistic kind of poetic vision has several drawbacks as an interpretation of *The Fall of Hyperion*. First, even in *Hyperion* we have seen that Keats revised his classical myth of generational warfare to show a complex individual development among the Titans, as well as from Titan to Olympian—a pattern described through development from sculpturesque to picturesque modes of consciousness. Thus dismissing the Titans in this poem as symbolic only of dreamers or of "poetic illusion" would suggest a less complex and developed role for them in the second poem. Because the second fragment breaks off even earlier in the Titans' story than the first one did, we might well accept a less developed pattern; but Wicker's argument also assumes Keats's intentions to include the original fragment as far as Apollo's transformation. Not only are the Titans more complex than his comparison suggests, but "dream" also carries too much ambiguity to be dismissed as simple "illusion." After *The Eve of St. Agnes* and *Lamia*, Moneta's fierce dismissal may indeed be Keats's palinode to their complexity. It seems far more likely, though, that he was continuing the debate and the redefinitions of dream.

Thus we might well find parallels between dream and Coelus's description of the Titans as sculptural forms who lived "solemn, undisturbed, unruffled" lives. Yet just as we must carefully evaluate the changing function of the sculptural analogue, so we must also evaluate the changing function of "dream" as analogue. For the *The Fall of Hyperion*, even more than in *Hyperion*, it is not the serenity of Winckelmannian gods that dominates the sculptural comparisons, but a more explicit comparison of those gods to sculpture as stony artifact.[3] Thus in much of the poem we see the Titans' experience not as dreamlike illusion but—in Van Ghent's image for the narrator—as a nightmarish consciousness of immobility.[4]

As Van Ghent's comment reminds us, moreover, the entire poem as we have it follows the narrative mode of a dream vision. Because Keats chooses this mode, we should look closely at the new structure he develops, instead of focusing too greatly upon the uncompleted narrative of Apollo's more epic struggle. By carefully examining these patterns, particularly the successive order and internal structure of the enclosed visions, I think we indeed can see Wicker's development from a serene, paradisal and thus dreamlike consciousness to Poesy; but it is a development that includes, not rejects, dream.[5] Nor does this development reject the falsely serene, sculpturesque Titans for the oxymoronic, picturesque Olympians who achieve an awakening to Poesy. Instead, Keats continues both his sculptural and his picturesque analogues, but he uses them within each scene, and from one scene to the next, to organize the education of his narrator. Through that scenic education, the narrator must reevaluate the significance of paradisal dream for Poesy. In each scene, and also in the fragment taken as a whole, he passes from a superficial experience of the scenic picturesque, through a confrontation with centered sculptural forms or figures, and finally develops in response to them a more profoundly, "metaphysically" picturesque consciousness of the contraries of life and death, process and immortality. Repeatedly, his new awareness tests the different idealizations of dream and of sculpture against the temporal processes of "a world of Circumstances." Before interpreting the complexity of those individual scenes, however, we should briefly map out their formal structure—as the narrator so constantly tries to do and finds he cannot, immersed in his senses' immediate experience.

Drawing upon the traditions of medieval dream vision, and also perhaps of the biblical narratives shown in the sequential frames of stained-glass windows or books of hours, Keats organizes a series of discrete scenes.[6] Within each scene the narrator explores visual details with an ordered detachment resembling Gilpin's version of the scenic picturesque. Yet, as the genre of dream vision promises, the narrator does not always control fully or even consciously the development and organization of scenes. Although he carefully stations himself to explore each scene with exact visual logic, sudden sleep or trance marks the abrupt, irrational transitions between scenes. The first scene, in the garden, begins abruptly in 1.19, with "Methought I stood" and ends with a "cloudy swoon" in line 55; the second, in Moneta's domed monument, ends with her "conjuration" in 1.291, so that the two of them "side by side . . . stood . . . Deep in the shady sadness of a vale." Moneta's narrative modulates between third and fourth scenes, but the fourth, incomplete scene still begins suddenly with the narrator's new station: "Now in clear light I stood, / Reliev'd from the dusk vale" (2.49–50).

Within these scenes, moreover, he repeatedly discovers an order transcending his own sequence of "I looked . . . I saw." In his first experience of each scene, a broad perspective that attempts to take in the whole setting, the narrator discovers that the place possesses a focal point which structures the landscape and limits his own aesthetic control. Three of the four scenes show this focusing; the fourth, left incomplete, points toward a similar pattern. As he looks more closely, its focal point appears first as altar or pedestal, then as statue or statuelike form. Particularly dominant because the scenes are so often empty of other figures, these statuelike forms recall Blake's Urizen, presiding over and symbolizing his own natural horizons—with the crucial difference that Keats's narrator sees but does not shape these forms. Finally, the narrator stations himself as participant not only in the landscapes but in a struggle with the values— aesthetic and moral—that the scenes and their focal sculptural figures seem determined to force upon him.[7] Beginning in the first two scenes, these struggles culminate as he witnesses the "scenes still swooning through [Moneta's] globed brain"—the scenes drawn from *Hyperion*, with their centered, sculptural Titanic figures.

In spite of the fragmentary nature of this poem, the four visionary scenes that follow the narrator's opening strictures on dream vision form a symmetrical pattern. The narrator moves from an enclosed garden to the vast architectural space of an "eternal domed monument." Then, within Moneta's vision he finds this pattern repeated and varied: after an enclosing, entrapping vale, he looks along the almost infinite architectural space of Hyperion's palace.[8] Given both imagistic and conceptual focus through the narrator's confrontation with Moneta at Saturn's altar, this alternating pattern of scenes might be described as one of "vexing" contrasts, to borrow a phrase from Moneta's criticism of the dreamer in that scene. Moreover, the portraitlike, oxymoronic description of Moneta's face and even more her challenging antithesis of "dreamer" and "physician" make her almost emblematic of Schlegel's picturesque or romantic consciousness.[9]

These vexing or "venoming" contrasts do not stop, however, when Moneta introduces the *Hyperion* narrative as her own series of visions. Instead, they become more intense. In the third scene, the first of two revised from *Hyperion*, the contrast between statue and setting becomes the focal point for the combined meditations of Moneta and the narrator. Like Oceanus's speech in *Hyperion*, her dialogue in scene 2 acts as a thematic hypothesis to be tested in the later scenes. To follow a suggestion by Harold Bloom, Moneta needs the narrator to help her understand the consequences of her antitheses that reject dream, or, better, to convert her antitheses to the dialectic that Keats calls Poesy.[10] The narrator needs Moneta, as well, so that he may develop a similar dialectic of contraries in which he neither totally rejects dream nor totally defends it. Their confrontation in the second half of the poem resembles the exchange between narrator and angel in Blake's *Marriage of Heaven and Hell*, in which each presents landscapes of hell for the other to interpret, and each can say, "All that I saw was owing to your metaphysics." The dramatic mutual definition of Moneta and the narrator does not end as the narrative drawn from the first *Hyperion* begins; instead the two antagonists must revise Moneta's visions in order to resee themselves.

Yet in contrast both to the cool poise with which Blake's narrator confronts theological monsters and to the detached exultation with which Apollo greets Mnemosyne's knowledge, neither Keats's narrator in *The Fall* nor Moneta herself can become detached from the emotional and moral consequences of commitment to such a vexing dialectic. In fact, they come to recognize their lack of detachment through the shared sight and narration of Moneta's visions. This narration develops ordinary sight, reflected in an impersonal, detached arrangement of picturesque scenes, into the metaphysical picturesque of Poesy.

The framing of these visions on the stage of Moneta's brain clearly exemplifies Schlegel's comparison of the "picturesque" consciousness to a framed, painted scene. Another aspect of that consciousness, its suggestion that vast visual perspectives are analogous to vast temporal perspectives, appears in the narrator's insistence on "telling." A "Poesy" based on telling partially supports Lessing's thesis that poetry, like music, is temporal and progressive in contrast to the spatial, static nature of sculpture and painting—and might suggest a turn toward the Burkean sort of sublimity Hazlitt sees in Schlegel's "romantic" consciousness. Yet in this poem, as in Lessing's examples, the pictorial and the sculptural form part of the basic fabric of the poetic: the separate scenes are almost like snapshots or tableaux as they organize themselves around a central sculptural focus. Furthermore, the time during and between scenes has a kind of dreamlike unreality—sometimes moving abruptly, sometimes unendurably slowly. In contrast to this erratic succession of fixed poses or scenes, however, Moneta's "telling" these scenes to the narrator as she shows them to him, and his own telling of the story to us, make the two tellers and the audience increasingly aware not only of temporal succession but of the symbolic references to past cultural stages. Both temporal contexts also frame and interpret their mutual narrative of the fallen Titans.

Although Keats partially changes his priestess from the Mnemosyne of *Hyperion* to Moneta, she ritually remembers her own long-past Saturnian world. As she offers glimpses back through enormous temporal distance into past human culture, that human culture also includes Saturnian dreams. No abstract memory-theater for recalling and indexing "names, deeds" and "dire rebellions" for an aspiring Apollo,[11] Moneta voices Keats's attacks on Milton's dogmatic and theological interpretation of a paradise lost. She also challenges Wordsworth's insistence in much of his poetry that such dreams of paradise—Edenic or Saturnian—are private and, as one leaves childhood, almost as irreversibly lost as Milton's. Through her retelling of the narrative first told in *Hyperion*, Moneta and the narrator can work out her role as a communal memory developing in time and in individual human encounters with time. Because her vision, her narrative commentary, and the poet-narrator's response are all interdependent in their development of this theme, Keats does not simply fall back upon the sculpturesque *Hyperion* narrative but uses it with great effectiveness to define a more profound "picturesque" consciousness— aware, we might say, of the hermeneutics of dream. In the narrator's proem and first two scenes, Keats explores the grounds for this transformation.

A "*dream now purposed to rehearse*": The Induction (1.1–18)

In *Hyperion*, the narrator's delayed but conventional invocation at the beginning of book 3 acknowledges centuries of other such attempts at epic vision, but it jars against the immediate mythic force of Titan and Olympian. In *The Fall of Hyperion*, awareness of those intervening centuries develops immediately as a specific and important theme; yet the poem still begins without an invocation to the muse. Keats's own statuesque form of epic had become so objective that it resisted even the conventionalized voice of poet invoking muse. When he turns to the dream vision, however, he can more easily adopt its conventional claims of privacy and subjectivity. Within this historical continuity, he also can find room to assert his individual challenge to convention. For, as Chaucer's dream visions show, an induction that announces the dream to come and weighs its claims to truth is a frequent, nearly conventional, way of beginning. On the other hand, *The Divine Comedy*, so clearly one of Keats's models for this passage, begins its dream vision with no assessment of its fictional value, no specific location of its events.[12] Only the urgent voice of its narrator and those threatening, mysterious animals define the serious-ness of his quest and the confusion of his having lost his way. As Keats chooses a conceptually detached intellectual and analytical frame, though one to which he adds a Dantean intensity of tone, he uses it to question not only the conventional modes of dream vision but poetry as a whole. Thus, he can assert both the private, subjective nature of his individual dream vision—"I saw"—and the universality of that private experience, marked in the literary convention of dream visions. Like the prose prefaces of Blake's *Milton* and Shelley's *Prometheus Unbound*, his sharply argued evaluation of poetic premises both announces and questions a near-prophetic connection between private vision and public mission. Although Keats raises his own questions, he uses, even subverts, conven-tion to phrase that self-questioning. Through this use of convention, Keats's technique in *The Fall* for relating individual, actual speaker of the preface and authorial presence in the work itself stands between that of Shelley and of Blake. Verse form, rhythm, and the convention of induc-tions in dream vision draw the specific "I" of the actual poet fluidly into the literary artifact, so that the subjectivity this speaker begins to discuss is ambiguous. Yet he expresses more vulnerability about his subjective stance than does either Blake or Shelley.

In a haunting image at the end of the induction, physical vulnerability acts as a test and then leads to a limited validation for dream vision: "Whether the dream now purposed to rehearse / Be poet's or fanatic's will be known / When this warm scribe my hand is in the grave." Our knowledge of Keats's own illness and death so soon after the writing of these lines gives almost too much historical presence to the visual and tactile image of the hand. Yet he speaks here not only as John Keats: he is any mortal poet, thinking both of the transmission from thought to the physical act of writing and of the weakness of the artist in contrast to his or her art. After reading the rest of the poem, we also become ironically aware of the difference between warm flesh and the cold stone of the sculptural images to follow.

This doubly tactile image of the hand that is "warm" both to our touch and to his sense of living concludes an almost compulsively reiterated chain of words that ties together the processes of artistic expression. First comes "vision," "imagination," and, most insistently, "dream" (five times in eighteen lines). Although the narrator argues that this inner vision is universal, its content, intensity, and significance must vary, because he next argues repeatedly a need to "tell" those "dreams"—to speak, to give them "melodious utterance . . . if he had lov'd / And been well nurtured in his mother tongue." Through a Miltonic ambiguity of syntax in lines 14–15, Keats underlines the importance of "telling" as escape from the possible solipsism of dreams. Is "every man" who "would speak" of his visions one who has loved his mother tongue or one who has loved another person? Is love here, as in Coleridge's Dejection Ode, the catalyst for the language of imagination? The end of the "Ode to Psyche" suggests as much.

Yet even that telling may not be enough: only writing, other lines suggest, can guarantee immortality for the dreamer as well as the dream. Lines 4 through 6 suggest that writing is the necessary next step: "pity these have not / Trac'd upon vellum or wild Indian leaf / The shadows of melodious utterance." So does line 18, as it describes "this warm scribe my hand." As in *Hyperion* 2.132ff. or in the passage on books in *The Prelude*, book 5, writing creates an artifact, however fragile or inaccurate, for the even more fragile and temporally evanescent dreams. The narrator also may suggest, however, that the conscious art of "Poesy" is more essential than the concrete physical record of those dreams to make them permanent: "For Poesy alone . . . with the fine spell of words alone can save / Imagination from the sable charm [or chain] / And dumb enchantment."[13] Beginning with the emotional commitment of "telling" one's dream to another, that conscious art continues, Keats suggests, through an artistic "rehearsing," whether in well-formed writing or in speech.

The telling by one who "has loved" seems a significant step in this paradoxical charm to free imagination from dumb enchantment; for an obvious danger, and in fact a powerful alternative to a completed "Poesy," is the fanatic's vision—the assertion of "paradise for a sect." If everyone tells his or her dreams and if each teller has loved others enough to recognize, even to share, the other's dreams, such a narrow dogmatism becomes less likely. In contrast to Blake's and Milton's plea from Numbers, "Would that all the Lord's people were prophets," Keats frees his claims for imagination from any religious creed; he bases them in "every man whose soul is not a clod." If the origin in dream is equal, then, what step in the chain leads to "Poesy," what to fanaticism? As his induction makes clear, in a geographical and temporal generosity Claude Lévi-Strauss might laud, people in all cultures, both primitive and advanced, are equally privileged in their dreams and even in the means to express them—"if he had lov'd / And been well nurtured in his mother tongue." Keats accepts now neither the evolutionary scheme of *Hyperion* nor that of the 4 May letter to Reynolds in which he argued that Milton's ideas—a paradise for a sect—are outmoded by a "Grand March of Intellect." No myth of historical progress, then, guarantees Keats's own superiority to Milton. He claims here no apotheosis into a new and confident Apollinian knowledge. Instead, he offers only a limited test of time for future audiences to measure their dreams against his: "Whether the dream now purposed to rehearse / Be poet's or fanatic's will be known / When this warm scribe my hand is in the grave."[14] Along with criticism of Milton's claims to absolute inspiration, he also revises Milton's vast claims in the induction to *Paradise Lost*, book 3, a claim that he has, like Virgil's Aeneas, entered the underworld and returned: "Taught by the heav'nly Muse to venture down / The dark descent, and up to reascend, / Though hard and rare" (3.14,19–21). Keats's understated if individually poignant claim that the truth of his dream will emerge when he is "in the grave" suggests that none of us can test the validity of our dreams of ultimate value until we have experienced the reality of the grave. His criticism resembles Blake's in *Milton:* in that poem, only life after death reveals to Milton the narrow inadequacy of his claims both to have seen all the cosmos in vision beforehand and to have understood its values.

Keats's narrator claims that his dream is to be tested in time; his dream is in part about the testing of dreams in time to discover the way in which they may become not doctrine but Poesy. As he confronts these vividly pictorial dreams, they become subject to thought. Yet, they also subject the thinking narrator to their patterns by focusing of scenes around altar, pedestal, and its statue or sculptural analogue. If the narrator thinks at first that his picturing is an art to subdue dream, he discovers that in the act of exercising his art—first in the stages of the dream itself and then in its rehearsal for us—he must shape a new and more complex art of the picturesque. Keats organizes the achieved poem neither by the sibling rivalry with which Blake tests his arts nor by the developmental analogues of sculpturesque and picturesque that he uses in *Hyperion*. Instead, as each pictorially, even picturesquely, organized scene focuses upon a sculptural image, the poem as a whole moves a step closer toward its "telling" of the metaphysical picturesque in Poesy.

Scene One: "Like a Silenus"

Our only guide into the first scene of the main "vision" (1.19–56) is the first phrase: "Methought I stood where trees of every clime. . . ." Although asserting a discovering consciousness, the archaic word "me-thought" implies that where he stands is only a matter of thought, a fiction more than a fact. Even more, it implies that such "thought" is a dreamlike recognition more than an act of will based on a rational analysis of possibilities.[15] Thus, though the "dream" arising from sleep or trance begins only as this scene ends and the next begins, this one marks the beginning of the visionary experience as a whole.[16]

In contrast to his sudden awareness at the beginning of the scene, the narrator's sense-perceptions slowly and carefully organize its details. Although the framework of those impressions is visual, his other senses are harmoniously involved, and all lead to the "appetite" that both completes and obliterates the scene. Dominant at the beginning, his sight organizes the setting in three stages—each of these carefully defined, as in the picturesque viewing of landscape, by the narrator's station. From stage to stage, however, he becomes less the composer of the scene and more a participant. These stages are his first broad survey (1.19–24), his turn to examine arbor and mound (1.25–29), and the "closer see[ing]" of the feast on the mound (1.30–38).

The initial detachment of his surveylike first view is increased by its use of a characteristic unifying method from the scenic picturesque: the screen that focuses the eye from foreground to distance or from peripheral to central elements of a composition:

Methought I stood where trees of every clime,
Palm, myrtle, oak, and sycamore, and beech,
With plantane, and spice-blossoms, made a screen.

(1.19–21)

Yet of course no single picturesque view of a natural scene could include all these species of trees; even as the narrator makes concrete his physical presence as witness, he defines the visionary and traditional nature of the scene as an earthly paradise. The "plantane," in particular, recalls one of Keats's examples of stationing from *Paradise Lost:* "So we see Adam 'Fair indeed and tall—under a plantane.' " Like Adam, the narrator stands within the scene as perceived object or "statuary"; but he is simultaneously the poet who is "not content to describe [but who] . . . stations" and organizes the elements of his scene. As he turns the "screen" that had limited his sight and his intellectual and emotional involvement gives way, and his other, more immediate senses come into play. Although he now recog-nizes that he stands in midscene, between foreground and background, his centrality is questioned as the scene begins to center itself: "Turning round, / I saw an arbour. . . . / Before its wreathed doorway, on a mound / Of moss, was spread a feast of summer fruits," and then that feast is "nearer seen." Strengthening the comparison of mound to altar, the arbor is hung with "blooms, / Like floral-censers." Garden, arbor, and feast "nearer seen" recall more and more specifically those in *Paradise Lost*.[17] The feast, finally and irreversibly, "seem'd refuse of a meal / By angel tasted, or our mother Eve" (1.30–31).

With this explicit allusion, the narrator implicitly raises the question of what he knows as he enters and surveys this visionary place.[18] Through the reference to Eve and the following one to Proserpine, he places himself not only physically in the midst of the landscape but consciously in the mythical, theological, and literary contexts of a loss of Eden. Thus the emptiness of this garden except for his own presence is defined as much in temporal as in spatial terms. Although it seems Edenic, he finds no greeting of a transcendent spirit, nor even another human to whom he might tell his dream of the place's meanings. Like Adam of *Paradise Lost*, imagining an exile into a merely natural landscape, he suggests that the connection between some sort of divine presence and earthly place has been broken: "On this Mount he appear'd, under this Tree / Stood visible. . . . / In yonder nether World where shall I seek / His bright appearances, or footstep trace?" (11.320–21, 28–29). For Keats's narrator, the world in which he stands has become a "nether World," emptied by the temporally irreversible act of Adam's fall—even if the final feast of innocence seems broken off just a moment before.

In contrast, the Dantean allusions acknowledge the fall but go on to suggest regeneration. As Matilda explains to the pilgrim Dante in *Purgatorio*, Canto 28, the garden is now empty but is to become a scene of redemption. And as the narrator recasts the comparison to Proserpine that both Dante and Milton have used before him, he echoes Dante's joyous expectation: "more plenty than the fabled horn . . . could pour forth . . . For Proserpine return'd to her own fields." The two allusions, then, bracket the sensuous immediacy of this garden as an expectant moment between the still innocent feast of Adam, Eve, and Raphael (before Eve's less innocent prohibited meal), and the regenerative feast of Proserpine's return (after her prohibited eating of the pomegranate seeds). That moment, like Blake's, expands almost to fill the time between fall and last judgment. Because the narrator does not mention those two feastings on prohibited fruit, his audience remains unsure whether he is a regenerated Adam or a redeemed Proserpine returning in celebration, or whether with the feasting that marks his full participation in the scene he now reenacts humanity's or nature's fall.

Although he does indeed act out the fall, I would argue, he redefines it as innocent of any moral culpability arising through the breaking of a prohibition. He replaces a specific account of Adam's and Eve's temptation and eating with his own unprohibited but not naive or ignorant eating and drinking. His participation in the feast comes as the culmination of a typically Keatsian hierarchy of senses: from sight, directed by a synaesthetic fusion of hearing, smelling, and touch (ll. 19–24), to taste—even, one might suggest, to an ingesting of the scene that has encircled and imposed its values on him, into himself. Although the scene becomes a celebration of human, natural senses, it is a celebration framed in the awareness of a mortality that is also natural: "pledging all the mortals of the world, / And all the dead whose names are in our lips" (ll. 44–45). Filling the empty scene with his own physical presence, he unites himself with it by a physical, not a transcendent act. Yet both as dream traveler and as later "rehearser" of his journey, he is aware of the limitations of that wholeness. Although he corrects his predecessors who gave that fall a moral basis, he also shares their longing for a transcendent presence that would make his sensuous wholeness eternal in some paradisal place, for his naturalistic interpretation also denies supernatural redemption or regeneration. One sort of regeneration that they all share, however, is their human propensity to dream of such places; and so his pledge to "all the mortals of the world, / And all the dead whose names are in our lips" is to all mortals and to the mortal poets who dreamed and then truthfully denied immortal gardens. The narrator, then, has gone beyond the chamber of maiden thought. Although he celebrates a sensuous wholeness in some ways like Schiller's sculptural harmony, his very celebration is based on the briefness of such harmony.[19]

Like Melancholy's "aching Pleasure nigh, / Turning to poison while the bee-mouth sips," his feasting leads him beyond the intellectual recognition of his pledge into a paradoxical experience of mortality. In the final tableau of this scene, the narrator suddenly finds that he himself has replaced the altarlike "mound of moss" as a central sculptural form whose stationing as object, not as envisaging subject, organizes the scene:

> Among the fragrant husks and berries crush'd,
> Upon the grass I struggled hard against
> The domineering potion; but in vain:
> The cloudy swoon came on, and down I sunk
> Like a Silenus on an antique vase.
>
> (1.52–56)

Such a sculptural image, a foreshadowing of death, tests Schiller's or Schlegel's harmonious, serene natural existence by placing it within temporal process.

The narrator's simile increases this tension in the sculptural analogue. Any figure on an antique vase would appear either as bas-relief or as a linear silhouette resembling a two-dimensional sculptural form more than a painting. In ancient Greece, moreover, roughly made pottery figures of Silenus were cult objects, artifacts for this minor god of fertility.[20] In *Endymion*, as Douglas Bush notes, Silenus is a follower of Bacchus and thus associated briefly with the apparently earthly Indian maid who finally reveals herself as Endymion's dreamed-of Cynthia.[21] Here the formally framed mythological figure suggests a later and more pessimistic version of Endymion's discovery of the transcendent in the immanent; for the transcendence this dreamer wakes to discover is Moneta's hostile challenge to dream, framed within her "antique" monument. Yet the narrator's shared inheritance for interpreting the myth of Silenus also includes Virgil's Sixth Eclogue, in which the half-drunk Silenus outsings Orpheus and rehearses all the world's myths from creation on. Virgil's Silenus suggests, then, that the whole inheritance of cultural myths can best be released through the suspension of art and almost of consciousness; in drunkenness or dream, not Poesy.[22] Finally, however, as the framing of the image on an "antique vase" suggests, the admonition to dream is a consciously received cultural inheritance. That cultural inheritance and consciousness of historical time, moreover, are not external to the dream vision he recounts. It would be neater to argue that the dream traveler is virtually unconscious of such complexity and that the narrator adds it, in the form of allusion and simile, as the man self-consciously tells his dream and becomes a poet. Instead, through the dream traveler's gradual participation in the scene, both the original scenic, picturesque landscape and the sculptural figure of the Silenus-poet within it embody the tension between mortal limits upon the fully explored senses and immortal longings. His telling only continues the process begun in the experience itself.

Scene Two: "that eternal domed monument"

In the second visionary scene (1.58–290), the narrator again searches for control through the order of his visual perception. Visual order contrasts sharply to the dreamlike suddenness of his finding himself there. It also contrasts, though more subtly, to the sense that others have come there before him and have shaped the scene with their preconceptions. Here the explicit analogues are not literary alone but are more broadly cultural. In fact, the broadest and most ancient cultural analogue we might discover is precisely the transformation of natural landscape into a sacred place that determines one's orientation. The centering that began in the first scene through the narrator's approach to its natural altar becomes more extensive and more painful in this scene, as the strange monument recalls and then transforms traditional religious architecture and its traditional orientation. These in turn further transform the allusions to Edenic serenity in the first scene. Each time the narrator frames a perspective, he finds that the perspective has framed, stationed, and evaluated him.

Looking "around," "high," and "at my feet," he first conveys a sense of enormous spatial and temporal perspectives. Guessing at the function of the building, he calls it an "old sanctuary." Strewn with paraphernalia of religious ritual, it seems "So old . . . the superannuations of sunk realms . . . seem'd but the faulture of decrepit things / To that eternal domed monument" (1.65, 69, 70–71). His second survey is more architecturally and spatially specific: "Turning from these with awe, once more I rais'd / My eyes to fathom the space every way" (1.81–82). Now, as in the moment of "turning round" in the first scene, we realize that he stands at a central point in the scene, close to a crossing of nave and transept that dictates his spiritual as well as his physical perspective. First following the mysterious transepts, that "silent massy range / Of columns north and south, ending in mist / Of nothing," he then turns

> . . . to eastward, where black gates
> Were shut against the sunrise evermore.
> Then to the west I look'd, and saw far off
> An image, huge of feature as a cloud,
> At level of whose feet an altar slept.
>
> (1.85–89)

As Bloom emphasizes, the cathedrallike "monument" is turned around, its altar west instead of east.[23]

The recession of the transepts into infinite distance confirms spatially the enormous temporal span suggested earlier and makes romantic and picturesque the indefinite yet neoclassical dome and columns. Anne Mellor has suggested that Keats modeled the building on accounts of the Parthenon, yet its floor plan is far more similar to a Gothic church.[24] Although it strongly resembles that baroque synthesis of Gothic and classical, Wren's design for Saint Paul's, the extreme view of the "columns north and south, ending in nothing" makes the style more a version of Rosenblum's romantic classicism than of the baroque. This distorted classical idiom, with its restless lack of serenity, makes the narrator's central location an "uneasy station." Moreover, as the next several lines show, the western altar, once seen, shapes its own imperatives visually even before its priestess pronounces her sudden ultimatum: ". . . an altar slept, / To be approach'd on either side by steps, / And marble balustrade, and patient travail" (1.89–91). Here his visual observations become a kind of discipline as they merge into moral imperatives for action.

As in the first episode, the narrator carefully marks the next stage of his observation: "coming nearer, [I] saw beside the shrine / One minist'ring" (1.95–96). Although that priestess soon dominates the scene and eventually replaces it with her own visions, it is crucially important to notice that the altar is dedicated to Saturn, whose enormous statue towers above it. Thus, though the second vision places the observer inside a massive work of architecture that manifests a sophisticated artistic and religious culture, all its perspectives focus upon a deity who recalls a pastoral or golden age like the one glimpsed by the narrator in his first vision—the Saturn of Roman paradisal myths. In the first *Hyperion* and later in this one, Saturn himself describes that world. At this point in the vision, his statue, so large that the narrator can see only its knees, is an hypostasizing center, a frozen memorial to the natural, spontaneous and sense-directed wholeness that the narrator has just experienced. If this "eternal domed monument" seems to include in its vast architecture and symbolic artifacts all earthly religions,[25] we must argue that all those religions memorialize a lost earthly wholeness—not a natural religion, but a wholeness of man, nature, and spirit. The Greek and Celtic traditions of searching for such paradises to the west, in a realm of life after death still lit by the westward-moving sun, suggest a positive interpretation for the anti-Christian direction of the sanctuary, as many of Keats's earlier lyrics suggest.[26] Yet the "black gates" "to eastward" that are "shut against the sunrise evermore" seem less to reject Christian or Asiatic mystery religion for a more joyous celebration of the senses than to exclude all new worshipers and indeed all illumination.[27] The westward turn of the sanctuary then points toward one traditional location of such earthly paradises but also suggests that their time is long past—that their sun is set. The fall of the Titans' sun-god would have made the metaphor narrative and concrete.

If the monument was built to worship an idyllic integrity of the senses and the natural world, that is, the "statuesque" or plastic world of the ancient Greeks as Schiller and Schlegel described it, its architecture modifies our perception of that world, by transforming classical limit and form to a more restless and romantic suggestiveness. In its contrast to the human figure of the strayed narrator, the scale and mysterious incompleteness of the building recall Piranesi. So do the objects that "all in a mingled heap confus'd . . . lay" on its marble floor. Finally, the "image huge of feature as a cloud" whose massive feet alone seem visible to the narrator's view recalls Fuseli's fragmentary foot of Constantine whose jolting discrepancy in scale works through Blake's *Milton*. Unlike Blake, however, who builds upon the discrepancy of proportion between scene and wanderer to transform conventional time and space, Keats is highly consistent both in maintaining the pictorial frame and in suggesting temporal distances that reach beyond the narrator's control. Fuseli's sketch expresses the monumental power and inaccessible distance of past culture through the discrepancy of spatial scale; the narrator in this scene, too, is overwhelmed by a discrepancy of temporal scale between his own brief existence and acts, and the mysterious age of the building. In the first scene, the inhabitants seem to have left moments before, and the narrator thus could participate easily in their undecayed feast. In the second, an enormous temporal distance seems to separate the building of the monument from the present. Moreover, because the building's massive architectural coldness is so far abstracted from the groves, fields, and forests of a pastoral paradise, Saturn's enshrining makes nearly inaccessible the actual state it tries to honor and thus becomes a kind of fall in itself. The second scene seeks in the continuity of human culture—religion and art—more than in any specific doctrines of transcendence or salvation, some compensation for the mortality of the individual humans and their private dreams.[28] Yet that very continuity seems to overwhelm the narrator.

In developing this architectural symbolism, Keats also may have kept in mind a more immediate model for this crisis of continuity: his comparison of Milton to Wordsworth in the 3 May 1818 letter to Reynolds. There his architectural model for the development of individual insight also becomes the model for a progress of poetry. Wordsworth's understanding of the human heart places him in "dark passages" that advance him beyond Milton. Through the narrator's participation in this scene, Keats seems to allude to Wordsworth's own subversive metaphors of ecclesiastical architecture to express his rivalry with Milton. The image of a vast cathedral, the struggle of the narrator to reach "the lowest step" of the altar for the enthroned Saturn, and above all the figure of a remembering Moneta who presides there, all revise images and functions drawn from Wordsworth's poetry. Although Keats of course did not know *The Prelude*, he would know Wordsworth's analyses of memory in the Immortality Ode and "Tintern Abbey"; he also would know the images of cathedral and throne from the prose preface and Prospectus to *The Recluse*.

In his prose preface Wordsworth explains, "The two Works [the unpublished *Prelude* and the unfinished *Recluse*] have the same kind of relation to each other . . . as the ante-chapel has to the body of a gothic church." Further, he continues the analogy to include all his "minor pieces" as "the little cells, oratories, and sepulchral recesses, ordinarily included in those edifices."[29] Like Blake, Wordsworth may find in Gothic architecture "living form" that opposes the rational forms of classicism. As an image for the vast, yet organic development of his own work, his choice of the cathedral seems a mirror image of his deliberate choice in "Lines written . . . above Tintern Abbey" to replace the famous Gothic ruins of the abbey with his more private and more naturally grounded shrine.[30] Watson points out that in "Tintern Abbey" Wordsworth carefully evokes and then avoids the prescribed stations and objects of the picturesque guides to the Wye valley. Turning from his culture's history as embodied in monuments to orthodox religious faith, he explores his own remembered history of a faith in nature; and turning half away from a visible landscape with its culturally formed views, he remembers what the individual mind half-creates. His later metaphor of the Gothic cathedral for his life's work as a poet draws upon that image of a past culture and its more public history to rebuild it as a monument, one might argue, for a private faith in his own continuity of memories.

True, his *Recluse* is planned to include all culture—to contain "views of Man, Nature, and Society"; and if *The Excursion* excludes much of that, it does so in part because Wordsworth is tracing the psychological cost of such exclusion.[31] Completing the criticism of isolation made in *The Excursion*, Keats suggests that the almost empty monument his narrator sees is a memorial in which private faith must be converted to necessarily if cautiously expressed public significance.

The image of Saturn that presides in Keats's "domed monument," moreover, makes it a temple to what Wordsworth's *Recluse* Prospectus calls "Paradise, and groves / Elysian, Fortunate Fields—like those of old / Sought in the Atlantic Main." In the 1797 optimism of these lines published with the preface to *The Excursion*, Wordsworth goes on to ask, "Why should they be / A history only of departed things, / Or a mere fiction of what never was?" For he locates the capacity to create these paradisal visions in "our Minds . . . the Mind of Man— / My haunt, and the main region of my song." The generic form "Man" hides here how private that enterprise becomes in much of Wordsworth's poetry, as the mutual fitting and fitted of the "individual Mind" and "external World" create that visionary new world to replace the old one. His optimistic phrasing in the Prospectus also excludes his own contemporary and later doubts of the adult's ability to maintain such "Paradise and groves" beyond childhood. Keats's doubts, however, reach beyond Wordsworth's as he turns from the mutability of sensuous paradises, a theme described in the first scene and shared with Wordsworth, to an attack in this scene on the isolation of the "individual Mind." Like Blake he refuses Wordsworth's "fitting and fitted" but for different reasons. Although both challenge natural religion, for Keats the external world cannot simply be repudiated and remolded like Urizen. Yet in this poem, as opposed to the "Ode to Psyche," the "individual Mind" must seek a communal stability, though not a tyrannical conformity, as it evaluates its yearning for "Paradise, and groves / Elysian."[32]

Toward the end of his *Recluse* Prospectus, Wordsworth does include an image that lessens the threat of solipsism. Another image from religious architecture, it lends both theme and vocabulary to the conversion of Moneta's temple from a memorial based on a solitary memory to a place of shared remembrance and a recalling of others who have shared such remembrances. Wordsworth pleads, "Descend, prophetic Spirit! that dost possess / A metropolitan temple in the hearts / Of mighty Poets: . . . that my Song . . . may shine, / Shedding benignant influence." Moneta's temple must become a "metropolitan temple," a monument to the encounters that make private dreams communal.

Thus the abbey ruin that Wordsworth refuses as lyric object but uses as metaphor to celebrate the whole of his poetic vision can become, as Keats transforms it to an "eternal domed monument," a new kind of "epic object." Yet his sanctuary becomes the locus for a poem that seeks neither a "Greek" objectivity and sculptural harmony of the divine, the human, and the natural, nor the egotistical sublime of an "individual Mind" that asserts the worship of its own, earlier childhood harmony with nature. Instead, this scene is, like the first one, a place in which natural limitations—of human lives in the first scene, of cultural lives in the second—are fused with the common dreams devised to escape such limitations. This monument to dreams of religions that have worshiped humanity's oneness with nature thus becomes the arena for a struggle to salvage that Wordsworthian hope of redemption—a hope recast in terms of shared vision and shared responsibility. Its struggle is far more darkly imaged, but its turn from "I" to "we," and from natural to urban models, recalls both Blake's "Jerusalem" stanzas in the lyric preface to *Milton* and Shelley's Athens in the "Ode to Liberty."

As the narrator struggles to recast Wordsworth's dream of salvation, he continues Keats's recasting of Wordsworth's images from the Prospectus. "In holiest mood" the Wordsworthian bard usurps Miltonic images and diction to acclaim his surpassing of Milton's deity. "Urania, I shall need / Thy guidance, or a greater Muse," he prays, as he announces that "I pass . . . unalarmed . . . All strength—all terror, single or in bands, /

That ever was put forth in personal form" to "breathe in worlds / To which the heaven of heavens is but a veil" (lines 25ff.). Keats's narrator, in contrast, succeeds only with great difficulty and with Moneta's grace in reaching the altar to Saturn—and from there can look up to see only the knees of the enthroned statue of Saturn. As Moneta's veils part, they reveal not a vision surpassing the "heaven of Heavens" but one poised in its moonlike images of "benignant influence" paradoxically between the sublunar, "nether sphere" of the mortal world (Prospectus, l. 93) and some realm more immortal. Finally, even that vision is given him, not claimed as an assertive poet's right.

The "dissociation of sensibility"[33] that almost keeps him from reaching the altar (1.122–34, 228–40) suggests both that man cannot surpass the "empyreal thrones" or outer limits of a natural realm presided over by Saturn, and that he cannot inhabit except momentarily or in dream the earthly harmonious paradises men surmise Saturn to have ruled.[34] Yet the mercy of even this admonitory Memory—that is, Moneta—gives him an alternate hope, though one formed upon dissociation, dissonance, and contrariety. The statue of Saturn, unattainable center of the scene, stands for an unattainable harmony; the presence of Moneta, both statuelike and picturelike, provides a model, though one that the narrator must challenge and partially revise, for a metaphysically picturesque consciousness. Bounded in mortality, it will yet recognize the necessity of Saturnian dream.

"Propitious parley": Moneta's Dialogue

Toward the end of this long second scene, Moneta's dialogue with the narrator and his emblematic description of her face form a central pivot of the poem. Between the narrator's pastoral and architectural visions (scenes 1 and 2) and Moneta's similar ones (scenes 3 and an incomplete 4), these two passages develop still further the tension between contraries already present in the first two scenes. In the first of these passages, an encounter built on oppositions, Moneta and the narrator must work to "interfuse" these contrarieties. First, in an acrimonious dialogue the still anonymous and veiled Moneta explains the narrator's presence and the necessity for his trial. As she attempts to distinguish between "physician" and "dreamer," she is ultimately forced, as Harold Bloom argues, to see those terms as dialectical opposites resolved in the term "poet."[35] Surprisingly, the first stage of her analysis also relates each pole of the debate to the Saturnian earthly paradise that the narrator has glimpsed earlier and that her own worship recalls. Although the physician is fully aware of the world's "misery," he sees these problems and his ability to cure them within the limits of the natural world. He is capable of "usurping" the height of the Saturnian altar because through, or in spite of, its painful discipline, it promises an earthly wholeness in which he believes. The dreamer, on the other hand, "venoms all his days" with a restlessness that mourns the visionary impossibility of Saturnian wholeness in a world of misery. Such a vision appears transcendently distanced from him, lost in a distant temporal and physical perspective. Paradoxically, then, the physician who "seek[s] no wonder but the human face, / No music but a happy-noted voice," can evoke as a hope the "Paradise, and groves / Elysian," whereas the dreamer, Moneta argues, is always conscious simultaneously of the paradises and the insistent presence of misery. Already, then, Moneta has begun to distinguish, within the category of useless people to whom she opposes the physician, those who "thoughtless sleep away their days" and the "dreaming thing" who "venoms all his days" by restlessness.[36] If the dreamer escapes from responsibility, he does so by too much incapacitating awareness of the human condition, not by thoughtless sleep. The jarring of his senses, the "suffering" she grants him, is—she suggests—a purification rite that will banish the jarring of the oxymoronic consciousness she already recognizes in this "dreamer."[37] He might then become a poet according to her definition, one who "pours out" balm upon the world.

In the bracketed passage from which this phrase is drawn,[38] the narrator, as Bloom argues, has forced Moneta to examine her two categories of "physician" and "dreamer" to suggest, in the third category of "poet," a psychological reconciliation that might accept the dreamer's restless "vexing" as means to a balm. Like Moneta's challenging dialogue, the vexing can be communicated not only as a disease but as "propitious parley medicin'd / In sickness not ignoble." The dreamer who vexes or venoms his days thus can become more than a dreamer—he can become a physician to restless minds, or even to minds lacking sufficient recognition to be restless—and thus he becomes a poet. Although this interfusion of contraries is incompletely worked out here, Keats has anticipated it in the preceding narrative, through the use of an earthly paradise to test the limits of "escapist" dream. Because the narrator as dreamer has experienced and recognized the deathlike trance at the center of the senses' earthly paradise, he is evicted from that paradisal place by his own "venoming" or vexing consciousness—even if his eviction makes him momentarily a sculpturesque figure who "sleeps away his days." More strongly than in the first scene, he now sees dream self-consciously as dream. Ironically, the resulting restlessness urges him on to worship Saturn, to overcome the fragmentation of his senses with a new and more active discipline that will reconstitute his vision of that paradise.

As his opening word, "Methought," showed, his earlier presence in this Eden was not a mindlessly naive one. To grow as poet, however, he must learn why the comforting, "thoughtless" dream of an earthly paradise, even if rejected as real possibility, must yet be treasured as temporary release. For in its unlimiting dream it becomes as much a measure of his humanness as are the limits of his senses and his biological existence. Although this painful and introspective reconstitution is far different from the triumphant surpassing of heaven Wordsworth describes in his Prospectus, it is in many ways similar to the "recompense" that knits together past and present in much of his other poetry, even if we exclude the unknown *Prelude*.

For Wordsworth, however, the solitary nature of such recompense is usually sufficient.[39] For the narrator of *The Fall of Hyperion*, the encounter with Moneta abruptly and thoroughly invades his isolation. Because she continues the discipline that the structure of the scene already has imposed on him, he is not simply fed with her sight, as the speaker of the "Ode on Melancholy" urges his initiate to do.[40] She resists becoming either an aesthetic object or a victim of his appetitive self-assertion. His struggle to reach the steps is not precisely self-sacrifice, for to stay in place would be to die; he ascends toward life, not to a sacrificial Christ-like death upon the altar.[41] Nevertheless, her discipline requires a self-effacing submission of his individual ego before the nature of his task, a direction of the dreamer's purpose beyond either self-gratification or self-criticism for failing physically to help humanity.

Through this direction, as the dialogue and the emblematic revelation of her face replace his physical struggle toward the steps, the Wordsworthian pattern of a solitary recompense, a returned vision of a Saturnian childhood of self or of culture, is transformed not only for him but for Moneta as well. As they clash with one another, they form a culture of two. Even as she speaks out peremptorily, she confirms her self as something more than a passive support system. Although the memory she offers is emotionally burdened with her own experiences, her mythic, Titanic status and stature make it far greater than the memory of a single person. As the narrator in turn challenges her, he couples that challenge with a concern for her as a person: "tell me where I am: / Whose altar this; . . . / What image this . . . and who thou art, / Of accent feminine, so courteous?" As a result, "by her voice I knew she shed / Long treasured tears." The shocking combination of his earlier anger and his "good will" releases her from her static role as "Sole priestess of [Saturn's] desolation" (1.211–15, 220–21, 227).

Moneta's *"wan face"*: Emblem of Contraries

The face of Saturn that Moneta describes in answer to the narrator's question prepares the way for his sight of her own face: "this old image here, / Whose carved features wrinkled as he fell, / Is Saturn's; I, Moneta, left supreme / Sole priestess of his desolation" (1.224–27). So vast is the statue that the narrator still sees Saturn's features only through Moneta's mediation. Her description illustrates even more sharply than in *Hyperion* the paradox of "statuary" as symbol, for her reference to "this old image here" is a curious fusion of a god and the sculptural representation of that god. It may show that Saturn himself was transformed into a statue as he fell from godhead; or that the face of the image, in a near-magical sympathetic response, wrinkled as the god's own face lost its marblelike divine serenity; or, finally, that the unknown sculptor could represent only an anguished mortal. Keats's sculptural image is no longer a simile, as in *Hyperion*, but is more directly tied to the actual Saturn.[42] Moreover, that sculpture no longer reflects only the serene realm and psyche of a god but becomes paintinglike as it reflects Saturn's loss of real power and his gain of emotion. The emotion is frozen in a single expression and pose, however, and at this point in the narrative we do not know whether Saturn exists as god or as statue alone. Focusing upon facial features and the portrayal of emotion almost eternally endured, Moneta's description of Saturn anticipates the pictorial framing of the rest of the narrative within her own iconic face and "hollow brain" and thus an increasingly pictorial, subjective narrative. Yet the oxymoronic nature of her description of Saturn as statue points toward a more complex version of Schlegel's or Coleridge's "picturesque" as structure for all of these narrative scenes. As noted above, her dialogue with the narrator and his description of her emblematic face form a central, pivotal section between the first two visions and the last two; the dialectical structures of these central passages epitomize the larger relationships of these two pairs of scenes. As the description of Saturn, the dialogue, and Moneta's face all suggest, this structure of contraries does not turn merely to subjective, inward vision but attempts both to criticize and to salvage inner dream confronted by an outer "world of Circumstances." Finally, the narrator and Moneta each attempts to share that perception of contraries with the other—who will keep it from being only a haunting, inward dream. Moneta's description of Saturn's statue and the narrator's description of her face become, then, closing images for the second scene, as those two statuelike figures force the narrator on to recognitions constituting the next scene, and they become larger pivotal images for the whole narrative structure.

The narrator's immediate response to Moneta's identification of Saturn as a Titan is to glance around repeatedly, almost compulsively, in a frenzied distortion of his earlier stationing as a picturesque observer. He can neither move toward the altar nor answer Moneta: this unresolved, almost meaningless alternation between contraries must shake his claim to define a poet as one who can become a physician by seeing and telling of vexing contraries, because these contraries neither progress nor interfuse to become a "balm." For the second time in this scene, his frantic immobility seems to approach the paradoxical stasis of Saturn's statue; for the second time, he seems to struggle like Blake's Milton against a malign force that attempts to freeze his footsteps into marble. Yet the "palsied chill" that "struck from the paved level up my limbs" (1.122–23) took place at a more elementary level of sense perception. More challenging to his physical self-preservation, that dissociation also challenged his Saturnian vision of a physical and "thoughtless" paradise. Now, in an encounter quite different from Milton's tactile encounter with Urizen, but equally corrective of the "abstract" grandeur of *Paradise Lost*, the narrator's hearing and sight—more abstract senses—must teach him to bear an emotional burden until now beyond his own experience. Incoherence and dissociation mark his attempt to assimilate his responses. Not only has Moneta's identification of Saturn confirmed his own experience of the mortality at the heart of that paradise, but she has made of their fall a world-shaping historical event. Like the sanctuary, their mythic history enlarges individual experience to a more universal experience of loss. The fall of the Titans is not an explanatory cause of human history and its ills, then, so much as a recognition of natural ills—as Shelley's Asia will interpret another version of this myth in her interview with Demogorgon. Moneta's historicizing of this recognition does not seem to represent any sentimental plea that, because a paradisal realm once existed, it may again exist.[43] Instead, the "electral changing misery" of her mourning has allowed so little change in her grief that the fallenness of the Titans, almost more than the memory of their paradise, seems an eternal painful present to her.[44] Her intention to "be kind to" the narrator, an intention ironically unobservant of his sympathetic involvement, shows her emerging hope that his poetic art might make of their history some consoling balm for the less visionary but still troubled inhabitants of earth—or perhaps a hope that her own visionlike presenting of those scenes "still swooning vivid through [her] globed brain" will achieve the same aesthetic yet not idealizing distance. That conversion is slower and more painful than she anticipates, however, because the narrator first must experience the Titans' universal history by sharing her individual, personal grief. Her historicizing of the end of a Saturnian paradise, however, points the way toward a release from grief, even for herself—for her role as Mnemosyne embodies the repeated human acknowledgments of that loss and also their repeated, shared myths of consolation. Thus the vision Moneta offers him is not, like the vision Michael offers Milton's Adam, a curse acknowledging the narrator's fallen state;[45] instead, it is a means of redemption for both, as they learn to share the sorrow of mortality. The narrator is learning to see not with "dull mortal eyes" but "as a god sees" (1.304). The nature of that godhead, however, is far different from that promised in the prelapsarian Saturnian visions or the detached apotheosis of Apollo in the earlier fragment. Instead, his sight of Moneta's face and its interfused contraries is a foreshadowing of his new knowledge.

When Moneta draws back her veils, the face she reveals fuses characteristics of sculpture and painting as if to emphasize the interfusion of the eternal and the natural, immortal and mortal:

. . . Then saw I a wan face,
Not pin'd by human sorrows, but bright blanch'd
By an immortal sickness which kills not;
It works a constant change, which happy death
Can put no end to; deathwards progressing
To no death was that visage; it had pass'd
The lily and the snow; and beyond these
I must not think now, though I saw that face.

(1.256–63)

Just as the veils frame her face, his repeated summaries frame its verbal details: "Then saw I a wan face. . . . I saw that face." Although the whiteness of the face as well as its size and her poise make her seem statuelike, she is caught between living person and statue. Her whiteness combined with the "constant change" that is evidence of life have something of the same unnerving mixture Flaxman claimed would result from the coloring of classical statues.[46] Because of this eerie whiteness, the evidence of life in her face is a Tithonuslike calculus, "deathwards progressing / To no death." Because it ironically recalls the confidence of Oceanus's speech in the first *Hyperion*, the word "progressing" here is all the more powerful. And further, the "constant change" reverses normal values in its "immortal sickness," making death "happy" in its desired but unattainable finality.

This verbal representation of a visual portrait resembles a blazon, an earlier literary form representing a visual heraldic shield, but here the Petrarchan hyperboles of a mistress like a goddess turn to horror.[47] As in "La Belle Dame," the natural comparisons of "lily" and "snow" point not toward the almost divine surpassing of natural, vivid beauty within natural process but to the unnatural or supernatural suspension of natural process. In the ballad, that unnaturalness includes the transfer of the mistress's springlike vitality to the knight's feverish autumnal sickness. In this poem, the temporal order of the narrator's words evokes a series of visual images that, though similar, conflict with one another in context and significance: the immortal and beautiful whiteness of marble or ivory in a statue, the mortal and beautiful whiteness of the courtly mistress's skin, and the eerie "wan" and "bright blanch'd" horror of a face in which the verge of mortality closest to death has become immortal. Traditionally, the blazon evokes specific visual images, usually drawn from nature, and then declares the inadequacy of such visual words for describing the lady's beauty. Usually, too, the naturalistic *carpe diem* motive defines all this beauty as urgently mortal: if the lady is like a goddess, she resembles one only for a moment or a day. As Keats's narrator concludes the first stage of his description, he extends even further his revision of this verbal and visual hyperbole. Her visage "had pass'd / The lily and the snow; and beyond these / I must not think now, though I saw that face." Although he has seen and thought beyond those traditional images of whiteness, what lies beyond is not conventional praise but unconventional terror. Ironically, too, that visual image becomes all too eternal in his mind. Because his personal memory of this "shade" of cultural memory remains painful, he too is caught in the same pattern of a process that never concludes.

In the second stage of the narrator's description, syntax again seems to reflect an endless and haunting repetition. Just as the first sentence begins and ends with "face," the second begins and ends with "eyes." Again the narrator uses a focusing visual pattern; but the pattern now reveals even more than before an oxymoronic, picturesque complexity. Like the whole face, her eyes show the features of sculpture, here in the very featurelessness of a classical sculpture ravaged by time: With "divinest lids / Half closed, . . . visionless entire they seem'd / Of all external things—they saw me not, / But in blank splendor beam'd like the mild moon, / Who comforts those she sees not, who knows not / What eyes are upward cast" (1.266–71). Mellor's suggestion that Keats echoes accounts of the Phidian statue of Athena in the Parthenon seems particularly forceful here.[48] Yet the thematic implications of that idea must be balanced against the function of Saturn's statue in the scene and even more against the mediating function of Moneta. Neither fully Titan nor fully mortal, she portrays in part the statuesque serenity of a god and in part the anguish of a "picturesque" consciousness aware of mortality.

Reflecting his own active, anguished struggle to communicate, the narrator describes directly as well as in the simile a viewer who looks at those eyes "visionless . . . Of all external things." Moreover, the images that make her eyes more than those of a statue describe not only "a benignant light" but a reflected light: they "beam'd like the mild moon." "What high tragedy," he goes on to conjecture, could "fill with such a light / Her planetary eyes [?]" (1.280–81). The phrase "benignant light" may again echo Wordsworth's *Prospectus:* the earlier poet asks "that my Song / With star-like virtue in its place may shine, / shedding benignant influence . . . secure / Of those mutations that extend their sway / Throughout the nether sphere." Although Wordsworth describes the effect of his song upon its readers and Keats's narrator describes the source of his vision and its effect on him, the allusion intensifies the boundarylike function of Moneta and her radiance. The light, more mutable than Wordsworth's "star-like . . . influence," comes from the internal things that "the hollow brain / Behind enwombed," giving her sadness "so dread a stress," and comes also from reflected light. In his metaphor, the source of that reflected light is the sun; on the literal level, the "high tragedy" whose light fills her "planetary eyes" may have its source in the human eyes that look up. When, a few lines further on, he calls her for the first time "Shade of Memory," we realize once more that she extends the narrator's consciousness with breadth and depth of history beyond his own. Reflecting his subjectivity and then leading it into a collective subjectivity, her "visage" is simultaneously an objective statue and subjective envisager or "seer" in the prophetic sense.

Yet the concept of a communal subjectivity is no easily established "harmonious interchange" any more than is Wordsworth's announcement of a fitting and fitted between the mind and the "external World" in his actual poetic demonstrations. The final simile in the narrator's portrait of Moneta shows the same sort of exploitation Blake's characters—for example, the speaker in "The Crystal Cabinet"—demonstrate and must overcome:

> As I had found
> A grain of gold upon a mountain's side,
> And twing'd with avarice strain'd out my eyes
> To search its sullen entrails rich with ore,
> So at the view of sad Moneta's brow,
> I ached to see what things the hollow brain

Behind enwombed: what high tragedy
In the dark secret chambers of her skull
Was acting, that could give so dread a stress
To her cold lips, and fill with such a light
Her planetary eyes; and touch her voice
With such a sorrow.

                                                  (1.271–82)

He interprets her face as he might a stone; yet his avaricious purpose is to
convert that opaque objectivity and its mysterious radiance into a subjectivity he can share—even invade.[49] In this invasion, however, his dominance is only temporary.

Scene Three: *"fixed shapes" in "eternal quietude"*

Like a proscenium stage, Moneta's "hollow brain" reveals behind its
white veils the scenes of her past. This visual and verbal framing, which
the narrator's "telling" in turn encloses, should draw our attention to two
important themes even more strongly developed in the second half of the
poem than in the first: the uncontrollable, if still beautiful, processes of
"chance, and death, and mutability," and the double-edged and treacher-
ous weapons used to establish some control over them, the forms of art.
Sculpture is the most obvious of these partially controlling arts, and not
surprisingly allusions to it become even more specific here than earlier in
the poem or in *Hyperion*. The enclosing narratives first of Moneta and then
of the narrator also represent poetry's art of "telling." Moreover, her
narrative, or more exactly the tableaux vivants she presents and on which
she comments, never fully develops its own fictional world but is constantly broken into by one teller or the other. Thus their telling fuses these
two forces, time and art, which Keats so often opposes to one another.
Each narrator adds a context of historical or even in Moneta's case a
prehistorical consciousness. Finally, the Titans themselves become conscious of time, though their irreversible history has just begun. Thus they
no longer lay claim to rule or to represent a Saturnian paradise; though
scene 3 is earthly and pastoral, it is no longer the emptied paradise of scene
1 but a world even more full of process than that of the hymn to Pan in
Endymion, which it closely echoes.[50] As a result, all of the characters now
consciously search for the same thing, for some consolation or stay against
their own entwining in natural process. The Titans, nevertheless, are
neither heroic surrogates for humanity, as they become in *Hyperion*, nor
equal to the human narrator. Instead, though they partially develop a
romantic subjectivity and a perception of their own ineffectualness in an

infinite natural world, they also act as focal points for the narrator's testing
of the effect and cost of art. They are still "stationed," and they still
represent a dream, but the dream they now represent is of an immortal,
saving art, not of an earthly or naive paradise of the senses. Thus the
function of their comparison to sculpture changes as well. Scene 4, a
return to Hyperion's sky-palace, is scarcely developed, although emblematic of the conclusion toward which Keats may have been moving in the
narrative. Scene 3, however, alternating between dramatic representation
of Thea and Saturn and narrative responses to them, works through two
crises in the symbolic meaning of sculpture. From these, in turn, emerges
a stronger definition of Poesy for the pilgrim narrator.

As he begins to see through Moneta's eyes and finds himself "deep in
the shady sadness of a vale," the narrator announces his new vision with
almost as much confidence as Apollo greeted Mnemosyne's "knowledge
enormous":

> There grew
> A power within me of enormous ken,
> To see as a God sees, and take the depth
> Of things as nimbly as the outward eye
> Can size and shape pervade . . .
>
> . . . .
> . . . I set myself
> Upon an eagle's watch, that I might see,
> And seeing ne'er forget.
>
> (1.302–06, 308–10)

Although these lines confirm his initiation into Moneta's vision, they raise
a series of questions. Like "an eagle's watch," the word "depth" immediately suggests a "station" that looks horizontally "deeper" into a picture or
a landscape. This pictorial frame reinforces the stage metaphor used
earlier and suggests his aesthetic distance from the narrative's events. Yet
"we stood," he says, "Deep in the shady sadness of a vale"; and, given the
myths of a fall from divinity or from dreamlike fulfillment that the
narrative has already evoked, this depth also suggests a psychological and
moral descent that involves him more than aesthetically. He may well
seem godlike because, like Orpheus or Christ, he already has made such a
descent in living through his collapses in scene 1 and again on approaching
the altar steps in scene 2.[51] Thus the "depth of things" is also an inner
knowledge for which his own experiences prepare him.

The ambiguity of this "power . . . To see as a God sees" increases
further with the Miltonic echoes not only of a "fall" but of its perceivers'
moral response. In the opening tableau of *Hyperion* Saturn looks and

sounds like Milton's Satan, though the resemblance is not so much an equation as a hypothesis that forces us to consider the cosmic framework of Keats's poem. As he revises this passage, Keats first stations his narrator in the vale and thus shifts the Satanic allusion from Saturn to the narrator. Not only does the narrator become for the moment the central objective figure in the vale, but his "power . . . of enormous ken, / To see as a God sees" closely resembles that of Satan as he surveys his new place: "As far as angels' ken he views / The dismal situation waste and wild." As he stations his fallen angels, "abject and lost," in the desolate landscape of hell, Satan seems the first of those spectators *ab extra* in Milton's poem who observe from a distance but morally must commit themselves to the consequences of their viewpoints. Yet Satan believes himself psychologically above his followers even as he condescends to lead them. In contrast, through the power of his godlike vision the narrator of Keats's *Fall* learns to share the lot of the fallen Titan. The kind of vision he must learn is one that would avoid such arrogant Satanic detachment.[52]

Furthermore, Keats's phrasing identifies the narrator not only with the observing Satan, who sees only an external depth, but also with Milton himself—who uses a remembered sight to "pervade" "size" and "shape" but turns inward with a glance made more profound through suffering. The characteristic tactile metaphors in which Keats describes this see-ing—"take the depth nimbly" and "pervade"—also recall the Milton who in Keats's marginal note "pursues his imagination to the utmost" and stations even his most visionary characters in a landscape precisely evoked for this world's senses. Yet if Milton sees "as a God sees," it is with the help of the Holy Spirit as muse. Although Keats's narrator thus far has lacked that certainty of revelation, his visionary trial on the altar steps has given him a new strength and self-confidence to rival Milton. The God whose capacities of vision he now emulates may be a form of hyperbole for Milton himself—and the very freedom in using the term "God" a declaration of freedom from Milton's sectarian imagination.

Yet of course the anonymous "God" in question also forces us to consider the Titans as his models for seeing. The narrator's "depth" and sight seem modeled on Moneta's eyes, "visionless entire . . . Of all external things." Though blank to immediate "external things," her vision painfully recognizes that larger pattern of "external things" that Oceanus in *Hyperion* calls the "envisaging of circumstances." Not only does she share this recognition with Saturn and the other Titans who are the central objects in the tableau she is to reveal, but she adds to it a consciousness of temporal duration almost unimaginable to the Titans. To see as the Titans do is in part to remember how gods once saw; to see as

Moneta does is to see, far more intensely than do her fellow Titans, the "contrarieties" in feeling the effects of splendor and loss, of a heavenly and an earthly station.

This ambiguous claim to a godlike sight prefaces a scene organized into two segments. In each of these segments Keats defines focal sculptural images through the speech of his gods and through the response of the narrator to the conflicting sight and sounds of those gods. Moneta and the narrator repeatedly point out in this scene and at the beginning of the next "how frail" is a feeble human tongue "To that large utterance of the early Gods!" (1.351ff., 466–67; 2.1–9). Yet although the Titans' speech in the first part of the scene corresponds to the grandeur of their sculptural images, in the second part a new dissonance between sight and sound is all the more obvious. Moreover, through this conflict between seeing sculpture and hearing it talk, the narrator develops two alternative ways of understanding the relationship of sculpture to time.

At the beginning of *Hyperion*, the narrator is enormously noncommittal about his own intervention as perceiver and about the border line between human art, natural feature, and divine presence. Saturn in his stillness is a vast phenomenon not immediately to be questioned. In *The Fall*, not only does the much more explicit narrator first see Saturn as a statue, but he carries into Moneta's shared vision the expectations associated initially with sculpture in *Hyperion*: the noble and sedate grandeur appropriate to unchallenged gods and to the Schlegelian synthesis of sculpturesque natural deities and Greek culture. The tension between this isolated image of deity and a more complex, indeed picturesque, integration of a human response to death, chance, and mutability redefines both the narrative tableau carried over from *Hyperion* and the two perceivers who confront it. Finally, as the original significance of sculpture as a metaphor for poetic art breaks apart for the narrator, he must redefine his own art through his redefinition of sculpture.

This growing tension between an image of isolated sculptural divinity and the mortal circumstances of the perceiver appears immediately. Instead of Saturn, Moneta and the narrator are stationed "deep" in the landscape:

> . . . side by side we stood,
> (Like a stunt bramble by a solemn pine)
> Deep in the shady sadness of a vale,
> Far sunken from the healthy breath of morn,
> Far from the fiery noon, and eve's one star.

> (1.292–96)

The parenthetical line, which seems such a jolting start to the long Miltonic sentence that originally had opened *Hyperion*, now no longer leads up to the statuelike, objective figure of Saturn. As the sentence breaks off in line 296, we realize that all its temporal and spatial remoteness now modifies the preceding subjects—and subjects who see themselves with a certain whimsical objectivity. Instead of the massive, yet delicately balanced, immersion of Saturn in the vale, "quiet as a stone," with "Forest on forest hung above his head," the grouping of narrator and priestess is thinner and stiffer: they are single forest trees, not sculpturesque natural masses. Saturn's position is now defined less by his own natural context than by the narrator's:

> Onward I look'd beneath the gloomy boughs,
> And saw, what first I thought an image huge,
> Like to the image pedestal'd so high
> In Saturn's temple. Then Moneta's voice
> Came brief upon mine ear,—"So Saturn sat
> When he had lost his realms."—
>
> (1.297–302)

As the lines ironically set the "high" pedestal against Saturn's fallen state, "When he had lost his realms," Keats reiterates the paradoxical relationship posed in *Hyperion*, in which sculpture is both immutable, transcendent immortality and static, immanent helplessness. The narrator's mistake, moreover, distances Saturn even further from the actual landscape. The earlier image "pedestal'd so high" reminds him that he sees and hears Moneta's vision. This conceptual distance reinforces the aesthetic distance already associated with sculpture, as Schlegel describes it. A still earlier image of the pedestal, in *Hyperion*, described not Saturn but Thea: "Her face was large as that of Memphian sphinx, / Pedestal'd haply in a palace court" (1.31–32). As Keats revises his description of Thea for this version of the poem, he seems at first to increase her immediate sense of living presence by editing out that temporally and spatially enlarging simile: not only has he used her "pedestal'd" station for Saturn, but he already has developed the paradox of a marble yet humanly emotional face for Moneta.[53] Both sphinx and pedestal thus have moved out of simile into a more literal mode of existence, in which Moneta and Saturn both show a highly ambiguous sort of life; in *Hyperion* the explicit simile compared Thea to the statue but defined her, in implicit contrast, as a living being. In the revised inner narrative of *The Fall of Hyperion*, the narrator "mark'd the goddess in fair statuary / Surpassing wan Moneta by the head," and yet the briefer phrase shows her thematic subordination to Moneta. Although she may be "in her sorrow nearer woman's tears" than is

Moneta, she is less explicitly separated from "statuary" than she was by the simile in *Hyperion*.

Although the narrator seems entranced with an unfallen definition of sculpture that includes both life and serenity, the lines that follow rigorously test the consequences of his commitment to this ideal: first by an extreme demonstration of that ideal, and second, as Saturn speaks, by its fragmentation. As if seeing in this very perfection a fictional element, the narrator cannot retain his belief in Thea's actuality any more easily than she can rouse Saturn from his statuelike and formal stasis. As the narrator watches these two static figures, time halts in a parody of eternity:

> Long, long, these two were postured motionless,
> Like sculpture builded up upon the grave
> Of their own power. A long awful time
> I look'd upon them; still they were the same;
> The frozen God still bending to the earth,
> And the sad Goddess weeping at his feet;
> Moneta silent.
>
> 　　　　　　　　　　　　　　　(1.382–88)

Now this, of course, is just what sculpture should do. The analogy, however, is deadly both in content and in effect. Although willing fifty lines earlier to call them "statuary" in an easy equation, the narrator now discovers that such stillness horrifies. As he returns to the simile, the implication that they are not sculpture but seem just as stony and unliving has the same effect as the whiteness of Moneta's face, beautiful if stone, terrible if flesh. The specific nature of the simile, moreover, answers clearly the hypothesis posed by Saturn's stillness at the opening of *Hyperion* and, though to a lesser extent, in this scene. In his statuesque stillness Saturn earlier prompted comparison to Keats's definition of "Poesy" as "might half slumb'ring on its own right arm," a Herculean figure with power in reserve. Here the power is explicitly ended. As the narrator compares the figures to those on funerary monuments, whether Gothic like those Blake copied in Westminster Abbey or more classical like those Flaxman was erecting in Saint Paul's,[54] we see them as artifacts—no longer are they "natural sculpture in cathedral cavern" (*Hyperion* 1.86).

Nor are they poised in the "moment" that conveys, in its stillness, further organic development in time. Fuseli's "expressive moment," we recall, modified Lessing's "fruitful moment" by substituting for the potential stages of further action potential stages for the self's psychological development. The Blakean moment, though prepared for by psychological analysis, reconstitutes the fallen, fragmented self by asserting that the moment which imagination hammers or sculpts into shape obliterates the period of time between fall and last judgment. It therefore rebuilds nature into the art of a "Human form" or a completed city. In much of his poetry, and particularly in the odes, Keats has the perceiving mind follow the organic curve of natural, "fruitful" and yet mortal, development. The perceiving mind then frequently discovers a moment at which it sees the future of that development and must decide whether knowingly to follow it toward biological death or to seek some alternative. Here Keats posits an alternative, but a terrifying one. As first Thea and then the narrator seem to collapse into the sculptural stasis of Saturn, this scene tests the cost of believing too fully that art offers a living return to the dream state of an earlier Saturnian harmony. The sculptural analogue becomes too dominant; the tension of "contrarieties" is lost as life is frozen. These figures seem to have no future and cannot change; even Moneta is drawn into the sculptural group, which, unlike those Schlegel defines as analogous with tragedy, suggests no reconciliation of eternity with process, only a terrible, unresolved tension.

Because he himself nearly succumbs to the power of his own near-fatal analogue, the narrator's vision offers no antidote. Nearly becoming what he beholds, he seems pulled out of nature into a Urizenic stoniness, an immortality that is not philosophically but artistically dogmatic and single-visioned:

> . . . Without stay or prop
> But my own weak mortality, I bore
> The load of this eternal quietude,
> The unchanging gloom, and the three fixed shapes
> Ponderous upon my senses, a whole moon.
> . . . .
> And every day by day methought I grew
> More gaunt and ghostly. Oftentimes I pray'd
> Intense, that death would take me from the vale
> And all its burthens. Gasping with despair
> Of change, hour after hour I curs'd myself.
>
> (1.388–92, 395–99)

This painful state is in some sense a triumph of his own imagination, a fearfully extended "moment" in which time, though not suspended, includes no process. The reference to the moon recalls Moneta's face, yet defines how these "three fixed shapes" worsen its earlier unresolved tension of that progress "to no death." As he experiences her vision, he resembles both the objects and the medium, both the Titans and their mediating priestess.

The primary effect of his self-absorption in sculpture is not visual but tactile. In contrast to the molding and liberating touch in Blake's metaphor of sculpture, however, the dominant sense-impression of the sculpture in this passage is that of weight: "Without stay or prop . . . I bore / The load" of those "three fixed shapes / Ponderous upon my senses." A line or two further he speaks of "the vale / And all its burthens." Although the narrator feels himself becoming a statue, even more he experiences the burden of the Titans as physical weight upon one less weighty, less statuelike, than they. This is indeed to endow his visionary tableau with feeling, though the feeling ironically narrows the term instead of expanding it.

To some extent this process is Blakean, however—not the harmonizing, sculpting touch with which Milton builds a human form for Urizen, but the "consolidation" and recognition of error as shown in the stony figure of Urizen earlier in *Milton*. As he simultaneously becomes statuelike and finds that he remains conscious of his difference from the statuelike Titans in his "weak mortality," the narrator must recognize painfully that art itself is not life: a very un-Blakean conclusion to a Blakean process of recognition. With such a recognition of aesthetic distance, however, he also can recognize the life that art reflects. Drawn into scenes that challenge his visual control and force him to explore the relationship of dream and Poesy, he must now recover some of his earlier aesthetic detachment to distinguish between an overpermanent art and Poesy.[55]

This chastisement of the narrator for his belief in a poetic art as immortal and transcendent as sculpture, then, becomes a way of showing that he had worshiped an artistic vision of a Saturnian golden world without acknowledging its central energy or impetus as a dream. Moreover, he discovers that its central energy is not invalidated by its being, to begin with, personal, private, even sectarian. By showing the relationship of many such dreams of a golden world to cosmic myth, and by showing that myth being frozen by worshipers of its religion (Moneta herself) or its art (the narrator), Moneta has led the narrator to confront the disintegration of his sculptural ideal as well as of the Saturnian, paradisal myth as dogmatic truth. The first, already dramatized in the crushing burden of those "three fixed shapes," is in part a metaphor for the second. The second appears in the next segment of the poem (1.412–59), when the narrator learns that the Titans' heroic, sculptural shapes neither dominate outer landscape nor express inner character. Both landscape and mind challenge a dogmatic belief in a benevolent personal, cosmic order. Both stages of the scene, then, challenge dream converted to dogmatic belief or its metaphoric correlative, sculptural form, and both celebrate the validity of dream as a recognized, necessary fiction—a "dream of what never was" in fact, existing only in the mind. From one point of view Saturn, like Psyche, becomes a god of the mind. Unlike Psyche, though, he betrays in this segment of scene 3 that he possesses a mind of his own. Psyche is stationed in the poet's mind; Saturn, once thought deity of external nature, must acquire a mind that then mocks his loss of peaceful sway, and his mind mirrors within the successive microcosms of Moneta's vision and of the narrator's dream a jarring disharmony those witnesses must face and absorb. As they do so, their dreams move from the relinquished sculptural mode of the middle of the poem to a picturesque perspective absorbing, yet changed from, those in the first two scenes of the poem.

Saturn's speech, far more self-pitying here than its earlier version in *Hyperion*,[56] uses a repeated vocabulary of "feebleness," "moaning," and death to challenge the narrator's earlier heroic and statuesque ideal. His rigid vision of heroic immortality seems less and less compatible with the "circumstances" of a world of natural process and a mind that recognizes those processes as alien from itself. Such a mind, in the shock of first recognition, is Saturn's; in a more delayed awareness of this demythologizing, it is the narrator's. Saturn changes, then, from the focal objective figure in a worship of nature to a focusing subjective witness in the process of discovering that such worship is only a recurrent, necessary, and enduring dream.

Ironically, this transformation parallels Satan's fictional transformation into a talking serpent: although the serpent tells Eve that his mind has been transformed, his body lags behind. Keats's narrator, more perceptive than Eve, finds Saturn's telling of these truths in painful conflict with his persistent yearning for statuesque divinity:

> Methought I heard some old man of the earth
> Bewailing earthly loss; nor could my eyes
> And ears act with that pleasant unison of sense
> Which marries sweet sound with the grace of form,
> And dolorous accent from a tragic harp
> With large limb'd visions.
>
> (1.440–45)

Several lines later, as sight again restores the ideal image, "his awful presence there / (Now all was silent) gave a deadly lie / To what I erewhile heard: only his lips / Trembled amid the white curls of his beard. / They told the truth . . ." (1.448–52). The facial portrait is less idealized and more accurate, again, at showing "the lightest movement of the mind."

This discrepancy between the narrator's sight and his hearing continues his instruction in the irony between an imagined ideal and a more ordinary human reality, and also between the "seeing" of dream vision or art and the intersubjective "telling" of Poesy. This dissociation recalls, moreover, both the physical and the intellectual challenge Moneta presented to him within Saturn's temple. There, as he reasserted a physical coordination and coherence, he also went on to assert in argument a dialectical union of the "contrarieties" of dreamer and physician in "Poesy." When she offers him the "scenes / Still swooning vivid through [her] globed brain," she seems to offer him the wreckage of a simpler sort of Poesy, in which the sculptural figures of the Titans would be models of wholeness and integration. They would symbolize both an integration of the senses, like the one the narrator experiences spontaneously in the first scene and must recreate more self-consciously or "picturesquely" in the second, and an integration of primary dream—the dream of a paradisal Saturnian age of gold—with art, a dream once told and mediated.

Sculpture, then, has changed from the "plastic" or naive natural wholeness defined by Schiller, Schlegel, and the insistent narrator, to a false vision of wholeness, a parody of the model of sensuous and visionary integration it becomes for Blake. Sculpture becomes a fallen art—its objects and its method a fallen but not a redemptive process. It is the rejection of sculpture that becomes redemptive, a rejection that must acknowledge a natural, mortal milieu and a natural, mortal consciousness. If the Saturn of the last scene has not quite acknowledged this, the perceiving narrator now does so. To move from a naive vision of wholeness to a self-conscious questioning of that dream is not enough; unlike either Urizen or Milton in Blake's poem, Saturn achieves no new coherence in a form molded of red clay. Finally, however, the narrator does achieve a similar wholeness, through recognition that to sympathize with others' dreams, emotionally to carry their burdens, is a way to integrate sight and emotion. The narrator learns this from his mixture of sympathy and revulsion for Saturn and from his mixture of sympathy for and terror of Moneta. Moneta, too, learns as she shares her vision and sees its effect on the narrator. Saturn cannot yet perceive or feel the emotions of another, absorbed as he is in his own loss, but he serves as an instructive example. His disintegration recalls the need for an integration that includes an awareness of self-loss and self-limitation. Dream may collapse in the encounter with others who recognize those limiting circumstances—until one sees and shares the dreams of others and builds Poesy out of that tension between circumstance and vision.

Because this poem gives us no equivalent of Oceanus's speech or Apollo's theophany, we have no explicit overarching scheme in which to interpret either Saturn's fall or the narrator's series of falls. Also, because his precede Saturn's, one is inclined to see them all in personal instead of cosmic terms, as explorations of extreme states that must, as in Blake, lead to some upheaval or fragmentation of the character's previous perceptions. Yet as the narrator moves from his sensuous paradise through his confrontation with the culture and history of Saturnian worship in the person and ideas of Moneta, to an encounter with her own vision of Saturn and his Titanian cohorts, it is clear that the poem works from individual to cultural to cosmic formulations of dream—and, at each stage, to a criticism and reevaluation of dream. The poem also works backward in time as it works outward in space and concept, so that as we see Saturn confronted with a fall from his world of dream, we are seeing a confrontation that took place long ago—and yet continues to repeat itself as others explore the limits and consequences of their dreams. The recognition of such universality in time and in place—the recognition that the need for dream extends back and out into the repetitions of myth—draws it out of solipsism and escape and makes it a route for comprehending and sharing the selves of others.[57] It gains no guarantee of fact, but of a common desire.

Scene Four: "Reliev'd from the dusk vale"

As shared sight can lead to a regenerated sight, the narrator's controlling sight runs through Hyperion's halls as quickly as the sun-god himself. The fact that the fragment breaks off with all this radiance and lucidity still intact is probably only an accident, but that final scene makes an apt image for sight exultant at its own regeneration. In the poem's surprising alternation between natural enclosure and architectural vastness, depth and a reaching toward transcendence, the narrator's controlling and now empathetic sight provides a narrative continuity in a series of mediated and meditated tableaux. It also provides a final framework for the visual and the metaphysical "picturesque" of a conscious yet not merely "sentimental" perception of the self. Separate from nature, it is yet bound to it by the very dreamlike longing to be part of its paradisal moments, and bound also to the communal dream lives of others who have achieved such recognitions. Moneta, now explicitly called Mnemosyne, "sitting on a square edg'd polished stone, / That in its lucid depth reflected pure / Her priestess-garments," symbolizes clearly at this stage of the poem a memory stationed in the images and memorials of human culture as well as in the alternately paradisal and nightmarish enclosed gardens of the natural world. Her drawing together of these contrarieties shapes a picturesque vision for the narrator that can turn from a view of the past as "deathwards progressing to no death," toward a recognition of the past as enlarging, not trapping, our visual designs.

Five

ᔕ

Shelley's *Prometheus Unbound*

"Wildernesses calm and green,
Peopled by shapes too bright to see"

*Dramatic Structure:
The Unbinding of Sculptural Form*

Shelley, writes G. Wilson Knight, "is usually averse from the weighty rondures and plastic forms of Milton and Keats."[1] Developing this observation, R. H. Fogle is more critical: "The figures of Keats's Titans are vast, bulky, Michelangelesque; one participates with them in the strains and stresses of their immense physical effort." In contrast, he goes on, "When was there ever so fine a subject for sculptural representation as Prometheus, bound to his rock? Yet Shelley does not utilize him. And without concrete shape or form empathy will not work."[2] Although Shelley indeed uses visual imagery, Fogle explains, it typically embraces vast distances. In the opening scene of *Prometheus Unbound*, for example, we can follow Prometheus's gaze outward over an expansive universe but we do not see the immediate physical limits of his body bound to its rock as clearly as we see Keats's Saturn, "quiet as a stone." Nor, to extend Fogle's protest, do we see body and rock placed as concretely within an immediate, enclosing physical world as are Saturn and his epic predecessors, the similarly downcast and static Odysseus, Aeneas, and Satan.

Yet although Keats's sculptural analogues do create vividly present human forms, sculpture also acts in both *Hyperion* poems as a monument to a lost calm of godlike transcendence. As much psychological as physical, the "stresses and strains" experienced by his characters develop because of their distance from a sculptural ideal of serenity. Like Moneta, all of Keats's characters must learn to enclose the sculptural, "epic" objects of ideal, transcendent self within the surrounding landscapes of mortal circumstances. To revise Fogle's point, it is exactly the heroic, "epic," though still physically human quality of those "muscular, Michelangelesque" Titans that first leads readers into a kinetic sort of empathy and then makes possible our sharing of their more limited and more inward consciousness of self.

A similar transformation, though a liberating one, occurs in *Prometheus Unbound*. Shelley's Titan, too, changes from an external sculptural form, one of Hazlitt's "epic objects," to a complex, picturesque consciousness that contains and expresses itself in "mental forms creating." Critics readily have seen the end point of this transformation, the apparent dissolving of all forms, human and natural alike, into a Turneresque and apocalyptic blaze of light. They also have acknowledged its starting point, though without recognizing its function, when they complain about either the lack of physical action in the first act or the lack of dramatic conflict in the following three acts.[3] For there is a sculptural starting point in Shelley's play that comes far closer to Keats's uses of sculpture than Fogle's criticism would suggest. Even before we read the blank verse of the opening speech, Shelley's stage directions should draw our attention to the obvious though difficult fact that *Prometheus Unbound* is a play. Although its only stage may be the minds of its readers, we must imagine that staging more fully than we have done before. Most important, we must imagine the play staged with human actors whose forms are visible on the stage, in most cases, as they speak. Thus the human figure of the actor playing Prometheus is a powerful visual, indeed sculptural, image that needs no narrative enhancement even by so apparently neutral and objective a speaker as the one who begins *Hyperion*. For Shelley's English audience, Fuseli's grim drawings that illustrate Aeschylus's Prometheus trilogy might well have reinforced such an imaginative staging. The Michelangelesque figure of Prometheus, lying flat in *Hephaestus, Bia and Crato securing Prometheus on Mount Caucasus* (ca. 1810), and almost falling from the horizontal rock in *Prometheus rescued by Heracles* (exhibited 1821), leans forward like a crucified Christ in *Prometheus and Io* (ca. 1800–1802).[4] Because of Prometheus's binding, that figure on stage is as kinetically, painfully sculptural as the figures of Keats's Titans that show the "strains and stresses of . . . immense physical effort." Both indeed test the premises of a Winckelmannian vision of sculpture possessing the "serene dignity and sedate grandeur" that Coelus describes as godlike; and both do so through the evoked physical presence of a human body. Keats's poem evokes this presence through narrative description, and Shelley's lyrical drama evokes it through dramatic presence.

Shelley's choice of genre becomes even more important as he attempts to challenge Milton. Like Keats, he makes critical use of Winckelmann's and Schlegel's analogues of sculpturesque and picturesque eras of artistic culture. Yet because he casts his revision of Milton in the form of Aeschylean drama, he raises even more directly the central debate between Winckelmann and Schlegel over the modern capacity either to recreate the Greek artistic achievement or to create an equally valuable equivalent. Criticizing Winckelmann's admiration for the southern, pagan, and "objective" classical era, Schlegel—as we have seen—praises the northern, Christian, and subjective era that begins with the medieval period and proves most intensely developed as he writes. According to Mary's journal, Shelley read Schlegel in March 1818 on his way to Italy.[5] On the other hand, as Shelley read Winckelmann's *History* in Italy, he surely saw its description of classical culture as the model for a civilization that might oppose the tyrannically oppressive Christian ethos of his most challenging modern precursors, Dante and Milton.[6] If he can write a successful modern version of a Greek drama, then he will have overcome Winckelmann's historical and geographical determinism and also have found a way to revise Milton's epic within his own drama. He will have challenged and overcome one predecessor by borrowing strength from the other. As he challenges Milton's theology with its definition of a personal God curbing man's potentiality, he uses the Aeschylean form of Greek drama to represent the possibility both of an alternate theological perspective and of a less didactic, single-voiced mode of presentation. In this respect, Milton's *Paradise Lost* seems to be a rigid, sculptural model, as monolithic as it is heroically grand in scale; and the "imagery drawn from the operations of the human mind," which Shelley borrows explicitly from Aeschylus for his own play, seems, ironically, to approach the subjective method of Schlegel's "picturesque" mode.[7]

So, in fact, does the powerful analysis of *Prometheus Bound* that Schlegel develops to represent the "sculpturesque" in ancient culture. Like his other specific discussions of Greek tragedy, this one is partially inconsistent with his larger developmental scheme. Although "too long a sacrifice," as Yeats says, "Can make a stone of the heart," the emotional intensity of Prometheus's opposition to a nearly demythologized Zeus resembles far more Schlegel's romantic or picturesque consciousness than it does a sculpturesque "serene dignity."[8] Far from weakening its appeal to Shelley, however, this interpretation might well have strengthened his strategy of opposing a revised, more romantic Aeschylean drama to Miltonic epic.

Shelley's drama diverges freely from its Aeschylean model after the first act, just as it also diverges further from explicit echoes of the struggle between God and Satan in *Paradise Lost*. Yet its new, freer form reflects another aspect of *Paradise Lost:* that epic's expansive earthly scenes, focused around figure by an observer's eye. Building on this scenic organization, it also develops a dramatic structure based on Schlegel's "metaphysical" and scenic picturesque. In short, the play moves from "statuary" to two versions of Miltonic "stationing."

Although this development becomes clearest in the contrast between the sharply defined dramatic conflict in act 1 and the lyric dialogue of contrary, evanescent forms in act 4, it also appears in the oppositions and reconciliations among all four acts. Frederick Pottle has shown the dramatic importance of Asia's quest in act 2 as a complement to Prometheus's resistance in act 1, and Donald Reiman has suggested that the four acts form an alternating pattern of dramatic and metaphysical modes.[9] Analyzing this alternative pattern in Schlegel's terms of sculptural and picturesque drama yields an even more precise sense of Shelley's art. In its close parallels to Aeschylus, in its use of a single scene, and in its use of a central, static figure set in tension with other figures, the "dramatic" quality of the first act fits Schlegel's definition of the sculpturesque. In sharp contrast, the second act moves from known to unknown realms of the universe, exploring in a series of scenes the symbolic geography that leads to its own transcendence. Its emphasis on vast perspectives of landscape and history perfectly expresses Schlegel's picturesque or "romantic" mode of drama. Shelley thus forces the reader to discard unity of place, even the vastness of Aeschylus's mountain peaks, for an interplay of scenes that recall symbolic romance and visionary epic. Moreover, by changing from Prometheus to Asia as protagonist, Shelley urges his audience to redefine unity of action not as the crucial, classical choice of a single protagonist but as a dialectical and thematic structure.

Because the confrontation of Jupiter and Demogorgon corresponds to the confrontation of Prometheus and Jupiter's phantasm, the third act returns in some ways to the more classical dramatic mode of the first. Its episodes also might be described as less metaphysical than those of acts 2 and 4; like the Furies' masque in act 1, the Spirit of the Hour's speech describes the human world directly. In addition, the characters in act 3 use a number of sculptural images that point toward a classically dramatic or sculpturesque mode. Yet further consideration shows that the more expansive, metaphysically picturesque mode of act 2 has modified strongly the dramatic sculptural mode of act 3. Its settings, for example, are almost as wide-ranging as those of act 2. More important, the unbinding of Prometheus and his reunion with Asia lead not to dramatic

action or even psychological conflict but to reconciliation of their comple-
mentary powers in a physically static but psychologically creative state;
and this state begins to renovate the world as it renovates a sculptural
mode of perception. Shelley balances the sculptural, bound form of
Prometheus in act 1 with the transfigured form of Asia at the end of act 2,
a form whose outlines dissolve in the radiant energy of love. Prometheus's
long speech of act 3, scene 3, and the Spirit of the Hour's speech at the end
of that act direct this renovating energy toward the human world. Thus
act 3 returns to the sculptural and dramatic modes of act 1 only to
transform their limits.

Because Shelley structures act 4 around the magnificent, lyrical dialogue of Earth- and Moon-Spirits as sexual contraries, and because that
dialogue describes the renovation of all landscapes, earthly and cosmic, it
continues the synthesis of act 3 but in a mode that becomes in Schlegel's
vocabulary more metaphysical and more picturesque. Most striking is the
transformation of Earth from speaker and from place, a desolate garden
like that in a now-ruined Babylon or Rome, to an image that is both place
and figure. In working out this transformation, Shelley uses neither a
Blakean reversal, in which landscape can be remolded into a human form,
nor a Keatsian usurpation, in which one figure moves aside from a central
focus to become the perceiver of another figure who replaces the first at
the center. By the end of the play, Shelley has developed a structural
mode that lies somewhere between these two—for acts 1 and 2 purge or
empty the stage of its central sculptural images.[10] In several cases these
images have proved to be phantasms, prompting Demogorgon in act 2 to
answer that the deep truth is imageless. In act 3 Prometheus confirms his
own peripheral role as witness and describes a complex way in which new
"apparitions" may be created from that witnessing and yet generative
mind. Finally, in act 4, two new "apparitions" appear in a clearing in the
woods and move to the center of the stage: the chariots bearing the Spirits
of Earth and Moon. Replacing Prometheus and Asia as central figures, the
evanescent children in these chariots symbolize landscapes made central.
Yet they dissolve both the surrounding landscape and its history—the
"world of Circumstances"—in order to recreate in greater freedom the
conditions of their stationing. Thus in Shelley's version of the "picturesque" as structural model, the limitations of scenic enclosure are far
fewer, and the encounter and fusion of contraries in a dialectical structure
are far sharper. Moreover, if the final action of *Prometheus* is to create a
drama that will reshape the universe, then Prometheus is unbound from a
dramatic form that in its assertion of classical and neoclassical unity also
asserted the supremacy of external circumstances. Natural causality,
which for Aristotle determines the dramatic plot, gives way at least

momentarily to the perceiving mind's creativity. Its ordering tableaux redefine sculptural form as visual and musical patterns of energy.

Statements on Sculpture: "to make intelligible in words [those] forms"

Differing sharply from Blake's insistence upon sculpture as molding, redemptive touch, and from Keats's increasing fear of it as burdening marble, Shelley tests his own more conceptual redefinitions of sculptural form both in poetry and in prose. Because several prose statements written during or just after the composition of *Prometheus* discuss sculpture both directly and metaphorically, these statements offer a clear starting point for the complexity of his metaphors in the poetic drama.

In the *Defence of Poetry* Shelley argues that all the arts in Greek culture, as well as its philosophy and politics, flourished in a mutually inspiring perfection. Athenian drama brought these arts even closer together.[11] Through their multiple but reinforcing "elements," the private vision of the poet became a public art capable of ordering communal life:

> Neither the eye nor the mind can see itself, unless reflected upon that which it resembles. The drama . . . is as a prismatic and many-sided mirror, which collects the brightest rays of human nature and divides and reproduces them from the simplicity of those elementary forms, and touches them with majesty and beauty, and multiplies all that it reflects, and endows it with the power of propagating its like.[12]

Although his dominant image of the "prismatic and many-sided mirror" is visual, each art in the "many-sided" dramatic production contributes to this analytic and then reconstitutive process.[13]

A few pages earlier in the *Defence*, however, Shelley interprets this range of expressive modes among the arts not as an advantage in their mutual defining of the dramatists' conception but as a disadvantage. Only poetry in its narrower sense as a verbal art can come close to expressing that conception, for "all other materials, instruments, and conditions of art, have relations among each other which limit and interpose between conception and expression." Language, on the other hand, "is arbitrarily produced by the Imagination and has relation to thoughts alone"; it is a "more direct representation of the actions and passions of our internal being than colour, form, or motion, and is more plastic and obedient to the controul of that faculty of which it is the creation." With a light-handed irony Shelley's words draw upon a sculptural metaphor: the imagination becomes a sculptor molding its "plastic and obedient" speech.

Thus even as he voices this skeptical awareness of their limits, he points toward his more synthetic arguments for the interdependence of these arts: although language may be more faithful to the artist's original thoughts, it may need to borrow the concreteness of other media.

In his "Notes on the Sculptures of Rome and Florence," Shelley's specific analyses of sculptural works constantly test this tension between his "plastic and obedient" language and the plastic art he describes.[14] It now appears, from E. B. Murray's careful arguments, that H. Buxton Forman's standard text of these notes did not come from a holograph Shelley notebook but probably from Claire Clairmont's flawed transcription. Thus "an eclectic text" based on Thomas Medwin's transcription from Shelley's own scrawled notes "written in pencil," on Forman's arrangement of Claire's transcription, and on guides to the Uffizi must yet be developed.[15] Yet with a great deal of caution, and with the guidance of Shelley's letters to Thomas Love Peacock, which develop similar concepts, we can examine in these notes not only Shelley's perception of the tension between the sculpture and language but also his response to sculpture as a form that emanates and dissolves into energy.

Even before he sends Peacock any specific descriptions of Roman sculptures, Shelley uses two dramatic images of their power to communicate an energy beyond their forms. Calling the Apollo Belvedere, the Laocoon, and others "the vital, the almost breathing creations of genius yet subsisting in their perfection," he apologizes for not yet describing them: "These things are best spoken of when the mind has drunk in the spirit of their forms." Later in the same letter, he describes "two winged figures of Victory" on the Arch of Titus, "whose hair floats on the wind of their own speed" and whose "lips are parted . . . to express the eager respiration of their speed." Classical artists, he goes on, scarcely ever showed an "ideal figure . . . with closed lips," "so essential to beauty were the forms expressive of the exercise of the imagination and the affections considered." Their speed and their breathing are thus not merely the artist's defiance of stone to represent an alien vitality but express the "fervor of their desire" to achieve the victory they personify. Although Shelley's focus upon this expression of imagination and emotion seems quite different from a Winckelmannian serenity, he also sought that serenity. The Monte Cavallo horse tamers "combine irresistible energy with the sublime and perfect loveliness supposed to have belonged to the divine nature."[16] As Timothy Webb writes, "This combination of calmness and vitality represented Shelley's own ideal in art and literature."[17] Yet as we compare Shelley's "Notes" on the sculptures in the Uffizi galleries to Winckelmann's and Schlegel's analyses, we can see that he repeatedly turns from the figures' paradoxical balance of vitality and calm to describe an energy emanating toward the perceiver.

Although his edition of Winckelmann's *History of Ancient Art* was too large to carry around the galleries, Shelley had been reading it carefully the preceding winter.[18] He also had read carefully Schlegel's analyses of dramatic form based upon extended analyses of several renowned sculptural groups. As a result, his own analyses of sculpture modify Winckelmann's valuing of unity and simplicity in a sculptural work, qualities that could encourage a direct and spontaneous response.[19] The unity Shelley defines in his "Notes on Sculpture" develops instead a more complex, romantic pattern based partly upon Winckelmann's own undeveloped reference to an Empedoclean conflict between static beauty and expression: "we . . . see an indication of the celebrated doctrine of Empedocles relative to discord and harmony, by whose opposing actions the things of this world are arranged. . . . from the action of one upon the other, and the union of the two opposing qualities, beauty derives additional power."[20] Although anticipating Schlegel's and Coleridge's definition of a "picturesque" or modern consciousness based on contraries, these words find little application in Winckelmann's practical criticism of individual works of classical art. Yet in his "Notes on Sculpture" Shelley makes use of this more complex sort of unity to revise his Winckelmannian classicism.

As Medwin noted, Shelley preferred the fluidity of the Praxitelean style to the more massive strength of the Phidian.[21] His responses to that fluidity unify sculptural object and perceiving subject as if barely acknowledging the difference between stone and living flesh. The fingers of a Bacchus, he writes, are "gently curved as with the burning spirit which animates their flexible joints," and "the flowing fulness and roundness of the breast and belly" are "Like some fine harmony which flows around the soul and enfolds it."[22] The Empedoclean "union of . . . opposing qualities" appears most dramatically in the two most famous sculptural groupings, the Laocoon (the Uffizi's Bandinelli copy) and the Niobe: their striking arrangement in these notes, as the first and last sculptures discussed, probably follows their arrangement in the galleries.[23] Paradigms for neoclassical analyses of sculpture, these two groups also can act as paradigms for Shelley's less classical responses. Works nearly equal in fame, both show mortal parents and children enduring divine punishment. Because their repeated subject recalled the loss of his own children so recently, each also must have carried personal significance for Shelley. Prompted by this involvement, he uses their similarity to point out his opposing, if subtly expressed, moral evaluation of the groups.

To compare Winckelmann's, Schlegel's, and Shelley's analyses of these sculptural groups is almost to undergo a "hateful siege of contraries." As we have seen, even though Winckelmann claims a "noble simplicity and sedate grandeur" for the central figure, his analysis of the original, Roman Laocoon in the 1755 *Gedancken* is already highly complex. In the 1765 *History*, Winckelmann emphasized more strongly the sufferings of Lao-coon: this "is a statue representing a man in extreme suffering who is striving to collect the conscious strength of his soul to bear it": yet "his own suffering seems to distress him less than that of his children."[24] Schlegel's brief discussion follows Winckelmann's closely but draws an image from the sculpture itself to describe this Empedoclean unity: "The convolving serpents exhibit to us the inevitable destiny which unites the characters . . . yet the beauty of proportion, the delightful flow of the attitude, are not lost in this violent struggle."[25]

Because Forman reprints Medwin's transcription of the Laocoon note, we have in this case a less acute textual problem than exists for the other notes.[26] Although Shelley echoes both Winckelmann and Schlegel in his note on the Laocoon group, he intensifies the flawed humanity of Lao-coon, decreasing his internal struggle but increasing the tension between father and son and between subject and medium: "Intense physical suffering . . . seems the predominant and overwhelming emotion," though he concedes a "nobleness in the expression and a majesty that dignifies torture." Yet in Shelley's view that majesty does not dignify the father's self-absorption, because in contrast the sons' "filial love . . . swallows up all other feelings." Through his greater concentration on the father's flawed humanness, a concentration recalling his criticism of other fathers and father-gods, Shelley anticipates more vividly than his prede-cessors the next moment of the serpent's attack: "his terrible fangs widely displayed, in a moment to . . . meet within its victim's [a son's] heart, make the spectator of this miracle of sculpture turn away with shuddering and awe, and doubt the reality of what he sees."[27] He doubts, most of all, that what he sees is stone: it is made living by the shared anguish of Laocoon and the perceiver. Thus horror and beauty, filial love and paternal self-absorption, immediate moment and eternal monument, all struggle in Shelley's description. The work is unified not in tranquillity but in pain.

In Shelley's final note, the description of the Niobe, his contrast with Winckelmann is tied more clearly to his greater interest in a psychological, expressive realism that arises from a structure of Empedoclean contraries. In this case Winckelmann and Shelley were looking at two different arrangements of this group, which consisted of a number of separate statues. From their discovery at the end of the sixteenth century until

1769, the group was on view in the gardens of the Villa Medici in Rome, and Winckelmann studied them there. By 1788 they were on display at the Uffizi. Shelley's analysis focuses upon the central statue, itself a group of two figures: Niobe, Shelley writes, is "a mother in the act of sheltering from some divine and inevitable peril, the last . . . of her surviving children." Winckelmann's glance around the Roman garden includes more of the subsidiary statues; in his description Niobe, in a less poignant grouping, has several children yet remaining.[28] It is not surprising, then, that Shelley is more moved than his predecessor.

The outcome of the mythic plot makes the Niobe group even more than the paradigm—almost the parody—of Winckelmann's aesthetic of a noble simplicity and sedate grandeur: "The daughters of Niobe . . . are represented . . . in that state of indescribable anguish, their senses horror-struck and benumbed, in which all the mental powers are completely overwhelmed and paralyzed by the near approach of inevitable death. The transformation of Niobe into a rock, in the fable, is an image of this state of deathlike anguish."[29] Because, Winckelmann writes, this "apathy does not disturb a limb or a . . . feature, the great artist has represented the highest beauty."[30]

When he speaks of the Niobe as an example of the grand style that develops historically between the ancient and the Praxitelean, Winckelmann becomes more Longinian: "so great is the unity of form and outline, that it appears to have been produced not without labor, but awakened like a thought, and blown out with a breath." Both the artist's creative impulse and the viewer's response dissolve the static and serene medium into a sublime and transcendent energy. Yet only in one phrase does Winckelmann suggest his own Empedoclean tension of contraries; the sculptor has found the secret of "uniting the anguish of death with the highest beauty."[31] Schlegel and Shelley, on the other hand, make these oppositions central.

Schlegel's description of the Niobe echoes Winckelmann and yet points toward Shelley. Because "The more than earthly dignity of the features are the less disfigured by pain. . . . [s]he appears . . . insensible and motionless." Yet he also praises her for seeming "to accuse the invisible wrath of Heaven." Thus "before this figure, twice transformed into stone, and yet so inimitably animated. . . . the most callous beholder is dissolved in tears."[32] In contrast to Winckelmann, he alludes to the redemptive aspect of the myth, in which the rock weeps eternal tears.

Shelley's emotional and moral involvement builds from child to mother, and from the immediate past of the preceding deaths to the all-too-immediate future of this child's death as well. Over and over, he points to the useless refuge of the sculptural moment: in the mother's face "is embodied a sense of the inevitable and rapid destiny which is consummating around her as if it were already over." And "As the motions of the form expressed the instinctive sense of the possibility of protecting the child . . . , so reason and imagination speak in the countenance the certainty that no mortal defense is of avail." Thus, though serene, she is far from showing the numbed stupor that Winckelmann sees in the Roman grouping. Instead, "her tender and serene despair . . . incapable of ever being worn away, is beyond any effect of sculpture." It is also, Shelley goes on, "difficult . . . to make intelligible in words the forms from which such astonishing loveliness results." Sculptural form transcends itself and the more fluid medium of words. Significantly, Shelley ignores the myth that turns her to stone—or, better, he uses the alternative myth of her metamorphosis into a fountain to dissolve the statue he sees into a living person: "As soon as the arrow shall have pierced her last child, the fable that she was dissolved into a fountain of tears, will be but a feeble emblem of the sadness of despair, in which the years of her remaining life, we feel, must flow away."[33]

His formal analysis begins and ends the note, acting as a distancing frame for its more intense, emotional center. At both beginning and end, he stations the group in relation to the viewer. Almost as Blake describes Milton, "like a sculptor walking round his work, viewing it from every side," Shelley appeals to the reader to "compare" by "moving" from one viewpoint to another. Yet the affective and musical language through which he shows how the contraries expressed in the Niobe lead to a similar reconciliation of opposites in himself is scarcely Blakean in its fluid dissolving of the barriers between sculptural and human figure. The sense of power shown in the face coexists with a "clear and tender beauty," which is, in turn, "the expression at once of innocence and sublimity of soul, of purity and strength, of all that which touches the most removed and divine of the strings of that which makes music within my thoughts, and which shakes with astonishment my most superficial faculties."[34]

Image, Shape, and Form: A Redemptive Vocabulary

When the individual "Notes" resolve the Empedoclean tension between sculptural form and subjective emotional response, they do so in metaphors of radiance or harmony; and these are the metaphors that resolve similar tensions in *Prometheus Unbound*. Here Shelley's contrast with Blake is especially clear. Because varying mythic traditions describe both Prometheus and Demogorgon as sculpting demiurges like Blake's Los or Milton, we might expect a more tactile renovation of sculptural form.[35]

Instead, to use Shelley's image from the *Defence*, Prometheus and even Demogorgon—in spite of the latter's "mighty darkness"— become "many-sided mirrors" of the characters who encounter them. Reflecting and idealizing microcosms of the drama Shelley presents, they teach and free their own audience and his larger one. This complex transformation of sculptural form into the energy of radiant or mirrored light pervades the vocabulary of the entire play; for Shelley's characters repeatedly use the apparently abstract terms "image," "shape," or "form" in their encounters with a series of spirits or presences. Through this vocabulary Shelley develops a precisely controlled range of visual and sculptural analogues.

These words give dramatic definition, Oscar Firkins suggests, to appearances that seem difficult to grasp or comprehend as specific, identifiable presences: the more formless the manifestation, he suggests, the more desperately the speaker uses such general, abstract expressions of concrete form to locate and specify what he sees.[36] Two other critics also have pointed out this recurrent vocabulary. In contrast to Firkins, Stephen Larrabee argues that Shelley's use of "form" and "shape" is almost always a metaphor pointing to sculptural concreteness. Because he also argues that Shelley's view of classical sculpture follows Winckelmann in seeing it as the manifestation of Platonic form, however, he comes close to Sarah Dyck's suggestion that Shelley uses this vocabulary to conjure up Platonic forms of aesthetic and moral value.[37] We can reconcile these viewpoints if we see act 1 moving from the central, rigidly sculptural form of Prometheus through a series of encounters with what the characters call "forms" and "shapes," visual manifestations of sculptural figure, toward an understanding of form as an inward, psychological and spiritual definition. Much of act 3 shows how these inward forms can find renewed outward expression, yet without returning to Prometheus's sculptural rigidity at the opening of the play.

A similar transformation also affects other visual images that are less explicitly sculptural and that seem to exist only within masquelike visionary tableaux. Although the same vocabulary of "image," "shape," and "form" describes them, to define these visual images as sculptural shape would seem to grant them a valid, externally separate existence and thus to beg the questions they raise; but they raise those questions through their association with sculpture. Two recent critics have suggested that in act 1 Prometheus must shake off not only the arrogant tone of his "high language" but also its dependence upon visual correlatives as exact verbal referents. Susan Brisman argues that we should call this dependence "Hermetic," in part because Mercury and his Furies enforce this viewpoint; a freer alternative we should call a "Promethean" language.[38] Daniel Hughes argues for a similar view when he points out that Prometheus in act 1 must endure "two woes—to speak and to behold." Beholding, Hughes argues, is passively to endure the Furies' impositions; speaking, though also painful, becomes a way to transform their tableaux.[39] Through the Furies' masquelike visual tortures, however, the problems of perception faced by their audience—Prometheus, Panthea, and Ione— eventually redefine the visual elements in Shelley's drama. They also redefine "form" in these images, to challenge the most "hermetic" of all perspectives: a Platonism that would scorn all language not ackowledging a priori transcendent forms.

These two redefinitions come together in Prometheus's change from sculptural, epic object to a perceiver seeing aspects of himself mirrored on an inner stage. Because he himself changes as he recognizes these images, no absolutely fixed referent for the images exists: he can establish not only a Promethean language but a Promethean drama of visual and verbal encounters that, again, redefines sculptural and dramatic form. The stationing of these self-images begins in act 1, as Earth describes "the magus Zoroaster" who "Met his own image walking in the garden" (1.192–93), and it continues on a larger scale in acts 3 and 4.

One notices almost immediately that "image," the most specifically visual of these words, is the one Shelley uses least often. Because he frequently makes it a synonym of "form" and "shape" in the same section of dialogue, and because its sound is less emphatic than those of the other two, we probably should not make too much of this distinction. Nevertheless, "image" is also the only one of the three terms to refer to itself as copy or mirroring of some other reality. Yet, though we may find a Platonic skepticism of the copy in this, we do not find a correspondingly greater emphasis upon "form" as the true or original model. Shelley uses "form" more frequently than image but far less frequently than "shape."[40] This pattern implies that the play explores not abstract or conceptual process alone but an artistic process finding expression in concrete, sculptural forms and shapes—and that these must be viewed with deliberate skepticism as artistic and not ontological forms. Another striking aspect of the distribution of these words is that they appear more frequently in acts 1 and 3 than in 2 and 4, though only act 4 is significantly lower.[41] "Image," moreover, occurs only twice in act 2—and one of those occurrences is "imageless"—and not at all in act 4.

Because it corresponds roughly to Reiman's description of acts 1 and 3 as dramatic and political, acts 2 and 4 as more metaphysical, the greater frequency of these words in acts 1 and 3 suggests two apparently opposing views. Either the "dramatic" qualities of acts 1 and 3 are partially defined through the presence of such shapes, seen as sculptural and nearly palpable figures, or the more speculative, metaphysical mode of acts 2 and

4 breaks through, at such points, into the dramatic mode. If we consider acts 1 and 3 as "sculpturesque" drama that is transformed toward the metaphysical picturesque of acts 2 and 4, however, we can integrate these two views. The fixed psychological attitudes of Prometheus and Jupiter, shown in their fixed dramatic positions at the beginning of these acts, begin to change through their confrontation with forms, shapes, and images that they must recognize, accept responsibility for, and transform. Although these shapes at first appear absolute and independent, their perceivers' acceptance of imaginative fatherhood allows these shapes to be recognized as imaginative. When Oscar Firkins points to the tension between sculptural form and an evasive insubstantiality, he also, implicitly, raises the question of parental responsibilities by citing Milton's figure of Death as the model for Shelley's repeated use of "shape": "The other shape, / If shape it might be call'd that shape had none / Distinguishable in member, joint, or limb, / Or substance might be call'd that shadow seem'd / For each seem'd either . . ." (2.666–70).[42] For Milton, death is both an absence of life and, because it has not yet come into the world, only potential in its force and form. In acts 1 and 3, Shelley's shapes and forms share the ambiguity of Milton's Death, but Shelley resolves the ambiguity quite differently: visualizable, sculptural grandeur of form gives way not to a Burkean verbal obscurity but to verbal clarity.

"Thy worn form pursues me": Sculpture as Torture in Act 1

Although the first act, with its massively centered, static figure of Prometheus, is the most obviously sculptural of the four, and although much of that effect comes from Shelley's following of *Prometheus Bound*,[43] much also comes—as I said earlier—from Prometheus's resemblance to Milton's Satan at the beginning of *Paradise Lost*. To free Prometheus from such a Satanic kind of sculpturesque consciousness, Shelley begins even in act 1 to transform his Aeschylean model of dramatic form—already a more liberating model than Milton's epic. Reducing Aeschylus's constant lyric chorus of Oceanides to the descriptive and analytical responses of only two daughters of Ocean, Panthea and Ione, he also endows a changing series of voices and speaking shapes with lyric lines, and he sets these as dramatic foils to Prometheus. Most important, they present masques that make Prometheus confront himself either directly or through his own shaping influence. Thus this fragmentation of the chorus into the two Oceanides and the visions they describe displaces one of its elements, surprisingly, to center stage. Prometheus, once the central sculptural shape, is now the tutored—and the tortured—observer in a

Keatsian witnessing of circumstances—but those circumstances are personified partially as "shape," "form," or "image." In the course of the act, Shelley turns Aeschylus's staging inside out.

In its unregenerate resistance to a tyrant, Prometheus's opening speech is close to those in *Prometheus Bound.* Yet as its point of view changes from the Titan's challenging outward gaze to an inward one and then to one in which he becomes object, the audience can see and hear the bonds that Prometheus has placed upon himself. In the opening lines, he expresses the conflict between himself and Jupiter as a struggle to "behold with sleepless eyes," as if to behold is to control "those bright and rolling worlds" (1.4, 2); Prometheus and Jupiter each struggle to enclose the other as epic object in this vast starscape. In sharp contrast to Milton's Adam stationing his God in the familiar landscapes of Eden so that he might recall and believe in him, Prometheus starts to deny Jupiter's power by replacing him as Berkeleyan perceiver and making him only the object of perception. As he usurps Jupiter's perspective, however, he begins to see himself, first from within and then from without. He first claims a bitterly ironic "paradise within":

> . . . torture and solitude,
> Scorn and despair,—these are mine empire:—
> More glorious far than that which thou surveyest
> From thine unenvied throne, O Mighty God!
>
> (1.14–17)

He then goes on to station himself as sculptural epic object in a sort of antigarden: "Black, wintry, dead, unmeasured; without herb, / Insect, or beast, or shape or sound of life" (1.21–22). One might interpret this final perspective, seeing himself from Jupiter's point of view, as a grim recognition of circumstance made bearable for Prometheus by his inner recognition of "scorn and despair." It is also, however, an apt image for his psychological rigidity. Drawing attention to the dramatic stage fact of his bound figure, this speech articulates the "mind-forged manacles" of that figure, to use Blake's phrase from "London." Thus the prologue ends with a clear, if negative, image of the "sculptural possibilities" Fogle and Webb did not see in Prometheus's situation.

Its real possibilities for Prometheus, however, lie in his understanding of this clear image so that he may move beyond its rigid sculptural stasis both physically and psychologically. In the first episode, Earth presents a substitute for this sculptural self-image, first in her story of Zoroaster and then in her calling-up of the phantasm of Jupiter. These figures, although described in the sculptural terms of "shape" and "form," are also "images" from a world that mirrors, mimics, and acts as imaginative source for this one.

When Prometheus acts upon Earth's revelation of this realm to call up the phantasm of Jupiter, Panthea and Ione call the phantasm "Shape." Yet Prometheus, echoing the phantasm's own self-description as a "frail and empty phantom," addresses him as "Tremendous Image" and urges him to "Speak the words which I would hear, / Although no thought inform thine empty voice" (1.246–49). The term "image" clearly describes an appearance without force or substance, without "informing" thought that would give it inner structure or soul. Ironically, the words of Prometheus's curse, which this shadowy image must repeat, make this distinction clearer still if they are applied to the phantasm: "An awful Image of calm power / Though now thou sittest, let the hour / Come, when thou must appear to be / That which thou art internally." With its internal emptiness, its lack of inner form, the phantasm fulfills Prometheus's exhortation now as the actual Jupiter will do in act 3. Jupiter, a number of critics have argued, represents in part a hardening of Prometheus's earlier belief in the power of knowledge without love. Even though Prometheus comes to hate him as a Manichean antagonist, he is still a projection of Prometheus himself.[44] Thus Jupiter and his more obviously shadowy phantasm are both examples of Earth's "Dreams and the light imaginings of men / And all that faith creates, or love desires, / Terrible, strange, sublime and beauteous shapes."

If these "Dreams and . . . light imaginings" are the source of human art and poetry, they are also the source of humans' structures of belief about their world, structures they see as objective and that Shelley sums up at the end of act 3 as Jupiter. Earth's description of this world as "underneath the grave" thus points to a sharper division between ghostly and living forms than proves true in the rest of the play. Yet by giving Prometheus a mirroring of this earlier self-voiced curse through the image of Jupiter early in the play, Shelley allows us to see the way dreams and imaginings can have an active life in this world. The most obvious reading of her lines describing "two worlds of life and death," and the one that Earth in her mortal language probably intends, is that the world she and Prometheus behold is the world of life, and the world beneath the grave is that of death. Yet Shelley's phrasing is carefully ambiguous: though Earth herself does not see it, each world may contain mere shadows and images, but each world also contains living things. The world "beneath the grave" is not simply an Odyssean underworld of pale phantoms but an Orphic world of potential forms, like Demogorgon's world explored by Asia in act 2.[45] It also resembles Prometheus's description in act 3 of the cave where he and Asia will intensify, complete, and return man's imaginings.

These potential forms, then, redefine sculpture not as external, objective, and fixed but as internally generated and plastic. Moreover, they begin to resolve the sharp contrast between the sculptural, rigid figure of Prometheus and the impalpable, invisible voices of the nature-spirits and even of Earth herself. Like Keats's Coelus, "but the voice of wind and tides," these spirits are not shaped and palpable gods; and yet the shape of Prometheus proves dangerously limited in the form of its heroism. Nor can Prometheus recognize an optimistic progress toward freestanding, anthropomorphic godhead, that Winckelmannian vision for which Coelus hoped, in the phantasm of Jupiter. Instead he sees only the dark side of Coelus's vision, as it appears in *The Fall of Hyperion*. When the phantasm first speaks (1.240–45), the incongruity between his "frail" speech and his "awful . . . Shape" (1.233) is like that of the fallen Saturn which Moneta reveals to Keats's poet-narrator; but this incongruity gives way to the grotesque because grimly harmonious moment in which the tyrant "Shape" of Jupiter's phantasm and the equally tyrannical voice of Prometheus's curse come together. In that moment heroic form is all too adequately spirited. But precisely because it is, Prometheus can see its sculptural rigidity of spirit and can repudiate its "shaped" if not palpable dramatizing of his curse. "It doth repent me," he responds to the phantasm. "Words are quick and vain; / Grief for awhile is blind, and so was mine" (1.303–05). His progress, then, comes from seeing and reflecting a sculptural past that more than met Coelus's aesthetic criteria for godhead, for it offered a visually perceived sculptural correlative of heroic speech or "high language."[46] In doing so, it denied moral criteria, the benevolent exercise of power Saturn recalls as his highest moment in *Hyperion*. If the vocabulary of "shape," "form," and "image" has begun to point toward a freer redefinition of sculpture, such words are not yet enough to complete the redefinition: the problematic relationship between words and the plastic or visual expression of their significance becomes the means of the Furies' torture in the next episode.

That episode begins and ends by focusing upon central, bound sculptural figures out of whose frustrated silence breaks prophetic speech. Prometheus, whose "worn form" is recalled in Mercury's insincere sympathy (1.359), refuses to "Clothe" the "secret" of Jupiter's downfall "in words, or bid it clasp his throne," as Mercury asks (1.375); in fact, he denies that he even knows "that fatal word." With that denial, however, he must endure the vision of a word made flesh, of a crucified Christ whose "words outlived him, like swift poison / Withering up truth, peace, and pity" (1.548–49), exactly the virtues he, like Prometheus, sought to support. Panthea's description of a "youth . . . nailed to a crucifix" (1.584–85) suggests the sculptural, if scarcely serene, images in Italian churches and thus also suggests that both Christ and Prometheus suffer further through that institutionalized worship of suffering.

These enforcedly sculptural though restless forms are unable to find release through the energy and freedom of speech. Between them a series of scenes, chaotic and unfocused fragments of history paintings, represent the French Revolution; lines 567–78 and 648–55 are the most specific. Because Prometheus recognizes and interprets these scenes, however, his own words begin to correct that history. If, as he says, "There are two woes: / To speak and to behold" (1.646–47), he accepts the suffering of his speaking as he has just accepted the suffering of his watching.

Both acceptances, moreover, develop from his recognition of the form taken by the Furies and by their tortures. Although both the solitary figure of the crucified Christ and the chaotic mobs of the French Revolution increase their torture of Prometheus because their tableaux create an aesthetic distance that enforces his passivity, the Furies' self-definition, shaped by their victim, already has denied this distance. As they arrived, Prometheus had addressed them as "Horrible forms," "Phantasms . . . foul," and "execrable shapes." So effective is their external appearance that, Prometheus says, "Methinks I grow like what I contemplate / And laugh and stare in loathsome sympathy" (1.450–51). In Blake such sympathy almost always marks the perceiver's downfall; here, it anticipates Prometheus's recognition that the Furies, though dramatically external to him, draw their specific and "horrible" forms from just that sympathetic perceiver:

> . . . from our victim's destined agony
> The shade which is our form invests us round,
> Else we are shapeless as our Mother Night.
>
> (1.470–72)

Not only are the grotesque forms of the Furies themselves physical projections of the "agony" and suffering of their victim, but the forms of their tableaux also derive from the victim's individual vulnerability. The "imaginings" or aspirations of what might be, the "Terrible, strange, sublime, and beauteous shapes" that inhabit the other world Earth describes, clash with the grim failure to realize them in human experience: this clash is the subject not only of the two "historical" tableaux but also of the final Fury's terrifying and eloquent speech. His torture is the more real because its form is the present inadequacy of the sympathetic imagination to transform what it so clearly sees and mourns.

In accepting both the validity of this description and its need as a torture that further develops sympathy, Prometheus now can attempt to move beyond sympathy toward a redemptive creativity. As he accepts the suffering imposed by words and images together, for "I pity those they torture not," he hopes that some day the Furies' "sights" "shall be no types of things which are." In his despairing acknowledgment of the Furies' accurate description, he hopes for release from a rigid bondage of visual sign to fact. This release, however, is only the first step. He also must reject the further torture of visionary words as poisonous because so far from human accomplishment; he must hope that his own or Christ's or the revolutionary idealist's visions *will* be "types of things which are."

The imagery of his despair points back toward the realm Earth described as "beneath the grave," for "Peace is in the grave— / The grave hides all things beautiful and good— / I am a God and cannot find it there" (1.638–40). Yet because Earth has begun to recognize the creative power of an imaginative vision independent of "things that are," she "bid[s] ascend those subtle and fair spirits / Whose homes are the dim caves of human thought." They behold, she goes on, "beyond that twilight realm, as in a glass, / The future" (1.658ff.). The future, we might speculate, is precisely the openness of imaginative vision to formulate its own realities; and thus Prometheus's desire to see the Furies' visions as eventually nonmimetic may come about, paradoxically, through the free generation of fictions in the "caves of human thought" or in Demogorgon's or Prometheus's caves later in the play.

The strongest images of this final episode in act 1, the visit of these spirits from the human mind, are visual and potentially sculptural analogues to verbal power; and, paradoxically, they deny conventional seeing. The poet neither "seeks nor finds . . . mortal blisses / But feeds on the aerial kisses / Of shapes that haunt thought's wildernesses." Although he watches an almost Edenic external world, which gives him rough models, he will neither "heed nor see, what things they be; / But from these create he can / Forms more real than living man" (1.740–42, 746–48).

These spirits do not resolve the tragic discrepancy between the poet's solitary creation of "Forms more real than living man," those verbal versions of sculptural shaping that celebrate human freedom, and humanity's recurrent loss of that freedom. Their final version of this discrepancy, however, the "shape" of Love endlessly pursued by ruin, turns Prometheus toward that resolution. As he acknowledges "Most vain all hope but Love" and turns his thoughts and dreams toward Asia, he makes possible both her quest in act 2 and the complete mutual redefinition of love and imagination in act 3. Although still externally bound, he has responded to the ambiguous "shapes" and "forms" of phantasm, Furies, and spirits and to their tableaux and lyric descriptions, acknowledging the force of their dramatic arts through a sympathy that recalls his own capacity to imagine, though not yet to sustain that imagining. Thus, as perceiver of images and forms that mirror himself as a central, objective, sculptural figure, he anticipates his role in acts 3 and 4. In this way he also defines the play's growing freedom from an Aeschylean model.

"progeny immortal": Sculpture in Act 3

Although the second main cluster of sculptural terms and images comes in act 3, two "transfigurations" in act 2 dramatize another Shelleyan redefinition of sculptural form: the Praxitelean unity that flows from a form's center to its extremities, finally expressing itself as a radiating energy. The first of these transformations occurs in Panthea's first, better-remembered dream described in scene 1. As "his pale, wound-worn limbs / Fell from Prometheus," she sees "the glory of that form / Which lives unchanged within . . ." (2.1.62–65). Although the inner "form" she describes had come almost through vengeance to resemble his constrained and sculptural outer form, its energy now shows its renewal:

—the overpowering light
Of that immortal shape was shadowed o'er
By love; which, from his soft and flowing limbs
And passion-parted lips, and keen faint eyes
Steam'd forth like vaporous fire; an atmosphere
Which wrapt me in its all-dissolving power.

(2.1.71–76)

At the end of the act, Asia's transfiguration into Love shows the same dissolving of sculptural form into an energy that envelops figure and perceiver alike. Both the first and the second stanzas sung by the "voice (in the air, singing)" celebrate this energy (2.5.48–65). In the next two stanzas, sculptural form dissolves both into radiant light and into emanating sound. As this voice becomes the medium for Asia's visionary voyage, her song describing the voyage becomes the "screen" or "shroud" hiding her renovation in reversed time, as her visual radiance hides her renovation in space. The phrase "liquid splendour" in the voice's song (2.5.63) floats between references to voice and form, unifying these two elements in her transformation.

In their images of sculptural form expressing energy, these radical transformations first of Prometheus and then of Asia anticipate the language Prometheus uses in act 3 to describe how the two of them will

preside over a renovated human creativity. In her interview with Demogorgon in act 2 Asia already had described the origin of human arts as a
Promethean gift, but a secondary one. Because Prometheus's gift of
knowledge to Jupiter, meant to ensure men a release from their unknow-
ing existence under Saturn, has led instead to a new tyranny, arts and
techniques come as "alleviators of [man's] state." In Asia's speech, sculpture, though neither origin nor culmination of those arts defining human
culture, nevertheless begins to suggest its more significant role in act 3 as
Shelley's—or Prometheus's—metaphor for all of artistic creativity:

> . . . human hands first mimicked and then mocked
> With moulded limbs more lovely than its own
> The human form, till marble grew divine,
> And mothers, gazing, drank the love men see
> Reflected in their race, behold, and perish.
>
> (2.4.80–84)

Not only does marble grow divine, but in a complex pattern of reflexive
and reflecting images the human race in turn grows more lovely by
contemplating its own artifacts with love.[47]

Asia's speech ends, however, with an assertion that even "while / Man
looks on his creation like a God / And sees that it is glorious" (2.101–03),
his creation—his culture and its artifacts—seems freer and more godlike
than he. Caught between natural process and the godlike serenity of his
art, he finds that each act of creation only increases his consciousness of
restless disappointment—and "drives him on, / The wreck of his own
will, the scorn of Earth, / The outcast, the abandoned, the alone" (2.103–
04). Thus Prometheus's alleviating gifts of culture and the arts intensify
the ambiguous first gift, the freedom that seems in retrospect only an
eviction from unthinking Saturnian harmony; and sculpture is the art that
most clearly defines the gap between ideal image and actual human
experience. As Asia questions Demogorgon about this split between
man's condition and his imaginative culture, his cryptic answer, "the deep
truth is imageless," suggests that man's condition is truer than his images.
The loveliness of those images, however—that is, their expression of
love—is another and more promising matter, for to "Fate, Time, Occasion, Chance, and Change . . . All things are subject but eternal Love"
(2.4.119–20). Significantly, it is Asia—playfully called "mother" in act
3—who manifests this loveliness.

Prometheus's crucial speech after his release in act 3 defines the positive
function of images: they are radically and mutually interdependent with
love. Each is the expression of the other. To define this relationship, he

uses a synaesthetic blending not of the senses but of the major sister arts that the play already has been exploring. Prometheus explains that in spite of their apparent isolation from the mutable processes of human experience, "hither come . . . / The echoes of the human world." Those echoes are

> . . . lovely apparitions dim at first
> Then radiant—as the mind, arising bright
> From the embrace of beauty (whence the forms
> Of which these are the phantoms) casts on them
> The gathered rays which are reality—
> Shall visit us, the progeny immortal
> Of Painting, Sculpture and rapt Poesy
> And arts, though unimagined, yet to be.
> The wandering voices and the shadows these
> Of all that man becomes, the mediators
> Of that best worship, love, by him and us
> Given and returned, swift shapes and sounds which grow
> More fair and soft as man grows wise and kind,
> And veil by veil evil and error fall.
>
> (3.3.40, 44, 49–62)

Because metaphor, personification, and the dramatic presence of Shelley's mythic Titans echo and influence one another, this passage is difficult. Yet its rhetorical structure reflects its themes, as the passage begins and ends with a love that both generates the arts and is generated by them. The first stage of this process, described in the first five lines, takes place on the human level: "the mind" is the mind of each individual artist, as it endows "lovely apparitions" with the "reality" of expression. The apparitions "shall visit us," Prometheus says, and in their prophetic idealism they become "the mediators / Of that best worship, love, by [man] and us / Given and returned." Both the creative initiative and the love first come from man, and these impulses are intertwined in a miniature myth of personified "mind" and "beauty" reflecting the larger myth of Prometheus's and Asia's reconciliation: the apparitions become "radiant—as the mind, arising bright / From the embrace of beauty . . . casts on them / The gathered rays which are reality." In that embrace of mind and beauty exist or originate the "forms / Of which these [the apparitions] are the phantoms." Because only as these apparitions become real do they visit the Titans' cave to confirm man's development through communicated love, their "forms" seem human and not transcendent in origin as Platonic ideas might be. Even though they begin as "apparitions" or "phantoms" of the prior forms, they also gain a "reality" that the mind draws from the same generative embrace, as if they come into consciousness when they gain definite, realized shape. Even if "copies" of the original "forms," they are no less real. Inner "form" becomes completed external form as its shape or phantom takes on radiance: this process is another version of the Praxitelean "flowing" shown in Asia's transformation. They are less real, however, than the reform of humanity that they prophesy, create, and then mirror: "The wandering voíces and the shadows these / Of all that man becomes. . . . swift shapes and sounds which grow / More fair and soft as man grows wise and kind." Although the word "form" continues Shelley's metaphoric redefinitions of sculpture from external to internal, organic definition, the realized "apparitions" are verbal, plastic, and visual: "voices" and "sounds," "shadows" and "shapes." As they grow more "soft," their external form moves even further from the marble images of heroism with which the play opened, to confirm the definition of a "form" generated in love, not hate.

All of this passage, then, answers Asia's description of a sculpture that "first mimicks and then mocks" its creators, having become an image of the gulf between ideal imaginative achievement and actual human experience in a world controlled by Jupiter. As these realized apparitions mediate in love between human and Titan, between the Titans themselves, and between humans themselves, we can define Prometheus: he becomes the conscious, public communication of the original human consciousness or "mind" that has given these apparitions their "reality." Like Moneta, Prometheus and Asia together act as mythic expressions of the communal, public aspirations of humanity. Instead of Moneta's ironic hedging of past paradisal, Saturnian dreams in the perpetual loss and isolation that seem their very guarantee of universality, Prometheus and Asia mediate private dream through a generating love that looks forward instead of back. The Saturnian realm, Asia has already explained to Demogorgon in act 2, allowed humanity neither remembered nor foreseeing dreams of perfect forms. If Jupiter's realm allowed the development of such creative images, the discrepancy between image and fact only mocked the limits of their creativity. Now, with the acknowledgment both of the limits of "Time, Occasion, Chance, and Change," and of "eternal Love" (2.4.119–20), the new Promethean paradise can correct the Saturnian one. Although Demogorgon had prefaced these crucial lines with the warning that "a voice / Is wanting, the deep truth is imageless," it is the creation of voice, image, and form through mediating love that can begin to overcome, if not totally to explain, the "deep truth" that emerges as the presence of impersonal evil or, rather, indifferent process. From the perspective of act 3, then, two kinds of "deep truth" appear: the "deep truth" that emerges as that unwilled process, but also the more explainable and interdependent sources of generative love and imagination, symbolized by Prometheus's and Asia's cave. There the mind, "arising bright / From the embrace of beauty," can create a "reality" aware of the first deep truth but compensating for it.

These generating ideal forms provide a context for several specific historical allusions to sculpture later in act 3. In the only two passages where Shelley describes sculptural monuments by alluding to specific historical sculptors, those references mediate between the ideally creative forms Prometheus has described and the rigid forms of the icons men had worshiped as Jupiter. Each of these specific references associates sculpture with the focusing of temple and sacred place. In the first passage Earth directs her torch bearer to lead Prometheus and Asia back to a temple and cave in Greece, once sacred to the fire bringer himself. As the sacred river Alph reflects the pleasure dome in "Kubla Khan," here "a windless and chrystalline pool" reflects "The image of a temple built above. . . . overwrought, / And populous most with living imagery— / Praxitelean shapes, whose marble smiles / Fill the hushed air with everlasting love" (3.3.159, 161, 163–66). Both the Coleridgean echoes of cave, water, and temple, and the repeated motifs of torch bearer and fire bringer point out Shelley's exploration of the sources and expressions of creativity. The human rituals of prophecy and torch races now can be grounded more thoroughly in the primal Promethean movement of mind flowing outward, through love, toward expression in human arts—appropriately, a Praxitelean process.

A scene later, another temple, this time filled with "Phidian forms," recalls the earlier and more powerful of the two most famous Greek sculptors and suggests that this temple described by the Spirit of the Hour is an archetype for the earthly temple Earth describes. As "I floated down," the spirit says, "My coursers sought their birthplace in the sun . . . / . . . Where my moonlike car will stand within / A temple, gazed upon by Phidian forms, / Of thee, and Asia and the Earth, and me / And you fair nymphs" (3.4.106ff.). "Yoked" to the chariot "by an amphisbaenic snake / The likeness of those winged steeds will mock / The flight from which they find repose." The polarity of energy and calm that so fascinates Shelley in sculpture aptly illustrates here a moment of historical transformation converted to a monument for the recurrent potentiality of such changes. Because this chariot brought first Asia and then Demogorgon from the abyss, rising as the moving expression of historical change to destroy Jupiter, its continued upward movement and its conversion to what Harold Bloom calls a "museum piece" mark its triumph over the Roman icons that later in the spirit's speech symbolize

Jupiter, and its role as image for a renewal of the original Phidian grandeur of Greek civilization.[48]

In the context of these two positive images for Greek sculpture as renewed ideals of human capability, the Spirit of the Hour goes on to measure human freedom by its ability to discard the sculptural shapes it had falsely worshiped as its own transcendent tyrants. It reports the abandonment of "Thrones, altars, judgement-seats and prisons" that nevertheless stand in witness "like those monstrous and barbaric shapes . . . Which from their unworn obelisks look forth / In triumph o'er the palaces and tombs / Of those who were their conquerors, mouldering round . . . even so the tools / And emblems of its last captivity . . . Stand, not o'erthrown, but unregarded now" (3.4.164ff.). Although Reiman glosses the "shapes" as the hieroglyphs inscribed on the obelisks, both picture-words and sculptural bas-reliefs "look forth" with silent commentary upon the ruins of civilizations like the Roman one. Repeating the word "shape," the Spirit of the Hour transforms sculptural simile into a false identification of spirit with external form:

> And those foul shapes, abhorred by God and man—
> Which under many a name and many a form
> Strange, savage, ghastly, dark and execrable
> Were Jupiter . . .
> Frown, mouldering fast, o'er their abandoned shrines.
>
> (3.4.180–83, 189)

From Roman, Egyptian, or still earlier cultures, these sculptural shapes worshiped not as human art but as incarnate gods manifest the ironic succession of one dehumanizing, petrifying tyranny by another. Now, the Spirit of the Hour suggests, that savage procession is ended, because men now can recognize that the spiritual shapes, like the stone forms that express them, are built by humans.

Shelleyan Landscape: Verbal and Visual Sketches for Prometheus

If a human builds the shapes of his or her cultural world, does that person also build the shape of the surrounding natural world? If the unbinding of Prometheus is also a psychological release of love and imagination, can those forces remold natural limits, as they do in *Milton*, or must they remain essentially enclosed or stationed within those limits, as in the *Hyperion* poems? These questions, emerging from Asia's journey and her cryptic encounter with Demogorgon in act 2, remain unclear even after the renewal of human society through the renewal of its generative sculptural forms at the end of act 3. In acts 2 and 4, as I suggested earlier, Shelley's dominant metaphoric method first for raising and then for answering these questions is a version of Miltonic stationing that moves through the scenic picturesque of landscape to the metaphysical picturesque of dramatic and cosmic structure. Beginning with the evaluation of landscape, Shelley's answers to these questions of a human place in the natural world ultimately emerge, in act 4, as lying between Blake's remolding of landscape into human figure and Keats's recognition of figures as immersed in a "world of Circumstances."

Like the images of sculptural form, landscape in *Prometheus Unbound* has been celebrated more for its absence than for its presence. Once Prometheus frees himself from the icy constraints of his own and Jupiter's mutual hatred in act 1, imaged in the peaks of the Caucasus, Shelley depicts the natural setting of the play as paradisal and almost without constraint on human fulfillment.[49] The image of Asia's flowering vale seems to dominate the remaining three acts, even though only in act 4, and not wholly there, does the play assert thematically that biological constraints fall away from human life. In fact, through much of act 2 Asia examines the significance both of powerful and of paradisal landscapes, as if to test the promise of her flowering vale; and among the questions she raises in Demogorgon's cave, she also seems to ask what significance lies beneath the surfaces of Earth's landscapes. In act 4 Shelley works out an even more complex image for exploring the significance of landscape as natural world. Earth changes to the Spirit of Earth and like a Blakean figure acts out a transforming masque that nearly dissolves nature; yet that Spirit remains stationed like a Keatsian character within a "clearing in the woods," immersed in the wildernesses of this natural world. Because this questioning, both in act 2 and in act 4, reaches beyond the visible surfaces of picturesque landscape settings, readers again, just as in searching for sculptural form, have seen the most extreme stage of the process without seeing its beginnings.

Although external to *Prometheus Unbound*, Shelley's acquaintance with picturesque theory and even with the picturesque uses of "stationing" is easier to establish than Blake's or Keats's. His prose, particularly the letters written from Switzerland in 1816 and the letters and prose written from Italy in 1818–1819, refers both to the picturesque and to the sublime in its description of landscape. Both the letters and the poetry, moreover, use the term "station" in hierarchical and picturesque senses. Further and striking evidence of his strong interest in landscape appears in page after page of his manuscript notebooks. Though also external to the completed drama in a way that Blake's illuminations are not, his ink and pencil sketches in these notebooks are intertwined closely with the drafts of

Prometheus Unbound and influence its development. A few central examples from this array of evidence must suffice to suggest his awareness of picturesque techniques in viewing landscape and also of their metaphoric implications for suggesting humanity's place in, and control over, the external natural world.

In his "Ode to Liberty," as we have seen, Shelley uses "station" as an almost Miltonic, metaphysical vantage point from which to see and hear Liberty's progress. Yet his successive location of Athens in visionary "battlemented cloud," "on the will of man," and on "that hill," the Acropolis, shows his revisionary awareness of conventional scenic description.

Probably the most important of his uses of "station" in the picturesque sense comes in *Julian and Maddalo*, where the two characters epitomize the dialectic of their different metaphysical perspectives with their differing scenic viewpoints: " 'Ere it [the magnificent sunset] fade,' / Said my Companion, 'I will shew you soon / A better station' "; and instead of the mountains' "very peaks transparent" in the setting sun, "I looked, and saw between us and the sun" a tower with "A bell," that "tolled / In strong and black relief" (ll. 85–88, 98, 103, 106–07). The bell is that of the madhouse which Maddalo makes "emblem and sign," as in Byron's "Prometheus," of man's "baffled" condition. The "better station" is thus a more honest perspective on the human condition, in Maddalo's view, though less beautiful.[50]

In the Italian letters of 1818 and 1819, the picturesque creating of a scene involves most often an interplay between architectural and natural setting, so that foreground and middle ground lead toward the vaster and less humanly limited spaces of the sublime. Though similar to Keats's focusing of landscapes toward architecture in *The Fall of Hyperion*, Shelley's scenes move the opposite way. Keats's scenes organize themselves around a central, statuesque figure set in a world of natural circumstances that frames the figure for the circumstantial, mortal witness. Shelley's more characteristic pattern in these letters is to focus toward and then through some enclosure, frequently an architectural monument like an amphitheater, almost as if the viewer passes through a Blakean vortex.[51]

In a prose-fiction fragment, "The Colosseum," begun in November 1818, Shelley carries these descriptions of amphitheaters furthest into symbol. Beginning with the repeated picturesque framing of "the wide, bright, blue sky" by "a great circle of arches built upon arches," the sketch then turns to a blind man's meditative response to this description. In its almost apocalyptic sublimity and then its affirmation of natural continuity, his language describes time's chastisement for the distortions of human culture enacted in the rituals of the arena. His final response, however, proposes an answer to those distortions not in the "enchantment of Nature" but in human emotions.

> The internal nature of each being is surrounded by a circle, not to be surmounted by his fellows . . . But there is a circle which comprehends, as well as one which mutually excludes, all things which feel. . . . [Man's] public and his private happiness consists in diminishing the circumference which includes those resembling himself, until they become one with him and he with them. It is because we enter into the meditations, designs and destinies of something beyond ourselves that the contemplation of the ruins of human power excites an elevating sense of awfulness and beauty.[52]

As the blind old man defines it, such stationing transcends the individual and subjective limits of scenic stationing alone, to avoid both solipsism and succumbing to an "objective" and alien external world. His blindness is not a necessary condition of such inner sympathy and thus not a complete freedom from the eye's tyranny, but it is a means of analyzing the steps from sight to speech to feeling. A similar and more complex gradation of descriptive narrator and mediating interpreter develops in *Prometheus*, as we consider the progression from Ione to Panthea to Asia, to Demogorgon's darkness. In all of these situations, the act of interpreting continues the description and presents it to another as an act of sharing one's horizon of significance. Meaning thus becomes not an individual and solitary point of view but an active, directed interpreting of the located, visual scene.

Shelley's own analogy of developing his finished poems from verbal "sketches" in his notebooks shows his strong interest in the relationship between visual image and verbal image, concept, or interpretation.[53] Scholars have published only a few of the drawings he habitually sketched as he drafted his poetry.[54] Yet a detailed study of the manuscript containing drafts of *Prometheus Unbound* shows an enormous complexity of such relationships.[55] From the greater frequency of sketches in the rough-draft as compared to the fair-copy notebooks, and from the evidence of simultaneity in visual and verbal sketches from the draft notebooks, it can be argued that these sketches frequently form a part of the drafting process. Moreover, because the drawings appear far more frequently as Shelley drafts poetry than as he drafts prose, they seem associated with the more concentrated rhythms and metaphors of poetry. Their frequency seems higher still in the lyrical than in the dramatic poetry; on the other hand, because the surviving notebooks contain more material from acts 2 and 4 than from the more dramatic acts 1 and 3, it is possible to weight this point too heavily. Of course, one might argue that prose drafts—or even blank-verse drafts—leave less white space on the notebook page for sketching; but more often than not the white space seems created deliberately for the sketch. Evaluated at the simplest level, these drawings keep the ink flowing as the poet works out lines in his head. The process of drawing is a kinetic action that parallels the impulses—and pulses—of the poetry. At the same time, as actual writing stops, the creation of a space and a spatial drawing accompanies "temporal" but mental exploration of rhyme, rhythm, and meter. These temporal and musical qualities of the verse are also, of course, formal qualities that shape and limit the fiery coal of inspiration and that lead, to use the language of the later *Defence*, both to its later fading and to its becoming known. Yet, though many of the sketches may have begun as kinetic gestures, empty of conscious content, the mutual respect between drawing space and text space suggests that at some point in this process Shelley becomes conscious of these drawings and their relationship to text. He would be confronted by the differences between his two arts and the senses with which they are most closely associated: "the temples high / Of man's ear and eye" (4.111–12). Though more marked by opposition and contrast, the interplay of his two modes of sketching on the page resembles the synaesthesia that premeates his verbal texts. If they show an interplay of senses, however, they also reflect an interplay between sense-perception and sense as significance. More specifically, from the examples of drawings that both mirror and prompt verbal revisions, Shelley also must become conscious of the sketches as motifs that reveal symbolic content. This significance, like the processes that create it, seems to explore the polarity of regenerative energy on the one hand, and formal or legislative limit on the other.

Both in expression and in their verbal context, a number of sketches of profiles suggest a tyrant's censorious rule that must be transformed from an externally imposed to an internally generated form. The architectural images in these notebooks might suggest a similar conversion to such a positive, humanized and humanly expressive form—as do the temples of ruined Rome and regenerative Greece in act 3—but there are too few of them to support adequate generalization. Apparently at the opposite pole are his reiterative sketches of trees and woodland landscapes. Obviously natural, organic, and generative in what they represent, these sketches in their very frequency also seem closest to the processes of poetic generation. Neville Rogers calls these trees symbols of regeneration; and in describing the dome as symbolic of imagination for Shelley, G. Wilson Knight also may have been describing these rounded treetops that spring up between stanzas of his choruses.[56]

Yet the relationship between the energy of the natural world and the sources of power for imagination is a problem repeatedly raised in acts 2 and 4 of *Prometheus*, the acts most fully represented in these draft notebooks. As spatial interruptions in the temporal sequence of writing out rhythms, these drawings may point to this ambiguous significance: for the repeated drawings of trees, and even the sketches of ponds, seem like returns to the English landscapes of Shelley's childhood or, more universally, like returns to a Wordsworthian source of energy and power that lies at times within natural phenomena and at times mysteriously behind and distanced from them. If these drawings point toward personal and epistemological origins, they also point toward the mythical origins of Eden— and to Asia's romantic criticism of Eden as a static and unconscious world:

> . . . such the state
> Of the earth's primal spirits beneath his sway
> As the calm joy of flowers and living leaves
> Before the wind or sun has withered them
> . . . but he [Saturn] refused
> The birthright of their being, knowledge, power,
> The skill which wields the elements, the thought
> Which pierces this dim Universe like light,
> Self-empire and the majesty of love.
>
> (2.4.34ff.)

Is this static if paradisal state the consequence of timelessness? Further, is it in any way a reflection of the state of the individual mind before it attempts a creation in time—before it casts vision into verse, or even before vision begins? Although these drawings raise such questions, only the greater complexity of the poetry can answer them.

The visual images that show most directly the dynamic process of conveying impulse into expression are those of boats and of chariots resembling boats. To consider the most literal drawings: as the impulse of the wind moves the sailboat, its sail shows which way the wind is blowing.[57] The very literalness of these drawings, in counterpoint to their verbal contexts, points to their function as metaphorical mediators, as a way of presenting invisible forces to us. The moon-boat or chariot not only signals a revelatory change in the cosmic weather but in its verbal context as *merkabah*, as Ezekiel's chariot of divine revelation, symbolizes the revelation of some ultimate power in "vehicular" symbol. To use Blake's language still further, as it reveals and gives form to energy this process contrasts with the unthinking "dull round" of natural cycles. At the beginning of act 4 Shelley's dialogue between Panthea and Ione mocks this revelatory function even as it confirms the redefinition of process from temporal cycle to expressive, regenerating energy attaining form. Hearing the voices of the unseen spirits who begin to celebrate their conquest of time, Ione asks, "What charioteers are these?" and Panthea, "Where are

their chariots?" Because boats and hourglass illustrate the notebook drafts
of this passage, the chariot is invisible in both media—or, rather, it is
delayed until the epiphanies of earth and moon at the center of the act. Yet
those mediating daughters of Ocean correctly, if somewhat comically,
anticipate the transformation from a sequential, irreversible time to dance
time. They hear what they cannot yet see, but seeing as well as music is an
essential part of the apocalypse, the freeing from covering, which follows.
Significantly, several of Shelley's moon-boat sketches, for example those
on the inside back cover of HM 2177, blend into visionary eyes that stare
at and past the reader. The chariot-boat is a medium for our seeing, for
our sharing a vision shaped by some transcendent, more Promethean,
force or consciousness.[58] From this visual starting point in Shelley's
sketches, the chariot indeed may symbolize a divinely human creativity
like the *merkabah* of Milton's Christ in *Paradise Lost;* its interpretation of a
creative logos is not restricted to ongoing speech or a "telling" like that in
Keats's *Hyperion* poems. From Shelley's verbal starting point in *Prometheus
Unbound,* however, the interplay between seeing and telling, and between
visual landscapes and temporal process, is more ambiguous. Although
Asia describes in act 2 how the landscape of a Saturnian Eden falls into
time, and Earth- and Moon-Spirits in act 4 describe how it is drawn nearly
out of time, these processes are not simply reversals of one another.
Instead, they represent different stages of seeing.

Asia's Descent, Jupiter's Fall, and Arguments from Design

In book 7 of *Paradise Lost* Milton's Christ rides out over the abyss of
Chaos in his chariot to create the universe "with his powerful Word": with
divine speech, the natural universe and its landscapes become wonderfully
visible. In act 2 of *Prometheus Unbound,* Shelley's Asia searches through an
expansive natural world and through a darker world beyond its limits for
the sources of its power and its magnificence. As she asks whether that
power is Jupiter or Demogorgon or some other, Shelley urges us to ask
whether that power—or those differing powers—resembles Milton's God.
The structural method of act 2, an alternation of contrasting scenes like
those in Spenserian romantic epic, emphasizes this questioning with an
alternation of visual and auditory scenes: the first, third, and fifth are
intensely visual, the second and fourth deny vision for sound and music,
or even for a dark silence. Yet though a denial of sight follows each visual
scene, these denials lead eventually to a correcting and a release of the
visual at the end of the act, and they lead also to a completion of Panthea's
dream at the beginning of scene 1—of the sculptural figure transformed

into energy. The second act, then, moves beyond Prometheus's negative and painful reading of historical and cultural emblems to Asia's positive reading, although one still in need of correction, of the book of nature. Her readings are positive because they are valid starting points; but as her journey gets underway, she is drawn beyond, beneath the surface of the visible natural world, led by sound. What finally emerges from the affirmation of sight in scenes 1, 3, and 5 and its denial in scenes 2 and 4, is Asia's transfiguration, revealed to sight at the end of the act. With its lyric accompaniment, it fuses sight, sound, and feeling.

Panthea's two dreams in act 2, scene 1 mediate not only between Prometheus and Asia but between the sculptural criticism of the first act and the scenic criticism of the second. They also mediate between the classical dramatic unity of the first and the romantic expansiveness of the second. Her first dream shows Asia once more the "glory of that form / Which lives unchanged within" Prometheus, as from "that immortal shape . . . an atmosphere," Panthea reports, "wrapt me in its all-dissolving power" (2.1.64–65, 72, 75–76). Although her response to this "form" or "shape" begins with perceptions like those prompted by Praxitelean sculpture in Shelley's "Notes on Sculpture," the virtually sexual merging of that presence into Panthea as mediator denies Prometheus's stasis, in order to prophesy his release. As Asia sees in her sister's dream "a shade—a shape—'tis He" (2.1.120), the shape is not yet dissolved in communicating power but "arrayed"—a word Shelley takes back to its origins—"In the soft light of his own smiles which spread / Like radiance from the cloud-surrounded moon" (2.1.120–22). Asia sees the second dream, too, as a "shape," but Panthea describes it as a series of messages written on natural things: "on each leaf was stamped . . . *O follow, follow!*" (2.1.139, 141). Asia, too, finds the same words "written" on clouds, "stamp'd" "on each herb," then "heard" from the wind in the pines, and finally seen in Panthea's eyes, which were the starting point for her reading of both dreams. In the style of the Duke of Arden finding "tongues in trees, books in the running brooks, / Sermons in stones," all this reading illustrates the traditional topos that Shakespeare also explores, that of reading the book of nature.[59] The first dream moves from the sculptural and human, though superhumanly grand, "form" of Prometheus to its subjective communication as energy. The second starts with an accelerated version of the first, moving from "shape" into mind, and then moves outward to interpret the natural world.

In this scene, the conscious, controlled act of "reading" contrasts with the uncontrollable method of dreaming. This counterpoint of willed and unwilled acts characterizes Asia's and Panthea's entire journey. Resembling the creative interplay between individual will and transcendent power in *The Defence*,[60] it also resembles the contrast between visual control and musical impulse in the act as a whole. The second half of scene 1 shows this principle of contrast at work, as Panthea and Asia try to locate the invisible echoes hiding within either the landscape or a "spirit-tongued" part of it. The contrast of the echoes' song continues this challenge to the visual, pictorial surface of landscape. The most frequent locating phrase, of those they musically repeat, is the nonplace, "through the caverns hollow" (2.1.175, 179, 197). The route of their journey seems a stationing that vanishes as it seeks a center within, not upon, the scene:

> By the forests, lakes, and fountains,
> Through the many-folded mountains,
> To the rents and gulphs and chasms
> Where the Earth reposed from spasms
> On the day when He and thou
> Parted—to commingle now.
>
> (2.1.200–205)

As the first three lines locate the next three scenes, the last line telescopes the time between the creation of a fallen landscape and its anticipated redemption, one subject of Asia's dialogue with Demogorgon in scene 4. That dialogue and her long speech responding to the "many-folded mountains" of scene 3 are particularly important because they discuss the far larger question on which the entire act turns: what animate, willing force finds power and expression in the landscape and the physical universe as a whole?

While the first scene presents the agents that direct Asia and Panthea on their journey, scene 2 begins to explore this crucial question. Both visually and musically, scene 2 is an exercise in oblique, indirect perspectives. By constantly vacating the expected center of the framed, described scene, Shelley creates a sense of motion and also alters our expectations about what or who should stand at the center.[61] As Asia and Panthea pass across the stage and into a forest, a chorus of unseen spirits comments on their journey; as they finish singing, a pair of fauns tries scientifically to locate those spirits and their significance; the fauns, in turn, will find Silenus; and he will distance all of these frames and the larger story as well into mythic and prophetic song. Because each commentator is framed or enclosed by the next, the structure of the scene becomes a "hollow cavern" opening toward a distant goal. In *The Fall of Hyperion*, Keats's narrator sinks down "like a Silenus on an antique vase," temporarily static as if caught in bas-relief, but potentially visionary. Shelley's Silenus, though offstage and unseen, is more active and vocal; he creates such "delightful strains" that he can "charm / To silence the unenvying nightingales" (2.2.95–97).

Although the next scene and the beginning of the fourth continue to explore intuitive and rational, musical and visual ways of knowing, they question not only what momentary music comes from cliff and caves but what larger force animates the whole natural scene. Breaking this inward-turning, enclosing descent, the journey in scene 3 tests scenic and literary mountain visions. Revising Miltonic heights and depths, Asia's observations and questions also begin to reevaluate the perspectives of sky-gods asserted from act 1 through act 3, scene 1.

As Asia describes the vast perspective, she stations herself precisely in relation to its pictorial composition: "Beneath is a wide plain of billowy mist, / As a lake, paving . . . Some Indian vale. . . . Behold it, . . . islanding / The peak whereon we stand—midway, around / Encinctured by the dark and blooming forests . . . / And far on high the keen sky-cleaving mountains" (2.3.19ff.). Although their position "midway" is the most highly recommended by theorists of the picturesque, the grandeur and vastness of the actual scene verge on the sublime. Yet evaluation of this magnificence, both for Asia and for Shelley's audience, proves difficult.

The opening lines of Asia's speech recall Raphael's warning about the problems of interpreting his myth of origins; for earth, the angel tells Adam, may be only the shadow of heaven.[62] Though cautiously conditional in her verbs, Asia implies that even if evil were to stain or in fact does stain both creator and creation, she would still "fall down and worship that and thee" (l. 16)—that is, "such a Power" (2.3.11) and "Earth" (2.3.12). Because of this recognition of possible evil, Asia's commitment to these is stronger than Wordsworth's in "Tintern Abbey," for in that earlier poem Wordsworth admits no evil stain in nature, only in man's infidelity to nature's teaching impulses. Because Asia's version of natural religion is based in beauty and seems to suspend morality, it echoes the abuses of the "picturesque moment" as Martin Price analyzes it. Yet because her conditional verbs also can be read as an experimental playing with such worship, and because she acknowledges this possible split between beauty and goodness, her neo-Wordsworthian meditation in fact serves as a severe analysis of the problems of inference from aesthetic effect to moral cause. This analytic prologue qualifies the later affirmation of her own beauty.

Her opening exclamation, "Fit throne for such a power," and her own exultation at the wide-ranging view from her pinnacle also associate supreme power with high places. From Aeschylus and mythic tradition, Shelley borrows the association of Jupiter with sky, storm, and Mount

Olympus. From Milton and his Biblical sources, he borrows the location of a supreme deity in a heaven above earth and accessible in vision from prophetic high places. Yet because Jupiter and thus indirectly the Miltonic God are shown in this play as tyrants, and because Prometheus is tortured by being pinioned on a mountain, Asia's apparent praise of high places and expansive visual perspectives must be seen either as misguided or as more complex than her scenic archetypes at first suggest. Shelley, we expect, will reverse the value of height and depth to show political and cosmic revolution. True enough, his agent of effective revolutionary power does emerge from the depths, from Demogorgon's "mighty portal, / Like a volcano's meteor-breathing chasm" (2.3.2–3). Prometheus, moreover, does not share that subterranean energy; both spatially and psychologically at this point in the play, he is too close to Jupiter.

Yet Demogorgon marks the turning-point of history in act 3, scene 1, by making Jupiter fall and by reclaiming the heights. More correctly, when Demogorgon rises he empties the heights. Not only is Jupiter thrown out, but Prometheus descends from the Caucasus to his Edenic cave and forest in Greece. "The tyranny of Heaven none may retain, / Or reassume, or hold succeeding thee," Demogorgon tells Jupiter (3.1.57–58). Modulating extremes of depth as well, Shelley will not quite allow his tyrant a hell.[63] Jupiter's last attempt at control of the universe is a piece of neo-Miltonic rant in which, denied heaven, he attempts to create a sublime hell for himself and for the "detested prodigy" Demogorgon. Echoing Satan in *Paradise Lost*, book 4, Demogorgon has announced simply, "we must dwell together / Henceforth in darkness—." Jupiter responds first by attempting to "trample" him "beneath the deep Titanian prisons"—and, that failing, calls up what he apparently sees as a fittingly dramatic end both for himself and for the universe:

—Let Hell unlock
Its mounded Oceans of tempestuous fire,
And whelm on them into the bottomless void
The desolated world and thee and me,
The conqueror and the conquered, and the wreck
Of that for which they combated.
                                        Ai! Ai!
The elements obey me not.

                                        (3.1.74–80)

Although his attempt at apocalypse has the air of a young boy picking up his marbles after the game goes against him, the marbles are "those bright and rolling Worlds" that he and Prometheus contemplate in the beginning of the play. Like Hyperion, struggling to control the dislocation of his universe by beginning the dawn early, Jupiter finds that the elements fail him, too. Although earth becomes a kind of hell for Keats's fallen and naturalized Titans, however, Shelley's falling Olympian gains no such definite place but becomes like one of Blake's falling figures in the later Lambeth prophecies. In the next scene, Ocean asks eagerly, "He fell to the abyss? To the dark void?" Apollo's answer is a complex simile: "An eagle so, caught in some bursting cloud / On Caucasus, . . . sinks at length / Prone, and the aerial ice clings over it" (3.2.11–12, 16–17). Yet as the open, unspecific end of the simile suggests, he refuses to give Jupiter even the rhetorical comfort of such grand words as "abyss" and "void." Even the "dark void," for all its sublimity, is a place or a denial of place far different in its indefiniteness from the more specific and torturing realm Jupiter calls either "Tartarus" or "Hell." Because Jupiter lacks the advantage of following Asia's quest downward in the preceding act, his rhetoric sounds all the more hollowly Miltonic in its absence of stationing.

Moreover, Jupiter's physical fall, though analogous to Satan's, responds to two earlier "falls." The first is the human loss of Eden Asia describes to Demogorgon in act 2, scene 4. Like Adam's and Eve's fall in *Paradise Lost*, it is not literal but spiritual, and yet like theirs it leads to their submission to a "world of Circumstances." The second "fall" preceding Jupiter's is of course Asia's descent to Demogorgon's cave, the setting for her telling of the earlier fall. Although Asia's curiosity, like Eve's, leads to her descent, her desire to know metaphysical truth and her love for Prometheus do not conflict with one another but are aspects of the same positive and ultimately creative impulse. Thus the abyss in act 2, scene 4, resembles not Milton's hell but the more creative, if passive, abyss over which his holy spirit "dove-like" sat brooding and out over which, in a different metaphor, Christ's chariot rode. In this scene (act 2, scene 3), Asia's images of mist first transforming mountains and valleys into metaphoric oceans and then transforming itself into "shapes" also suggest the interchange of height and depth, vision and darkness, in Wordsworth's two most powerful evaluations of mountain vision, the Simplon and Snowdon passages in *The Prelude*. Although Shelley could not have known these, their assertions first of power in the "mind's abyss" and then of power in the "unremitting interchange" of mind and nature, sound and sight, suggest new answers to Asia's quest for the sources of power and creativity behind the natural landscape. Shelley's portrayal of the abyss of Demogorgon and the transfiguring of Asia, "issuing forth in . . . light," in scenes 4 and 5, explores such a possibility. As prologue, scene 3 shows an interchangeable supremacy or, better, a skeptical dialectic between visual magnificence and, in the temporary denial of light, the impulse of music and sound.

In scene 4 Asia attempts to define man's fallen natural circumstances in a complex speech of origins. First, she reviews the interdependent responsibilities of Prometheus and Jupiter, then questions the extent of Jupiters's new responsibility. Although Demogorgon's answers are as cryptic as those of any oracle, his answers, his setting, and Shelley's dramatic technique all begin to reassign a portion of that responsibility to the individual listener or perceiver. The knowledge Asia seeks about the power ordering the phenomenal surfaces of this natural world thus begins to resemble Schlegel's ideas of a "picturesque" or romantic consciousness. As she examines the prior stages of man's "world of Circumstances," Asia describes four separate settings, but the first is so abstract as to deny both person and place: "There was the Heaven and Earth at first / And Light and Love;—" (2.4.32–34). As in the preceding scenes, place and power seem two pairs that her syntax lacks energy to couple more fully. As a result, there is no real explanation of the origins of the next stage, a Saturnian realm that seems at first glance paradisal: without time, "the earth's primal spirits beneath his sway" live "As the calm joy of flowers and living leaves / Before the wind or sun has withered them / And semi-vital worms." Yet, though their almost Edenic garden is full of "calm joy," they lack both light and love: "he refused / The birthright of their being, knowledge, power, / The skill which wields the elements, the thought / Which pierces this dim Universe like light, / Self-empire and the majesty of love." They do not lack all energy, however, because they recognize the lack of these, "for thirst of which they fainted"; that thirst establishes their birthright. Prometheus's first gift to man, then, is that freedom of consciousness; but Jupiter's administration of the gift leads to a third, "fallen" stage in Asia's chronicle.

Ignoring the politics of Prometheus's alliance with Jupiter, Shelley focuses upon its humanitarian intentions: Prometheus "gave wisdom, which is strength, to Jupiter, / And with this law alone: 'Let man be free,' / Clothed him with the dominion of wide Heaven." This gift, however, seems flawed because Prometheus, not Shelley, has ignored the politics of power; or, we might say, he has ignored or has not yet learned the meaning of "freedom" as it applies to Jupiter and to humanity. Like Milton's Adam and Eve, Prometheus, Jupiter, and humanity all learn that they are "free to fall." In Shelley's or more precisely Asia's version of this myth, however, there seems no alternative for growth within the garden. In its dramatic position and its thematic function, her speech fuses Raphael's and Adam's inner narratives of universal and human origin in *Paradise Lost*, but she offers no diagram of body working up to spirit. Described as "earth's primal spirits" in line 35, the human race becomes those spirits with Prometheus's injunction for their freedom in line 45:

"man" seems defined, then, by the ideal of his own freedom, but the shift from spirit to man also points toward the "fallen" world they inhabit under Jupiter's rule, ". . . ruining the lair wherein they raged" (2.4.58).

According to Asia's narrative, the fallen landscape is caused not by any human action but by Jupiter's abuse of power. Because he is too free, knowing "nor faith nor love nor law," and yet exercising his omnipotence, he causes "famine," "toil," "disease," extreme seasons, and the psychological conflicts among people that make this now alien setting even more painful: "Strife, wounds . . . fierce wants . . . And mad disquietudes, and shadows idle / Of unreal good, which levied mutual war." Both external conditions and internal resistance and frustration lead to "ghastly death unseen before." As Mildred McGill points out, in act 1 Earth gives a somewhat different version of the origins of this "fallen" nature. Earth suggests, though not with total clarity, that Prometheus's curse either caused it or made it far worse; and the curse itself asks for just such a completion of evil.[64] Both Earth's remembering and the phantasm's repetition of the curse refer to a time after Prometheus's second, and direct, gift giving to humanity—the "alleviations of his state" under Jupiter, the arts of culture. Nowhere in the first act does anyone suggest the Saturnian realm we see in Asia's speech, so the question of Jupiter's original responsibility does not arise at that point. It is as if, almost like those "primal spirits" under Saturn, Prometheus and Earth had only a limited consciousness either of past or of future time.

Yet, though Asia assumes Jupiter's responsibility for this world when she first describes it, by the end of her speech—at line 100—she seems dissatisfied with that hypothesis. Her dissatisfaction apparently rises out of the third of her settings for human existence, a partially renovated and civilized Eden built out of Prometheus's second and more humanly fortunate gift giving. That description may lead her, as it leads the reader, to recognize that the "fall" apparent in Jupiter's reign is in fact a developing recognition of the consciousness denied in the vegetative Saturnian garden. Human beings become free, then, only by seeing before and after—and recognizing the significance of their own choices within biological limits. The fall that apparently subjects them to Jupiter subjects them only to those biological limits that may have existed all along unrecognized, as Asia's dialogue with Demogorgon from line 105 on seems to indicate. This is not to deny Jupiter's guilt entirely, for he too seems to believe in his omnipotence over the natural world and, in his insistence upon being worshiped as omnipotent, apparently has forced this belief upon humanity. As a character, he is as "real" as Prometheus and Asia are; but as cosmic power, he is only an administrator and an exploiter of Prometheus's ambiguous first gift: a mental freedom that leads to a sudden sense of physical powerlessness and an awareness of mortality. For Shelley, the tree of knowledge and that of conscious life are the same, but eating of that tree leads also to a consciousness of mortality. Human immortality exists only in the past, in the ignorance of death.[65]

This fall is in some sense fortunate, then, even though it reveals human vulnerability to random fortune. Even in the interpretation of the fall that Michael offers to Milton's Adam we may see it as fortunate, for without that burst of terrifying awareness humanity would not have had the secondary gifts of hopes, technology, and arts that make human culture an image of partial control over fortune. As in Shelley's Italian letters, nature and art are harmonious: "Cities then / Were built, and through their snow-like columns flowed / The warm winds, and the azure aether shone, / And the blue sea and shadowy hills were seen" (2.4.94–97). Instead of a Blakean Eden of art, however, or a new Jerusalem built in a green and pleasant land, this apparently perfect human civilization contains a restlessness of spirit that is not creative "mental warfare" but self-destructive conflict. Because the artifices of culture still remain within the world of natural process, not in a fully imaginative realm, time is suspended only momentarily amid these "snow-like columns."

It is the recognition of time, however, that leads to the downfall of Jupiter, because the recognition that "Fate, Time, Occasion, Chance, and Change" are ultimate conditions places them beyond Jupiter as well. Through this acknowledgment of the power of temporal process can come the "destined hour." And through this acknowledgment also can come a return to the visual, as Asia's "beholding" the shape of the destined hour, and our beholding the transformation of Asia and the universe together, make clear. What is not clear is why these impersonal and cosmic forces should exist independent of all human accessibility.[66]

Demogorgon denies both visual and auditory access to truth: "If the Abysm / Could vomit forth its secrets:—but a voice / Is wanting, the deep truth is imageless" (2.4.114–16). Through its denial of sight and its forced reliance on voice and temporal sequence, his own dark abysm has led Asia first to the chronology of places—gardens, ruined lairs, and idyllic, if still flawed, temples—and then, through Demogorgon's minimal answers, to the ironic interdependence of temporal process and freedom of human consciousness. By explaining not only that the "deep truth is imageless," a declaration that would assert his own dark power as supreme, but also that "a voice is wanting,"[67] Demogorgon implies that secrets which would explain why process, change, and mortality exist are unavailable to his voice as well. He offers the evidence of these forces' existence simply as phenomenal fact, evident to both major senses: "For what would it avail to bid thee gaze / On the revolving world? What to bid speak / Fate, Time, Occasion, Chance, and Change?" (2.117–19). In one sense, his lines bury the argument from design in the processes and accidents of the natural world. Gazing or listening will yield immediate causes or repeated patterns but no ultimate cause: neither sense has advantage here.

By refusing the role of ultimate cause, he prevents our reading the symbolic landscapes of the play as a simple inversion from the Miltonic heights of an omnipotent sky-god to the depths of a Demogorgon seen as an early Blakean Satan, in all the fiery energy of *The Marriage of Heaven and Hell*. For, he begins, "Fate, Time, Occasion, Chance, and Change. . . . To these / All things are subject." Yet though he still uses the language of master and slave, ruler and subject, which has dominated the play thus far,[68] his completed statement—"To these / All things are subject but eternal Love"—suggests an alternative relationship. In a note to *Shelley's Poetry and Prose*, Reiman and Powers suggest that "Demogorgon makes sense only if we read Shelley's use of the term 'Love' here as Eros or Desire; the *desire* for good eternally outlasts all the evils of mortality."[69] One merit of this emphasis upon desire is that it converts humanity's restless striving into a Faustian virtue. Yet if that striving desire is not to become a continued restless torture for the possessor who, like Prometheus in act 1 and those Asia describes in lines 100–105 of this scene, sees the gap between desire and accomplishment, we must interpret Demogorgon's "Love" differently. Instead of a Platonic Eros reaching toward a transcendent good that it lacks, it seems a Coleridgean love making possible, as in the Dejection Ode, a reconciling imagination—or, as in Shelley's fragment "On Love" and in his later *Defence*, an imagination that makes love possible.[70]

Like Coleridge's imagination, this reconciling imaginative love not only unites individuals with one another but also allows the mind to unite disparate phenomena or perceptions into a unified whole. That whole may be an epistemological one, a significant view of the universe, or an artistic expression of that view. Although Demogorgon's "Mighty Darkness / Filling the seat of Power" at first suggests a sculptural center to the scene, as in *The Fall of Hyperion*, in fact its empty throne denies such shape and all other visual context as well. In this way the scene continues the alternation of sight and musical impulse that has stimulated Asia's quest and yet made the evidence of her senses seem disharmonious and difficult to reconcile with one another. Yet because this scene lies beyond "the cloudy strife / Of Death and of Life," beyond "the veil and the bar / Of things which seem and are" (2.3.57–60), it is an appropriate place in which to create such unity out of strife. Demogorgon's acknowledgment of the limits of natural perception, sound as well as sight, redeems them from the absolutism of an epistemological tyranny of the senses over the emotions.

The contrast between the tragically arrested process of *The Fall*, even if partially redeemed by the narrator's recognition of shared dream, and the released energy of this play, a Promethean imagining come true, clarifies further how Shelley supplements Schlegel's romantic or picturesque consciousness of contraries with Coleridge's reconciling imagination. Although the two are of course similar in their reconciliation of contraries, Schlegel's picturesque consciousness is optimistic more in its heroic envisaging of circumstances than in its ability to transform them, and more in its claim that such a view is an advance over the ancients' claim to dominate those powers than in that evisaging itself. His claim, echoed by Hazlitt, that it is the romantic or picturesque consciousness which perceives the infinite, uncontrollable nature of space and time, has stronger affinities with his portrait of Prometheus's stoicism in defying a mysterious and alien universe than does his claim for the Greeks' joyous control over nature. To use Demogorgon's phrasing, he thus emphasizes the perceiving mind's inability to eliminate "Time, Occasion, Chance, and Change," accepting their vast, mysterious, yet patterned powers as the context for the mind's heroism in "to envisage circumstance" and make these powers coherent. If Demogorgon describes how unavailing is any appeal to those anonymous forces for human sympathy, however, he only partially represents the mysterious sources of a "Nature's law" of which Oceanus speaks and against which Hyperion strives in Keats's first fragment.[71] As the end of his answer to Asia suggests, he also speaks for and seems to dramatize a more Coleridgean and optimistic imaginative consciousness that reconciles and even creates its world, though in a more limited way than do Blake's characters. We might speculate that he represents a mythic and cosmic version of Coleridge's primary imagination, enacting a skeptical confrontation of mind—that is, all human minds—with natural effects and even with some speculative, conjectural cause, while remaining invisible as object to the mind's consciousness.[72] Enlarging the perceiver's construction of the universe, Demogorgon includes both the human awareness of natural process as a kind of immutable mutability, as Wasserman suggests, and the human imaginative power to build this recognition, too, into a larger harmony.

Once Asia recognizes that she has asked her question before and that "my heart gave / The response thou hast given," she becomes the radiant force of love that will establish imaginative relationship not only between persons but also between the perceiving mind and landscape. Thus love replaces the Furies' futile alternation of conflicting emotions and attitudes.

As a transfigured, Venus-like figure, she mediates among all of the opposing figures and forces drawn into harmonious relationship, and in her restored relationship with Prometheus she also becomes one of the contraries so reconciled. In contrast to Blake's redemptive and sculpting touch, however, this feeling—love—that comes in aid of Demogorgon's refusal of both sight and sound is more emotional than physical because it must accept, as Blake's sculptors do not, the unavailing strength of "Fate, Time, Occasion, Chance, and Change" over everything but that love.

As the final scene in act 2 moves from the darkness and depth of scene 4 to a mountaintop and to light, the focus turns toward Asia. Instead of reading the visible landscape, Panthea and the spirit must interpret her. As the "veil" hiding her radiance falls or turns translucent (2.5.18–20, 54–55), both the static, torturing "emblem" of the crucified Christ and the static sculptural figure of Prometheus are replaced by this source of energy emanating from figure out toward landscape: "Child of Light! Thy limbs are burning / Though the vest which seems to hide them." Because the spirit who sings this interpretation of vision is unseen, the scene repeats in itself the act's larger pattern of turning from sight to music. Yet its music and Asia's concluding lyric, which makes landscape visible from musical impulse, tie together the two senses and their ways of knowing—rational and intuitive, spatially organizing and temporally accepting. Asia's song, finally, provides a new alternative to her earlier myth of origins and to its flawed Saturnian paradise: "through Elysian garden islets / . . . The boat of my desire is guided— / Realms where the air we breathe is Love / Which in the winds and on the waves doth move, / Harmonizing this Earth with what we feel above." As the journey passes age, manhood, and youth, even "Beyond the glassy gulphs . . . / Of shadow-peopled Infancy," it can recreate the past as a paradisal image for the future: they will pass "Through Death and Birth to a diviner day."

Recreating time and place, her song acts as a model for the "Promethean" world of achieved imagination in the third and fourth acts.

A Cosmic Dance of Contraries

In its paradisal renewal, act 4 of *Prometheus Unbound* continues Shelley's exultant but cautious balance between Schlegel's dialectic that envisages circumstances and Coleridge's more optimistic one that would transform those circumstances. As the Spirits of Earth and Moon celebrate the union of Prometheus and Asia by demonstrating its effects on the universe, the broad structural pattern of the act increasingly reflects that harmonious reconciliation of opposites. Two major changes in dramatic focus, both

revision of landscape, illustrate Schlegel's metaphysical picturesque moti-
vated by Coleridgean love. In the more radical of these, the constitutive,
shaping power of that love appears in an almost Blakean conversion of
landscape to figure: the character Earth, a speaking but unshaped place in
the first three acts, is transformed at the end of act 3 and in act 4 to a
human shape. Nearly annihilating ordinary landscape in its radiance, the
Spirit of Earth joins a similarly apocalyptic Spirit of the Moon at the
center of the play's dramatic action. Shelley controls these radical transformations, however, by stationing the spirits in a natural landscape and a
temporal process only partially suspended. Even more immersed in the
natural setting, Prometheus and Asia move from the center of the stage to
their oracular cave in the background, nearly obscured with "the dark
linked ivy tangling wild" (3.3.136). There they represent in part the
human world become audience for the spirits' prophetic masque. Like
Prometheus and Asia, themselves free from mutability though set within
its "budding, blown or odour-faded blooms" (3.3.137), the masque points
beyond but does not abandon the natural world.

   Similarly, the transformation of Earth from speaking place to singing
figure is not quite a full metamorphosis into human form. Even though the
songs of the two spirits in act 4 celebrate universal regeneration through a
profoundly sexual energy of love, the relationship between figurative and
literal language in their lyrics is ambiguous. That resistance to a Blakean
transformation appears even more strongly, though still benevolently, in
the spatial and temporal stationing of these visions. Because the transformation of Earth from place to figure in act 4 develops out of her role in act
1, analysis of the background must precede any discussion of the new
figure, a Spirit of the Earth "Like to a child" (3.4.263), and its companion
spirit, the "winged infant" asleep in the crescent moon.

   From the beginning of the play, Shelley's dramatic presentation of
Earth is puzzling, and it becomes more so as she is replaced by the male
"Spirit of the Earth" who first appears in act 3, scene 4.[73] The first surprise
in her dramatic characterization is her apparent lack of development as an
anthropomorphic figure. Like Keats's Coelus she seems in acts 1 and 2
"but a voice," not a "shap'd and palpable" god; or, better, she is palpable
but only as the ground or soil, the literal earth, is palpable. Critics point to
Prometheus's early difficulties in understanding her mortal language; yet
it is also true that, even though he gradually develops a sense of what she
says, he cannot see the speaker as a separate figure. Although Shelley does
not list her among the *dramatis personae* for act 1, he does list her in act 3,
scene 3. The omission in the first act probably represents simply Shelley's
wish to emphasize Prometheus's solitude at the beginning of the play. For
in act 3, scene 3, even more explicitly than in act 1, she is as much place as

person. When Prometheus turns to address her—"And thou, O Mother Earth!"—the stage directions immediately preceding this line describe him as "[Kissing the ground]." She answers, "I hear—I feel— / Thy lips are on me, and their touch runs down / Even to the adamantine central gloom / Along these marble nerves—'tis life, 'tis joy" (3.3.84–87). Although (like Wordsworth's Lucy) she neither sees nor is seen, she can now feel. This is probably the most tactile imagery in the play, appropriate for her materiality.

Later in the same speech, a complex simile draws into focus the archetypal relationship between Earth as ground and Earth as mother. As she anticipates the new age to follow Prometheus's unbinding, she announces the end of her nurturing of despair and exults that even death will be painless; for "death shall be the last embrace of her / Who takes the life she gave, even as a mother / Folding her child, says, 'Leave me not again!' " (3.3.105–07). In a mixture of happiness and poignance, the simile suggests a secure reconciliation of human mother and child. Yet Earth, substituting herself for the mother, appropriates the child in death—as in another Lucy poem. Through this figure, we are reminded that she is not only Earth-mother, both womb and tomb, but also, in the mythic tradition, Prometheus's mother. Although Shelley handles this aspect of the myth very lightly and not very literally, it leads us to a further interpretation of Earth's role in act 1. A tone in the simile above, an overprotectiveness that approaches suffocation and death, points back toward Earth's conservative, fearful, and rigid attitudes in act 1. McGill aptly interprets Earth as "Memory" in this act.[74] For in act 1 the ghosts of imagination "underneath the grave" are no more alive or capable of action for her than those of the dead. As material earth, she is a passive and uncreative container.

Unlike McGill, however, I do not see Earth in act 3 as a passive hoarder—a Mnemosyne who mothers no muses. Instead, the scene she guides the Titans toward can be interpreted as symbolic of a new and more creative motherhood that points toward the triumphant images of children in act 4.[75] This creativity develops from an almost Oedipal characterization of Earth not only as surface but as a womblike cave, not destructive but creative. This characterization develops by a process of association, as Earth describes the Greek cave that has become a shrine for Prometheus and will now, she hopes, gain new significance with his actual presence. Topographically it is an aspect of Earth, and symbolically it begins to redefine her significance as a medium for nurturing the future out of the past.

Although Shelley's caves are recurrent images both in his writing and in his notebook sketches, their symbolic significance varies. Although closely related in their meaning, the cave Earth describes in act 3, scene 3, lines 124ff., should be distinguished not only from her earlier description of an almost Odyssean "world beneath the grave" but also from Demogorgon's oracular cave in act 2 and from Prometheus's more hypothetical description of a cave earlier in the same scene. In act 1 the ghosts of the "world beneath the grave" include imagination's images, but Earth at that point does not believe them capable of much except absorbing punishment. Nature is on the surface of the earth, and those images lurk shadowlike within it—except when they meet, eerily, in Zoroaster's emblematic garden. In act 2 Demogorgon's cave lies beyond "the strife" of the relationship between imagination and nature and thus is the presiding center for the mind's comprehension of each and of their relationship. Prometheus describes the cave he and Asia propose to inhabit as a sort of sacred recess in Eden, "a Cave / All overgrown with trailing odorous plants . . . a simple dwelling" (3.3.10ff.), where they will "make / Strange combinations out of common things / Like human babes in their brief innocence" (3.3.31–33). Although this making is physically located in the natural world, they themselves can "talk of time and change / As the world ebbs and flows, ourselves unchanged—" without experiencing that change as humans must, for "What can hide Man from Mutability?" Their creativity seems free of the world of natural process, a process Demogorgon describes as one face of the cosmic structure that the questing mind discovers by descending into his cave.

As Earth tells Prometheus of the specific cave she recommends, it unites the insights of those two earlier caves: human awareness of mutability with the human art and ritual to make its acceptance a part of the beauty of Promethean art. With the sculptured forms of its temple and its reflecting lake, the complex setting of this cave and its surroundings reconciles opposites—nature and art, depth and height, dark and light—as in Coleridge's "Kubla Khan."[76] Through the oracular vapor that has expressed Earth's anguish and now will express her happiness, through the rituals of the torch carriers who emulated Prometheus's light bringing, it is also the focus of a human culture that is continuous without enslaving its participants. This context or consciousness Prometheus and Asia must share, Earth seems to suggest, in order to be more than "babes." Though all too conscious of their own freedom from mutability, they cannot retreat into playing a prelapsarian Adam and Eve, roles all to close to the Saturnian realm from which Prometheus freed humanity. Prometheus's great paean to the arts as mediators of love must, in other words, accommodate the recognition of human mutability as a circumstantial grounding for the arts. Hence Earth's cave is less remote than the cave Prometheus first describes from the historical processes of the human world. Because this cave is Earth's own, moreover, it is also less remote from natural process: from her surface landscapes of mutability and materiality, Earth allows access through descent to the ultimate and unknowable nature of such process. Earth's cave, like Demogorgon's, suggests powers beyond the brightness of the conscious mind contemplating the beautiful; in contrast to Demogorgon's cave, however, hers seems to include a practical and existential accommodation to those powers in its arts.

At the end of her speech Earth must remind Asia, as she reminded Prometheus in act 1, that she speaks a mortal language which the Titans cannot fully understand. The humans whom they inspire, however, must also speak Earth's language even in their visions of transforming art.

Earth's function, then, already has changed greatly from the first act to this scene in the third. In one sense, she has learned to point beyond the realm of specific, individual, and mirroring memory—exact "own image," exact words of a curse—to broader patterns of biological limit, of cultural continuity, of human artistic effort, however flawed and distorted, and finally to the oracular possibilities that emerge from confronting these. In this sense of cultural continuity she resembles Keats's Moneta, his more profound reworking of Mnemosyne. In her total image of mortal process, however, she clearly does not resemble Moneta, for she can allow death as well as participate in it. In her formlessness, too, she lacks the tragic effect of Moneta's painfully immortal, painfully sculptural and yet "picturesque" face and figure. Yet through that cave, apparently even more formless than the surfaces of Earth's landscape, develops the regenerative, optimistic figure of the "Spirit of the Earth," the effect of Prometheus's and Asia's reconciliation in that cave.

This spirit is not explicitly the child of Earth, the character he replaces. In fact he explicitly, if playfully, calls Asia "mother." Asia is the mother of this child in the same way that Jupiter is the father of Demogorgon: each "parent" has triggered a series of events that leads to the timely arrival of this nonbiological and preexistent child. Her motherhood, however whimsically introduced, seems appropriate because this spirit manifests the animating power of love as energy; witness his teasing dialogue with Asia. His report of a journey to a "somewhat changed" earth and its cities shows that same energy on a wider scale.

Although this playful "spirit of Earth" can claim to be Asia's child because he shares her regenerating energy, she herself is to be distinguished from Earth's role as mythic mother of phenomenal natural process. Earth speaks of "The many children fair / Folded in my sustaining arms—all plants, / And creeping forms, and insects rainbow-winged / And birds and beasts and fish and human shapes" (3.3.90–93). Critics who have argued that Asia is a symbolic figure for the natural world must discount her attempts at nature worship and at "reading" the natural world in act 2 and above all Demogorgon's assertion of relentless mutability as dominant. Thus the delayed dawn and the resurgent spring at the end of act 2 represent Asia's recognition of a freedom from the intention of evil but not an assertion of her own control over natural process. Paradoxically, the sympathetic response of the natural world seems to celebrate a positive freedom from willed, anthropomorphic control of natural process. "The sun will rise not until noon.—Apollo / Is held in Heaven by wonder" (2.5.10–11).

Paradoxically, too, this situation resembles the demythologizing in Keats's first epic fragment, when Hyperion finds that he is not god enough of the sun to overcome natural process and bring about an early dawn. Asia's radiance substitutes for the suspended dawn in Shelley's poem in much the same way that Keats's Apollo substitutes an aesthetic perception or shaping for actual physical control over the universe. At least two crucial differences exist between these radiant figures, however. First, at this point Asia seems the means, almost the object, of such an aesthetic substitution, more than its perceiver. Prometheus addresses her in act 3, scene 3, as "light of life, / Shadow of beauty unbeheld"; and later in the same speech his more abstract analysis of human and Titanic imagination uses the apparent analogue of "the mind, arising bright / From the embrace of beauty." Second, Keats's Apollo yearns for knowledge and gains a tragic exultation, but his exultation is not love; the source of Asia's beauty, as act 2 has made clear, is her love. Thus Panthea's memory of Asia as a version of the Botticelli Venus properly emphasizes her radiance and not her material engendering of forms, so that beauty seems an objectified expression of the energy of love, and interdependent with it.[77] If she is a Venus genetrix, she engenders light. Through that manifestation of light and love, she mediates between Prometheus as foreseeing, conscious mind and the realm of process she has explored.

In act 4, the Spirit of Earth shows the parentage it has laughingly claimed in Asia's radiant love by appearing in the human shape of a child. Surrounded by the energy of that radiance, he seems to dissolve the surrounding landscape, grinding not only the brook but the entire setting "into an azure mist / Of elemental sublety" (4.254–55). His transformation of Earth from landscape into a humanizing, loving control over the physical universe appears further in the dancelike, even masquelike, choruses of this spirit with the similarly childlike Spirit of the Moon. Projecting themselves into their future development as male and female sexual beings, Earth- and Moon-Spirits act out a new wedding masque for Prometheus and Asia which suggests that their Titanic renewal extends beyond human society to natural landscape and cosmic configuration. Their reconciliation of sexual opposites, present now in Prometheus and Asia and prophetic for these children as symbolic of the larger universe, is a triumphant Coleridgean example of romantic imagination, the metaphysical picturesque in its happiest mode. Like Coleridge's "new heaven and new earth" in the Dejection Ode, they "Emblem . . . Heaven and Earth united now": new Moon and new Earth celebrate the wedding of their renewed nature—and its landscapes—to the human mind.

The literary origins of their chariots further support the reconciliation of the opposites of mind and nature. In the Dejection Ode, Coleridge converts the sight of the new moon with the old moon in its arc, an omen of foul weather, into an omen of a natural storm that parallels and participates in the renewal of the speaker's imaginative gifts. Here Shelley converts the moon's "chariot like that thinnest boat / In which the Mother of the Months is borne" (4.206–07) into an omen of natural readiness for renewal. The second chariot, as it resembles Ezekiel's "chariot of paternal Deity," suggests that the Earth-Spirit already has absorbed landscape into creative spirit and will extend that energy, as their lyrics attest, to the moon.[78]

In the children's shapes at the center of these chariots, then, and in the reconciled contraries of their celebratory songs, Shelley integrates a new version of sculptural form with a version of the metaphysical picturesque. These sculptural forms extend themselves into dissolving radiance, like Prometheus's form at the beginning of act 2 and Asia's at the end of that act; and they extend beyond rigid limits of self because they resemble children and have a child's capacity for change.[79] They do not absorb all surroundings into human form, however; Shelley qualifies this Coleridgean, almost Blakean metaphysical picturesque with a persistent, residual version of Schlegel's or Keats's picturesque. He stations its optimism within larger perspectives of space and time that resist any final human control but the artistic recognition of their power.

The spatial elements in this resistance include both the dramatic stage setting, "two openings in the forest" that merge into a larger clearing before the cave of Asia and Prometheus, and the settings upon the spheres of Earth and Moon as astronomical bodies. Although both of these spatial settings are almost Edenic, the first also stations its visions in lush organic enclosures that recall not only the nature-bound landscapes of Keats's "Hymn to Pan" in *Endymion* but also the limiting frames of *The Fall of Hyperion*:

> . . . see, where through two openings in the forest
> Which hanging branches overcanopy,

And where two runnels of a rivulet
Between the close moss violet-inwoven
Have made their path of melody . . .

.   .   .   .

Two visions of strange radiance float upon
The Ocean-like inchantment of strong sound.

(4.194–98, 202–03)

The final stationing of Panthea's description, of course, dissolves this Keatsian solidity; for Shelley modulates from music as simile to music as actual, literal medium for these chariots. With this "path of melody," he reinforces the harmonic metaphor, which also becomes increasingly literal as the vision continues. Its visual correlative is the Earth-Spirit's "multitudinous Orb,"

A sphere, which is as many thousand spheres,
Solid as chrystal, yet through all its mass
Flow, as through empty space, music and light:
Ten thousand orbs involving and involved,

.   .   .   .

Sphere within sphere. . . .

.   .   .   .

Yet each intertranspicuous, and they whirl
Over each other with a thousand motions
Upon a thousand sightless axles spinning.

(4.238–41, 243, 246–48)

Yet this magnificent microcosm of a universe, this visual representation of the traditional crystal spheres that chime in a harmony perceived by the unfallen, has emerged from this world's "forest" and is framed within that setting, as if to suggest that we must see this renewed and harmonious universe in the context of some natural limitations.

Like this one, the second scenic limit upon a Blakean humanization of the natural world also exists in enormous tension with the most exultant of transforming moments. Although Panthea and Ione see these spirits as children in their cool but fiery chariots, the spirits describe themselves not only as sexual adult humans but as global landscapes. The metaphor is traditional enough, but Shelley's balance is so careful that we cannot distinguish between tenor and vehicle. The Moon first addresses Earth as "Calm wanderer [or planet], / Happy globe of land and air" (4.325–26), and speaks of the transformation of its own "lifeless mountains" and "solid Oceans" into energy and vegetation, so that "living shapes upon my bosom move . . . 'Tis Love, all Love!" (4.356–57, 365, 369). In spite of the fact that the Moon addresses him as "brother," Earth continues the imagery of a maternal landscape that the earlier, unshaped character Earth had used: "the caverns of my hollow mountains, / My cloven fire-crags, sound-exulting fountains" (4.332–33). In a longer chorus, he declares that Love "interpenetrates my granite mass, / Through tangled roots and trodden clay doth pass / Into the utmost leaves and delicatest flowers" (4.370–72). Finally, the Moon's dancelike tetrameter chorus emphasizes again the more distanced, astronomical perspective: "Thou art speeding round the Sun, / Brightest World of many a one, / Green and azure sphere" (4.457–59). In a delicate displacement, the human lovers are sometimes figurative descriptions of astronomical bodies: "As in the soft and sweet eclipse / When soul meets soul on lovers' lips . . . So when thy shadow falls on me / Then I am mute and still,—by thee / Covered; of thy love, Orb most beautiful, / Full, oh, too full!" (4.450–51, 453–56). Even when apparently literal, the human sexual images remain fully consistent with the astronomical images:

> I, thy chrystal paramour,
> .   .   .   .
> I, a most enamoured maiden
> .   .   .   .
> Maniac-like around thee move,
> Gazing, an insatiate bride,
> On thy form from every side.
>
> (4.463, 467, 470–72)

These cosmic landscapes not only remain the context for measuring the regenerative changes brought about by Prometheus's release, but they also remind the audience that like itself these singers are stationed within a still mutable natural world and are also, themselves, such mutable worlds. The qualification upon apocalypse is delicate, but it is present.[80]

Another qualification, a temporal one, also finds support in the distinction between Panthea's and Ione's description of these spirits and their own self-description, but it begins with a distinction earlier in the act. The procession of dead hours who "bear Time to his tomb in eternity," a kind of antimasque at the beginning of the act, signals a radical change from the revolution completed at the end of act 3, which was individual and political but not biological. The "spirits from the human mind" continue a triumphant and apparently complete transcending of biological limits. Announcing that they come "From the temples high / Of man's ear and eye / Roofed over Sculpture and Poesy," they plan to build a real projection of the "human love . . . / Which makes all it gazes on, Paradise":

> We'll pass the Eyes
> Of the starry skies
> Into the hoar Deep to colonize;
>   Death, Chaos, and Night,
>   From the sound of our flight
> Shall flee, like mist from a Tempest's might.
>
> And Earth, Air and Light
> And the Spirit of Might
> Which drives round the stars in their fiery flight;
>   And Love, Thought, and Breath,
>   The powers that quell Death,
> Wherever we soar shall assemble beneath!
>
>   (4.141–52)

Thematically, this reformation is as radical as anything in Blake; all of the personified forces of mutability become subordinate to the now combined forces of an energetic human art based in "the temples high / Of man's ear and eye" and "the Spirit of Might." These forces, finally, are no longer at odds, as they were in the Furies' oxymoronic speech. When this chorus of spirits merges with a new chorus of hours and then divides into semi-choruses, however, it defines two realms for the operation of time. The first semichorus is more radical: "We, beyond Heaven, are drive along— . . . Ceaseless and rapid and fierce and free / With the spirits which build a new earth and sea" (4.161, 163–64); and in an acceleration, not a dissolution or suspension of time, these spirits build an apocalyptic new heaven and new earth. The second semichorus, on the other hand, is less radical as it suggests a temporal process not unlike the unredeemed present, except in mood. "Us, the inchantments of Earth retain—. . . Solemn and slow and serene and bright / Leading the Day and outspeed-ing the Night / With the Powers of a world of perfect light—. . . We encircle the Oceans and Mountains of Earth / And the happy forms of its death and birth / Change to the music of our sweet mirth" (4.162, 166–68, 172–74). In this world, neither death nor change is annihilated, but both are made "happy forms," musically orchestrated by those ordering but not apocalyptic hours.

Reinforcing this double perspective upon millenial time is the striking distinction already noted between the childlike appearance of the Earth- and Moon-Spirits to the Oceanides, and their adult songs. In a passage pencilled into his fair-copy version of act 3 (Bodleian Ms. Sh. e. 3), Shelley added the brief, teasing interlude between Asia and the Spirit of the Earth, just after that puckish spirit has reported on his visit to Earth, and before the Spirit of the Hour adds its eloquent final description of

Earth's transformation. In this moment of comic relief Asia claims that the Earth-Spirit will remain with her until the "frozen and inconstant moon" will thaw "And love thee"—a piece of hyperbole that, one suspects, is almost the equivalent of "till hell freezes over." In fact Asia's time scheme is less extreme. As the spirit asks, "What, as Asia loves Prometheus?" she answers, "thou art yet not old enough." The appearance of brother and sister as shining children in act 4 confirms Asia's estimate of their ages; but their lyrical dialogue reaches beyond their age in a visionary rebellion against maternal solicitude that is also a fulfillment of desire: the once "frozen moon" celebrates the thawing of its oceans. In their lyrics, the two places and two forces that Asia described in act 2 as existing originally— Heaven and Earth, Light and Love—now work harmoniously together.

Puzzlingly however, those Ezekiel-like chariots that Panthea and Ione describe seem more extreme in their transformation of natural time and place than are the spirits' own self-descriptions of rebirth. In one perspective these children sing prophetic songs of their maturity to come; in another, their present childlike appearances, like Asia's return "through Death and Birth to a diviner day," symbolize a more radical potentiality for change than do their adult songs of regeneration. Those appearances correspond to the chorus of spirits from the human mind earlier in the act who claim triumphantly that "Death, Chaos and Night, / From the sound of our flight / Shall flee, like mist from a Tempest's might" (4.144–46). Like the first semichorus of those spirits, they seem to reach out "beyond Heaven" to "build a new earth and sea" (4.161–64). Their adult songs, working their transformations within the bounds of an existing nature and the patterns of its mutability, seem to correspond to the less radical changes planned by the second semichorus. This paradox can best be resolved by interpreting the sight of these children and their chariots as an imaginative vision, even as imagination in process. Such imaginative vision at its most radical can act as a purgation that prepares for the somewhat less radical, more naturalized transformations of which the spirits sing, just as the Earth-Spirit's visionary archaeology described by Panthea in lines 270–318 reveals a total fluidity in the development and collapse of earlier civilizations and thus makes possible a new, imaginative culture. In this sight of the spirits, imagination is freed from temporal process. In the spirits' Orphic songs, preceded by that sense of possibility, time is accepted: their spoken or sung redemptive vision embraces and reforms—without eliminating—biological limits. Though "Man['s] . . . nature is its own divine controul," though he works at "Compelling the elements with adamantine stress," this humanizing order is still one of imposing pattern over an "unquiet Republic" of elements that, like the planets, are "struggling fierce toward Heaven's free wilderness" (4.394ff.).

And though "Labour and Pain and Grief in life's green grove / Sport like tame beasts—none knew how gentle they could be," the implication is that they still exist, though less poisonously destructive of humanity's sense of self-worth than before. Time, Occasion, Chance, and Change still exist—but not as a Fate that opposes. The "green grove" of this new paradise, then, still must depend upon the communication of love through imagination and upon the moral virtues Demogorgon cites in his final speech: "Gentleness, Virtue, Wisdom, and Endurance." So a visionary near-apocalypse is made a mode of vision, a rehearsal for the integration of imagination and natural process.

Because of his mediation between natural process and imagination in act 2, it is not surprising that Demogorgon should speak to conclude both the millenial masque and the play as a whole. Here, as in act 2, his oracular voice also mediates between that indifferent process, so delicately shown in the renovated "green grove" of the Earth-Spirit's song, and Asia's imaginative recognition of the heart's power, a recognition that has transformed society. Demogorgon's own appeal to the heart's power now can be more explicit than in his dialogue with Asia precisely because she has made that earlier discovery. If his emotional involvement in this speech seems to risk violating the natural indifference that he communicated to the Titans and to us in act 2, it nevertheless is balanced by his prophetic warning: humanity's misdirection or loss of emotional intensity will bring about a social and political counter-revolution. In the eternally continuing "acts and hours" of future time, a newly "disentangled Doom" again might build natural and political tyranny into an idol for worship. Demogorgon also mediates, then, between the magnificent hopes for natural transformation in act 4 and the no less magnificent, but less visionary, hopes for social transformation in act 3.

Thus, after invoking all the forces that act in the cosmos, including "Man," Demogorgon draws upon the landscapes of a sublime natural world to describe the self's struggle to maintain and to extend its victory. To express this struggle, his rhetoric first defines traditional Christian topography for the triumph of absolute good over absolute evil, and, second, it delineates figures on the narrow verge between mental act and personification. In the first two of these three declamatory, yet lyrical, stanzas, the triumphant images from I Corinthians 15 and from Revelation make Prometheus's victory over Jupiter analogous to Christ's resurrection and his final triumph over Satan, without making either victory a less real figure for the other. "Despotism," "Conquest," "Destruction's strength," "serpent," and "disentangled Doom," all names or images for the biblical Satan or for the Shelleyan Jupiter, are consigned to a hellish depth—"the void Abysm," "the Deep," "the pit"—by a victor seemingly intent on punishing external, absolute evil. As if to avoid falling into that abyss, Love has been perched giddily on the "slippery, steep, and narrow verge" of a crag. Moreover, Demogorgon's prophetic warning of the serpent's emergence from the pit describes its attack upon the female Eternity as a rape like the one implicitly suggested in Blake's *Paradise Lost* illustration of Eve's fall.

Yet the serpent, at first reading so powerfully negative, is also powerfully positive. Even without alluding to Blake's mythic figure of Orc as phallic revolutionary, we should recall the "snake-like Doom" coiled beneath Demogorgon's throne in act 2, scene 3, and released through Asia's quest. In act 2 and in act 4 the coiled serpent represents the potential for revolutionary social change, but because acts 2 and 3 have presented a change toward liberty, any new uncoiling would lead toward tyranny. To read Demogorgon's rhetoric of triumph as absolute, then, is to forget a liberating and yet dangerous ambiguity in his images. This serpent can work for either party.

In another transforming rhetorical pattern, Demogorgon internalizes both landscape and figure to show the individual responsibility for such revolutionary change. Although Love is stationed precariously on a "narrow verge," that cliff is not the outward Caucasus of Prometheus's suffering but a "crag-like Agony" that is also an "awful throne of patient power / In the wise heart" (4.557–60). Here myth changes to an allegorical personification of our own possible strengths. In the same way, the mythic Jupiter is not named; instead, our own weakness which constituted that figure—despotism and conquest—must be conquered. Because of this internalization even "the void Abysm" or "the pit" are more than negative prisons for evil and thus metonymically evil themselves. They also house the oracular and generative powers of Demogorgon's "void Abysm" in act 2. Though mouths that "yawn" to swallow the tyrant, like medieval hell-mouths, they are also images for the creative cave from which the "Earth-born" Prometheus utters his "spell" of redeeming, imaginative love. In Corinthians, Death is swallowed up in victory, absorbed and annihilated; in Demogorgon's speech, tyranny is recognized as internal and endemic to the self; but out of the self may issue "spells by which to reassume / An empire o'er the disentangled Doom" (4.568–69).

As Demogorgon recites these spells, his last stanza turns from the cosmic topography with which he began. Instead, he tells us the words that can act as "seals" against a new uncoiling of tyranny from within ourselves and from within society. In his rhetoric, these words for psychological qualities balance between personification and act. More abstract and less dramatized than the mysterious "shapes" and "forms" earlier in the play, they mediate between that dramatic representation and the "operations of the human mind" that both Demorgorgon's audience and Shelley's must go on to perform. As Donald Reiman and Sharon Powers point out, the dominant rhetorical device in the final stanza is the "timeless" infinitive.[81] Yet both Power and Hope are personified; and in the final line of the play, a ninth-line alexandrine added to the eight-line pentameter stanza, the substantive nouns return. If sustained, this almost infinite struggle can itself create "Life, Joy, Empire, and Victory."

Demogorgon's word "Hope" epitomizes this process and in doing so also points toward a further, final reason for his speaking here. In the first line of this stanza (4.570), Hope is personified enough to have a range of emotions, including a self-contradictory despair: "To suffer woes which Hope thinks infinite." In the fourth and fifth lines, however, the infinitive verbal action of hoping transforms this minimally visualized figure, if we may call it even that, into a Promethean creator, a visionary sculptor working from the fragments of its own self-image: "To love, and bear; to hope, till Hope creates / From its own wreck the thing it contemplates." Although the sculptural metaphor is subdued, these lines recall both Asia's description of human creativity in act 2, scene 4, and that of Prometheus in act 3, scene 3, lines 49–63. When Asia questions Demogorgon, she describes how human hands "first mimicked and then mocked . . . the human form," the beauty of the sculpture leading only to restless dissatisfaction with humanity's actual lot: what evil, she asks, "while Man looks on his creation like a God, / And sees that it is glorious, drives him on, / The wreck of his own will?" An act later Prometheus answers with jubilant optimism that if artistic forms express harmonious love, they can lessen or even overcome that ironic gap between envisioned or sculpted ideal and human experience. Demogorgon's Hope, creating the aesthetic object from its own destroyed desires, is a somewhat more somber mediator between these ironic and idealistic views. It also offers a model for our reading of the play as the "thing" Hope "contemplates," as a "beautiful idealism," yet one grounded in a world that repeatedly threatens to turn it to wreckage.

Finally, interpreting this personification as a sculptor points toward Demogorgon's stage presence as a concluding metaphor for the ambiguity of sculptural form in the play. Panthea speaks in line 510 of a "mighty Power which is as Darkness." Although she seems to hear a voice, she and Panthea can station neither voice nor figure precisely in their landscapes: that unseen Power "Is rising out o' Earth and from the sky / Is showered like Night, and from within the air / Bursts, like eclipse" (4.511–13). A force immanent and yet triumphing "like eclipse" over a visually realized natural setting, Demogorgon recalls by contrast the more limited situation of his human audience. Though working to redeem and humanize Earth's "green groves," they still are placed within the biological constraints of a natural "world of Circumstances." Demogorgon's freedom from these natural constraints seems a far goal for humanity as it frees itself from the sculptural form of the bound Prometheus, rigid with hatred. Although the "monstrous and barbaric shapes" worshiped as Jupiter and too closely emulated by Prometheus now are replaced by the Titans' radiant "glory" (4.576), even the emanative, energetic human forms shown in act 4 may become idols. Eclipse instead of glory, Demogorgon protects that glory by skeptically denying us a final image to worship. Yet with that warning, human creativity is finally affirmed. Demogorgon's liminal personification Hope, a sculptor so unshaped in his own rhetoric that figure scarcely emerges from concept, remains to affirm the "Empire, and Victory" possible to Shelley's mental forms. Like the poet, Hope is a stubborn sculptor for the mind's most vulnerable, tenuous, and yet necessary visions.

Six

Sculptural Figure and a "world of Circumstances"

In Keats's most dramatic example of stationing from *Paradise Lost*, Uriel's "eye pursu'd" Satan "down / The way he went" and then saw him "disfigur'd . . . on th' *Assyrian* mount." Yet in these romantic poems the perceiver is less serenely detached than Uriel from the Satanic figure poised before him. Again and again his spatial perception of the sculptural figure enclosed in natural landscape emphasizes the romantic observer's own ambiguous, existential station between the divine and the natural. Although Uriel's eye leads him to a clear moral judgment of Satan, its very clarity prevents him from seeing in himself either a longing to test the freedom he and Satan both have been given, or its abuse, a tendency toward absolutism. As Blake showed in the Bard's song, the Satan who rebels from his station is a part of Los and of Milton, both in his rebellion and in his impulse to mar that rebellion by establishing himself as a new god, a "disfigur'd" sculptural object of worship. Like Blake's Milton, Shelley's Prometheus confronting the phantasm of Jupiter also must learn to see both of these traits in himself. Though less guilty of this moral distance, Keats's witnesses still must struggle to share the emotions of the fallen figures they perceive, earning salvation for themselves as they do so.

Instead of moral detachment, Keats's characters suffer, as Uriel does, from an aesthetic detachment almost like the tyranny of the eye that so disturbed Wordsworth in the cult of the scenic picturesque. Although Uriel's detachment does not suspend moral judgment, it does suspend moral sympathy. Furthermore, his moral judgment seems based on the same aesthetic criterion that Coelus applies to Hyperion. Satan's disfiguring expressions of violent emotion Uriel judges inconsistent first with

Satan's heroic, sculptural figure and second with the serene harmony of inner and outer self that defines a "Spirit of happy sort" (6.128). Uriel's rejection of the "hateful siege / Of contraries" (9.121–22) in Satan's stance and expression also rejects a human complexity for himself. Thus although Uriel's eye has provided a model for the romantic consciousness in these poems, Milton's unfallen as much as his fallen angel is a model that demands revision—for it is the humanness of the perceiver, in its powers and its limits, that these poems have defined.

Although originating in Milton's descriptive moments or scenes, the perceiver's "envisaging" of the tension between godlike sculptural figure and its stationing becomes, we recall, a model for the larger dramatic and narrative patterns of these romantic poems. In their revisions of *Paradise Lost*, this critically evaluative stationing includes not only the spatial perspectives of landscape but the temporal perspectives of the perceiver's individual memory and his or her perception of historical and cultural eras. In Blake's poem, Milton comes to share Blake's perspective on *Paradise Lost* and its effects on recent history. He thus can contend with the distortions of imagination in his personal history and even in eras that have preceded him. Another sort of extended temporal consciousness develops from this model of "statuary" and its "stationing" as Keats and Shelley draw upon Schlegel's analogies of sculpturesque and picturesque eras in history to shape their Miltonic emulations. Because these analogues extend Milton's descriptive methods into metaphors describing conflicting eras of historical development, both Keats and Shelley can use these analogues to reinterpret the classical myth of a conflict between Titans and Olympians as a more exact parallel to their own problems and aims in emulating Milton. Like Blake, they evaluate each art, sculpture and painting, as analogue to define the powers and limits of their poetry. In addition, they also evaluate Schlegel's pattern of progressive historical development to challenge Milton's pattern of history as paradise, fall, and redemption. Their most obvious purpose is to define their own complex, self-conscious independence from their sculpturesque predecessor. Yet implicit in the close readings developed through the preceding chapters is a further purpose at work in these poems: to redeem Milton from that fallen and static sculptural mode.

In Chapter 1 I suggested that these poets identify Milton's poetry either with sculpture or painting, analyze the limitations of his poetry through the limitations of one of those two arts, and then reaffirm the worth of their own poetry through the worth of the other art. Criticizing Milton, by arguing that his poetic art is too close to a neoclassical and naturalistic painting, Blake's *Milton* shows the limits of such a pictorial perspective by a "stationing" that asserts the greater imaginative freedom of poetry and, even more powerfully, by a sculpture in which Milton reshapes Urizen, the deity of a rational, objective natural world. In broad terms, Keats's *Hyperion* poems and Shelley's *Prometheus Unbound* reverse Blake's evaluation of these analogues. Keats and to a lesser extent Shelley also reverse the position of Milton in Schlegel's pattern of historical development. Instead of belonging to the romantic and "picturesque" moderns, defined for Schlegel by the advent of Christianity, Milton now seems to become a classical, "sculpturesque" writer, remote from the exigencies of actual human experience in the natural world. In contrast, their own more intense awareness of natural and historical forces defined in dialectical contrast to an earlier, simpler, and less self-divided consciousness makes Keats's and Shelley's poems experiments in Schlegel's metaphysical picturesque. As we have seen, however, the poems then move beyond this apparent rejection: they begin to redeem Milton. Explicit in the discussion of Blake's *Milton*, this partial redemption has remained largely implicit in the Keats and Shelley chapters. A brief comparison and contrast of the way each poem defines the significance of sculpture and painting will draw out these implications.

The modern poet's redemption of Milton is clearest in Blake's illuminated book: there Blake allows Milton himself to become a modern poet and to save himself from his own past. Blake confronts that past in two ways: through his own provisional but then radically transformed stationing of figures in landscapes, and through Milton's remolding of a human form for Urizen out of red clay. The placing of figures upon a definite ground plane in Blake's illuminations to *Milton* reinforces the placing of figures within specific "local habitations" described in his poetic text. Yet this *ut pictura poesis* conjunction of Blake's arts is only temporary, for the recurrent "stationing" of feet in landscapes soon becomes a way to show how his poetry can depict a more radical transformation of the ordinary world of space and time than can his illuminations. In the verbal text's radical changes of scale, for example, Milton enters Blake's left foot, and Blake fastens on the entire vegetal world as a brilliant sandal, "to walk forward thro' Eternity." By thus evoking specific "stationings" of figure in landscape and then verbally transforming them, Blake purges Milton's poetry and his own of an unimaginative fidelity to literary pictorialism that accepts rational Newtonian—or Urizenic—space and time as absolute.

Milton also works out his own salvation by becoming a sculptor; his remolding of Urizen, who is both Old Testament deity and horizon of this world's landscapes, uses a material from landscape itself—red clay—to humanize this abstract and resistant form. Although Milton's redemption of Urizen and thus himself reshapes the external landscape into sculpted form, that form does not reject earthly corporeality for the transcendent, eternal realm of Winckelmann's serene marble forms. Urizen resists Milton's sculpting by turning the ground around him into marble, the symbol of a sculptural ideal that denies the vital corporeality of touch and of sexuality; Milton's new sculpture uses Adam's red clay to unify human corporeal existence and the "human form divine." Ultimately, Blake suggests in *Jerusalem*, the human form divine will transcend this sensual existence, absorbing its landscapes and its figures into the giant form of a risen Albion. But in *Milton* Blake urges the joyous acceptance of a subjectively and individually experienced corporeal world as the ground for such renovation. Appropriately, at the end of the poem Blake as witness stations the divine figures who complete Milton's salvation within his local "world of Circumstances," his cottage garden at Felpham.

In *Hyperion*, as shown in Chapter 3, the "world of Circumstances" is far more intransigeant. Early in the poem, Coelus suggests that the Titans once ruled the natural universe almost by virtue of their serene aesthetic detachment and "distinct" sculptural form. In his account of origins, Oceanus seems to confirm Coelus's judgment by claiming that the new order of Olympians succeeds to power through their superior aesthetic merit as beautiful sculptural objects. This Winckelmannian ideal, however, is challenged in two ways: first, by a more negative definition of the sculptural metaphor itself in contrast to a surrounding natural world; and second, by the inclusion of even an ideal sculptural analogue as the earlier stage of Schlegel's development toward a picturesque consciousness.

In the first of these challenges, the Titans who find themselves suddenly stationed "Deep in the shady sadness of a vale" appear as static sculptural objects trapped in their monumental passivity. Seemingly naturalized by their submission to the forces of mutability, they offer only a negative model for human response to the same forces. Although Oceanus urges the Titans to accept the "force / Of Nature's law," his recommendation that they "envisage circumstance" urges a new and picturesque sovereignty. Keats's descriptions of Apollo develop more fully the same "picturesque" consciousness as the basis of his Olympian power. Apollo learns to rule not as a natural deity but as a human poet whose consciousness orders and seeks to reconcile the oxymoronic contraries within the "gray legends, dire events, rebellions" he reads in Mnemosyne's face—legends and myths that include the Titans' experiences. Thus Oceanus's pattern of successively more beautiful sculptural deities ruling nature has developed into Schlegel's pattern of a single transformation from such a sculpturesque mode of experience into a picturesque one.

Yet because the Titans, too, begin to develop this more picturesque and romantic consciousness, and because it is their own fall they must confront in those "gray legends," now framed as much in the "wide hollows" of their own perceiving minds as in Apollo's, Keats tempers the force of Oceanus's natural law and finds a way to begin resolving his ambivalence toward *Paradise Lost*. His imitation of Miltonic epic in *Hyperion* created a stylistically magnificent but apparently static fragment that seemed on the one hand to mark his own failure in that imitative mode, but on the other to symbolize the sterility of such a sculptural mode for his own new era. Yet because he develops the Titans as well as Apollo into picturesque poets who acknowledge the confrontation of change as the source of their power, he suggests a partial regeneration of Milton rather like Blake's. In this regeneration, the "stationing" of sculptural figures in "worlds of Circumstances" plays a significant symbolic role.

In *The Fall of Hyperion*, Keats replaces Coelus's association of sculptural form with serene divinity over nature by the physical weight and stasis of sculpture as artifact. The statue of Saturn in the mysterious "domed monument" becomes all too apt a prefiguring for the vision of the Titans that Moneta shares with the narrator. In that vision, all divinity has become associated with their visual and palpably weighty sculptural appearance, but their voices reveal a humanness stripped both of divinity and of dignity: it is as if the cost of preserving an eternal art has drained them of any nobility in confronting the loss of their natural powers.

Yet although the changlessness of this scene is a terrifying burden for the narrator, its new place within a series of subjective dream visions, each scene organized pictorially and thematically around a sculpture or sculpturelike focus, ultimately makes the scene redemptive. Tutored by Moneta, the narrator learns to reject a rigid sculptural permanence in art while celebrating the more elemental impulse, in art and religion alike, to dream of timeless Saturnian paradises. These dreams become the material for the narrator's "telling" of Poesy, a telling that retains the dreams' sculpturesque harmony within a context that acknowledges the loss of such harmony in mortal process; Poesy thus becomes picturesque. Finally, in symbolizing the human cultural memory of all such dreams, not only of a remote Titanic art, Moneta gains a partial release, in the temporal art of poetry, from her own too permanent confrontation of endless but never completed loss.

Through their perceivers' picturesque awareness, then, ongoing time and its comprehension become redemptive instead of torturing. Praising those who come later in time, such as the narrator and his modern contemporaries, Keats also praises those who have recognized the oxymoronic tension between a universal, spontaneous paradisal dream and an art that becomes too rigid in its claims both for eternity and for its own uniqueness. Because Milton, like Moneta, sensed the first even as he succumbed to the second, Keats's portrayal of Moneta with eyes "vision-less entire . . . of all external things" might suggest, finally, a version of Milton himself, both tutor to the modern poet and redeemed by his new dialectic.

In *Prometheus Unbound*, Shelley also challenges sculpturesque analogues with picturesque ones: from the central sculptural figure of the bound Prometheus the play moves toward the regenerated landscapes of Earth- and Moon-Spirits, their contraries reconciled in a wedding masque for the Titans. Like Keats, Shelley challenges Milton by associating the earlier poet with an objective, sculpturesque art, but he identifies this sculptur-esque art only partially with the civilization of classical Greece. In acts 1 and 3 both Aeschylus and Milton offer models for tyrants worshiped as idols and for protagonists superb in their resistance to such tyrants yet bound by hatred. Thus they both share responsibility for the negative sculptural qualities of these two acts. Yet Shelley's development of the lyrical forms of Aeschylean drama in order to rival Milton's objective epic manifests the power of the classical Greek world to engender a liberating, imaginative subjectivity. This subjectivity, beginning in Aeschylus, can redeem the sculptural elements in the later Milton. For in these two acts sculpture is not simply condemned. Instead, it develops from external, rigid shape to a revelation of internal, imaginative form in radiant energy.

Milton's own more picturesque elements, however, complete this re-generation of a Greek freedom for the imagination. In acts 2 and 4 Shelley uses the vast perspectives of Milton's landscapes from *Paradise Lost* to define a new kind of picturesque stationing. He corrects the mind's persistent attempts to worship external nature by his lyric hypothesis of a nature humanized through an interdependent love and imagination. This alternation of sculptural drama and picturesque landscape journeys is itself, of course, a structure that demonstrates Schlegel's interfusion of contraries in the "metaphysical" picturesque. Supporting his Platonic and Coleridgean definition of an imaginative love that reconciles contraries, this structure draws both Aeschylus and Milton gracefully into his final celebration of a renewed Promethean world, their own rebel forms now made humane as well as heroic. Even if finally qualified by their more pessimistic Keatsian stationing in a world of "Time, Occasion, Chance, and Change," those Titanic figures from past eras now are transformed into "far goals" for mortal human aspiration.

Although in figurative terms each of these four poems originates in the margins of *Paradise Lost*, each also shapes its own independent, imagina-tive, and humanized form. Each begins by stationing an antagonistic aspect of Milton's imaginative vision at the center of its own critical but redemptive perspective. Like his Satan, "disfigur'd . . . on th' *Assyrian* mount," Milton's monumental and transcendent forms reveal their short-comings, tested in this world's landscapes and in the perception of witnesses who imagine a higher because freer humanity for such figures and for their author alike. That humanity may dominate and transform those natural landscapes through a redefined sculpture that builds a "human form divine," as in *Milton* and partially in act 4 of *Prometheus*, or it may recognize its biological limits stationed within a world of those circumstances, as in Keats's poems. Nevertheless it celebrates a rebellious but ultimately generous imaginative freedom. In *Paradise Lost*, Uriel's eye pursues Satan's descent in a foreshadowing of his final downfall. With very different intent, these poets and the witnesses within their poems pursue Milton's imagination to the utmost in order, finally, to redeem his vision. Extending its descriptive technique of "stationing or statuary" and developing the metaphors of sculpture and painting implicit within that technique, they release him and themselves from the "monstrous and barbaric shapes" of religious and imaginative tyranny.

Notes

Abbreviations

BNYPL   *Bulletin of the New York Public Library*
BS   *Blake Studies*
ELH   *English Literary History*
HLQ   *Huntington Library Quarterly*
JAAC   *Journal of Aesthetics and Art Criticism*
JEGP   *Journal of English and Germanic Philology*
JHI   *Journal of the History of Ideas*
K-SJ   *Keats-Shelley Journal*
MLA   Modern Language Association
MLR   *Modern Language Review*
MP   *Modern Philology*
PQ   *Philological Quarterly*
SiR   *Studies in Romanticism*

Chapter 1: "Bright appearances"

1. Citations from Milton in my text are to *John Milton, Complete Poems and Major Prose*, ed. Merritt Y. Hughes (New York: Odyssey, 1957). References are to books and lines.

2. See Louis L. Martz, *The Paradise Within* (New Haven: Yale University Press, 1964).

3. *The Poetical Works and Other Writings of John Keats*, ed. H. Buxton Forman, rev. Maurice Buxton Forman, 8 vols. (New York: Scribners, 1939), 5:303–04. Keats writes the actual note by the first of these phrases, from bk. 7, ll. 420–23. Douglas Bush, in *Mythology and the Romantic Tradition* (1937; rpt., New York:

197

Norton, 1963), p. 116, notes this "subtle lesson that Keats learns from Milton" and
quotes in n. 52 the passage cited above. My earlier discussion of this passage, in
Nancy M. Goslee, " 'Under a Cloud in Prospect': Keats, Milton, and Stationing,"
PQ 53 (1974): 205–19, appears in revised form in the second section of this chapter.

4. See Rachel Trickett, "The Augustan Pantheon: Mythology and Personification in Eighteenth-Century Poetry," *Essays and Studies*, n.s., 6 (1953): 81, and Jean
H. Hagstrum, *The Sister Arts: The Tradition of Literary Pictorialism and English Poetry
from Dryden to Gray* (Chicago: University of Chicago Press, 1958), pp. 147–48.

5. *The Poems of John Keats*, ed. Jack Stillinger (Cambridge, Mass.: Harvard
University Press, 1978). All subsequent citations to Keats's poetry are to this
edition and will be noted in the text; references are to book and line. See also
Walter Jackson Bate's discussion of this line in *John Keats* (1963; rpt., New York:
Oxford Galaxy, 1966), p. 243, and Nancy M. Goslee, "Phidian Lore: Sculpture
and Personification in Keats's Odes," *SiR* 21 (1982): 75.

6. See Mario Praz, *Mnemosyne: The Parallel Between Literature and the Visual
Arts*, A. W. Mellon Lectures, 1967 (Princeton: Princeton University Press, 1970),
p. 12, and John Dixon Hunt, *The Figure in the Landscape: Poetry, Painting, and
Gardening during the Eighteenth Century* (Baltimore: Johns Hopkins University
Press, 1976), pp. 20–21, and 60, where he quotes Pope's *Guardian* no. 173 satire on
Adam and Eve in topiary. For Milton's earlier use of traditional garden images, see
Roland Mushat Frye, *Milton's Imagery and the Visual Arts* (Princeton: Princeton
University Press, 1978), pp. 6, 218ff.

7. For charges of stasis, see Bush, *Mythology and the Romantic Tradition*, p. 119;
John D. Rosenberg, "Keats and Milton: The Paradox of Rejection," *K-SJ* 6 (1957):
87–97; Bate, *Keats*, pp. 404–05 (though he argues that Keats's main problem here is
how to deal with a stylistic massiveness); and *Shelley's "Prometheus Unbound": A
Variorum Edition*, ed. Lawrence John Zillman (Seattle: University of Washington
Press, 1959), pp. 48–49. For recent arguments that consider the romantics as more
successful in their epic emulation, yet develop neither Bloom's theory of influence
nor my theory of analogues from the other arts, see Northrop Frye, "The
Drunken Boat," in *Romanticism Reconsidered*, ed. Northrop Frye (1963; rpt., New
York: Columbia University Press, 1968), pp. 5–19; Karl Kroeber, *Romantic
Narrative Art* (1960; rpt., Madison: University of Wisconsin Press, 1966); Brian
Wilkie, *Romantic Poets and Epic Tradition* (Madison: University of Wisconsin Press,
1965); and Joseph Anthony Wittreich, Jr., "Opening the Seals: Blake's Epics and
the Milton Tradition," in *Blake's Sublime Allegory*, ed. Wittreich and Stuart Curran
(Madison: University of Wisconsin Press, 1973), pp. 23–58.

8. See Walter Jackson Bate, *The Burden of the Past and the English Poet* (Cambridge, Mass.: Harvard University Press, 1970), and Harold Bloom, "Keats and
the Embarrassments of Poetic Tradition" in *From Sensibility to Romanticism*, ed.
Frederick W. Hilles and Bloom (New York: Oxford University Press, 1965), pp.
513–26; idem, *The Anxiety of Influence* (New York: Oxford University Press, 1973);
idem, *A Map of Misreading* (New York: Oxford University Press, 1975); and idem,
Poetry and Repression: Revisionism from Blake to Stevens (New Haven: Yale University
Press, 1976). For a more optimistic view of the romantic achievement, yet one that

uses Bloom's categories to develop that view, see Leslie Brisman's *Milton's Poetry of Choice and Its Romantic Heirs* (Ithaca: Cornell University Press, 1973) and his *Romantic Origins* (Ithaca: Cornell University Press, 1978). For the view that only other literature or literary myth can be the direct means of influence upon later poetry, see Northrop Frye, *The Anatomy of Criticism* (Princeton: Princeton University Press, 1957), pp. 95–128.

9. From *The Letters of John Keats, 1814–1821*, ed. Hyder Edward Rollins, 2 vols. (Cambridge, Mass.: Harvard University Press, 1958), 2:104 (21 April 1819).

10. For the tendency to identify plastic and picturesque arts, see Hagstrum, *Sister Arts*, p. xxii and throughout the body of his discussion. M. H. Abrams argues in *The Mirror and the Lamp* (New York: Oxford University Press, 1953), pp. 50–51, that the romantics replace *ut pictura poesis* with *ut musica poesis;* Roy Park, however, points out the continuity of the tradition and Schlegel's revisions of it in "*Ut pictura poesis*: The Nineteenth-Century Aftermath," *JAAC* 28 (1969): 156–57.

11. See Ian Jack's discussion of the picturesque in *Keats and the Mirror of Art* (Oxford: Clarendon Press, 1967), pp. 114–15. See also Elizabeth Wheeler Manwaring, *Italian Landscape in Eighteenth-Century England* (1925; rpt., New York: Russell and Russell, 1965); Christopher Hussey, *The Picturesque: Studies in a Point of View* (London: Putnam, 1929); Henry V. S. Ogden and Margaret S. Ogden, *English Taste in Landscape in the Seventeenth Century* (Ann Arbor: University of Michigan Press, 1955); Walter J. Hipple, Jr., *The Beautiful, the Sublime, and the Picturesque in Eighteenth-Century British Aesthetic Theory* (Carbondale: Southern Illinois University Press, 1957); Edward G. Malins, *English Landscaping and Literature, 1660–1840* (London: Oxford University Press, 1966); and J. R. Watson, *Picturesque Landscape and English Romantic Poetry* (London: Hutchinson Educational, 1970).

12. Z. A. Fink, *The Early Wordsworthian Milieu* (Oxford: Clarendon Press, 1958), pp. 22, 77ff. The primary sources from which Wordsworth and probably Keats drew their vocabulary will be discussed in the second section of this chapter. Because of the careful step-by-step viewing of a scene that such stations emphasize, my analysis of this process as a central one for these romantic poets considers both kinds of landscape consciousness John Dixon Hunt describes in Thomson's *Seasons*: the distanced, wide-ranging picturesque perspective and the "local" involvement in "changing vistas" of the "gardenist" perspective.

13. See *Coleridge's Shakespeare Criticism*, ed. Thomas Middleton Raysor, 2 vols. (Cambridge, Mass.: Harvard University Press, 1930), 2:159–60, 262; and Augustus William Schlegel, *A Course of Lectures on Dramatic Art and Literature*, trans. John Black, 2 vols. (London: Baldwin, Cradock and Joy, 1815), 1:9. For Coleridge's earlier uses of "statuesque" and "picturesque," see Stephen A. Larrabee, *English Bards and Grecian Marbles* (New York: Columbia University Press, 1943), p. 135.

14. See Wayne C. Booth's discussions in *The Rhetoric of Fiction* (1961; rpt., Chicago: University of Chicago Press, 1965), esp. pp. 45–46 and 154; and Susan Sniader Lanser, *The Narrative Act: Point of View in Prose Fiction* (Princeton: Princeton University Press, 1981), chap. 1 for a review of critical problems, pp.

191–98 for spatial stance, and fig. 21, p. 224, for an overview of her discussion.

15. See John Walter Good, "Studies in the Milton Tradition," app. 1, "Milton's Eden and English Landscape Gardening," *Illinois University Studies in Language and Literature* 1 (1915): 268–73; Malins, *Landscaping and Literature*, p. 141; and Marcia R. Pointon, *Milton and English Art* (Toronto: University of Toronto Press, 1970), p. xli.

16. See M. H. Abrams, *Natural Supernaturalism: Tradition and Revolution in Romantic Literature* (New York: Norton, 1971), pp. 90–92, and Ralph Cohen, *The Art of Discrimination: Thomson's "The Seasons" and the Art of Criticism* (Berkeley and Los Angeles: University of California Press, 1964), p. 279.

17. These references come from entries for "station" in William Ingram and Kathleen Swaim, eds., *A Concordance to Milton's Poetry*, (Oxford: Clarendon Press, 1972).

18. "Summer," ll. 1648–50, in *The Complete Poetical Works of James Thomson*, ed. J. Logie Robertson, Oxford Standard Authors (1980; rpt., London: Oxford University Press, 1963), p. 114.

19. See Chester F. Chapin, *Personification in Eighteenth-Century Poetry* (New York: Columbia University Press, 1955), pp. 40, 75, and Watson, *Picturesque Landscape*, p. 33; see also R. A. Aubin, *Topographical Poetry in Eighteenth-Century England* (New York: MLA, 1936), p. 87; Alan McKillop, *The Background of Thomson's "Seasons"* (Minneapolis: University of Minnesota Press, 1942), p. 12; and William Gilpin, *Observations on the River Wye, and Several Parts of South Wales, Relative Chiefly to Picturesque Beauty . . .*, 3d ed. (London: R. Blamire, 1782), p. 61.

20. [Thomas West], *A Guide to the Lakes in Cumberland, Westmoreland, and Lancashire*, 6th ed. (London: W. Richardson, 1796), pp. 2–3, 89.

21. "Arthur's seat," Gilpin writes, "presents an unpleasing view from every station," and "in composition alone she [Nature] fails." See Gilpin's *Observations on Several Parts of Great Britain, particularly the High-lands of Scotland, relative chiefly to Picturesque Beauty, made in the year 1776*, 3d ed., 2 vols. (London: R. Blamire, 1808), 1:88; and idem, *Observations on Several Parts of the Counties of Cambridge, Norfolk, Suffolk, and Essex. Also on Several Parts of North Wales; Relative Chiefly to Picturesque Beauty . . .* (London: T. Cadell and W. Davies, 1809), p. 174.

22. Gilpin's *Observations relative chiefly to Picturesque Beauty made in the year 1772, On several parts of England; particularly the Mountains, and Lakes of Cumberland and Westmoreland*, 2d ed., 2 vols. (London: R. Blamire, 1788) first was published in 1786; that on the Highlands in 1789; and on North Wales in 1809. See Carl Paul Barbier, *William Gilpin: His Drawings, Teachings, and Theory of the Picturesque* (Oxford: Clarendon Press, 1963), chap. 6. The Lake Country guide discusses similarities and differences of the "sister arts" in its introduction (1:xxii) and the effect of placing various kinds of human figures in "a scene of grandeur" (2:45).

23. Joseph Wilkinson, *Select Views in Cumberland, Westmoreland, and Lancashire* (London: R. Ackermann, 1810); I have examined a copy of this work at the Huntington Library. For Wordsworth's ownership of Gilpin's works and discussion of their influence, see Watson, *Picturesque Landscape*, p. 80, and James W. Heffernan, *Wordsworth's Theory of Poetry: The Transforming Imagination* (Ithaca: Cornell University Press, 1969), p. 19.

24. See Mary Moorman, *William Wordsworth*, 2 vols. (1957; rpt., Oxford: Oxford University Press, 1968), 2:159n.

25. The introduction was published under Wordsworth's name for the first time in 1820, in *The River Duddon, a Series of Sonnets: Vaudracour and Julia: and Other Poems. To Which Is Annexed, A Topographical Description Of The Country of The Lakes, in the North of England*. It appeared again, on its own, in 1822; again, slightly enlarged, in 1823; and substantially enlarged in 1835. See W. M. Merchant's introduction to William Wordsworth, *A Guide Through the District of the Lakes* (London: Rupert Hart-Davis, 1959), pp. 30–31. Although only the 1810 version could have directly influenced the poems I discuss here, Wordsworth's continued and in fact expanded use of the term "station" suggests its continued currency; see Wordsworth, *Guide*, pp. 81, 83, 163, and see p. ii in the 1810 edition.

26. All citations to Wordsworth's poetry other than *The Prelude* are to *The Poetical Works of William Wordsworth*, ed. Ernest de Selincourt and Helen Darbishire, 5 vols. (Oxford: Clarendon Press, 1940–1949). *The Excursion* is contained in vol. 5. References in text are to books and lines.

27. Keats, *Letters*, ed. Rollins, 1:178.

28. Noted in Dane Lewis Baldwin et al., eds., *A Concordance to the Poems of John Keats* (Washington: Carnegie Institution, 1917), entry for "stationed."

29. Keats, *Letters*, ed. Rollins, 1:403 (24 October 1818).

30. Dorothy Van Ghent, in her recently published *Keats: The Myth of the Hero*, rev. ed., ed. Jeffrey Cane Robinson (Princeton: Princeton University Press, 1983), pp. 206–07, quotes this passage in her discussion of stationing as a realization of sculptural presence.

31. Bate, *Keats*, p. 243. According to Bate, Keats unites this "ideal of dynamic poise, of power kept in reserve," with another one, "range of implication." Bate defines the latter largely in temporal terms: "Process, though slowed to an insistent present, is carried in active solution." Bate includes only the first of these concepts in his interpretation of stationing. For articles that discuss the relationship of temporal narrative to spatial form, though a collection largely emphasizing modernist literature, see Jeffrey R. Smitten and Ann Daghistany, eds., *Spatial Form in Narrative* (Ithaca: Cornell University Press, 1981).

32. In his discussion of "Autumn" Bate does seem to consider setting as closely related to stationing, but again he defines the setting more as temporal process than as spatial location of figure and process. See Bate, *Keats*, pp. 582ff.

33. See Claude Lee Finney, *The Evolution of Keats's Poetry*, 2 vols. (Cambridge, Mass.: Harvard University Press, 1936), 1:337, and Stuart M. Sperry, *Keats the Poet* (Princeton: Princeton University Press, 1973), p. 51.

34. See *The Letters of Charles Armitage Brown*, ed. Jack Stillinger (Cambridge, Mass.: Harvard University Press, 1966), pp. 43–44; and see Keats, *Letters*, ed. Rollins, 1:174; 1:322; 2:52; 2:130; 2:135; and 2:142ff. See also Watson's chapter on Keats (in *Picturesque Landscape*) for an analysis of the poet's uneasiness at confronting a setting so unlike his own southern England.

35. *The Prelude*, ed. Jonathan Wordsworth, M. H. Abrams, and Stephen Gill, a Norton Critical Edition (New York: Norton, 1979), p. 425. I am using the 1850 text here. References in text are to books and lines.

36. Martin Price, "The Picturesque Moment," in Hilles and Bloom, *From Sensibility to Romanticism*, p. 260.

37. Samuel Monk, *The Sublime* (1935; rpt., Ann Arbor: University of Michigan Press, 1960), p. 225; for a more recent, psychological analysis of the visual or scenic sublime, see Thomas Weiskel, *The Romantic Sublime* (Baltimore: Johns Hopkins University Press, 1976), pp. 12–22, 136–64.

38. See Watson, *Picturesque Landscape*, pp. 79–87, for a discussion of "Lines . . . above Tintern Abbey" (Wordsworth, *Works*, vol. 2) as an antipicturesque poem.

39. Heinrich Wölfflin, *Principles of Art History*, trans. from 7th ed. by M. D. Hottinger (1929; rpt., New York: Dover, n.d.), p. 24. Two eighteenth-century theorists of landscape, Richard Payne Knight and Uvedale Price, argued at length over the objectivity of the picturesque. Wordsworth and Coleridge read and annotated a copy of Knight's *Analytical Inquiry into the Principles of Taste*, a copy I have examined in the Huntington Library (11577). See also Edna A. Shearer, "Wordsworth and Coleridge Marginalia in a Copy of Richard Payne Knight's *Analytical Inquiry into the Principles of Taste*," *HLQ* 1 (1937): 63–94, and Julian I. Lindsay, "A Note on the Marginalia," ibid., pp. 95–99. Shelley and Thomas Love Peacock jokingly compared their controversy over the "Four Ages of Poetry" to the Price-Knight argument, and Peacock further satirized the debate in *Headlong Hall*. See Watson's chapter on Shelley in *Picturesque Landscape*. I also have consulted a copy of Knight's 4th ed. of *Analytical Inquiry* (London: Payne and White, 1805).

40. See Goslee, "Phidian Lore," p. 80. James Bunn mentions "stationing" briefly in "Keats's *Ode to Psyche* and the Transformation to Mental Landscape," *ELH* 37 (1970): 593–94.

41. A longer version of this discussion appeared in Goslee, " 'In Englands green & pleasant Land': The Building of Vision in Blake's Stanzas from *Milton*," *SiR* 13 (1974); 105–25. I have omitted here most of the explication of Blake's allusions to British and biblical mythology.

42. *The Complete Poetry and Prose of William Blake*, ed. David V. Erdman, with commentary by Harold Bloom, newly rev. ed. (Berkeley and Los Angeles: University of California Press, 1982), pp. 95–96. All references to Blake's poetry and prose, unless otherwise noted, are to this edition (cited as E) and will be identified by page, plate, and line numbers.

43. Much of the preface is an angrily ironic condemnation of classical literature and all literature celebrating corporeal war. The substance of his accusation parallels Milton's attack upon traditional epic in *Paradise Lost*, book 9; the method is a subversion of Milton's distinction, in *Reason of Church Government* (Milton, *Poems and Prose*, p. 671), between the Daughters of Memory and the Daughters of Inspiration.

44. In *Milton* itself, as John E. Grant has noted in reading an earlier version of my 1974 *SiR* essay ("Building of Vision"), Blake's clear focus on the actors' feet repeatedly indicates encounters of one realm of existence with another. Here the images lack that sharp-edged quality.

45. Here I disagree with Edward J. Rose's suggestion in "Blake's *Milton*: The Poet as Poem," *BS* 1 (1968): 25, that Blake ironically describes eighteenth-century England as a "pleasant Land." I see the "pleasant Land" as ironic because it refers to the distant past (first stanza) and the future (last line) but not to the present—though of course it should.

46. See Thomas A. Vogler, *Prefaces to Vision: The Epic Venture in Blake, Wordsworth, Keats, and Hart Crane* (Berkeley and Los Angeles: University of California Press, 1971), p. 9. Although Vogler considers *Milton* he does not discuss this lyric.

47. For a thorough discussion of the connection between fiery chariot, archer's bow, and rainbow in *Jerusalem*, see Edward J. Rose, " 'Forms Eternal Exist Forever': The Covenant of the Harvest . . . ," in *Blake's Visionary Forms Dramatic*, ed. David V. Erdman and John E. Grant (Princeton: Princeton University Press, 1970), pp. 451, 453–54, 456, 460–62. For a fuller discussion of classical and biblical patterns of imagery in this highly compressed stanza, images that extend through Milton, Henry Vaughan, and Thomas Gray's "Progress of Poesy," see my fuller *SiR* version, "Building of Vision," pp. 113–23 and notes.

48. See Nehemiah 4:13, 17–18, and Ezra 5:2; see also Martha Winburn England, "Blake and the Hymns of John Wesley," *BNYPL* 70 (1966): 26. England and John Sparrow, *Hymns Unbidden* (New York: New York Public Library, 1966), is a more general discussion of the relationship between Blake and Wesley.

49. *Shelley's Poetry and Prose*, ed. Donald H. Reiman and Sharon B. Powers, a Norton Critical Edition (New York: Norton, 1977), p. 229. All references to Shelley's poetry and prose, unless otherwise indicated, are to this edition and will be included in the text. All references to *Prometheus Unbound* are to acts, scenes, and lines.

50. Reiman and Powers (ibid., p. 231n) suggest that "thou" in line 72 refers to "Athens, treated as the permanent idea of human civilization made possible by the spirit of Liberty." I read "thou" as addressed to Liberty herself, a sculptor as she is in Collins's "Ode to Liberty."

51. Rensselaer Lee, *Ut Pictura Poesis: The Humanistic Theory of Painting* (New York: Norton, 1967), p. 25; rev. from *Art Bulletin* 22 (1940).

52. Trickett, "Augustan Pantheon"; Lee, *Ut Pictura Poesis*; and Earl R. Wasserman, "The Internal Values of Eighteenth-Century Personification," *PMLA* 65 (1950): 435–63.

53. The *OED* lists a 1684 use of "figure" as facial expression: "To have devout figures of the face, and uncomely postures of the soul"; a figure in heraldry is the representation of a face.

54. For a discussion of the *"spectator ab extra"* in *Paradise Lost*, see Geoffrey Hartman, "Milton's Counterplot," in *Beyond Formalism* (1970; rpt., New Haven: Yale University Press, 1971), pp. 113–23. Bloom's discussion of a "primal scene of instruction" (*Map of Misreading*, p. 47) also has influenced my analysis here.

55. See Mildred Sloan McGill, "The Role of Earth in Shelley's *Prometheus Unbound*," *SiR* 7 (1968): 117–28.

Chapter 2: Blake's Milton

1. As noted in Chapter 1, all citations to Blake's poetry and prose, unless otherwise stated, are to Erdman's rev. ed. of *The Complete Poetry and Prose of William Blake* (cited as E), and references are to page and to plate and line when citing engraved works. I have based discussion of the *Milton* illuminations on limited examination of Copy B (Huntington Library), on the Trianon Press facsimile of Copy D (Clairvaux: William Blake Trust, London, 1967), and on Erdman's reproduction of Copy A in the order of Copy D, in his *The Illuminated Blake* (Garden City, N.Y.: Doubleday Anchor, 1974). All references to illuminated plates unless otherwise indicated are to *The Illuminated Blake* (also cited in text as *IB*). Erdman follows the order of Copy D but does not include the plates of full-page illuminations in his numbering; see E:806.

2. In *Blake's Apocalypse* (Garden City, N.Y.: Doubleday, 1963), p. 341, Harold Bloom reads the poem as purgatorial. For more historically focused discussion of Blake's uncertainty of vocation during this period, see G. E. Bentley, Jr., *Blake Records* (Oxford: Clarendon Press, 1969), particularly pt. 3, "Patronage and Dependence," pp. 62ff. and 173–74. See also W. J. T. Mitchell, "Style and Iconography in the Illustrations of Blake's *Milton*," *BS* 6 (1973): 48–49. Although I disagree with Joseph Wittreich's view in *Angel of Apocalypse* (Madison: University of Wisconsin Press, 1974), p. 247, that Blake's quarrel is not with Milton himself but only with his more establishmentarian followers, I do find convincing his suggestion of a mellowing attitude through the four copies of *Milton*. For another evaluation of Milton's reputation in the eighteenth century, see David E. James, *Written Within and Without: A Study of Blake's "Milton,"* Europaische Hochschulschriften, Series 14 (Frankfurt: Peter Lang, 1977), pp. 57–64. I find myself also in partial agreement with Bloom's view of Blake as a "strong poet" more able to wrestle with the burden of the past than are other romantic poets; I have not attempted in this chapter, however, to relate my analysis more closely to the premises or the schemata of Bloom's recent studies of poetic influence. See Susan Fox, *Poetic Form in Blake's "Milton"* (Princeton: Princeton University Press, 1976), pp. xiv–xv, n. 4, for a bibliography listing studies of Blake's relationship to Milton.

3. For a discussion of Blake's response to Milton's blindness, see Wittreich, *Angel of Apocalypse*, pp. 6ff. See also Viktor Lowenfeld, "Psycho-Aesthetic Implications of the Art of the Blind," *JAAC* 10 (1951): 1–9, and F. David Martin, "The Autonomy of Sculpture," *JAAC* 34 (1976): 273–86. In *Blake's "Milton"* (Rutherford, N.J.: Fairleigh Dickinson University Press, 1976), p. 226, John Howard suggests that Milton's molding a clay form for Urizen echoes Christ's healing of blindness with clay (John 9:1–41); he links the passage not with Milton's physical blindness but with his spiritual blindness as manifested in Urizen. Northrop Frye also notes this biblical parallel in "Notes for a Commentary on *Milton*," in *The Divine Vision*, ed. Vivian de Sola Pinto (London: Gollancz, 1957), p. 134. For further discussion of the particular qualities of sculpture as a separate art, see my discussion later in this chapter. Suzanne Hoover's paper, "Blake and the Poetry of Stone," read at the 1976 MLA Blake Seminar, also develops an argument for Blake's awareness of sculpture.

4. Jonathan Richardson, *Explanatory Notes and Remarks on Milton's "Paradise Lost"* (1734; facsimile rpt., New York: Garland, 1970), pp. 156–57 and passim; and Edmund Burke, *A Philosophical Inquiry into the Origins of Our Ideas of the Sublime and the Beautiful*, ed. J. J. Boulton (New York: Columbia University Press, 1958), p. 170. For Blake's awareness of involvement in the *ut pictura poesis* controversy over Milton, see Bentley, *Blake Records*, pp. 195ff.; Marcia Pointon, *Milton and English Art*, Appendix D, "Fuseli's Milton Gallery"; and David Bindman, *Blake as an Artist* (London: Phaidon; New York: Dutton, 1977), pp. 91ff. Blake's defense of Fuseli's Milton Gallery, his later defense of his own illustrations to Blair's *Grave*, and by implication his own illustrations to Milton's work all assert that visual art is indeed capable of spiritual significance; in *Milton* he shows the earning of that significance. For further discussion of the correction of visual perception in *Milton*, see Thomas W. Herzing, "Book I of Blake's *Milton*: Natural Religion as Optical Fallacy," *BS* 6 (1973): 25. Recent debate over the relationship of Blake's two arts has been frequent and furious. For a summary of recent positions, see Jean H. Hagstrum, "Blake and the Sister-Arts Tradition," in Erdman and Grant, *Blake's Visionary Forms Dramatic*, p. 82 and n; for an argument of verbal over visual art, see Thomas R. Frosch, *The Awakening of Albion* (Ithaca: Cornell University Press, 1974), pp. 103ff.; for suggestions of conscious rivalry similar to the one I will propose here, see Mitchell, "Style and Iconography"; idem, *Blake's Composite Art* (Princeton: Princeton University Press, 1978); and David M. Wyatt, "The Woman Jerusalem: *Pictura* versus *Poesis*," *BS* 7 (1974): 105–24.

5. Anne Kostelanetz Mellor, *Blake's Human Form Divine* (Berkeley and Los Angeles: University of California Press, 1974), pp. xv–xvi, and Mitchell, *Composite Art*, pp. 48, 59.

6. Robert Rosenblum, *Transformations in Late Eighteenth Century Art* (Princeton: Princeton University Press, 1967), especially pp. 154ff. See also Mellor, *Blake's Human Form Divine*, chap. 4, and *SiR* 15 (1976), a special issue on romantic classicism, edited by Morton D. Paley. For the development of three-dimensional pictorial space in painting, see John White, *The Birth and Rebirth of Pictorial Space*, 2d ed. (Boston: Boston Book and Art Shop, 1967); for the transformation from the absolute space of the rationalists to an increasing emphasis upon point of view, see Claudio Guillen, "On the Concept and Metaphor of Perspective," in *Comparatists at Work: Studies in Comparative Literature*, ed. Stephen G. Nichols, Jr., and Richard B. Vowles (Waltham, Mass.: Blaisdell, 1968), pp. 34–47. Guillen cites Erwin Panovsky's essay, "Die Perspektive als 'Symbolische Form' " (1924). See also John T. Ogden, "From Spatial to Aesthetic Distance in the Eighteenth Century," *JHI* 35 (1974): 63–78. For a denial of three-dimensional space in romantic classicism, and specifically in Blake, see Rosenblum, *Transformations*, pp. 57n, 169n, 189ff.

7. Mitchell, *Composite Art*, p. 36.

8. Bindman, in *Blake as Artist*, p. 187, cites Blake's increasing interest in landscape after 1810, as shown in the *Paradise Regained* watercolors and in his later friendship with John Constable (pp. 196, 203).

9. Mitchell, *Composite Art*, pp. 108, 138–39: Karl Kroeber, "Graphic-Poetic Structure in Blake's *Book of Urizen*," *BS* 3 (1970): 10–14; Mitchell, "Style and

Iconography," pp. 48–49; on his new consciousness of a prophetic stance, Bloom, *Blake's Apocalypse*, pp. 340–41; and E:915.

10. "Blake's Frame of Language," in *William Blake: Essays in Honour of Sir Geoffrey Keynes*, ed. Morton D. Paley and Michael Phillips (Oxford: Clarendon Press, 1973), p. 88.

11. Mitchell, *Composite Art*, pp. 48ff.

12. Marshall McLuhan, *The Gutenberg Galaxy: The Making of Typographic Man* (Toronto: University of Toronto Press, 1973), p. 88; Mitchell, *Composite Art*, p. 74.

13. In Hagstrum, *Sister Arts*, chap. 5, "English Neoclassicism." His distinction between *enargeia* and *energeia* is on pp. 11–12. See also Morris Eaves, *William Blake's Theory of Art* (Princeton: Princeton University Press, 1982), pp. 18–38, 66.

14. McLuhan, *Gutenberg Galaxy*, pp. 265–66, quoted in Mitchell, *Composite Art*, p. 74.

15. *Letters of William Blake*, 3d ed., ed. Geoffrey Keynes (Oxford: Clarendon Press, 1980), p. 41. In the same letter (p. 42) Blake describes his spiritual state in metaphors he will develop for his *Milton*. Anthony Blunt in *The Art of William Blake* (New York: Columbia University Press, 1959), p. 68, draws attention to Blake's "only two landscapes from life," done at Felpham, and comments that his "command of the techniques of watercolor could have made him successful in landscape painting."

16. Sir Joshua Reynolds, *Discourses on Art*, ed. Robert R. Wark (New Haven: Yale University Press, for the Paul Mellon Centre for Studies in British Art, 1975), pp. 175–76, and William Gilpin, *Three Essays: On Picturesque Beauty; On Picturesque Travel; and On Sketching Landscape*, 2d ed. (London: R. Blamire, 1794), pp. 48ff. Frederick W. Hilles, in *The Letters of Sir Joshua Reynolds* (Cambridge: Cambridge University Press, 1929), p. 217, points out Gilpin's quotation of Reynolds in his *Three Essays*, which first appeared in 1792.

17. For discussion of a spectator who must judge, see Hartman, "Milton's Counterplot," in *Beyond Formalism*, pp. 118ff. Walter Jackson Bate discusses Coleridge's recurrent use of this viewpoint in *Coleridge* (New York: Macmillan, 1968), esp. p. 44.

18. See Eaves, *Blake's Theory of Art*, p. 113, for a discussion of these "experiment pictures" as parodies of color theory.

19. Noted by Jean H. Hagstrum, *William Blake: Poet and Painter* (Chicago: University of Chicago Press, 1964), pp. 60–62. As Hagstrum also points out, Blake's friend George Cumberland wrote in 1780 *A Poem on the Landscapes of Great-Britain*. The poem celebrates the way those British landscapes echo the paintings of Ruysdael, Rosa, and other landscapists favored by the picturesque school. In a note written at the work's belated 1793 publication (London: W. Wilson), Cumberland confesses that new awareness of classical sculpture has led him to "see the face of nature with discriminate delight" (p. 29n)—yet he still admires the Welsh mountains. Blake surely also knew of Fuseli's 1794 reviews of Richard Payne Knight's and Uvedale Price's works on picturesque theory in Joseph Johnson's *Analytical Review*. See Eudo C. Mason, *The Mind of Henry Fuseli*

(London: Routledge and Kegan Paul, 1951), app. 2. David Irwin, *English Neoclassical Art: Studies in Inspiration and Taste* (Greenwich, Conn.: New York Graphic Society, 1966), p. 139, cites Fuseli's antipicturesque challenge to Price to "produce one passage from Milton, describing the ground on which Satan stood." Keats's citation of Milton stationing Satan "disfigured—on the Assyrian Mount" does just that, though admittedly without the detailed "roughness of surface and intricacy of motion" which Fuseli criticizes Price for making a characteristic of the picturesque.

20. Here I disagree with James's and Eaves's arguments that conception and execution occur, for Blake's theory, in the same moment; *Milton* seems to describe his "[herculean] Labours" to bring the two closer by a conscious recognition and reworking of others' defective execution. See D. E. James, *Written Within*, p. 2, and Eaves, *Blake's Theory of Art*, pp. 80ff.

21. Critics disagree on which of the figures in this illumination (*IB* 10A) is Rintrah and which is Satan; see Erdman's commentary in *Illuminated Bible* and see Mitchell, "Style and Iconography," pp. 64–66.

22. See D. E. James, *Written Within*, pp. 147ff.

23. Northrop Frye, *Fearful Symmetry* (1947; rpt., Boston: Beacon, 1962), pp. 312–13; a few pages later, however, he suggests that book 1 corresponds to *Paradise Lost*, book 2 to *Paradise Regained*. See also Bloom, *Blake's Apocalypse*, p. 304; Wilkie, *Romantic Poets*, p. 130; Stuart Curran, "The Mental Pinnacle: *Paradise Regained* and the Romantic Four-Book Epic," in *Calm of Mind: Tercentenary Essays on "Paradise Regained" and "Samson Agonistes," in Honor of John S. Deikhoff*, ed. Joseph Anthony Wittreich, Jr. (Cleveland: Press of Case Western Reserve University, 1971), pp. 136, 139; and Wittreich, "Opening the Seals," pp. 26–27. Wittreich goes on, however, to argue that revelation and prophecy are more crucial than dialogue in shaping both *Paradise Regained* and Blake's epics.

24. See Joseph Anthony Wittreich, Jr., "William Blake: Illustrator-Interpreter of *Paradise Regained*," in *Calm of Mind*, pp. 112–17; J. M. Q. Davies, " 'Embraces and Cominglings': Passion and Apocalypse in Blake's *Paradise Regained* Designs," *Durham University Journal* 74, n.s. 43 (1981): 75–96; and Stephen C. Behrendt, *The Moment of Explosion: Blake and the Illustration of Milton* (Lincoln and London: University of Nebraska Press, 1983), esp. pp. 48–49. Because he reads both *Paradise Lost* and *Milton* through the "interiority" of *Paradise Regained*, Behrendt suggests (p. 99) that illustrators to *Paradise Lost* who chose Satan's encounter with Uriel focused upon mere dramatic action, an imbalance corrected by Blake's two versions of *The Son Offers to Redeem Man* (plates 6–7), illustrating an earlier narrative moment in book 3. Without denying the significance of Blake's choice as he illustrates this moment, I think we nevertheless can explore the dramatic confrontation of Satan and Uriel as part of an external epic structure that becomes symbolic.

25. Northrop Frye, "The Road of Excess," in *The Stubborn Structure: Essays on Criticism and Society* (Ithaca: Cornell University Press, 1970), pp. 161–62; Rose, "Blake's *Milton*," p. 17; Wittreich, "Opening the Seals," p. 30; and D. E. James, *Written Within*, pp. 5ff.; later, however, James qualifies his assertion (pp. 92ff.).

26. See Thomas M. Greene, *The Descent from Heaven: A Study in Epic Continuity* (1963; rpt., New Haven: Yale University Press, 1975), for discussion of this recurrent element of epic structure through Milton.

27. See Fox, *Poetic Form*, p. 18, for this judicious modifying of the instantaneous-action theory. In "Blake's Radical Comedy," in Wittreich and Curran, *Sublime Allegory*, p. 287, W. J. T. Mitchell also suggests modification of the "moment" as he speaks of an "apocalyptic . . . current . . . running against both the cyclic and progressive movements of the poem."

28. See Roland Barthes, "An Introduction to the Structural Analysis of Narrative," *Communications* 8 (1969), rpt. in *New Literary History* 6 (1975): 243; and see Seymour Chatman, "Towards a Theory of Narrative," ibid., pp. 295ff.

29. See Peter Alan Taylor, "Providence and the Moment in Blake's *Milton*," *BS* 4 (1971): 48.

30. Here I disagree with D. E. James's assertion that these hells are similar to those in Blake's *The Marriage of Heaven and Hell* (*Written Within*, p. 76).

31. The listings for "station" and "stations" in *A Concordance to the Writing of William Blake*, ed. David V. Erdman, assisted by John E. Thiesmeyer and others (Ithaca: Cornell University Press, 1967), show even as early as *The French Revolution* and *America* the military sense of "battle station" and the more transcendent sense of responsibility defined by place. The only approximately picturesque use comes in *The Marriage of Heaven and Hell*: "the angel climbed from his station into the mill." At least three writers Blake was reading use the picturesque sense of "station." Edward Davies, in *Celtic Researches* . . . (London: J. Booth, 1804), p. viii, describes a group that "reached a kind of station, which commanded a fair view." Charles Dunster's 1795 edition of *Paradise Regained*, in *Milton's "Paradise Regained"*: *Two Eighteenth-Century Critiques* by Richard Meadowcourt and Charles Dunster, facsimile rpt., intro. Joseph Anthony Wittreich, Jr. (Gainesville, Fla.: Scholars' Facsimiles and Reprints, 1971), not only discusses the "picturesque" qualities of *Paradise Lost* as they recur in the later poem (p. 34n) but discusses whether both poems might be used as guides to landscape gardening (p. 93). Further, he debates whether Satan carries Christ to Mount Niphates, "as in such station," the Assyrian perspective would be impossible (p. 151). Keats, we recall, uses Satan "disfigured—on the Assyrian Mount" as one of his examples of "stationing." In his *Essay on Painting*, William Hayley proclaims, "Let the fond Muse, tho' with a transient view, / The progress of her sister art pursue. . . . To praise [Painting's] dearest sons, whose daring air / Gain'd their bright stations on the heights of fame, / And mark the paths by which her partial hand / Conducts her *Romney* to this radiant band"; ll. 13–20, in *Poems and Plays*, 6 vols. (London: T. Cadell, 1785), 1:3–4. Blake surely has Los usurp this angelic picturesque station.

32. The Hayley-Blake interpretation of the Bard's song appears to begin with S. Foster Damon's *William Blake: His Philosophy and Symbols* (Boston: Houghton Mifflin, 1924), p. 175, as James Rieger notes in " 'The Hem of their Garments': The Bard's Song in *Milton*," in Wittreich and Curran, *Sublime Allegory*, p. 260. Frederick E. Pierce, in "The Genesis and General Meaning of Blake's *Milton*," *MP* 25 (1927–1928): 166–67, suggests that Hayley's *Life of Milton* (2d ed., 1796; facsimile rpt., intro. Joseph Anthony Wittreich, Jr. [Gainesville, Fla.: Scholars'

Facsimiles and Reprints, 1970]), pp. 78 and 229, contains the seeds of Blake's idea for Milton's return.

33. See Bloom, *Blake's Apocalypse*, p. 310, and Mary Lynn Johnson, " 'Separating What Has Been Mixed': A Suggestion for a Perspective on *Milton*," *BS* 6 (1973): 11–17.

34. Donald Ault, *Visionary Physics* (Chicago: University of Chicago Press, 1974), p. 74.

35. See Leopold Damrosch, Jr., *Symbol and Truth in Blake's Myth* (Princeton: Princeton University Press, 1980), pp. 154–55 and 291ff., for a more pessimistic view both of "states" and of the capacity for redemption through the flesh.

36. Fox, *Poetic Form*, p. 23. A similar, earlier warning is sounded by Edward J. Rose in "Blake's Metaphorical States," *BS* 4 (1971): 10–12. Rose tends to equate "State" with "Class," except on p. 18.

37. See Mitchell, *Composite Art*, esp. pp. 3–4, 60. Thomas Frosch, in reviewing Mitchell's *Composite Art* (*Blake Quarterly* 13 [1979]: 41), suggests that Mitchell tends to emphasize the verbal element more strongly.

38. Northrop Frye, "Poetry and Design in William Blake," *JAAC* 10 (1951): 41.

39. Mitchell, *Composite Art*, pp. 69ff. Pointon (*Milton and English Art*, pp. 187–88) emphasizes this artistic, not scientific, basis for Blake's use of the vortex by suggesting that he may have borrowed it from Turner, specifically from his *Hannibal Crossing the Alps* (1812).

40. See for example John E. Grant's interpretation of a drawing in the Vala Manuscript (p. 74) as "a roughly drawn helix or vortex ring"; "Visions in Vala," in Wittreich and Curran, *Sublime Allegory*, p. 178n. Frosch, in *Awakening of Albion*, p. 71, also argues that the vortex cannot be diagrammed, and he criticizes Hazard Adams's attempt to do so in *Blake and Yeats: The Contrary Vision* (Ithaca: Cornell University Press, 1955), pp. 104–10.

41. Sir William Cecil Dampier, *A History of Science*, 4th ed. (1948; rpt., Cambridge: Cambridge University Press, 1961), p. 136.

42. Ibid., p. 137. For the vortex as "visionary," the *OED* cites Swift, *The Battle of the Books;* see *A Tale of a Tub, to which is added The Battle of the Books . . .* , ed. A. C. Guthkelch and D. Nichol Smith, 2d ed. (Oxford: Clarendon Press, 1958), p. 244. In *A Tale of a Tub*, its link to "imagination," "Madness or Phrenzy" is even more explicit; see p. 167. Interestingly, the *clinamen* (one of Bloom's categories of revisionary ratios) is part of Swift's satire on the same page; see Bloom, *Anxiety of Influence*, pp. 38ff., for a discussion of Blake's responses to Descartes's vortices and their Lucretian origin. Bloom does not mention Swift as intermediary, though *A Tale of a Tub* might lend itself to such a study of influence. Milton's arrival at Blake's foot, "Swift as a swallow or swift," may refer to this origin.

43. Ault, *Visionary Physics*, p. 24, argues that Blake criticizes both Descartes and Newton as ruled by the logic of excluded opposites; the Cartesian vortex and the Newtonian void are for Blake equally inadequate.

44. N. Frye, *Fearful Symmetry*, p. 350, and Ault, *Visionary Physics*, pp. 158–60. White, *Pictorial Space*, p. 253, cites Euclid's discussion of the "visual cone . . . with its vertex in the eye and its base at the limits of the object seen." Frye explains that the vertex or "apex" is in the *object* but that in unfallen vision the object would not

be external; Ault cites conflicts in eighteenth-century theories of vision, some (Voltaire's explanation of Newton, for example) placing the apex of emitted rays in the object, and others (Robert Smith, for example) placing the apex in the perceiver's eye. Blake "collapses" these two ideas into one another, Ault says.

45. N. Frye, *Fearful Symmetry*, p. 334.

46. See White, *Pictorial Space*, pp. 123–24. White suggests, however, that Italian painters and theorists between Giotto and Alberti saw space as radiating from the central object or figure in the painting; see, for example, his discussion of Lorenzetti's fresco in Siena (p. 94).

47. Ault, *Visionary Physics*, p. 156, and Frosch, *Awakening of Albion*, pp. 72–73.

48. Martin K. Nurmi, "Negative Sources in Blake," in Alvin H. Rosenfeld, ed., *William Blake: Essays for S. Foster Damon* (Providence: Brown University Press, 1969), pp. 310–11. See also D. E. James, *Written Within*, pp. 108–09, who describes the vortex briefly as an "open center" for vision.

49. Frosch, *Awakening of Albion*, p. 74.

50. See Michael J. Tolley's "*Europe*: 'to those ychained in sleep,' " in Erdman and Grant, *Visionary Forms Dramatic*, p. 121.

51. Rosenblum, *Transformations*, esp. pp. 154ff. See also Mellor, *Blake's Human Form Divine*, chap. 4.

52. Peter Tomory, *The Life and Art of Henry Fuseli* (New York and Washington: Praeger, 1972), p. 49. Though Fuseli undoubtedly saw these fragments in their Roman setting, Tomory points out that the foot—or a left foot—was brought to England in 1790. Fuseli's red-chalk and sepia-wash drawing appears on the cover of *SiR*'s romantic classicism issue cited in n. 6.

53. L. Brisman, *Choice*, pp. xi–xii.

54. See David V. Erdman, "The Steps (of Dance and Stone) that Order Blake's *Milton*," *BS* 6 (1973): 73.

55. Joseph Wicksteed first proposed this thesis in *Blake's Vision of the Book of Job* (1910); a revised version appeared in 1924 (New York: Dutton). For a recent challenge to this interpretation, see W. J. T. Mitchell, "Blake's Composite Art," in Erdman and Grant, *Visionary Forms Dramatic*, p. 73n.

56. N. Frye, "Drunken Boat"; see also Harold Bloom, "The Internalization of Quest-Romance," in *Romanticism and Consciousness*, ed. Bloom (New York: Norton, 1970), pp. 3–24, and Abrams, *Natural Supernaturalism*, pp. 149ff.

57. As Erdman points out in *Illuminated Blake*, Blake moves this plate closer to the end in successive copies of *Milton*. For an analysis of this plate that suggests a sexual relationship between Blake and Los as model for inspiration, see Mitchell, "Style and Iconography," p. 67. The figure of Los as a burning sun who suddenly approaches Blake also recalls Uriel and Satan in *Paradise Lost*, 3.620ff. D. E. James (*Written Within*, p. 147) suggests that the change from one to both sandals represents a gain in confidence.

58. In *Illuminated Blake*, p. 234.

59. See Irene Tayler's essay, "Blake's Laocoön," *Blake Newsletter* 10 (1976): 72–81; it includes a reproduction of Blake's engraving. She also analyzes the dimensionality of the engraving much as I do. See also Donald Brook, "Perception and the Appraisal of Sculpture," *JAAC* 27 (1968): 323–30.

60. See E:728, Erdman's textual note.

61. Vincent A. De Luca, "Ariston's Immortal Palace: Icon and Allegory in Blake's Prophecies," *Criticism* 12 (1970): 12, 14; see also *Jerusalem* 16: 61ff.

62. See entries for sculpture, statue, statuary, sculptor, and similar terms in Erdman, *Concordance to Blake*. See also Morton D. Paley, " 'Wonderful Originals': Blake and Ancient Sculpture," in *Blake in his Time*, ed. Robert N. Essick and Donald Pearce (Bloomington: Indiana University Press, 1978), pp. 172–73; and Francis Haskell and Nicholas Penny, *Taste and the Antique: The Lure of Classical Sculpture 1500–1900* (New Haven and London: Yale University Press, 1981).

63. See Bentley, *Blake Records*, pp. 62ff., 173–74.

64. In Nancy M. Goslee, "From Marble to Living Form: Sculpture as Art and Analogue from the Renaissance to Blake," *JEGP* 77 (1978): 188–211.

65. Hagstrum, *Sister Arts*, p. 66.

66. William K. Wimsatt, Jr., and Cleanth Brooks, *Literary Criticism: A Short History* (New York: Knopf, 1962), p. 262, citing Thomas Munro, *The Arts and their Interrelationships* (1949; rpt., Cleveland: Press of Case Western Reserve University, 1967), pp. 32–33, and *The Literary Works of Leonardo da Vinci*, comp. and ed. J. P. Richter; see 3d ed., 2 vols. (London: Phaidon, 1970), 1:82–101, 367–69.

67. Paul O. Kristeller, "The Modern System of the Arts: A Study in the History of Aesthetics," *JHI* 12 (1951): 516.

68. See Hagstrum, *Sister Arts*, p. 66. An Italian Renaissance paragone between painting and sculpture was reprinted in Rome in 1754; see Kristeller, "Modern System," p. 516n.

69. See Irwin, *English Neoclassical Art*, pp. 23–25 and sections on Flaxman and Fuseli. For English Renaissance versions, see Hagstrum, *Sister Arts*, pp. 66–67; *Queen Elizabeth's Entertainment at Mitcham: Poet, Painter, and Musician*, attributed to John Lyly, ed. Leslie Hotson (New Haven: Yale University Press, 1953); and *Timon of Athens* (1.1.157–60). For Blake's familiarity with *Timon*, see Tomory, *Fuseli*, pp. 206–11, and Bentley, *Blake Records*, pp. 614, 616.

70. See Margarete Bieber, *Laocoon: The Influence of the Group Since its Discovery*, rev. and enl. ed. (Detroit: Wayne State University Press, 1967). As she points out, this sculpture is in fact Hellenistic.

71. Reynolds, Discourse 3, *Discourses*, pp. 44–45, and John Flaxman, *Lectures on Sculpture* (London: John Murray, 1829). For earlier publications of Flaxman's ideas about the distinction between sculpture and painting, see his "Cursory Strictures on Modern Art, and particularly Sculpture, in England, previous to the establishment of the Royal Academy," in *The Artist*, ed. Prince Hoare, No. 12 (Sat., 30 May 1807), republished as 2 vols. 1810, 1:3, 14. For an account of Blake's relationship to Flaxman, see G. E. Bentley, Jr., "Blake's Engravings and his Friendship with Flaxman," *Studies in Bibliography* 12 (1959): 161–88. Paley, " 'Wonderful Originals,' " p. 182, argues that Flaxman's views were probably well developed much earlier.

72. See Blake's *Annotations to Reynolds*, esp. E:638, 641, and, for the point below, *A Descriptive Catalogue*, E:541–42 in particular, in which he answers Robert Hunt's attacks upon his designs for Blair's *Grave*; Hunt's attack is reprinted in Bentley, *Blake Records*, pp. 195–97. For an early and useful survey of Blake's debt

to Greek sculpture (but one which concludes that he is a Platonist strongly influenced by Reynolds), see Larrabee, *English Bards and Grecian Marbles*, chap. 5. See also Hazard Adams, "Revisiting Reynolds' *Discourses* and Blake's Annotations," in Essick and Pearce, *Blake in his Time*, pp. 135–36, for a useful discussion of "abstract" versus "imaginative" universals.

73. Johann Joachim Winckelmann, *Reflections on the Painting and Sculpture of the Greeks; with Instructions for the Connoisseur and an Essay on Grace in Works of Art*, trans. Henry Fuseli (1765; facsimile rpt., Menston, Yorks.: Scolar Press, 1972), p. 34; and Gotthold Ephraim Lessing, *Laocoon* [1766], trans. Edward Allen McCormick, Library of Liberal Arts (New York: Bobbs-Merrill, 1962), chaps. 1 and 2, esp. p. 15.

74. Marcia Allentuck, "Fuseli's Translations of Winckelmann; A Phase in the Rise of British Hellenism, with an Aside on William Blake," in *Studies in the Eighteenth Century II; Papers Presented at the Second David Nichol Smith Memorial Seminar*, Canberra, 1970, ed. R. F. Brissenden (Toronto: University of Toronto Press, 1973), pp. 163–64; Flaxman, *Lectures*, pp. 76–77, where he cites an Italian edition; William Hayley, *An Essay on Sculpture. In a Series of Epistles to John Flaxman, Esq., R. A.* (London: T. Cadell and W. Davies, 1800), pp. 75, 149, 347.

75. Erdman textual note, E:885–86; see also Adams, "Revisiting," pp. 128–44. Flaxman had been mulling over the *Discourses* about the same time; see Joseph Farington, *The Farington Diary*, ed. James Grieg, 4th ed., 2 vols. (London: Hutchinson, 1923), 2:82–83 (16–17 February). Flaxman's plans for an article on sculpture in Rees's *Cyclopaedia* may have led to Blake's later Laocoon engraving; see Tayler, "Blake's Laocoon," pp. 72, 74, and Bentley, *Blake Records*, pp. 238, 618.

76. See Wilhelm Todt, *Lessing in England, 1767–1850* (Heidelberg: Carl Winters Universitätsbuchhandlung, 1912), p. 41; Mason, *Mind of Fuseli*, p. 203; and Marcia Allentuck, "Henry Fuseli (Johann Heinrich Füssli) and Lessing," *Lessing Yearbook* 1 (1969): 179–80. Coleridge, while in Germany, evidently considered translating all of Lessing (Todt, *Lessing in England*, p. 57).

77. The work reviewed was Uvedale Price's *Essay on the Picturesque*. See Irwin, *English Neoclassical Art*, p. 134; Mason, *Mind of Fuseli*, pp. 206–07; and Allentuck, "Fuseli and Lessing," pp. 182–83.

78. In an earlier published version of this discussion, I suggested that Yvonne M. Carothers might have included this idea in her "Space and Time in *Milton*: the 'Bard's Song,' " published only in abstract at that time. She does not, in the full essay published in Essick and Pearce, *Blake in his Time*, pp. 116–27; but W. J. T. Mitchell has, meanwhile, suggested a similar idea in *Composite Art*, pp. 30ff. For the probable beginning of *Milton*, see Blake's *Letters*, p. 55 (25 April 1803); for a study of Los as line, see Edward J. Rose, "The Spirit of the Bounding Line," *Criticism* 13 (1971): 54–76.

79. Frederick Antal, in *Fuseli Studies* (London: Routledge and Kegan Paul, 1956), labels Fuseli emphatically an idealist.

80. See Marcia Allentuck, "Fuseli and Herder's *Ideen zur Philosophie der Geschichte der Menschheit* in Britain: An Unmarked Connection," *JHI* 35 (1974): 113–20; and Antal, *Fuseli Studies*, p. 165. Both note that Fuseli praises Herder in his first

Academy lecture; see *The Life and Writings of Henry Fuseli, Esq.*, ed. John Knowles, 3 vols. (London: Colburn and Bentley, 1831), 3:24n.

81. James Harris, *Three Treatises: the first concerning art, the second concerning music, painting, and poetry, the third concerning happiness*, 2d ed. rev. and corr. (1765; facsimile rpt., New York: Garland, 1970), p. 55. For Herder see René Wellek, *A History of Modern Criticism, Vol. 1, The Later Eighteenth Century* (New Haven: Yale University Press, 1955), pp. 185–86; Munro, *Arts and Interrelationships*, p. 166; and Robert C. Clark, Jr., *Herder: His Life and Thought* (Berkeley and Los Angeles: University of California Press, 1955, pp. 81, 202–03; Joe K. Fugate, *The Psychological Basis of Herder's Aesthetics*, Studies in Philosophy, vol. 10 (The Hague: Mouton, 1966), pp. 142–43.

82. Clark, *Herder*, p. 224.

83. George Cumberland, *Thoughts on Outline; Sculpture, and the System that Guided the Ancient Artists in Composing their Figures and Groupes* (London: W. Wilson, 1796), pp. 40, 8, and 47.

84. Blake, *Letters*, pp. 10–11 (to Cumberland, 26 August 1799), and pp. 16–17 (to Cumberland, 2 July 1800).

85. Hayley, *Essay on Sculpture*, epistle 2, pp. 34–35.

86. See Allentuck, "Fuseli and Lessing," p. 183. See also Fuseli, *Life and Writings*, vol. 1, chap. 8; Pointon, *Milton and English Art*, app. D; and Bentley, *Blake Records*, pp. 47, 110, 117 n. 1, for accounts of the controversy over Fuseli's Milton Gallery during the 1790s, a controversy turning on the capacity of painting to represent sublime poetry.

87. Fuseli, *Life and Writings*, 2:259; see also Eaves, *Blake's Theory of Art*, pp. 47ff. and 176.

88. Ault, *Visionary Physics*, pp. 58, 102ff.

89. Coleridge, *Shakespeare Criticism*, 1:xxvii–xxviii, and 2:159. For a recent debate on the fidelity of these texts to Coleridge himself, see John F. Andrews, "*The Ipsissima Verba* in My Diary?" *Shakespeare Studies* 8 (1975): 333–67, a review of the work of R. A. Foakes in re-editing the Shakespeare lectures of 1811–1812; and Foakes's later discussion, "What Did Coleridge Say? John Payne Collier and the Reports of the 1811–12 Lectures," in *Reading Coleridge: Approaches and Applications*, ed. Walter B. Crawford (Ithaca: Cornell University Press, 1979), pp. 191–210. For other aspects of Coleridge's interest in the fine arts, see Hagstrum, *Sister Arts*, p. 160, and Park, "Nineteenth-Century Aftermath," pp. 155–64.

90. See Larrabee, *English Bards and Grecian Marbles*, p. 135.

91. R. P. Knight, *Analytical Inquiry*, pp. 105, 189, 303. For Knight's place in debate on picturesque theory, see M. Price, "Picturesque Moment," pp. 259–92; Hipple, *The Beautiful, the Sublime, and the Picturesque*; and Malins, *Landscaping and Literature*.

92. Farington, *Diary*, 2:211; see also Bentley, *Blake Records*, p. 365. Most direct communication between Blake and Coleridge comes late in Blake's life, though Henry Crabb Robinson is an early intermediary.

93. D. E. James does not discuss the metaphor of sculpture but emphasizes the importance of this episode in saying that "the creation of an accurate image of God . . . becomes . . . the primary activity of the poem" (*Written Within*, p. 127).

94. Mellor, *Blake's Human Form Divine*, p. xv. See also Janet A. Warner, "Blakes's Use of Gesture," in Erdman and Grant, *Visionary Forms Dramatic*, p. 174.

95. De Luca, "Ariston's Immortal Palace," pp. 4, 17.

96. See Mitchell, "Blake's Composite Art," *Visionary Forms Dramatic*, p. 61; although he does not mention Lessing specifically in this paragraph, his discussion grows out of an analysis of the Laocoon several pages earlier. See also Mitchell's fuller discussion in *Composite Art*, pp. 30ff.

97. For a discussion of these two plates, see Mitchell, "Style and Iconography," p. 55, and, for differing views, Erdman, "Steps," p. 76; Bindman, *Blake as Artist*, pp. 174–76; and Behrendt, *Explosion*, p. 25.

98. Hazard Adams, *William Blake: "Jerusalem," Selected Poems and Prose* (New York: Holt, Rinehart, Winston, 1971), p. 724. S. Foster Damon, in *A Blake Dictionary* (1965; rpt., New York: Dutton, 1971), p. 140, suggests that the left foot symbolized Urizen and thus that "Milton became part of Blake primarily through his ideas."

99. See Fox, *Poetic Form*, pp. 116–17; Edward J. Rose, "Los, Pilgrim of Eternity," in Wittreich and Curran, *Sublime Allegory*, pp. 83–99, esp. p. 85; and D. E. James, *Written Within*, p. 88.

Chapter 3: Keats's Hyperion

1. Christopher Ricks, *Keats and Embarrassment* (Oxford: Clarendon Press, 1974), p. 7, tracks the beginning of this debate back to Leavis; see also John Jones, *John Keats's Dream of Truth* (London: Chatto and Windus, 1969), pp. 76ff.; however, his later discussion on pp. 159–64 takes a momentarily more positive view of Keats's Miltonic stationing as a sculptural stasis no longer "servile"— though ultimately leading toward "a blighted moonscape of the spatial imagination's own making, . . . a country without feel."

2. See particularly Jack, *Mirror of Art*. For discussion of this description as impeding the narrative, see Bush, *Mythology and the Romantic Tradition*, p. 119, and Bate, *Keats*, chap. 16.

3. Although focus upon the anxiety of this search begins with Bate's *Burden of the Past*, Bloom's *Anxiety of Influence*, and more recent studies, the centrality of this theme in *Hyperion* has long been noted; for example, Clarence Thorpe, *The Mind of John Keats* (New York: Oxford University Press, 1926), pp. 43–45; Kenneth Muir, "The Meaning of *Hyperion*," in *Keats: A Reassessment*, ed. Muir (1958; rpt., Liverpool: University of Liverpool Press, 1959), pp. 104–05, arguing for a broad cultural and political view of progress; and Edward B. Hungerford, *Shores of Darkness* (1941; rpt., Cleveland: Meridian, 1963), pp. 147ff., arguing for a progress of poetry. Leslie Brisman's two books, *Milton's Poetry of Choice* and *Romantic Origins*, both claim a greater freedom than does Bloom for the romantics and especially for Keats in emulating Milton; see esp. *Choice*, p. 97, and *Origins*, chap.

2. In *Keats the Poet*, p. 165, Sperry argues that if *Hyperion* challenges Milton in style and method, its primary thematic challenge is to Keats's more immediate predecessor Wordsworth; and that *The Fall of Hyperion* is in fact more, yet independently, Miltonic as it revises Milton's myth of suffering and redemption. Stuart Ende, in *Keats and the Sublime* (New Haven: Yale University Press, 1976), p. xiv, includes Milton as part of "an idealized or sublime otherness" toward which the poet feels ambivalence; Ende uses Freudian theories to analyze that ambivalence.

4. John Middleton Murry, "Keats and Wordsworth" in *Keats* (New York: Noonday, 1955), p. 279.

5. Van Ghent, *Myth*, pp. 192ff.

6. Tilottama Rajan, *Dark Interpreter: The Discourse of Romanticism* (Ithaca: Cornell University Press, 1980); see chap. 1 and pp. 183, 194ff. For anticipations of this developmental argument, see Geoffrey Hartman's essays, "Spectral Symbolism and Authorial Self in Keats's *Hyperion*," in Hartman, *The Fate of Reading and Other Essays* (Chicago: University of Chicago Press, 1975), p. 69, and "Blake and the Progress of Poesy," in *Beyond Formalism*, pp. 193–205. Karl Kroeber notes a shift from simple to complex, "mechanical" to "organic" harmony within *Hyperion*, but he relates this shift neither to Schlegel nor to plastic and pictorial analogues; see "The Commemorative Prophecy of *Hyperion*," *Transactions of the Wisconsin Academy of Sciences, Arts, and Letters* 52 (1963): 190. Ronald A. Sharp, in *Keats, Scepticism, and the Religion of Beauty* (Athens: University of Georgia Press, 1979), pp. 139ff, suggests that Titan is to Olympian as Christianity to Keats's new religion of beauty.

7. An earlier version of my argument appeared in Nancy M. Goslee, "Plastic to Picturesque: Schlegel's Analogue and Keats's *Hyperion* Poems," *K-SJ* 30 (1981): 118–51.

8. Almost all Keats critics have noted the sculpturesque quality of the Titans, Jack even quoting a passage from Schlegel's lectures in support (*Mirror of Art*, p. 174); Jack also notes the pictorial, Titian-like qualities of book 3. He does not relate the two characteristics to Schlegel's theories, however.

9. See René Wellek, *A History of Modern Criticism*, Vol. 2, *The Romantic Age* (New Haven: Yale University Press, 1955), pp. 57–58. See also Rajan, *Dark Interpreter*, p. 52n.

10. Schlegel, *Lectures*, 1:9. Because my essay argues that Keats may well have known this translation, I have used it as the basis for my discussion of Schlegel; further citations to this work will appear in the text with volume and page numbers. For the origin of his ideas and earlier versions of his thesis, see Wellek, *Romantic Age*, pp. 57ff.

11. Coleridge, *Shakespeare Criticism*, 2:159–60. A later version (1813) is in 2:262. The parallel passages in Schlegel are in *Lectures*, 1:9ff. For Schelling's use of this analogue, see his "On the Relation of the Plastic Arts to Nature," rpt. in Hazard Adams, ed., *Critical Theory Since Plato* (New York: Harcourt Brace Jovanovich, 1971), p. 455; Wellek, *Romantic Age*, p. 79; Munro, *Arts and Interrelationships*, p. 173; Coleridge, *Shakespeare Criticism*, 1:xxvii–xxviii. In *Coleridge's Miscellaneous Criticism*, ed. Thomas Middleton Raysor (1936; rpt., Folcroft, Pa.: Folcroft Press, 1969), the report of Coleridge's 1818 lecture based on Schelling omits this crucial

analogue—though perhaps because he had used Schlegel's version of it so frequently earlier in his lectures that year. For Coleridge's earlier use of "statuesque" and "picturesque," see Larrabee, *English Bards and Grecian Marbles*, p. 135.

12. Johann Joachim Winckelmann, *History of Ancient Art*, trans. G. Henry Lodge, 4 vols. in 2 (New York: Ungar, 1968), 2:52ff. This edition is essentially a reprint of Lodge's 1873 translation, the only English translation, but published in two volumes instead of the original four. Although pagination is continuous for each of the two 1968 volumes, the original volume numbers for the four volumes are preserved.

13. These musical analogues probably are derived from his brother Friedrich Schlegel and from Schiller. See Coleridge, *Shakespeare Criticism*, 1:xxx–xxxi; Wellek, *Later Eighteenth Century* for Schiller and *Romantic Age* for Friedrich Schlegel; and Friedrich von Schiller, *"Naive and Sentimental Poetry" and "On the Sublime,"* trans. Julius A. Elias (New York: Ungar, 1966), p. 133 and n.

14. See Reynolds, *Discourses*, 3 and 10, opening paragraphs; Flaxman, *Lectures*, pp. 170, 191, 225–26; and Hagstrum, *Sister Arts*, p. 144. See also Chapter 2.

15. Roy Park, *Hazlitt and the Spirit of the Age: Abstraction and Critical Theory* (Oxford: Clarendon Press, 1971), p. 119.

16. See *The Diary of Benjamin Robert Haydon*, ed. Willard Bissell Pope, 5 vols. (Cambridge, Mass.: Harvard University Press, 1960), 2:38 and n.

17. Ibid., 2:120. Pope notes the Black translation.

18. See Keats, *Poems*, ed. Stillinger, pp. 564–65.

19. See Coleridge, *Miscellaneous Criticism*, pp. 3–5. For Keats's attendance at the Hazlitt lectures, see Bate, *Keats*, pp. 259–60. Although Charles Lamb did not attend those Coleridge lectures, he is a possible intermediary because Crabb Robinson reports going to both series, seeing Lamb frequently, and earlier agreeing with him about Coleridge's debts to Schlegel's *Lectures*; Keats also saw Lamb frequently. See *Henry Crabb Robinson on Books and their Writers*, ed. Edith J. Morley, 3 vols. (London: Dent, 1938), 1:63, 178, 219. Leigh Hunt also had read Schlegel's lectures. See his "Preface [to Foliage]," 1818, in *Leigh Hunt's Literary Criticism*, ed. Lawrence Houston Houtchens and Carolyn Washburn Houtchens (New York: Columbia University Press, 1956), p. 140, cited by Timothy Webb in *The Violet in the Crucible: Shelley and Translation* (Oxford: Clarendon Press, 1976), p. 59. In their broadest terms, of course, these ideas of classical and romantic, Mediterranean and northern, had become cultural clichés for the cognoscenti such as Crabb Robinson, who prided himself on having introduced the popularizing Mme de Stael to the Schlegel brothers in Jena fifteen years earlier. He attended many of Coleridge's series of lectures and debated German literature with him frequently. Although he knew many members of Keats's circle, he apparently did not know Keats directly.

20. William Hazlitt, "Schlegel on the Drama," in *Complete Works of William Hazlitt*, ed. P. P. Howe, Centenary Edition, 21 vols. (London: Dent, 1931–1934), 16:65–66. All quotations from Hazlitt are from this edition.

21. Paul Sherwin's essay, "Dying into Life: Keats's Struggle with Milton in *Hyperion*," *PMLA* 93 (1978): 383–95, also uses these metaphors from Blake's *Milton*—following Bloom and Murry.

22. Both context and form of Hazlitt's examples from the "pagan systems" offer another link to Keats's emulation of Milton in the *Hyperion* poems and suggest strongly that Keats had read Hazlitt's review. The marginal discussion of Milton's "stationing or statuary" in Keats's copy of *Paradise Lost* uses examples that, though drawn from Milton, sound strikingly like Hazlitt's placing of the pagan statues "in airy porticos, in solemn temples and consecrated groves." Moreover, the context of Hazlitt's line from *Hamlet* (3.4.53ff.) ties "stationing" to the image of Hyperion in a way that must have helped to suggest Keats's analysis of "stationing" both in Miltonic epic and in his own epic.

23. Judy Little, *Keats as a Narrative Poet: A Test of Invention* (Lincoln: University of Nebraska Press, 1975), pp. 127ff. Her discussion and references directed me to the following Hazlitt passages on epic objects.

24. See, for example, *Lectures on the English Poets* 5:22 ("On Chaucer and Spenser"), and 5:53 ("On Shakespeare and Milton"). Park (*Hazlitt*, p. 144) notes that Hazlitt's comparison of Kemble and Kean is essentially a contrast between "statuesque" and "picturesque."

25. See Gilpin, *Mountains and Lakes* 1:184, and Coleridge, *Miscellaneous Criticism*, p. 165 (from Lecture 10, 27 February 1818). Raysor notes that Schiller had so described Klopstock in "On Naive and Sentimental Poetry."

26. Little, *Narrative Poet*, p. 140.

27. Sperry, *Keats the Poet*, pp. 169–79.

28. Bate, *Keats*, pp. 246–47; *Hyperion*, 1.4, 31–32, 85–86.

29. See Jack, *Mirror of Art*, pp. 163ff., for a discussion of possible Greek models and definite Egyptian ones. He does not suggest archaic Greek models. Winckelmann's *History*, however, does describe a Greek style preceding the Phidian or grand style and resembling the Egyptian; see 1:34ff. and 2:119ff. Van Ghent, *Myth*, pp. 189–90, suggests Winckelmann's distinction of archaic and Praxitelean styles as models for the Titans and Apollo.

30. The parallel is Bate's, in *Keats*, pp. 510, 584; from "Sleep and Poetry," l. 237.

31. Jack, *Mirror of Art*, p. 174, compares these figures to "Michelangelo," probably thinking—to judge from the context—of his frescoes of the Last Judgment; they also seem similar to his half-completed, half-carved slave figures.

32. See N. Frye, "Drunken Boat," and M. H. Abrams, "English Romanticism: The Spirit of the Age," in N. Frye, *Romanticism Reconsidered*.

33. Van Ghent's argument (*Myth*, p. 187) that the poem shows beneath its superficial conflict of generations a rebirth of individual heroes into full development is a similar idea but sets the process within myth; Keats's characters move beyond myth, as I interpret them.

34. In his note to these lines in *John Keats: The Collected Poems*, 2d ed. (1977; rpt., New York: Penguin, 1978), p. 612, John Barnard states that Saturn "is depicted as the creator of the ordered universe"; but Oceanus does not seem to know this. James Land Jones implies that creation of a world separate from self is a result of the fall into self-consciousness. See *Adam's Dream: Mythic Consciousness in Keats and Yeats* (Athens: University of Georgia Press, 1975), p. 184. Ende, in *Keats and the Sublime*, p. 101, interprets Saturn as one who "in easing his heart of love . . . falls

victim to the danger faced by poets as well—he surrenders self without retaining power or self-possession." As a result "the mind" attempts "to retain objects" but fails (ibid., p. 105).

35. See Martin Meisel's essay, "The Material Sublime: John Martin, Byron, Turner, and the Theatre," in *Images of Romanticism: Verbal and Visual Affinities*, ed. Karl Kroeber and William Walling (New Haven: Yale University Press, 1978), pp. 211–32, and Jack, *Mirror of Art*, pp. 171ff.

36. Although Michael G. Cooke does not discuss this passage in *The Romantic Will* (New Haven: Yale University Press, 1976) and his discussion of Keats there focuses more specifically on a "will to art," his book has drawn my attention to the importance of will in these lines.

37. See *John Keats: Selected Poems and Letters*, ed. Douglas Bush (Boston: Houghton Mifflin, 1959), p. 337.

38. See Jack, *Mirror of Art*, pp. 167–71, for possible sculptural sources and for the conventional image of sunrise striking the statue as topics in minor eighteenth-century poetry.

39. See J[ohn] Lempriere, *Bibliotheca Classica: A Classical Dictionary*, containing a full account of all the Proper Names mentioned in Antient Authors . . . , 4th ed. (London: T. Cadell and W. Davies, 1801), entries for "Hyperion" and "Apollo." Gray's "Progress of Poesy," though it vividly evokes both Hyperion and poetic development, also restricts Hyperion to the sun. See *The Complete Poems of Thomas Gray, English, Latin, and Greek*, ed. H. W. Starr and J. R. Hendrickson (Oxford: Oxford University Press, 1966), 2.1; p. 14. Interestingly, variants of Gray's lines all show Hyperion in more active violence. Editors of an 1832 text suggest that Hyperion is analogous to the muse. See *The Poetical Works of Milton, Young, Gray, Beattie, and Collins*, no ed. given (Philadelphia: John Grigg, 1832), p. 36n. In *Milton*, Blake transforms Gray's Hyperion to himself as prophet wielding a "Bow of burning gold"; see Irene Tayler, *Blake's Illustrations to Gray* (Princeton: Princeton University Press, 1971), p. 87n, and Goslee, "Blake's Stanzas from *Milton*," pp. 121–22.

40. Douglas Bush, in *Science and English Poetry: A Historical Sketch, 1590–1950* (New York: Oxford University Press, 1950), pp. 105–07, suggests that the setting of the Reynolds epistle on the beach "happens to resemble" a setting in which William Paley "Saw multitudes of shrimps leaping in sheer exuberance of happiness" (*Natural Theology; or, Evidence of the Existence and Attributes of the Deity, collected from the Appearances of Nature* [London: R. Foulder, 1802], p. 492); see also Keats, *Selected Poems*, ed. Bush, p. 328, for earlier theories of an amoral and bloody nature.

41. Coleridge, *Shakespearean Criticism*, 1:196–97; Raysor cites Schlegel, *Sammtliche Werke*, ed. Edouard Böcking, 12 vols. (Leipzig: Weidmann, 1846–1847), 6:158ff., and Reynolds, *Idler*, no. 82, "The true idea of beauty," in *The Yale Edition of the Works of Samuel Johnson. Volume II: Samuel Johnson, "The Idler" and "The Adventurer,"* ed. W. J. Bate, John M. Bullitt, and L. F. Powell (New Haven and London: Yale University Press, 1963), pp. 254–58. Coleridge's passage seems strikingly close to Oceanus's rhetoric in its themes and images.

42. This bird's-eye view of Wordsworth's challenges to sight is based upon Geoffrey Hartman's *Wordsworth's Poetry 1787–1814* (New Haven: Yale University Press, 1964) and Bloom's *Romanticism and Consciousness*, pt. 1 and pp. 273–304. For a detailed discussion of the visual and its relation to the sublime, see Weiskel, *Romantic Sublime*.

43. William Hazlitt, "Schlegel on the Drama," *Edinburgh Review*, *Works* 16:65–66.

44. Ibid.

45. Cited by Park, *Hazlitt*, p. 129. He gives several contemporary parallels; Reynolds probably gave the idea currency in his Discourse 10, and Fuseli repeats it in his Royal Academy lectures. Haydon had been his student and occasional assistant; see *Diary*, 1:32.

46. See most recently Anne Kostelanetz Mellor in "Keats's Face of Moneta: Source and Meaning," *K-SJ* 25 (1976): 65–80.

47. See Little, *Narrative Poet*, pp. 138–39; but see also Van Ghent, *Myth*, pp. 196ff.

48. Little, *Narrative Poet*, pp. 139–40.

49. D. G. James, *The Romantic Comedy* (1948; rpt., London: Oxford University Press, 1963), p. 141.

50. See Reynolds, *Discourses*, 10, paragraphs 20ff.

51. The *OED* notes under the latter meaning that "the stress *conte'nt* is historical and still common among the educated, but *co. ntent* is now used by many, esp. young people" (1981 correspondent).

52. See Abrams, *Mirror and Lamp*, pp. 50–51, and n. 13 above.

53. See Sperry, *Keats the Poet*, p. 183n.

Chapter 4: Keats's The Fall of Hyperion

1. Perkins goes on, in his headnote to *The Fall of Hyperion*, to say that "it is doubtful whether the two could have been combined"; in David Perkins, ed., *English Romantic Writers* (New York: Harcourt Brace Jovanovich, 1967), p. 1197. See also Keats, *Selected Poems*, ed. Bush, p. 356; Bush quotes Muir ("Meaning of *Hyperion*," in Muir, *Keats: A Reassessment*, p. 120), saying that Keats "had already used up the climax" of *Hyperion* in canto 1 of *The Fall*; but see Sperry, *Keats the Poet*, p. 313, for a more positive view. In *Narrative Poet*, Little has a useful survey of the debate.

2. Brian Wicker, "The Disputed Lines in *The Fall of Hyperion*," *Essays in Criticism* 7 (1975): 38.

3. See Little, *Narrative Poet*, p. 147, and Rajan, *Dark Interpreter*, pp. 192–93.

4. See Van Ghent, *Myth*, p. 232.

5. See Brisman, *Origins*, p. 385. On this point I disagree with Rajan; see *Dark Interpreter*, pp. 186ff., although her earlier statement on p. 169 is more positive.

6. See Bate, *Keats*, p. 438n, for Keats's acquaintance with Gothic windows.

7. Here I diverge from Paul D. Sheats, "Stylistic Discipline in *The Fall of Hyperion*," *K-SJ* 17 (1968): 82, though I do agree that the "stationed" observer's "perception results in . . . self-consciousness" (p. 83). Bernice Slote, in *Keats and the Dramatic Principle* (Lincoln: University of Nebraska Press, 1958), pp. 127–29, points to Keats's development of "organic relationships in figure and scene"; she cites *Lamia* particularly. In "Phenomenology and Process: Perception in Keats's 'I Stood Tip-Toe.' " *K-SJ* 25 (1976): 44, 48, Marjorie Norris emphasizes the subjective nature of "perceived space" in Keats's poetry.

8. See Arthur H. Bell, " 'The Depth of Things': Keats and Human Space," *K-SJ* 23 (1974): 77–94, esp. pp. 91ff., which briefly discuss *The Fall of Hyperion*. Bell suggests that vast space is less disorienting in Moneta's temple than in earlier poems because the narrator is directed. For a discussion of the enclosing vale as bower, see Morris Dickstein, *Keats and his Poetry* (Chicago: University of Chicago Press, 1971), pp. 26ff.; the motif is central to the book.

9. See Wicker, "Disputed Lines," pp. 29–30.

10. See Harold Bloom, *The Visionary Company: A Reading of English Romantic Poetry*, rev., enl. ed. (Ithaca: Cornell University Press, 1971), p. 428.

11. See Frances A. Yates, *The Art of Memory* (1966; rpt., Harmondsworth: Penguin, 1969).

12. Although Robert Gittings claims in *The Mask of Keats: A Study of Problems* (Cambridge, Mass.: Harvard University Press, 1956) that volumes 2 and 3 of Keats's copy of Dante were unopened, John Saly argues, with Bridges, Lowes, and Hewlett, that the Purgatorio and the Paradiso both influenced *The Fall*; see John Saly, "Keats's Answer to Dante: *The Fall*," *K-SJ* 14 (1965): 65–78. See also Little, *Narrative Poet*, pp. 120ff., for a general discussion of Keats's use of dream vision as genre.

13. Bush's text of Keats's *Selected Poems* has "chain." Stillinger (*Poems of John Keats*) prints "charm" and explains that the W² transcript has "cham"; as Stillinger explains (pp. 670–71), Keats's letter to Woodhouse (21–22 September 1819, now at Harvard) has "charm"; and Charlotte Reynolds's transcript has " 'chain'—presumably . . . an attempt to make sense of W²'s 'cham.' "

14. Such a test of time was advocated strongly by Samuel Johnson in the 1765 preface to his edition of Shakespeare; see *The Yale Edition of the Works of Samuel Johnson, Volume VII: Johnson on Shakespeare*, ed. Arthur Sherbo, 1st of 2 vols. (New Haven: Yale University Press, 1968), pp. 59–60.

15. *OED*; all the entries for "methought" are drawn from dream visions, even as early as 1300–1400.

16. Sperry includes the first 56 lines as part of the "induction" (see *Keats the Poet*, p. 319), as does Little (*Narrative Poet*, p. 125). A few pages earlier, however, Little notes that the grove or garden is typically the first stage of the dream in medieval dream vision (p. 122). Bush's notes to Keats, *Selected Poems*, call lines 1–293 the induction—hence not an induction to dream but to Moneta's vision, the revised narrative of *Hyperion* (p. 355).

17. See *The Poems of John Keats*, ed. Miriam Allott (London: Longman, 1970), p. 658n; Allott notes that Keats marked *Paradise Lost* 5.377–79.

18. See William C. Stephenson, "The Performing Narrator in Keats's Poetry," *K-SJ* 26 (1977): 69, for a similar view of the narrator's refusal to interpret explicitly.

19. Ernest de Selincourt, in Keats, *"Hyperion": A Facsimile of Keats's Autograph Manuscript. With a transliteration of the manuscript of "The Fall of Hyperion, A Dream,"* with introduction and notes by de Selincourt (Oxford: Clarendon Press, 1905), p. 24, proposes that garden, temple, and shrine are analogous to the "three stages in the poet's development toward the attainment of his ideal"—in *Sleep and Poetry* and in the 3 May 1818 letter to Reynolds. Several later critics, however, suggest ambiguity in the opening scene, based on its parallels to *Paradise Lost*. Sperry's intriguing reading argues that the poet reenacts Adam's fall because imagination is the knowledge of good and evil (*Keats the Poet*, p. 320); this becomes largely a fortunate but somewhat ambiguous "fall." Wicker paradoxically sees the "meal and potion" as "sacramental union between the poet in his present disordered state and the state of primordial human innocence" ("Disputed Lines," p. 40). Saly ("Keats's Answer," p. 77) suggests that the poet is defiant in his repetition of Adam's sin. I am suggesting some consciousness of fallen disorder even before he eats, and surely before he drinks.

20. Although it is unlikely that Keats was directly familiar with Alcibiades' speech in the *Symposium* describing Socrates as a clay Silenus figure, Shelley translated it in July 1818; see James A. Notopoulos, *The Platonism of Shelley: A Study of Platonism and the Literary Mind* (Durham: Duke University Press, 1949), p. 453, and Webb, *Violet in the Crucible*, pp. 32, 40. See also Jack, *Mirror of Art*, p. 159; pl. 19, Poussin's *Indian Triumph of Bacchus*, and pl. 37, the Borghese Vase.

21. See Bush's textual note in Keats's *Selected Poems*, p. 357.

22. See Bate, *Keats*, pp. 25–26.

23. Bloom, *Visionary Company*, p. 423.

24. Mellor, "Moneta," p. 71. For earlier, more eclectic speculation on Keats's sources, see John Livingston Lowes, "Moneta's Temple," *PMLA* 51 (1936): 1098–1113, and D. S. Bland, "Painting and the Poetry of Keats: Some Further Identifications," *MLR* 50 (1955): 502–04.

25. Bloom, *Visionary Company*, p. 423.

26. See Hartman, "Blake and the Progress of Poesy," in *Beyond Formalism*, pp. 196ff., for a discussion of "westering myth"; this one differs from his pattern because Saturn's myth appears original or primal, not derived and made less mysterious as it moves from the east.

27. In *Visionary Company*, pp. 423–24, Bloom suggests that this westward turn makes the sanctuary a temple acknowledging the failure of all religions to overcome man's mortality.

28. See Sperry, *Keats the Poet*, p. 321. Kenneth Muir suggests earlier that "Mnemosyne . . . [in *Hyperion*] is the personification of the vision and understanding of human history," a reading that points toward this reading of the continuity of human culture. See Muir, "Meaning of *Hyperion*," p. 108.

29. Passages from the Preface and the Prospectus are from Wordsworth, *Works*, vol. 5; this passage from p. 2.

30. See Watson, *Picturesque Landscape*, p. 83.

31. Sperry interprets the first *Hyperion* as Keats's challenge to Wordsworth's near-despairing portrayal of withdrawal into isolation; see *Keats the Poet*, chap. 7.

32. In this assessment I follow critics such as Bate and Bloom, not the idealist readings culminating in Earl R. Wasserman's *The Finer Tone* (1953; rpt., Baltimore: Johns Hopkins University Press, 1967).

33. Although John Jones does not use this phrase, his discussion of *The Fall* suggests a widespread split between the snail-horn perception and abstract idea; see *Dream of Truth*, pp. 91–104. Bloom, *Poetry and Repression*, p. 130, describes "various reductions of" the past as "reified" fragments.

34. On "surmise," see Hartman, *Wordsworth's Poetry*, pp. 8ff.

35. Bloom, *Visionary Company*, p. 428.

36. See Murry, *Keats*, p. 245, for a differing analysis of subcategories; he says the "imaginative" or morally perceptive are divided into dreamers and useful humanitarians.

37. For Moneta's significance in rites of purification for the "twice-born," see Dorothy Van Ghent, "Keats's Myth of the Hero," *K-SJ* 3 (1954): 13; and for a more recent expansion, idem, *Myth*, pp. 224ff.

38. See textual notes in Keats, *Poems*, ed. Stillinger, p. 672. In contrast, see an earlier discussion in Wicker, "Disputed Lines," p. 28n, where he agrees with Murry that this passage should be excluded but argues against Murry that there would still remain "an extraordinary degree of confusion" in the main text minus these lines.

39. See Bloom, *Visionary Company*, pp. 138–40, for an interpretation of Wordsworth's response to Dorothy's presence in "Tintern Abbey."

40. See Hartman, "Spectral Symbolism," p. 72.

41. See D. G. James, *Romantic Comedy*, p. 150.

42. Rajan, *Dark Interpreter*, pp. 192–93, argues that the Titans are *only* statues or masks we cannot see beyond.

43. See ibid., chap. 1, for a discussion of sentimental apocalyptics.

44. For an analysis of Moneta's successive misinterpretations of the poet that make her "the Muse of repression" of the sort of "death marked by privation" that she is in effect describing here, see Bloom, *Poetry and Repression*, pp. 130–42.

45. See Sperry, *Keats the Poet*, p. 325.

46. See Chapter 2, final section. In a long review, "Flaxman's Lectures on Sculptures," at their publication in 1829, Hazlitt finds Flaxman's objections to color inconsistent, but he supports the objection on the grounds that "A statue is the utmost possible development of form; and that on which the whole powers . . . of the artist have been bent: it has a right, then, by the laws of intellectual creation, to stand alone in that simplicity and unsullied nakedness in which it has been wrought" (Hazlitt, *Complete Works*, 16:361–62). This seems an expressive theory of form.

47. See John B. Bender, *Spenser and Literary Pictorialism* (Princeton: Princeton University Press, 1972), chap. 2, for a description of "focusing" that shows how Spenser goes beyond a conventional catalogue of stereotyped attributes.

48. See Mellor, "Moneta," p. 66.

49. See Dickstein, *Keats and his Poetry*, p. 260.

50. But, as Leslie Brisman points out, there are no singers here capable of a parallel hymn; see *Origins*, p. 99.

51. Van Ghent, *Myth*, pp. 228–32.

52. See Murry, "Keats and Blake," in *Keats*, pp. 292ff.

53. Sheats suggests that the sculptural comparison is transferred to Saturn, now compared to his own statue in the temple; see "Stylistic Discipline," p. 79.

54. See Haydon, *Diary*, 1:264 (1812), for his resentment that sculpture instead of painting was always the chosen medium for such large public commissions. For sketches of Flaxman's monuments, see *Drawings by John Flaxman in the Huntington Collection*, ed. Robert R. Wark (San Marino, Calif.: Henry E. Huntington Library and Art Gallery, 1970); see also Bindman, *Blake as Artist*, p. 129.

55. In a discussion of James Thomson's "use of one element of the sublime—the 'statuesque,' " Cohen suggests that such sculptural images illustrate not only static Greek beauty but a silence that shows "the inadequacy of poetic expression by comparison with non-verbal art. . . . Thomson's *silence* is a recognition of the inscrutableness of nature, and sculpture and 'fixity' represent the buried yet insoluble life of man. Silence constitutes one mode of response to unanswerable dilemmas"; in *Art of Discrimination*, pp. 274–75. My argument is rather that sculpture in Keats's poetry represents a too-permanent possibility in his own verbal art; yet this reading of Thomson underscores the availability of such poetic modes for Keats. See Rajan's discussion of Schopenhauer's concept of the sublime; his description includes what I would call a strong picturesque element (*Dark Interpreter*, pp. 195–96).

56. See Muir, "Meaning of *Hyperion*," pp. 116–18; cited in Keats, *Selected Poems*, ed. Bush, p. 358.

57. Here I find myself arguing against the "return to the earth" that Leslie Brisman proposes in his reading of *The Fall of the Hyperion* in *Origins*, pp. 92–102, and affirming something like his sceptically framed affirmation of dream in his "Reintroduction" at the end of *Origins*, p. 385.

Chapter 5: Shelley's Prometheus Unbound

1. G. Wilson Knight, *The Starlit Dome: Studies in the Poetry of Vision* (1941; rpt., London: Oxford University Press, 1971), p. 179.

2. Richard Harter Fogle, *The Imagery of Keats and Shelley* (Chapel Hill: University of North Carolina Press, 1949), p. 178.

3. See Shelley, *Variorum*, pp. 48–49, 336. Zillman cites Sidney Lanier, but the complaint has persisted.

4. See *The Drawings of Henry Fuseli*, ed. Nicholas Powell (London: Faber and Faber, 1951), for a reproduction of *Prometheus Rescued by Heracles* (pl. 17), now in the British Museum; Gert Schiff, in *L'Opera Completa di Johann Heinrich Fuseli* (Milan: Rizzoli Editore, 1977), reproduces a painting of this subject and dates it as early as the 1780s. *A Collection of Drawings by Henry Fuseli, R. A.*, ed. Peter Tomory (Auckland: Auckland City Art Gallery, 1967), contains reproductions of the other two: *Prometheus and Io* (no. 15) and *Hephaestus . . . securing Prometheus* (no. 24).

Tomory also reproduces the latter in *Fuseli*, pl. 113. Tomory's notes for the recently discovered Auckland drawings suggest that the group belonged to Moses Haughton, Jr., an engraver who lived with Fuseli from 1803 to 1819 (*Collection*, p. 10); in *Fuseli*, p. 204, Tomory points out that Fuseli "dined" at Godwin's house "as late as 1813" and speculates on links between Fuseli's Promethean treatment of Satan and Mary Shelley's *Frankenstein*. Schiff identifies the drawing of *Prometheus and Io*, according to Tomory, as *Prometheus and Gaia*, thus possibly making it an illustration for the missing second play of Aeschylus's trilogy—and for Shelley's Prometheus listening to Earth, though a more humanized Earth than the one I understand in the play.

5. See *Mary Shelley's Journal*, ed. Frederick L. Jones (Norman: University of Oklahoma Press, 1947), p. 225. Claire Clairmont, traveling with them, was apparently rereading this English translation in Rome during 1819, as she had not begun learning German; see Donald H. Reiman, ed., *Shelley and his Circle*, (Cambridge, Mass.: Harvard University Press, 1973), 6:527, n. 8. In May 1818, however, the Shelley family had lent their copy to the Gisbornes: see *The Letters of Percy Bysshe Shelley*, ed. Frederick L. Jones, 2 vols. (Oxford: Clarendon Press, 1964), 2:17. For Shelley's reading of Coleridge's *Biographia*, see Mary's *Journal*, listing it read on 8 December 1817; for possible Shelley attendance at Coleridge's 27 February 1818 lecture see Reiman, *Shelley Circle*, 6:915n.

6. For Shelley's reading of Winckelmann in December 1818 and January and March 1819, see Mary Shelley, *Journal*, pp. 114–15. He begins reading the *History* during the evenings in Naples and continues in Rome while visiting galleries during the day. Neither he nor Mary mentions it specifically during their fall 1819 stay in Florence. His French text is apparently *Histoire de l'Art Chez les Anciens*, trans. Huber, rev. Jansen, 2 vols. bound as 3 (Paris: Bossange, Masson et Besson, 1802). I have used a copy of this French edition as well as the later English translation; book, chapter, and section divisions are not the same. All English quotations are from Winckelmann, *History*, trans. Lodge, cited in ch. 3, n. 12; the description of classical culture here comes from 1:61.

7. From the preface to *Prometheus Unbound*, in Shelley, *Poetry and Prose*, p. 133.

8. For Schlegel's analysis of Aeschylus's *Prometheus Bound*, see his *Lectures*, 1:112–13.

9. See Frederick A. Pottle, "The Role of Asia in the Dramatic Action of Shelley's *Prometheus Unbound*," in *Shelley: A Collection of Critical Essays*, ed. George M. Ridenour (Englewood Cliffs, N.J.: Prentice-Hall, 1965), pp. 133–43, and Donald H. Reiman, *Percy Bysshe Shelley* (New York: Twayne, 1969), p. 87.

10. See Bloom's discussion of *askesis* or purgation in *Anxiety of Influence*, chap. 5, though I do not pursue here the full implications of his theory for my use of the term. See also Daniel J. Hughes, "Prometheus Made Capable Poet in Act I of *Prometheus Unbound*," *SiR* 17 (1978): 4: "After establishing Prometheus' capacity to create, Shelley lets the rest of the poem use him up; he is *sacrificed* like the Bard of the West Wind."

11. Shelley, *Poetry and Prose*, p. 489.

12. Ibid., pp. 490–91. John Sewell Flagg, in *"Prometheus Unbound" and "Hellas": An Approach to Shelley's Lyrical Dramas*, Romantic Reassessment, no. 14 (Salzburg:

Institut für Englische Sprache und Literatur, 1972), discusses this passage from the *Defence* and Schlegel on pp. 194–95, though he does not explicitly link them; the Schlegel analogue is in Lecture 2.

13. This mirroring that completes its original is similar to the idea of the epipsyche that Shelley explores from *Alastor* through the 1818 essay "On Love." For its date, see Reiman, *Shelley Circle*, 6:633–47.

14. For a fuller discussion of these "Notes" as exemplifying a "romantic" or metaphysical picturesque structure, see Nancy M. Goslee, "Shelley's 'Notes on Sculpture': Toward a Romantic Classicism in *Prometheus Unbound*," *Comparatist* 4 (1980): 11–22. My claims there for interpreting the individual notes in this way still hold, I believe; my claim for the organization of the "Notes" as a whole must be modified in light of E. B. Murray's research (see following discussion in text).

15. See E. B. Murray, "Shelley's *Notes on Sculptures:* The Provenance and Authority of the Text," *K-SJ* 32 (1983): 150–71, esp. 170n.

16. Shelley, *Letters*, 2:84, 86, 88–89 (23 March 1819).

17. See Timothy Webb, *Shelley: A Voice Not Understood* (Manchester: Manchester University Press, 1977), p. 211.

18. The volumes are large quartos (26½ by 20¼ cm.). The edition consists of two volumes, but the second one is bound in two parts. For a description of Shelley writing these notes, see Thomas Medwin, *The Life of Percy Bysshe Shelley. A New Edition printed from a copy copiously emended and extended by the Author and left unpublished at his death.* Intro., comm. by H. Buxton Forman (London: Oxford University Press, 1913), p. 222. See also Webb, *Voice*, p. 224.

19. See the letter to Peacock in Shelley, *Letters*, 2:88 (23 March 1819). See also Webb, *Voice*, p. 213.

20. Winckelmann, *History*, 2:246.

21. Medwin, *Shelley*, pp. 216–17.

22. *The Complete Works of Percy Bysshe Shelley*, ed. Roger Ingpen and Walter E. Peck, 10 vols., the Julian Edition (New York: Scribner's Sons; London: Benn, 1929), 6:319. All citations to the "Notes on Sculpture" are to this edition, cited as Julian, unless otherwise noted.

23. See Frederic S. Colwell, "Shelley on Sculpture: The Uffizi Notes," *K-SJ* 28 (1979): 59–77, and Murray, "Shelley's *Notes*," pp. 166–69. Ingpen and Peck have used H. Buxton Forman's edition of the "Notes," first published privately in 1879 and then in *The Works of Percy Bysshe Shelley*, ed. Forman, 8 vols. (London: Reeves and Turner, 1880); the "Notes" are in vol. 7. Ingpen and Peck include variants from Forman's text in their textual notes. *Shelley's Prose, or The Trumpet of a Prophecy*, ed. David Lee Clark (1954; rpt., Albuquerque: University of New Mexico Press, 1966), follows Forman most of the time and Medwin occasionally, but does not indicate where the text changes. I have examined Bod. MS. Shelley adds. c. 4, several loose folio sheets, which contain a fair copy of "The Arch of Titus," included by Forman as Note 1, evidently because he thought the Laocoon Shelley described was in Rome and should be introduced by this Roman gateway, just as the series was to be concluded by the "Pitti Gardens"; see Murray, "Shelley's *Notes*," p. 157.

24. Winckelmann, *History*, 4:85.

25. Schlegel, *Lectures*, 1:88.

26. See Murray, "Shelley's *Notes*," p. 169.

27. Julian, pp. 310–11; Medwin, *Shelley*, pp. 223–24.

28. Julian, p. 330; Haskell and Penny, *Taste and the Antique*, pp. 274–79 on the Niobe and pp. 100–107 on Winckelmann. The editors of the French text criticize Winckelmann for thinking that he is seeing the most significant version of the Niobe group; that one, they explain, is in Florence (Winckelmann, *Histoire*, 2:286n); by the time they write, indeed it is. Two of Shelley's tour guides to Italy mention the Niobe group specifically. Joseph Forsyth, *Remarks on Antiquities, Arts, and Letters during an Excursion in Italy in the years 1802 and 1803*, 2d ed. (London: John Murray, 1816), praises the Niobe as the high point of sculpture in Florence but says little else about the group; he does describe a modern anatomist-sculptor in Florence, however, as "this active Prometheus" (p. 37). John Chetwode Eustace, *A Classical Tour Through Italy (1802)*, 3d ed., rev. and enl., 4 vols. (London: J. Mawman, 1815), 3:363–64, is more specific in describing the gallery in the Uffizi that contains the group and in reporting critical debate over whether this is the original group Pliny describes or a Roman copy.

29. For the first phrase, the French text reads, "Niobe et ses filles." In a note, the editor admits, "j'ai ajouté ici Niobe, à cause que tout l'ensemble de ce paragraphe le demande, et parce que Winckelmann en a fait de même dans *le Traité preliminaire* de son *Expl. de Mon. de l'ant.* ch. iv. C.F." (Winckelmann, *Histoire*, 1:424n).

30. Winckelmann, *History*, 2:251.

31. Ibid., 3:132, 136.

32. Schlegel, *Lectures*, 1:89.

33. Julian, pp. 331–32. Mary Shelley's text for this Note, in *Essays, Letters from Abroad, Translations, and Fragments, by Percy Bysshe Shelley*, 2 vols. (London: Edward Moxon, 1840), 2:263–66, does include a reference to stone as well as to the fountain. See also Julian, p. 379; it quotes Medwin's 1833 version, which also alludes to the metamorphosis into stone.

34. Julian, pp. 330, 332.

35. See Robert A. Hartley, "The Uroboros in Shelley's Poetry," *JEGP* 73 (1974): 536–38; Plato, *Timaeus, Cleitophon, Critias, Menexenus, Epistles*, Loeb Classical Library (1929; rpt., Cambridge, Mass.: Harvard University Press, 1942), pp. 90–91; and Notopoulos, *Platonism of Shelley*, p. 116, for a discussion of a "nature plastique." Notopoulos cites Ralph Cudworth's *The True Intellectual System of the Universe* (London: R. Royston, 1678) though saying Shelley probably had not read it directly; Notopoulos (p. 138) points to Diderot's encyclopedia article on *Nature Plastique*. Thomas McFarland (*Coleridge and the Pantheist Tradition* [Oxford: Clarendon Press, 1969], pp. 260–61) traces Coleridge's exposure to this idea before reading Schlegel by citing Cudworth's *System*, pp. 147, 155–56. See also Peacock's footnote to *Rhododaphne* in Shelley, *Variorum*, p. 313n. For late classical sources of Prometheus as creator of men, see Shelley, *Variorum*, pp. 727–28 (Apollodorus, fl. 140 B.C., and Lucian, A.D. 125–190). See also Anthony Ashley Cooper, Third Earl of Shaftesbury, *Characteristicks of Men, Manners, Opinions, Times, etc.*, ed., intro., and notes by John M. Robertson, 2 vols. (London: Grant Richards, 1900), 1:335,

in a passage cited by McFarland, *Coleridge and the Pantheist Tradition*, p. 34, as he argues that the Germans found the Platonic idea through Shaftesbury, but Coleridge more directly through Plotinus.

36. Oscar W. Firkins, *Power and Elusiveness in Shelley* (Minneapolis: University of Minnesota Press, 1937), p. 82.

37. Sarah Dyck, in "The Presence of that Shape: Shelley's *Prometheus Unbound*," *Costerus* 1 (1972): 21, suggests that "shape" reflects "the image of a mind struggling to create order." Larrabee, *English Bards and Grecian Marbles*, p. 184, points out that "form" for Shelley usually refers to sculpture.

38. Susan Hawk Brisman, " 'Unsaying His High Language': The Problem of Voice in *Prometheus Unbound*," *SiR* 16 (1977): 66–67.

39. Hughes, "Prometheus Made Capable Poet," p. 5.

40. "Shape" (including "shapes" and "shapeless") occurs forty-one times, "form" twenty-six, and "image" (including "imaged" and "imageless") nine. See F. S. Ellis, *A Lexical Concordance to the Poetical Works of Percy Bysshe Shelley* (1892; rpt., New York: Burt Franklin, 1968). The concordance, however, omits some references that I have found, so that my numbers here are drawn from the concordance checked and supplemented with my reading. As my analysis of these terms will indicate, I see a greater specificity in Shelley's vocabulary than does Jean Hall in *The Transforming Image: A Study of Shelley's Major Poetry* (Urbana: University of Illinois Press, 1980); see esp. pp. 5, 14. Two recent articles, both in *K-SJ* 31 (1982), support, though in quite different ways, this attempt to read Shelley's language closely, especially his language about the relationship of language to some external reality; see Frederick Burwick, "The Language of Causality in *Prometheus Unbound*," pp. 136–58, and Jerrold E. Hogle, "Shelley's Poetics: The Power as Metaphor," pp. 159–97.

41. Act 1, twenty-three times; act 2, eighteen; act 3, twenty-one; act 4, thirteen.

42. Firkins, *Power and Elusiveness*, p. 82; cited in Shelley, *Variorum*, p. 407.

43. See Stephen Rogers, *Classical Greece and the Poetry of Chenier, Shelley, and Leopardi* (South Bend: University of Notre Dame Press, 1974), p. 74; George Thomson, *Aeschylus and Athens*, 3d ed. (1966; rpt., New York: Grosset and Dunlap, 1968), pp. 307ff. Rogers, following Thomson and traditional analyses, actually describes a prologue and then four episodes both in Aeschylus and in Shelley's act 1. See also Reiman, who sees only three main "movements" in the act, including Prometheus's opening monologue through his confrontation with the phantasm of Jupiter as one section; he argues that this structure parallels the three movements of act 4 (*Percy Bysshe Shelley*, p. 75). One can preserve the parallel, however, in a four-part division for each of these acts: the masques of the Furies then correspond to the lyric dialogue of Earth and Moon.

44. See Richard Harter Fogle, "Image and Imagelessness: A Limited Reading of *Prometheus Unbound*," *K-SJ* 1 (1952): 26; modified by Harold Bloom in *Shelley's Mythmaking* (New Haven: Yale University Press, 1959), p. 106, where he argues that Prometheus, Jupiter, and "a number of other energies" are contained "as component[s]" in the human mind. See also Earl R. Wasserman, *Shelley: A Critical Reading* (Baltimore: Johns Hopkins University Press, 1971), p. 307; Charles E. Robinson, *Shelley and Byron: The Snake and Eagle Wreathed in Fight* (Baltimore: Johns

Hopkins University Press, 1976), pp. 123–24, for Jupiter as an aspect of Prometheus's mind. Barnard, however, cited in Shelley, *Variorum*, p. 468, would
make him responsible for *all* evil, not only that manifested in distorted religious or
social structures; and Stuart Curran in *Shelley's Annus Mirabilis: The Maturing of an
Epic Vision* (San Marino, Calif.: The Huntington Library and Art Gallery, 1975)
surely implies the same in his application of Zoroastrian dualism, though he argues
on p. 104 that "Jupiter . . . is not a fact, but a woefully misconceived interpretation."

45. See Daniel J. Hughes, "Potentiality in *Prometheus Unbound*," *SiR* 2 (1963):
107–26, rpt. in Shelley, *Poetry and Prose*, pp. 603–20.

46. See S. Brisman, "Problem of Voice," pp. 56–59.

47. See Shelley, *Variorum*, p. 471, where Zillman cites Swinburne, "Notes on
the Text of Shelley," in *The Complete Works of Algernon Charles Swinburne*, ed. Sir
Edmund Gosse and Thomas J. Wise, 20 vols., Bonchurch Edition (London:
William Heinemann; New York: Gabriel Wells, 1925), 15:361; but Swinburne, in
turn, probably had read Winckelmann's discussion of Spartan women who kept
statues of Apollo, Narcissus, and Hyacinth in their bedrooms, to have beautiful
children (*History*, 2:178).

48. See Bloom, *Mythmaking*, p. 137; see also Donald H. Reiman, "Roman
Scenes in *Prometheus Unbound* III. iv," *PQ* 46 (1967): 70–73.

49. See Fogle, *Imagery*, pp. 42–43, and Bloom, *Mythmaking*, p. 91, for a sense of
icy alienation. Webb, *Voice*, p. 140, notes a parallel between Shelley's reference to
Ahrimanes in his *Letters*, 1:499, and act 1; Webb goes on to comment, however, on
the lushness of the Italian landscape as a shaping force for his vision of Greece
(*Voice*, p. 191).

50. See C. E. Robinson, *Snake and Eagle*, pp. 113ff. For other uses of a
picturesque "station," see *Peter Bell the Third*, ll. 268–72, 298–302; "Ode to
Naples," l. 123; Shelley, *Letters*, 1:377 (4 October 1813, describing the Lake
Country) and 1:481. For an excellent demonstration of Shelley's interest in making
landscape specific, as noted by Webb in *Violet in the Crucible*, p. 139, see Shelley's
translation of the *Hymn to Mercury*, l. 160. This passage shows the relationship
between "station" as picturesque vantage point and Jay Appleton's habitat theory;
see *The Experience of Landscape* (New York: John Wiley, 1975), pp. 68–70.

51. See Shelley, *Letters*, 2:73, 77, 79, 84, for examples of this pattern from late
1818 through early 1819. For earlier awareness of picturesque theory, see his
letters from Switzerland of 17 May 1816 (1:475–76) and July 1816 (1:495ff.) and
also Mary's use of those letters in the *History of a Six Weeks' Tour* through a part of
France, Switzerland, Germany, and Holland; with Letters descriptive of a Sail
Round the Lake of Geneva, and of the Glaciers of Chamouni, by Percy Bysshe
Shelley (London: T. Hookham, and C. and J. Ollier, 1817), p. 93. Some of the
"tourist" vocabulary in this *History* may come from William Coxe, *Travels in
Switzerland and in the Country of the Grisons*, 4th ed., in 3 vols. (London: T. Cadell
and W. Davies, 1801); he uses "prospect" frequently (e.g., 2:2) and also uses a
geometrical vocabulary, particularly in describing Mont Blanc (2:31). I am in-
debted to Jim Borck for suggesting Shelley's use of Coxe. For other discussion of

Shelley's interest in perspectives, see Webb, *Voice*, pp. 140, 255, and Reiman, *Shelley Circle*, 6:616, SC 486.

52. Julian, pp. 303–04. Part of this fragment appears in Bod. MS. Shelley adds. e. 12; I have examined it but have not collated it with the Julian text, derived from Mary Shelley's 1840 edition of *Essays*. John W. Wright, in *Shelley's Myth of Metaphor* (Athens: University of Georgia Press, 1970), p. 38, suggests that after 1818 images of "a 'magic circle' gradually displace" cave images.

53. Neville Rogers draws attention to Shelley's use of this metaphor in *Shelley at Work*, 2d ed. (Oxford: Clarendon Press, 1967), pp. 4, 225. The occasion is a conversation with Edward Trelawny, from *Recollections of the Last Days of Shelley and Byron* (London: Edward Moxon, 1858, rpt., in Humbert Wolfe, ed., *The Life of Percy Bysshe Shelley* [London: Dent, 1933], 2 vols., 2:197). In *Shelley at Work*, the fullest discussion of these drawings so far, Rogers makes this interdependence his starting point for a Platonic interpretation of both visual and verbal motifs. Much evidence exists, of course, for Shelley's deep interest in Plato, particularly from 1817 on; see Notopoulos, *Platonism of Shelley*. Yet in spite of Rogers's diligent and often very perceptive readings of the notebooks, his assumptions lead him not only into false emphases concerning the manuscripts of *Prometheus Unbound*, but also into a self-contradictory position. If much of Shelley's skepticism about the validity or stability of sense-perception comes from the empiricists (see C. E. Pulos, *The Deep Truth: A Study of Shelley's Scepticism* [1954; rpt., Lincoln: University of Nebraska Press, 1962]), it is reinforced by his reading of Plato, in whom the image is as much a distortion as a medium, and the visual image is more distorting than the verbal and more conceptual one. If one presses hard for a Platonic reading of both visual and verbal symbols, then, one needs to raise the very problems about the relationship of image and significance that Shelley himself raises, most strikingly in Demogorgon's assertion that "the deep truth is imageless." This problem appears in the relationship of visual image on the page to verbally conveyed visual image, and in the further relationship between both expressions and their generative source, whether a Platonic ideal or an unknowable Power or something else altogether. Because Rogers starts from Platonic passages in the notebooks, it is understandable that his Ariadne's thread leads him through that particular maze, a maze that surely exists in the wide wilderness of Shelley's speculations. In drawing upon these visual and verbal images, which Rogers has traced so well, I take a wider and more literal, or perhaps more pictorial, view of that wilderness. For at first glance, the most dominant images of the sketches are those of trees, forests, and mountainous landscapes. By surveying the sketches in the notebooks that contain the drafts of *Prometheus Unbound*, starting as descriptively as possible, we may then interpret more successfully the stationing of sketch in text, or text in sketch.

54. See *Notebooks of Percy Bysshe Shelley, from the originals in the library of W. K. Bixby*. Deciphered, transcribed, and edited with a full commentary by H. Buxton Forman, 3 vols. (Boston: printed for Bibliophile Society, 1911), vol. 1, facing pp. 136 and 156; vol. 2, p. 3 and facing pp. 60, 106, and 186. The first two volumes discuss the materials in the notebooks that now are identified as HM (Huntington

Manuscript) 2176 and 2177, at the Huntington Library. Both of these notebooks contain *Prometheus* drafts, but only the plate facing vol. 2, p. 106 (HM 2177, *21r), contains both a sketch and lines from the play. (Shelley often reused his notebooks from back to front, turning them upside down; the asterisk indicates this reverse pagination.) Forman's volumes also describe a number of other non-*Prometheus* drawings. Neville Rogers, in *Shelley at Work*, reproduces six of Shelley's drawings, all from Bodleian mss. but none associated with *Prometheus* drafts. His plate Ia is from Bod. MS. Shelley e. 4; Ib and IIa and b are from Bod. MS. Shelley adds. e. 9; IIc is a sketch of Shelley's Tan-y-rallt assailant; and plate III is from Bod. MS. Shelley adds. e. 6. In *The Shelley Circle*, vol. 6, Reiman reproduces two pages containing *Prometheus* drafts from the *Philosophical Reform* notebook, owned by the Carl H. Pforzheimer Library (numbered SC 549, p. 1073), one of which also contains a sketch; on p. 1005 he also reproduces the front cover of the notebook, which is a finished sketch of trees, lake, and mountains, and the front pasted-down endpaper, full of profiles and a full face or two. Also included in the Pforzheimer collection are three leaves torn from HM 2177; Reiman reproduces two of these (SC 548, p. 867), which have lines from act 2 of *Prometheus*, and one of them also includes a sketch. For perceptive analyses of a very few sketches, see Webb, *Voice*, pp. 208–14.

55. This study is based on examination of thirteen of Shelley's manuscript notebooks. Of the thirteen notebooks examined, seven contain substantial *Prometheus* material: Bod. MSS. Shelley adds. e. 11, 12 (draft notebooks) and Bod. MSS. Shelley e. 1–3 (fair-copy notebooks), described by permission of the curators of the Bodleian Library; Huntington Manuscripts (HM, formerly Bixby) 2176, 2177, described by permission of the Huntington Library, San Marino, California. The eighth (the *Philosophical Reform* notebook), described here by permission of the Carl and Lily Pforzheimer Foundation, Inc., contains only two passages, and the ninth (Bod. MS. Shelley adds. e. 6) only a line. I have also looked at Bod. MS. Shelley e. 4, which contains a passage related to *Prometheus Unbound*, act 2, scene 5; and I have examined the facsimile of the British Library *Mask of Anarchy* notebook. I have also examined the third Shelley notebook at the Huntington, HM 2178 ("Cyprian"), though Shelley apparently did not use it until 1821; and Bod. MS. Shelley adds. c. 4, loose pages in 1818–1819 but containing no lines from *Prometheus*.

56. G. W. Knight, *Starlit Dome*, p. 179, and N. Rogers, *Shelley at Work*, p. 68.

57. See Flagg, *"Prometheus Unbound" and "Hellas,"* pp. 91ff.

58. See N. Rogers, *Shelley at Work*, chap. 6, "Boats. Isles," pp. 91ff.; his interpretation is more specifically Platonic than mine, however.

59. See Ernst Curtius, *European Literature and the Latin Middle Ages*, trans. Willard Trask (1953; rpt., New York: Harper and Row, 1963), pp. 319ff. Flagg (*"Prometheus Unbound" and "Hellas,"* pp. 80–81) suggests that Panthea's dream is "a visionary reconstruction of the first act"; L. Brisman (*Origins*, pp. 153–57) discusses it as a valorizing of voice in reading and in the dream-vision sequences of act 2.

60. See Flagg, *"Prometheus Unbound" and "Hellas,"* pp. 83ff., and Hughes, "Potentiality," p. 613.

61. See Hughes, "Potentiality," p. 612.

62. See Shelley, *Poetry and Prose*, p. 169n.

63. See Webb, *Violet in the Crucible*, chap. 8, for a discussion of Shelley's criticisms of Dante and his Inferno.

64. See McGill, "Role of Earth," pp. 117–28.

65. See C. E. Robinson's discussion of this theme in chap. 8, "The Trees of Knowledge and of Life," in *Snake and Eagle*.

66. For an argument that Shelley had not abandoned but had made more subtle his earlier adherence to the doctrine of Necessity, see Stuart M. Sperry, "Necessity and the Role of the Hero in Shelley's *Prometheus Unbound*," *PMLA* 96 (1981): 242–54. I tend to see more distinction between natural and social patterns of change than his reading suggests.

67. S. Brisman, "Problem of Voice," p. 82.

68. See P. M. S. Dawson, *The Unacknowledged Legislator: Shelley and Politics* (Oxford: Clarendon Press, 1980), p. 90. He cites R. Cronin, "Shelley's Language of Dissent," *Essays in Criticism* 27 (1977): 203–15.

69. Shelley, *Poetry and Prose*, p. 175n.

70. See Shelley, *Poetry and Prose*, pp. 473–74 and 504–05.

71. For the range of interpretations before 1959, see Shelley, *Variorum*, p. 317; Zillman categorized these as (1) a "Primal Power behind the world"; (2) "Necessity, Destiny, or Fate"; (3) "an aspect of divinity"; (4) "Eternity"; and (5) "Reason." Several of the more recent interpretations attempt to reconcile the idea of Demogorgon as a power alien to or at least transcending man's imaginative power, and that human power. See C. E. Robinson, *Snake and Eagle*, pp. 133–34; Ridenour, *Critical Essays*, p. 10; to some extent, Bloom, *Mythmaking*, pp. 99–100; Hall, *Transforming Image*, p. 70, who suggests that Demogorgon is "the Humean habitual way of seeing that follows the transforming moment of Vision"; and Melanie Bandy, *Mind Forg'd Manacles: Evil in the Poetry of Blake and Shelley* (University: University of Alabama Press, 1981), p. 71. Wasserman (in *Shelley*, pp. 318, 321ff.), however, argues that Demogorgon lies beyond even Necessity.

72. For Demogorgon as imagination, see G. W. Knight, *Starlit Dome*, p. 204, who equates him with "the human imagination or Holy Spirit"; Fogle, in "Image and Imagelessness," p. 28, who says he "represents the ultimate in the testing of systematic thought by the demands of poetic imagination"; and Bloom, in *Mythmaking*, pp. 99–100, who says he is "mythopoeic process" but does not restrict that process to human mind; instead, it represents "relational" or "dialectic" "confrontations" of human and inhuman.

73. See McGill, "Role of Earth," pp. 126ff.

74. Ibid., p. 122.

75. See Webb, *Voice*, pp. 248, 254, and idem, *Violet in the Crucible*, pp. 75ff.

76. See Peter Butter, *Shelley's Idols of the Cave* (Edinburgh: Edinburgh University Press, 1954), pp. 56, 60. See also McGill, "Role of Earth," p. 124; she in turn cites Hungerford, *Shores of Darkness*, p. 203, who discusses Earth's cave as transformed haunt of Aeschylus's Furies.

77. See Colwell, "Uffizi Notes," p. 61n, who argues that Shelley could not have seen Botticelli's *Birth of Venus* until his late-1819 visit to the Uffizi.

78. See Bloom, *Mythmaking*, p. 140, for the association with Ezekiel. Lawrence John Zillman in *The Complete Known Drafts of Shelley's "Prometheus Unbound"* (Ann Arbor: University Microfilms International, 1978), p. 67, quotes the lines from the ballad in noting Shelley's sketch over his verbal draft in Bod. MS. Shelley adds. e. 12.

79. See Webb, *Voice*, pp. 248, 254, and Hughes, "Potentiality," p. 608. Hughes cites G. W. Knight, *Starlit Dome*, p. 222.

80. For Shelley's careful stylistic qualifications of apocalypse or even millennium, see Vincent A. De Luca, "The Style of Millenial Announcement in *Prometheus Unbound*," *K-SJ* 28 (1979): 78–101. See also Wasserman, *Shelley*, p. 360, who argues that at the end of act 3 Prometheus has moved out of the world of time, but that act 4 "is a commentary on [the Promethean drama] . . . conducted on the human plane." When man transcends time, he will "be absorbed into the unity of Existence. . . . man, as man can never transcend those relationships among thoughts called time" (p. 361). Earlier (p. 356) Wasserman points to the different paradisal realms, one heavenly and one its earthly mirror, defined by the Spirits of the Human Mind, though he does not link this distinction explicitly to the temporal one. I think we can accept this careful distinction of a transformed but not eliminated time without accepting Wasserman's definition of a further apocalypse as man's absorption into One Mind. See also Ridenour, *Critical Essays*, p. 7. This qualification, I would argue, at least partially meets Rajan's objection in *Dark Interpreter* that act 4 "press[es] beyond the ambiguities of scepticism to the finality of a holistic view of the universe" (p. 89). She notes (p. 93) in the first three acts a doubling similar to the one I develop, but she does not extend it to act 4.

81. In Shelley, *Poetry and Prose*, p. 210, n. 3.

Bibliography

Abrams, M. H. *The Mirror and the Lamp: Romantic Theory and the Critical Tradition.* New York: Oxford University Press, 1953.

_____. *Natural Supernaturalism: Tradition and Revolution in Romantic Literature.* New York: Norton, 1971.

Adams, Hazard. *Blake and Yeats: The Contrary Vision.* Ithaca: Cornell University Press, 1955.

_____. "Revisiting Reynolds' *Discourses* and Blake's Annotations." In *Blake in his Time,* edited by Robert N. Essick and Donald Pearce. Bloomington: Indiana University Press, 1978. Pp. 128–44.

_____, ed. *Critical Theory Since Plato.* New York: Harcourt Brace Jovanovich, 1971.

_____, ed. *William Blake: "Jerusalem," Selected Poems and Prose.* New York: Holt, Rinehart, Winston, 1971.

Allentuck, Marcia. "Fuseli and Herder's *Ideen zur Philosophie der Geschichte der Menschheit* in Britain: An Unmarked Connection." *Journal of the History of Ideas* 35 (1974): 113–20.

_____. "Fuseli's Translations of Winckelmann; A Phase in the Rise of British Hellenism, with an Aside on William Blake." In *Studies in the Eighteenth Century II; Papers Presented at the Second David Nichol Smith Memorial Seminar,* Canberra, 1970, edited by R. F. Brissenden. Toronto: University of Toronto Press, 1973. Pp. 163–85.

_____. "Henry Fuseli (Johann Heinrich Füssli) and Lessing." *Lessing Yearbook* 1 (1969): 178–86.

Altizer, Thomas J. J. *The New Apocalypse: The Radical Christian Vision of William Blake.* East Lansing: Michigan State University Press, 1967.

Andrews, John F. "The *Ipsissima Verba* in My Diary?" *Shakespeare Studies* 8 (1975): 333–67.

Antal, Frederick. *Fuseli Studies.* London: Routledge and Kegan Paul, 1956.

233

Appleton, Jay. *The Experience of Landscape*. London: John Wiley, 1975.

Arthos, John. *On the Poetry of Spenser and the Form of Romances*. London: Allen and Unwin, 1956.

Aubin, R. A. *Topographical Poetry in Eighteenth-Century England*. New York: Modern Language Association, 1936.

Ault, Donald. *Visionary Physics: Blake's Response to Newton*. Chicago: University of Chicago Press, 1974.

Baldwin, Dane Lewis, Leslie Norton Broughton, Laura Cooper Evans, John William Hekel, Benjamin F. Stelter, and Mary Rebecca Thayer, eds. *A Concordance to the Poems of John Keats*. Washington: Carnegie Institution, 1917.

Baker, Carlos. *Shelley's Major Poetry: The Fabric of A Vision*. 1948. Reprint. Princeton: Princeton University Press, 1973.

Baker, Herschel. *William Hazlitt*. Cambridge, Mass.: Harvard University Press, 1962.

Bandy, Melanie. *Mind Forg'd Manacles: Evil in the Poetry of Blake and Shelley*. University: University of Alabama Press, 1981.

Barbier, Carl Paul. *William Gilpin: His Drawings, Teachings, and Theory of the Picturesque*. Oxford: Clarendon Press, 1963.

Barrell, Joseph. *Shelley and the Thought of his Time; a Study in the History of Ideas*. New Haven: Yale University Press, 1947.

Barthes, Roland. "An Introduction to the Structural Analysis of Narrative." *Communications*: 8 (1969). Reprinted in *New Literary History* 6 (1975): 237–72.

Bate, Walter Jackson. *The Burden of the Past and the English Poet*. Cambridge, Mass.: Harvard University Press, 1970.

––––––. *Coleridge*. New York: Macmillan, 1968.

––––––. "The English Poet and the Burden of the Past." In *Aspects of the Eighteenth Century*, edited by Earl R. Wasserman. Baltimore: Johns Hopkins University Press, 1965. Pp. 245–64.

––––––. *John Keats*. 1963. Reprint. New York: Oxford Galaxy, 1966.

––––––. *The Stylistic Development of Keats*. 1945. Reprint. New York: Humanities Press, 1958.

Beer, John. "Blake, Coleridge, and Wordsworth: Some Cross-Currents and Parallels, 1789–1805." In *William Blake: Essays in Honour of Sir Geoffrey Keynes*, edited by Morton D. Paley and Michael Phillips. Oxford: Clarendon Press, 1973. Pp. 231–59.

––––––. *Blake's Visionary Universe*. Manchester: Manchester University Press, 1969.

Behrendt, Stephen C. *The Moment of Explosion: Blake and the Illustration of Milton*. Lincoln and London: University of Nebraska Press, 1983.

Bell, Arthur H. " 'The Depth of Things': Keats and Human Space." *Keats-Shelley Journal* 23 (1974): 77–94.

Bender, John B. *Spenser and Literary Pictorialism*. Princeton: Princeton University Press, 1972.

Bennett, James R. "*Prometheus Unbound*, Act I, 'The Play's the Thing.' " *Keats-Shelley Journal* 23 (1974): 32–51.

Bentley, G. E., Jr. *Blake Books*. Rev. ed. Oxford: Clarendon Press, 1977.

_____. *Blake Records.* Oxford: Clarendon Press, 1969.

_____. "Blake's Engravings and his Friendship with Flaxman." *Studies in Bibliography* 12 (1959): 161–88.

_____, ed. *William Blake, The Critical Heritage.* London: Routledge and Kegan Paul, 1975.

Beyer, Werner W. *Keats and the Daemon King.* New York: Oxford University Press, 1947.

Bieber, Margarete. *Laocoon: The Influence of the Group Since its Discovery.* Rev. and enl. ed. Detroit: Wayne State University Press, 1967.

Bindman, David. *Blake as an Artist.* Oxford: Phaidon; New York: Dutton, 1977.

Blake, William. *Blake's Grave, A Prophetic Book . . .* Illustrations for Robert Blair's *The Grave,* arranged as Blake directed, with a commentary by S. Foster Damon. Providence: Brown University Press, 1963.

_____. *Blake's Pencil Drawings,* 2d series. Edited by Geoffrey Keynes. London: Nonesuch Press, 1956.

_____. *The Complete Poetry and Prose of William Blake.* Newly rev. ed. Edited by David V. Erdman, with commentary by Harold Bloom. Berkeley and Los Angeles: University of California Press, 1982.

_____. *Drawings by William Blake: 92 Pencil Studies.* Selections, introduction, and commentary by Sir Geoffrey Keynes. New York: Dover, 1970.

_____. *The Illuminated Blake.* Edited and with commentary by David V. Erdman. Garden City, N.Y.: Doubleday Anchor, 1974.

_____. *Letters of William Blake.* 3d ed. Edited by Geoffrey Keynes. Oxford: Clarendon Press, 1980.

_____. *Milton.* Copy B. Huntington Library and Art Gallery.

_____. *Milton.* Trianon Press facsimile of Copy D. Clairvaux: William Blake Trust, London, 1967.

Bland, D. S. "Painting and the Poetry of Keats: Some Further Identifications." *Modern Language Review* 50 (1955): 502–04.

Bloom, Harold. *The Anxiety of Influence.* New York: Oxford University Press, 1973.

_____. *Blake's Apocalypse.* Garden City, N.Y.: Doubleday, 1963.

_____. "The Internalization of the Quest-Romance." In *Romanticism and Consciousness: Essays in Criticism,* edited by Harold Bloom. New York: Norton, 1970. Pp. 3–24.

_____. "Keats and the Embarrassments of Tradition." In *From Sensibility to Romanticism: Essays Presented to Frederick A. Pottle,* edited by Frederick W. Hilles and Harold Bloom. New York: Oxford University Press, 1965. Pp. 513–26.

_____. *A Map of Misreading.* New York: Oxford University Press, 1975.

_____. *Poetry and Repression: Revisionism from Blake to Stevens.* New Haven: Yale University Press, 1976.

_____. *The Ringers in the Tower: Studies in Romantic Tradition.* Chicago: University of Chicago Press, 1971.

_____. *Shelley's Mythmaking.* New Haven: Yale University Press, 1959.

_____. *The Visionary Company: A Reading of English Romantic Poetry.* Rev. and enl. ed. Ithaca: Cornell University Press, 1971.

_____, ed. *Romanticism and Consciousness: Essays in Criticism.* New York: Norton, 1970.

Blunt, Anthony. *The Art of William Blake.* New York: Columbia University Press, 1959.

Booth, Wayne C. *The Rhetoric of Fiction.* 1961. Reprint. Chicago: University of Chicago Press, 1965.

Brisman, Leslie. *Milton's Poetry of Choice and Its Romantic Heirs.* Ithaca: Cornell University Press, 1973.

_____. *Romantic Origins.* Ithaca: Cornell University Press, 1978.

Brisman, Susan Hawk. " 'Unsaying His High Language': The Problem of Voice in *Prometheus Unbound.*" *Studies in Romanticism* 16 (1977): 51–86.

Brook, Donald. "Perception and the Appraisal of Sculpture." *Journal of Aesthetics and Art Criticism* 27 (1968): 323–30.

Brown, Allan R. "Blake's Drawings for the Book of Enoch." *Burlington Magazine* 27 (1940): 80–85.

Brown, Charles Armitage. *The Letters of Charles Armitage Brown.* Edited by Jack Stillinger. Cambridge, Mass.: Harvard University Press, 1966.

Brown, Nathaniel. *Sexuality and Feminism in Shelley.* Cambridge, Mass.: Harvard University Press, 1979.

Bunn, James. "Keats's *Ode to Psyche* and the Transformation to Mental Landscape." *English Literary History* 37 (1970): 581–94.

Burke, Edmund. *A Philosophical Inquiry into the Origins of Our Ideas of the Sublime and the Beautiful.* Edited and with introduction by J. J. Boulton. New York: Columbia University Press, 1958.

Burwick, Frederick. "The Language of Causality in *Prometheus Unbound.*" *Keats-Shelley Journal* 31 (1982): 136–58.

Bush, Douglas. *Mythology and the Romantic Tradition.* 1937. Reprint. New York: Norton, 1963.

_____. *Science and English Poetry: A Historical Sketch, 1590–1950.* New York: Oxford University Press, 1950.

Butter, Peter. *Shelley's Idols of the Cave.* Edinburgh: Edinburgh University Press, 1954.

Buxton, John. "Greece and the Imagination of Byron and Shelley." *Byron Journal* 4 (1976): 76–89.

_____. "Shelley and the Tradition of the Progress Piece." *Keats-Shelley Memorial Bulletin* 23 (1972): 1–5.

_____. "Shelley's Neoclassical Taste." *Apollo* (1972): 276–81.

Caldwell, James Ralston. *John Keats' Fancy: The Effect on Keats of the Psychology of his Day.* Ithaca: Cornell University Press, 1945.

_____. "The Meaning of *Hyperion.*" *PMLA* 51 (1936): 1080–97.

Campbell, William Royce. "Shelley's Philosophy of History: A Reconsideration." *Keats-Shelley Journal* 21–22 (1972–1973): 43–63.

Cameron, Kenneth Neill. *Shelley: The Golden Years.* Cambridge, Mass.: Harvard University Press, 1974.

_____. *The Young Shelley: Genesis of a Radical.* 1950. Reprint. New York: Collier, 1962.

_____, ed. *Shelley and his Circle.* Vols. 1–4. The Carl H. Pforzheimer Library. Cambridge, Mass.: Harvard University Press, 1961–70.

Carothers, Yvonne M. "Space and Time in *Milton:* The 'Bard's Song.' " In *Blake in his Time,* edited by Robert N. Essick and Donald Pearce. Bloomington: Indiana University Press, 1978. Pp. 116–27.

Chapin, Chester F. *Personification in Eighteenth-Century Poetry.* New York: Columbia University Press, 1955.

Chatman, Seymour. "Towards a Theory of Narrative." *New Literary History* 6 (1975): 295–318.

Chayes, Irene. "Plato's Statesman Myth in Shelley and Blake." *Comparative Literature* 13 (1961): 358–69.

Chernaik, Judith A. "The Figure of the Poet in Shelley." *English Literary History* 35 (1968): 566–90.

Clark, Robert C., Jr. *Herder: His Life and Thought.* Berkeley and Los Angeles: University of California Press, 1955.

Cohen, Ralph. *The Art of Discrimination: Thomson's "The Seasons" and the Art of Criticism.* Berkeley and Los Angeles: University of California Press, 1964.

Coleridge, Samuel Taylor. *Coleridge's Miscellaneous Criticism.* Edited by Thomas Middleton Raysor. 1936. Reprint. Folcroft, Pa.: Folcroft Press, 1969.

_____. *Coleridge's Shakespearean Criticism.* Edited by Thomas Middleton Raysor. 2 vols. Cambridge, Mass.: Harvard University Press, 1930.

_____. *The Collected Works of Samuel Taylor Coleridge.* Vol. 4, *The Friend, II.* Edited by Barbara E. Rooke. Princeton: Princeton University Press, 1969.

Collins Baker, C. H. "The Sources of Blake's Pictorial Expression." *Huntington Library Quarterly* 4 (1941): 359–67.

Colwell, Frederic S. "Shelley on Sculpture: The Uffizi Notes." *Keats-Shelley Journal* 28 (1979): 59–77.

Cooke, Michael G. *The Romantic Will.* New Haven: Yale University Press, 1976.

Cooper, Anthony Ashley, Third Earl of Shaftesbury. *Characteristicks of Men, Manners, Opinions, Times, etc.* Edited with introduction and notes by John M. Robertson. 2 vols. London: Grant Richards, 1900.

Coxe, William. *Travels in Switzerland and in the Country of the Grisons,* in a series of letters to William Melmoth, Esq. 4th ed. in 3 vols. London: T. Cadell and W. Davies, 1801.

Crawford, Walter B., ed. *Reading Coleridge: Approaches and Applications.* Ithaca: Cornell University Press, 1979.

Cudworth, Ralph. *The True Intellectual System of the Universe.* London: R. Royston, 1678.

Cumberland, George. *A Poem on the Landscapes of Great-Britain.* London: W. Wilson, 1793.

_____. *Thoughts on Outline; Sculpture, and the System that Guided the Ancient Artists in Composing their Figures and Groupes.* London: W. Wilson, 1796.

Curran, Stuart. "The Mental Pinnacle: *Paradise Regained* and the Romantic Four-Book Epic." In *Calm of Mind: Tercentenary Essays on "Paradise Regained" and "Samson Agonistes," in Honor of John S. Diekhoff,* edited by Joseph Anthony

Wittreich, Jr. Cleveland: Press of Case Western Reserve University, 1971. Pp. 133–62.

_____. *Shelley's Annus Mirabilis: The Maturing of an Epic Vision.* San Marino, Calif.: Huntington Library and Art Gallery, 1975.

Curtius, Ernst. *European Literature and the Latin Middle Ages.* Translated by Willard Trask. 1953. Reprint. New York: Harper and Row, 1963.

Damon, S. Foster. *A Blake Dictionary.* 1965. Reprint. New York: Dutton, 1971.

_____. *William Blake: His Philosophy and Symbols.* Boston: Houghton Mifflin, 1924.

Dampier, Sir William Cecil. *A History of Science.* 4th ed. 1948. Reprint. Cambridge: Cambridge University Press, 1961.

Damrosch, Leopold, Jr. *Symbol and Truth in Blake's Myth.* Princeton: Princeton University Press, 1980.

Davies, Edward. *Celtic Researches on the Origins, Traditions, and Language of the Ancient Britons;* with some introductory sketches on Primitive Society. London: J. Booth, 1804.

Davies, J. M. Q. " 'Embraces and Cominglings': Passion and Apocalypse in Blake's *Paradise Regained* Designs." *Durham University Journal* 74, n.s. 43 (1981): 75–96.

Davis, Michael. *William Blake: A New Kind of Man.* Berkeley and Los Angeles: University of California Press, 1977.

Dawson, P. M. S. *The Unacknowledged Legislator: Shelley and Politics.* Oxford: Clarendon Press, 1980.

De Luca, Vincent A. "Ariston's Immortal Palace: Icon and Allegory in Blake's Prophecies." *Criticism* 12 (1970): 1–19.

_____. "The Style of Millenial Announcement in *Prometheus Unbound*." *Keats-Shelley Journal* 28 (1979): 78–101.

Dickstein, Morris. *Keats and his Poetry: A Study in Development.* Chicago: University of Chicago Press, 1971.

Digby, George Wingfield. *Symbol and Image in William Blake.* Oxford: Clarendon Press, 1957.

Dyck, Sarah. "The Presence of that Shape: Shelley's *Prometheus Unbound*." *Costerus* 1 (1972): 13–80.

Eaves, Morris. *William Blake's Theory of Art.* Princeton: Princeton University Press, 1982.

Eggers, J. Philip. "Memory in Mankind: Keats's Historical Imagination." *PMLA* 86 (1971): 990–97.

Ellis, F. S. *A Lexical Concordance to the Poetical Works of Percy Bysshe Shelley.* 1892. Reprint. New York: Burt Franklin, 1968.

Ende, Stuart. *Keats and the Sublime.* New Haven: Yale University Press, 1976.

England, Martha Winburn. "Blake and the Hymns of John Wesley." *Bulletin of the New York Public Library* 70 (1966): 7–26, 93–112, 153–68, 251–64.

England, Martha Winburn, and John Sparrow. *Hymns Unbidden.* New York: New York Public Library, 1966.

Erdman, David V. *Blake: Prophet Against Empire: A Poet's Interpretation of the History of his Own Times.* Rev. ed. Reprint. Garden City, N.Y.: Doubleday Anchor, 1969.

_____. "The Steps (of Dance and Stone) that Order Blake's *Milton.*" *Blake Studies* 6 (1973): 73–87.

_____, ed., assisted by John E. Thiesmeyer and others. *A Concordance to the Writings of William Blake.* Ithaca: Cornell University Press, 1967.

Erdman, David V., and John E. Grant, eds. *Blake's Visionary Forms Dramatic.* Princeton: Princeton University Press, 1970.

Essick, Robert N., and Donald Pearce, eds. *Blake in his Time.* Bloomington: Indiana University Press, 1978.

Eustace, John Chetwode. *A Classical Tour Through Italy (1802).* 3d ed., rev. and enl. 4 vols. London: J. Mawman, 1815.

Evans, James C. "Masks of the Poet: A Study of Self-Confrontation in Shelley's Poetry." *Keats-Shelley Journal* 24 (1975): 70–88.

Farington, Joseph. *The Farington Diary.* Edited by James Grieg. 4th ed. 2 vols. London: Hutchinson, 1923.

Fink, Z. A. *The Early Wordsworthian Milieu.* Oxford: Clarendon Press, 1958.

Finney, Claude Lee. *The Evolution of Keats's Poetry.* 2 vols. Cambridge, Mass.: Harvard University Press, 1936.

Firkins, Oscar W. *Power and Elusiveness in Shelley.* Minneapolis: University of Minnesota Press, 1937.

Fisch, Harold. "Blake's Miltonic Moment." In *William Blake: Essays for S. Foster Damon,* edited by Alvin Rosenfeld. Providence: Brown University Press, 1969. Pp. 36–56.

Fisher, Peter F. "Blake and the Druids." *Journal of English and Germanic Philology* 58 (1959): 589–612. Reprinted in *Discussion of William Blake,* edited by John E. Grant. Boston: D. C. Heath, 1961. Pp. 28–43.

_____. *The Valley of Vision: Blake as Prophet and Revolutionary.* Edited by Northrop Frye. Toronto: University of Toronto Press, 1961.

Flagg, John Sewell. *"Prometheus Unbound" and "Hellas": An Approach to Shelley's Lyrical Dramas.* Romantic Reassessment, no. 14. Salzburg: Institut für Englische Sprache und Literatur, 1972.

Flaxman, John. "Cursory Strictures on Modern Art, and particularly Sculpture, in England, previous to the establishment of the Royal Academy." In *The Artist,* edited by Prince Hoare, No. 12 (Sat., 30 May 1807), republished as 2 vols. 1810; vol. 1, 1810.

_____. *Drawings by John Flaxman in the Huntington Collection.* Edited and with commentary by Robert R. Wark. San Marino, Calif.: Henry E. Huntington Library and Art Gallery, 1970.

_____. *Lectures on Sculpture.* London: John Murray, 1829.

Foakes, R. A. "What Did Coleridge Say? John Payne Collier and the Reports of the 1811–12 Lectures." In *Reading Coleridge: Approaches and Applications,* edited by Walter B. Crawford. Ithaca: Cornell University Press, 1979. Pp. 191–210.

Fogle, Richard Harter. "Image and Imagelessness: A Limited Reading of *Prometheus Unbound.*" *Keats-Shelley Journal* 1 (1952): 23–36.

_____. *The Imagery of Keats and Shelley: A Comparative Study.* Chapel Hill: University of North Carolina Press, 1949.

Ford, Newell F. *The Prefigurative Imagination of John Keats: A Study of the Beauty—*

Truth Identification and Its Implications. 1951. Reprint. Hamden, Conn.: Archon, 1966.

Forsyth, Joseph. *Remarks on Antiquities, Arts, and Letters during an Excursion in Italy in the years 1802 and 1803.* 2d ed. London: John Murray, 1816.

Fox, Susan. *Poetic Form in Blake's "Milton."* Princeton: Princeton University Press, 1976.

Frosch, Thomas R. *The Awakening of Albion.* Ithaca: Cornell University Press, 1974.

_____. Review of *Composite Art,* by W. J. T. Mitchell. *Blake Quarterly* 13 (1979): 40–48.

Frye, Northrop. *The Anatomy of Criticism.* Princeton: Princeton University Press, 1957.

_____. "The Drunken Boat: The Revolutionary Element in Romanticism." In *Romanticism Reconsidered: Selected Papers from the English Institute,* edited by Northrop Frye. 1963. Reprint. New York: Columbia University Press, 1968.

_____. *Fearful Symmetry: A Study of William Blake.* 1947. Reprint. Boston: Beacon, 1962.

_____. "Notes for a Commentary on Milton." In *The Divine Vision: Studies in the Poetry of William Blake,* edited by Vivian de Sola Pinto. London: Gollancz, 1957. Pp. 99–137.

_____. "Poetry and Design in William Blake." *Journal of Aesthetics and Art Criticism* 10 (1951): 35–42.

_____. *The Stubborn Structure: Essays on Criticism and Society.* Ithaca: Cornell University Press, 1970.

_____. *A Study of English Romanticism.* New York: Random House, 1968.

_____, ed. *Romanticism Reconsidered: Selected Papers from the English Institute.* 1963. Reprint. New York: Columbia University Press, 1968.

Frye, Roland Mushat. *Milton's Imagery and the Visual Arts.* Princeton: Princeton University Press, 1978.

Fugate, Joe K. *The Philosophical Basis of Herder's Aesthetics.* Studies in Philosophy, X. The Hague: Mouton, 1966.

Fuseli, Henry. *A Collection of Drawings by Henry Fuseli, R. A.* Edited by Peter Tomory. Auckland: Auckland City Art Gallery, 1967.

_____. *The Drawings of Henry Fuseli.* Edited by Nicholas Powell. London: Faber and Faber, 1951.

_____. *The Life and Writings of Henry Fuseli, Esq.* Edited by John Knowles. 3 vols. London: Colburn and Bentley, 1831.

_____. *L'Opera Completa di Johann Heinrich Fuseli.* Introdotta e coordinata da Gert Schiff. Apparati critici e filologica di Paolo Viotto. Milan: Rizzoli Editore, 1977.

Gilpin, William. *Observations on Several Parts of Great Britain, particularly the High-lands of Scotland, relative chiefly to Picturesque Beauty, made in the year 1776.* 3d. ed. 2 vols. London: R. Blamire, 1808.

_____. *Observations on Several Parts of the Counties of Cambridge, Norfolk, Suffolk, and Essex. Also on Several Parts of North Wales; Relative Chiefly to Picturesque Beauty. . . .* London: T. Cadell and W. Davies, 1809.

_____. *Observations on the River Wye, and Several Parts of South Wales, Relative Chiefly to Picturesque Beauty. . . .* 3d ed. London: R. Blamire, 1782.

_____. *Observations Relative Chiefly to Picturesque Beauty made in the year 1772, On Several Parts of England; particularly the Mountains, and Lakes of Cumberland and Westmoreland.* 2d. ed. 2 vols. London: R. Blamire, 1788.

_____. *Three Essays: On Picturesque Beauty; On Picturesque Travel; and On Sketching Landscape.* 2d ed. London: R. Blamire, 1794.

Giovannini, G. "Method in the Study of Literature in its Relation to the Other Arts." *Journal of Aesthetics and Art Criticism* 8 (1950): 185–95.

Gittings, Robert. *John Keats.* Boston: Little, Brown, 1968.

_____. *John Keats: The Living Year.* 1954. Reprint. London: Heinemann, 1962.

_____. *The Mask of Keats: A Study of Problems.* Cambridge, Mass.: Harvard University Press, 1956.

Gleckner, Robert. *William Blake: Selected Writings.* New York: Appleton-Century-Crofts, 1967.

Good, John Walter. "Studies in the Milton Tradition." In *Illinois University Studies in Language and Literature* 1 (1915): 93–291.

Goslee, Nancy M. "From Marble to Living Form: Sculpture as Art and Analogue from the Renaissance to Blake." *Journal of English and Germanic Philology* 77 (1978): 188–211.

_____. " 'In Englands green & pleasant Land': The Building of Vision in Blake's Stanzas from *Milton*." *Studies in Romanticism* 13 (1974): 105–25.

_____. "Phidian Lore: Sculpture and Personification in Keats's Odes." *Studies in Romanticism* 21 (1982): 73–85.

_____. "Plastic to Picturesque: Schlegel's Analogue and Keats's *Hyperion* Poems." *Keats-Shelley Journal* 30 (1981): 118–51.

_____. "Shelley's 'Notes on Sculpture': Toward a Romantic Classicism in *Prometheus Unbound*." *Comparatist* 4 (1980): 11–22.

_____. " 'Under a Cloud in Prospect': Keats, Milton, and Stationing." *Philological Quarterly* 53 (1974): 205–19.

Grabo, Carl. *"Prometheus Unbound": An Interpretation.* Chapel Hill: University of North Carolina Press, 1935.

Grant, John E. "Visions in Vala; A Consideration of Some Pictures in the Manuscript." In *Blake's Sublime Allegory*, edited by Joseph Anthony Wittreich, Jr., and Stuart Curran. Madison: University of Wisconsin Press, 1973. Pp. 141–202.

_____, ed. *Discussions of William Blake.* Boston: D. C. Heath, 1961.

Gray, Thomas. *The Complete Poems of Thomas Gray, English, Latin, and Greek.* Edited by H. W. Starr and J. R. Hendrickson. Oxford: Oxford University Press, 1966.

_____. *The Poetical Works of Milton, Young, Gray, Beattie, and Collins.* No editor given. Philadelphia: John Grigg, 1832.

Greene, Thomas M. *The Descent from Heaven: A Study in Epic Continuity.* 1963. Reprint. New Haven: Yale University Press, 1975.

Grierson, H. J. C. *Lyrical Poetry of the Nineteenth Century.* New York: Harcourt Brace, 1929.

Guillen, Claudio. "On the Concept and Metaphor of Perspective." In *Comparatists at Work: Studies in Comparative Literature*, edited by Stephen G. Nichols, Jr., and Richard B. Vowles. Waltham, Mass.: Blaisdell, 1968. Pp. 28–90.

Hagstrum, Jean H. "Blake and the Sister-Arts Tradition." In *Blake's Visionary Forms Dramatic*, edited by David V. Erdman and John E. Grant. Princeton: Princeton University Press, 1970. Pp. 82–91.

_____. "Christ's Body." In *William Blake: Essays in Honour of Sir Geoffrey Keynes*, edited by Morton D. Paley and Michael Phillips. Oxford: Clarendon Press, 1973. Pp. 129–56.

_____. *The Sister Arts: The Tradition of Literary Pictorialism and English Poetry from Dryden to Gray*. Chicago: University of Chicago Press, 1958.

_____. *William Blake: Poet and Painter*. Chicago: University of Chicago Press, 1964.

Hall, Jean. *The Transforming Image: A Study of Shelley's Major Poetry*. Urbana: University of Illinois Press, 1980.

Harris, James. *Three Treatises: the first concerning art, the second concerning music, painting, and poetry, the third concerning happiness*. 2d ed. rev. and corr. 1765. Facsimile reprint. New York: Garland, 1970.

Hartley, Robert A. "The Uroboros in Shelley's Poetry." *Journal of English and Germanic Philology* 73 (1974): 524–42.

Hartman, Geoffrey. *Beyond Formalism*. 1970. Reprint. New Haven: Yale University Press, 1971.

_____. *The Fate of Reading and Other Essays*. Chicago: University of Chicago Press, 1975.

_____. *Wordsworth's Poetry 1787–1814*. New Haven: Yale University Press, 1964.

Haskell, Francis, and Nicholas Penny. *Taste and the Antique: The Lure of Classical Sculpture 1500–1900*. New Haven and London: Yale University Press, 1981.

Haydon, Benjamin Robert. *The Diary of Benjamin Robert Haydon*. Edited by Willard Bissell Pope. 5 vols. Cambridge, Mass.: Harvard University Press, 1960.

Hayley, William. *An Essay on Sculpture. In a Series of Epistles to John Flaxman, Esq., R. A.* London: T. Cadell and W. Davies, 1800.

_____. *The Life and Posthumous Writings of William Cowper, Esq.* New and enl. ed. 4 vols. Chicester: J. Seagraves, for J. Johnson. St. Paul's Church-yard, London, 1806.

_____. *The Life of Milton*. 2d ed. 1796. Facsimile reprint. Introduction by Joseph Anthony Wittreich, Jr. Gainesville, Fla.: Scholar's Facsimiles and Reprints, 1970.

_____. *Poems and Plays*. 6 vols. London: T. Cadell, 1785.

Hazlitt, William. *Complete Works of William Hazlitt*. Edited by P. P. Howe. Centenary Edition. 21 vols. London: Dent, 1931–1934.

Heffernan, James W. *Wordsworth's Theory of Poetry: The Transforming Imagination*. Ithaca: Cornell University Press, 1969.

Herzing, Thomas W. "Book I of Blake's *Milton*: Natural Religion as Optical Fallacy." *Blake Studies* 6 (1973): 19–34.

Hildebrand, William H. "A Look at the Third and Fourth Spirit Songs: *Prometheus Unbound I*." *Keats-Shelley Journal* 20 (1971): 87–99.

Hilles, Frederick W., and Harold Bloom, eds. *From Sensibility to Romanticism: Essays Presented to Frederick A. Pottle.* New York: Oxford University Press, 1965.

Hipple, Walter J., Jr. *The Beautiful, the Sublime, and the Picturesque in Eighteenth-Century British Aesthetic Theory.* Carbondale: Southern Illinois University Press, 1957.

Hoare, Prince. *Epochs of the Arts; Including Hints on the Use and Progress of Painting and Sculpture in Great Britain.* London: John Murray, 1813.

_____, ed. *The Artist,* a Collection of Essays, relative to Painting, Poetry, Sculpture, Architecture, the Drama, Discoveries of Science, and Various other subjects. London: John Murray, John White, W. Miller, J. Harding, J. Asperne; Edinburgh: Archibald Constable, 1807.

Hogle, Jerrold E. "Shelley's Poetics: The Power as Metaphor." *Keats-Shelley Journal* 31 (1982): 159–97.

Hoover, Suzanne. "Blake and the Poetry of Stone." Paper presented at Blake Seminar, annual meeting of Modern Language Association, New York, 28 December 1976.

Howard, John. *Blake's "Milton."* Rutherford, N.J.: Fairleigh Dickinson University Press, 1976.

Hughes, Daniel J. "Kindling and Dwindling: The Poetic Process in Shelley." *Keats-Shelley Journal* 13 (1964) : 13–28.

_____. "Potentiality in *Prometheus Unbound.*" *Studies in Romanticism* 2 (1963): 107–26. Reprinted in *Shelley's Poetry and Prose,* edited by Donald H. Reiman and Sharon B. Powers. A Norton Critical Edition. New York: Norton, 1977. Pp. 603–20.

_____. "Prometheus Made Capable Poet in Act I of *Prometheus Unbound.*" *Studies in Romanticism* 17 (1978): 3–12.

Hungerford, Edward B. *Shores of Darkness.* 1941. Reprint. Cleveland: Meridian, 1963.

Hunt, John Dixon. *The Figure in the Landscape: Poetry, Painting, and Gardening during the Eighteenth Century.* Baltimore: Johns Hopkins University Press, 1976.

Hunt, Leigh. *Leigh Hunt's Literary Criticism.* Edited by Lawrence Houston Houtchens and Carolyn Washburn Houtchens. New York: Columbia University Press, 1956.

Hurt, James R. "*Prometheus Unbound* and Aeschylean Dramaturgy." *Keats-Shelley Journal* 15 (1966): 43–48.

Hussey, Christopher. *The Picturesque: Studies in a Point of View.* London: Putnam, 1929.

Ingram, William, and Kathleen Swaim, eds. *A Concordance to Milton's Poetry.* Oxford: Clarendon Press, 1972.

Irwin, David. *English Neoclassical Art: Studies in Inspiration and Taste.* Greenwich, Conn.: New York Graphic Society, 1966.

Jack, Ian. *Keats and the Mirror of Art.* Oxford: Clarendon Press, 1967.

James, D. G. *The Romantic Comedy.* 1948. Reprint. London: Oxford University Press, 1963.

James, David E. *Written Within and Without: A Study of Blake's "Milton."* Europäische Hochschulschriften, Series 14. Frankfurt: Peter Lang, 1977.

Johnson, Mary Lynn. " 'Separating What Has Been Mixed': A Suggestion for a Perspective on *Milton*." *Blake Studies* 6 (1973): 11–17.

Johnson, Samuel. *The Yale Edition of the Works of Samuel Johnson. Volume VII: Johnson on Shakespeare*. Edited by Arthur Sherbo. 1st of 2 vols. New Haven: Yale University Press, 1968.

Jones, James Land. *Adam's Dream: Mythic Consciousness in Keats and Yeats*. Athens: University of Georgia Press, 1975.

Jones, John. *John Keats's Dream of Truth*. London: Chatto and Windus, 1969.

Keach, William. "Reflexive Imagery in Keats and Shelley." *Keats-Shelley Journal* 24 (1975): 49–69.

Keats, John. *"Hyperion": A Facsimile of Keats's Autograph Manuscript. With a transliteration of the manuscript of "The Fall of Hyperion, A Dream."* Introduction and notes by Ernest de Selincourt. Oxford: Clarendon Press, 1905.

_____. *John Keats. Poems, 1820. Lamia, Isabella, The Eve of St. Agnes, and Other Poems*. The English Replicas. New York: Payson and Clark, 1927.

_____. *John Keats: Selected Poems and Letters*. Edited by Douglas Bush. Boston: Houghton Mifflin, 1959.

_____. *John Keats: The Collected Poems*. Edited by John Barnard. 2d ed. 1977. Reprint. New York: Penguin, 1978.

_____. *The Letters of John Keats, 1814–1821*. Edited by Hyder Edward Rollins. 2 vols. Cambridge, Mass.: Harvard University Press, 1958.

_____. *The Poems of John Keats*. Edited by Miriam Allott. London: Longman, 1970.

_____. *The Poems of John Keats*. Edited by Jack Stillinger. Cambridge, Mass.: Harvard University Press, 1978.

_____. *The Poetical Works and Other Writings by John Keats*. Edited by H. Buxton Forman. Revised by Maurice Buxton Forman. 8 vols. New York: Scribners, 1939.

Keynes, Geoffrey. *Blake Studies: Essays on his Life and Work*. 2d ed. Oxford: Clarendon Press, 1971.

Kiralis, Karl. "A Guide to the Intellectual Symbolism of William Blake's Later Prophetic Writings." *Criticism* 1 (1959): 190–210.

Knight, G. Wilson. *The Starlit Dome: Studies in the Poetry of Vision*. 1941. Reprint. London: Oxford University Press, 1971.

Knight, Richard Payne. *Analytical Inquiry into the Principles of Taste*. 4th ed. London: Payne and White, 1805.

Kristeller, Paul O. "The Modern System of the Arts: A Study in the History of Aesthetics." Parts 1, 2. *Journal of the History of Ideas* 12 (1951): 496–525; 13 (1952): 17–46.

Kroeber, Karl. "The Commemorative Prophecy of *Hyperion*." *Transactions of the Wisconsin Academy of Sciences, Arts, and Letters* 52 (1963): 189–204.

_____. "Experience and History: Shelley's Venice, Turner's Carthage." *English Literary History* 41 (1974): 321–39.

_____. "Graphic-Poetic Structuring in Blake's *Book of Urizen*." *Blake Studies* 3 (1970): 7–18.

_____. *Romantic Landscape Vision: Constable and Wordsworth*. Madison: University of Wisconsin Press, 1975.

_____. *Romantic Narrative Art*. 1960. Reprint. Madison: University of Wisconsin Press, 1966.

Kroeber, Karl, and William Walling, eds. *Images of Romanticism: Verbal and Visual Affinities*. New Haven: Yale University Press, 1978.

Lang, S. "The Genesis of the English Landscape Garden." In *The Picturesque Garden and its Influence Outside the British Isles*, edited by Nikolaus Pevsner. Dumbarton Oaks Colloquium on the History of Landscape Architecture, II. Washington, D.C.: Trustees for Harvard University. Pp. 1–29.

Lanser, Susan Sniader. *The Narrative Act: Point of View in Prose Fiction*. Princeton: Princeton University Press, 1981.

Larrabee, Stephen A. "Critical Terms for the Art of Sculpture." *Notes and Queries* 172 (3 April 1937): 239–40.

_____. *English Bards and Grecian Marbles: The Relationship Between Sculpture and Poetry Especially in the Romantic Period*. New York: Columbia University Press, 1943.

Leavis, F. R. "Justifying One's Valuation of Blake." In *William Blake: Essays in Honour of Sir Geoffrey Keynes*, edited by Morton D. Paley and Michael Phillips. Oxford: Clarendon Press, 1973. Pp. 66–85.

Lee, Rensselaer. *Ut Pictura Poesis: The Humanistic Theory of Painting*. New York: Norton, 1967. Revised from *Art Bulletin* 22 (1940).

Lempriere, J[ohn]. *Bibliotheca Classica: A Classical Dictionary*, containing a full account of all the Proper Names mentioned in Antient Authors. . . . 4th ed. London: T. Cadell and W. Davies, 1801.

Leonardo da Vinci. *The Literary Works of Leonardo da Vinci*. Compiled and edited by J. P. Richter. 3d ed. 2 vols. London: Phaidon, 1970.

Lessing, Gotthold Ephraim. *Laocoon: An Essay Upon the Limits of Painting and Poetry*. [1766] Translated with introduction and notes by Edward Allen McCormick. Library of Liberal Arts. New York: Bobbs-Merrill, 1962.

Levin, Harry. *The Broken Column: A Study in Romantic Hellenism*. Cambridge, Mass.: Harvard University Press, 1931.

Lindsay, Julian I. "A Note on the Marginalia." *Huntington Library Quarterly* 1 (1937): 95–99.

Lipking, Lawrence. *The Ordering of the Arts in Eighteenth-Century England*. Princeton: Princeton University Press, 1970.

Little, Judy. *Keats as a Narrative Poet: A Test of Invention*. Lincoln: University of Nebraska Press, 1975.

Lowenfeld, Viktor. "Psycho-Aesthetic Implications of the Art of the Blind." *Journal of Aesthetics and Art Criticism* 10 (1951): 1–9.

Lowes, John Livingston. "Moneta's Temple." *PMLA* 51 (1936): 1098–1113.

[Lyly, John.] *Queen Elizabeth's Entertainment at Mitcham: Poet, Painter, and Musician*. Edited by Leslie Hotson. New Haven: Yale University Press, 1953.

McCarthy, Michael. "Eighteenth Century Amateur Architects and their Gardens." In *The Picturesque Garden and its Influence Outside the British Isles*, edited by

Nikolaus Pevsner. Dumbarton Oaks Colloquium on the History of Landscape Architecture, II. Washington D.C.: Trustees for Harvard University. Pp. 31–55.

McCormick, D. Allen. "*Poema Pictura Loquens:* Literary Pictorialism and the Psychology of Landscape." *Comparative Literary Studies* 13 (1976): 196–211.

McFarland, Thomas. *Coleridge and the Pantheist Tradition.* Oxford: Clarendon Press, 1969.

McGill, Mildred Sloan. "The Role of Earth in Shelley's *Prometheus Unbound.*" *Studies in Romanticism* 7 (1968): 117–28.

McKillop, Alan. *The Background of Thomson's "Seasons."* Minneapolis: University of Minnesota Press, 1942.

McLuhan, Marshall. *The Gutenberg Galaxy. The Making of Typographic Man.* Toronto: University of Toronto Press, 1962.

Malek, James S. *The Arts Compared: An Aspect of Eighteenth-Century British Aesthetics.* Detroit: Wayne State University Press, 1974.

Malins, Edward G. *English Landscaping and Literature, 1660–1840.* London: Oxford University Press, 1966.

Manwaring, Elizabeth Wheeler. *Italian Landscape in Eighteenth-Century England.* 1925. Reprint. New York: Russell and Russell, 1965.

Marken, Ronald. " 'Eternity in an Hour': Blake and Time." *Discourse* 9 (1966) 167–92.

Martin, F. David. "The Autonomy of Sculpture." *Journal of Aesthetics and Art Criticism* 34 (1976): 273–86.

Martz, Louis L. *The Paradise Within.* New Haven: Yale University Press, 1964.

Mason, Eudo C. *The Mind of Henry Fuseli.* London: Routledge and Kegan Paul, 1951.

Matthews, G. M. "A Volcano's Voice in Shelley." *English Literary History* 24 (1957): 191–228. Reprinted in *Shelley: A Collection of Critical Essays,* edited by George M. Ridenour. Englewood Cliffs, N.J.: Prentice-Hall, 1965. Pp. 111–31.

Meadowcourt, Richard, and Charles Dunster. *Milton's "Paradise Regained": Two Eighteenth-Century Critiques.* Facsimile reprint. Introduction by Joseph Anthony Wittreich, Jr. Gainesville, Fla.: Scholars' Facsimiles and Reprints, 1971.

Medwin, Thomas. *The Life of Percy Bysshe Shelley.* A New Edition printed from a copy copiously emended and extended by the Author and left unpublished at his death. Introduction and commentary by H. Buxton Forman. London: Oxford University Press, 1913.

Meisel, Martin. "The Material Sublime: John Martin, Byron, Turner, and the Theatre." In *Images of Romanticism: Verbal and Visual Affinities,* edited by Karl Kroeber and William Walling. New Haven: Yale University Press, 1978. Pp. 211–32.

Mellor, Anne Kostelanetz. *Blake's Human Form Divine.* Berkeley and Los Angeles: University of California Press, 1974.

———. "Keats's Face of Moneta: Source and Meanings." *Keats-Shelley Journal* 25 (1976): 65–80.

Messman, Frank J. *Richard Payne Knight: The Twilight of Virtuosity.* The Hague: Mouton, 1974.

Miles, Josephine. "Blake's Frame of Language." In *William Blake: Essays in Honour of Sir Geoffrey Keynes*, edited by Morton D. Paley and Michael Phillips. Oxford: Clarendon Press, 1973. Pp. 86–95.

Milton, John. *John Milton, Complete Poems and Major Prose*. Edited by Merritt Y. Hughes. New York: Odyssey, 1957.

Miner, Paul. "William Blake: Two Notes on Sources." *Bulletin of the New York Public Library* 62 (1958): 203–07.

Mitchell, W. J. T. "Blake's Composite Art." In *Blake's Visionary Forms Dramatic*, edited by David V. Erdman and John E. Grant. Princeton: Princeton University Press, 1970. Pp. 57–81.

_____. *Blake's Composite Art*. Princeton: Princeton University Press, 1978.

_____. "Blake's Radical Comedy." In *Blake's Sublime Allegory*, edited by Joseph Anthony Wittreich, Jr., and Stuart Curran. Madison: University of Wisconsin Press, 1973. Pp. 281–307.

_____. "Style and Iconography in the Illustrations of Blake's *Milton*." *Blake Studies* 6 (1973): 47–71.

Monk, Samuel. *The Sublime*. 1935. Reprint. Ann Arbor: University of Michigan Press, 1960.

Moorman, Mary. *William Wordsworth: A Biography*. 2 vols. 1957. Reprint. London: Oxford University Press, 1968.

Muir, Kenneth. "The Meaning of *Hyperion*." In *Keats: A Reassessment*, edited by Kenneth Muir. 1958. Reprint. Liverpool: University of Liverpool Press, 1959. Pp. 102–22.

_____, ed. *Keats: A Reassessment*. 1958. Reprint. Liverpool: University of Liverpool Press, 1959.

Munro, Thomas. *The Arts and their Interrelationships*. 1949. Reprint. Cleveland: Press of Case Western Reserve University, 1967.

Murray, E. B. "Shelley's *Notes on Sculptures:* The Provenance and Authority of the Text." *Keats-Shelley Journal* 32 (1983): 150–71.

Murry, John Middleton. *Keats*. New York: Noonday, 1955.

_____. *William Blake*. 1933. Reprint. New York: McGraw-Hill, 1964.

Nichols, Stephen G., Jr., and Richard B. Vowles, eds. *Comparatists at Work: Studies in Comparative Literature*. Waltham, Mass.: Blaisdell, 1968.

Norris, Marjorie. "Phenomenology and Process: Perception in Keats's 'I Stood Tip-Toe.' " *Keats-Shelley Journal* 25 (1976): 43–54.

Notopoulos, James A. "New Texts of Shelley's Plato." *Keats-Shelley Journal* 15 (1966): 99–115.

_____. *The Platonism of Shelley: A Study of Platonism and the Literary Mind*. Durham: Duke University Press, 1949.

Nurmi, Martin K. "Negative Sources in Blake." In *William Blake: Essays for S. Foster Damon*, edited by Alvin H. Rosenfeld. Providence: Brown University Press, 1969. Pp. 303–18.

Ogden, Henry V. S., and Margaret S. Ogden. *English Taste in Landscape in the Seventeenth Century*. Ann Arbor: University of Michigan Press, 1955.

Ogden, John T. "From Spatial to Aesthetic Distance in the Eighteenth Century." *Journal of the History of Ideas* 35 (1974): 63–78.

O'Hara, J. D. "Hazlitt and Romantic Criticism of the Fine Arts." *Journal of Aesthetics and Art Criticism* 27 (1968): 73–87.

Paley, Morton D. *Energy and the Imagination: A Study of the Development of Blake's Thought.* Oxford: Clarendon Press, 1970.

———. "William Blake, the Prince of the Hebrews, and the Woman Clothed with the Sun." In *William Blake: Essays in Honour of Sir Geoffrey Keynes,* edited by Morton D. Paley and Michael Phillips. Oxford: Clarendon Press, 1973. Pp. 260–93.

———. " 'Wonderful Originals': Blake and Ancient Sculpture." In *Blake in his Time,* edited by Robert N. Essick and Donald Pearce. Bloomington: Indiana University Press, 1978. Pp. 170–97.

———, ed. Special issue on romantic classicism. *Studies in Romanticism* 15 (1976).

Paley, Morton D., and Michael Phillips, eds. *William Blake: Essays in Honour of Sir Geoffrey Keynes.* Oxford: Clarendon Press, 1973.

Paley, William. *Natural Theology; or, Evidences of the Existence and Attributes of the Deity, collected from the Appearances of Nature.* London: R. Foulder, 1802.

Park, Roy. *Hazlitt and the Spirit of the Age: Abstraction and Critical Theory.* Oxford: Clarendon Press, 1971.

———. "*Ut Pictura Poesis:* The Nineteenth-Century Aftermath." *Journal of Aesthetics and Art Criticism* 28 (1969): 155–64.

Paulson, Ronald. *Emblem and Expression: Meaning in English Art of the Eighteenth Century.* London: Thames and Hudson, 1975.

———. "The Pictorial Circuit and Related Structures in Eighteenth Century England." In *The Varied Pattern: Studies in the Eighteenth Century,* edited by Peter Hughes and David Williams. Toronto: A. M. Hackett, 1971. Pp. 165–87.

Peckham, Morse. "Blake, Milton, and Edward Burney." *Princeton University Library Chronicle* 11 (Spring 1950): 107–26.

Perkins, David. *The Quest for Permanence: The Symbolism of Wordsworth, Shelley and Keats.* Cambridge, Mass.: Harvard University Press, 1959.

———, ed. *English Romantic Writers.* New York: Harcourt Brace Jovanovich, 1967.

Pevsner, Nikolaus, ed. *The Picturesque Garden and its Influence Outside the British Isles.* Dumbarton Oaks Colloquium on the History of Landscape Architecture, II. Washington, D.C.: Trustees for Harvard University, 1974.

Pierce, Frederick E. "The Genesis and General Meaning of Blake's *Milton.*" *Modern Philology* 25 (1927–28): 165–78.

———. "Two Notes on Blake." *Modern Language Notes* 41 (1926): 169–70.

Pilkington, M. *A Dictionary of Painters from the Revival of the Art to the Present Period.* Edited by Henry Fuseli, R. A. New, rev. ed. London: J. Johnson and others, 1805.

Pinto, Vivian de Sola. "Isaac Watts and William Blake." *Review of English Studies* 20 (1944): 214–23.

———, ed. *The Divine Vision: Studies in the Poetry of William Blake.* London: Gollancz, 1957.

Plato. *Timaeus, Cleitophon, Critias, Menexenus, Epistles.* Loeb Classical Library. 1929. Reprint. Cambridge, Mass.: Harvard University Press, 1942.

Pointon, Marcia R. *Milton and English Art*. Toronto: University of Toronto Press, 1970.

Pottle, Frederick A. "The Role of Asia in the Dramatic Action of Shelley's *Prometheus Unbound*." In *Shelley: A Collection of Critical Essays*, edited by George M. Ridenour. Englewood Cliffs, N.J.: Prentice-Hall, 1965. Pp. 133–43.

———. *Shelley and Browning: A Myth and Some Facts*. 1923. Reprint with new preface by author. Hamden, Conn.: Archon, 1965.

Praz, Mario. *Mnemosyne: The Parallel Between Literature and the Visual Arts*. A. W. Mellon Lectures, 1967. Princeton: Princeton University Press, 1970.

Price, Martin. "The Picturesque Moment." In *From Sensibility to Romanticism: Essays Presented to Frederick A. Pottle*, edited by Frederick W. Hilles and Harold Bloom. New York: Oxford University Press, 1965. Pp. 259–92.

Pulos, C. E. *The Deep Truth: A Study of Shelley's Scepticism*. 1954. Reprint. Lincoln: University of Nebraska Press, 1962.

Rajan, Tilottama. *Dark Interpreter: The Discourse of Romanticism*. Ithaca: Cornell University Press, 1980.

Reiman, Donald H. *Percy Bysshe Shelley*. New York: Twayne, 1969.

———. "Roman Scenes in *Prometheus Unbound* III. iv." *Philological Quarterly* 46 (1967): 69–78.

———, ed. *Shelley and his Circle*. Vols. 5–6. The Carl H. Pforzheimer Library. Cambridge, Mass.: Harvard University Press, 1973.

Reynolds, Sir Joshua. *Discourses on Art*. Edited by Robert R. Wark. New Haven: Yale University Press, for the Paul Mellon Centre for Studies in British Art, 1975.

———. *Letters of Sir Joshua Reynolds*. Edited by Frederick Hilles. Cambridge: Cambridge University Press, 1929.

———. *The Yale Edition of the Works of Samuel Johnson. Volume II: Samuel Johnson, "The Idler" and "The Adventurer."* Edited by W. J. Bate, John M. Bullitt, and L. F. Powell. New Haven and London: Yale University Press, 1963.

Richards, George D. "Shelley's Urn of Bitter Prophecy." *Keats-Shelley Journal* 21–22 (1972–1973): 112–25.

Richardson, Jonathan. *Explanatory Notes and Remarks on Milton's "Paradise Lost."* 1734. Facsimile reprint. New York: Garland, 1970.

Ricks, Christopher. *Keats and Embarrassment*. Oxford: Clarendon Press, 1974.

Ridenour, George M., ed. *Shelley: A Collection of Critical Essays*. Englewood Cliffs, N.J.: Prentice-Hall, 1965.

Rieger, James. " 'The Hem of their Garments': The Bard's Song in *Milton*." In *Blake's Sublime Allegory*, edited by Joseph Anthony Wittreich, Jr., and Stuart Curran. Madison: University of Wisconsin Press, 1973. Pp. 259–80.

Robinson, Charles E. *Shelley and Byron: The Snake and Eagle Wreathed in Fight*. Baltimore: Johns Hopkins University Press, 1976.

Robinson, Henry Crabb. *Diary, Reminiscences, and Correspondence of Henry Crabb Robinson, Barrister at Law*. Selected and edited by Thomas Sadler. 3 vols. London: Macmillan, 1869.

———. *Henry Crabb Robinson on Books and their Writers*. Edited by Edith J. Morley. 3 vols. London: Dent, 1938.

Rogers, Neville, *Shelley at Work: A Critical Inquiry*. 2d ed. Oxford: Clarendon Press, 1967.

Rogers, Stephen. *Classical Greece and the Poetry of Chenier, Shelley, and Leopardi.* South Bend: University of Notre Dame Press, 1974.

Rollins, Hyder Edward, ed. *The Keats Circle: Letters and Papers.* 2 vols. Cambridge, Mass.: Harvard University Press, 1965.

Rose, Edward J. "Blake's Fourfold Art." *Philological Quarterly* 49 (1970): 400–423.

———. "Blake's Human Insect: Symbol, Theory, and Design." *Texas Studies in Literature and Language* 10 (1968): 215–32.

———. "Blake's Metaphorical States." *Blake Studies* 4 (1971): 9–32.

———. "Blake's *Milton*: The Poet as Poem." *Blake Studies* 1 (1968): 16–38.

———. "Circumcision Symbolism in Blake's *Jerusalem*." *Studies in Romanticism* 8 (1968): 16–25.

———. " 'Forms Eternal Exist Forever': The Covenant of the Harvest in Blake's Prophetic Poems." In *Blake's Visionary Forms Dramatic*, edited by David V. Erdman and John E. Grant. Princeton: Princeton University Press, 1970. Pp. 443–62.

———. "Los, Pilgrim of Eternity." In *Blake's Sublime Allegory*, edited by Joseph Anthony Wittreich, Jr., and Stuart Curran. Madison: University of Wisconsin Press, 1973. Pp. 83–99.

———. " 'Mental Forms Creating': Fourfold Vision and the Poet as Prophet in Blake's Design and Verse." *Journal of Aesthetics and Art Criticism* 23 (1964–65): 173–83.

———. "The Spirit of the Bounding Line." *Criticism* 13 (1971): 54–76.

———. "The Structure of Blake's *Jerusalem*." *Bucknell Review* 11 (1962–1963): 35–54.

———. "The Symbolism of the Opened Center and Poetic Theory in Blake's *Jerusalem*." *Studies in English Literature* 5 (1965): 587–606.

———. " 'Visionary Forms Dramatic': Grammatical and Iconographical Movement in Blake's Verse and Design." *Criticism* 8 (1966): 111–25.

Rosen, Charles, and Henri Zerner. Review of *Romanticism*, by Hugh Honour. *New York Review of Books*, 22 November 1979. Pp. 23–29.

Rosenberg, John D. "Keats and Milton: The Paradox of Rejection." *Keats-Shelley Journal* 6 (1957): 87–97.

Rosenblum, Robert. *Transformations in Late Eighteenth Century Art.* Princeton: Princeton University Press, 1967.

Rosenfeld, Alvin H., ed. *William Blake: Essays for S. Foster Damon.* Providence: Brown University Press, 1969.

Ruben, Joseph. "Shelley's *Prometheus Unbound* and the Indian Caucasus." *Keats-Shelley Journal* 12 (1963): 95–106.

Saly, John. "Keats's Answer to Dante: *The Fall*." *Keats-Shelley Journal* 14 (1965): 65–78.

Sandler, Florence. "The Iconoclastic Enterprise: Blake's Critique of Milton's Religion." *Blake Studies* 5 (1972): 13–57.

Schiller, Friedrich von. *"Naive and Sentimental Poetry" and "On the Sublime."* Translated with an introduction by Julius A. Elias. New York: Ungar, 1966.

Schlegel, Augustus William. *A Course of Lectures on Dramatic Art and Literature.* Translated by John Black. 2 vols. London: Baldwin, Cradock and Joy, 1815.

_____. [August Wilhelm von Schlegel.] *Sammtliche Werke.* Edited by Edouard Böcking. 12 vols. Leipzig: Weidmann, 1846–1847.

_____. *Vorlesungen über Dramatische Kunst und Literatur.* Edited by Giovanni Vittorio Amoretti. 2 vols. Bonn and Leipzig: Kurt Schroeder, 1923.

Sharp, Ronald A. *Keats, Scepticism, and the Religion of Beauty.* Athens: University of Georgia Press, 1979.

Shearer, Edna A. "Wordsworth and Coleridge Marginalia in a Copy of Richard Payne Knight's *Analytical Inquiry into the Principles of Taste.*" *Huntington Library Quarterly* 1 (1937): 63–94.

Sheats, Paul D. "Stylistic Discipline in *The Fall of Hyperion.*" *Keats-Shelley Journal* 17 (1968): 75–88.

Shelley, Mary. *The Letters of Mary Wollstonecraft Shelley.* Vol. 1, 'A part of the Elect.' Edited by Betty T. Bennett. Baltimore: Johns Hopkins University Press, 1980.

_____. *Mary Shelley's Journal.* Edited by Frederick L. Jones. Norman: University of Oklahoma Press, 1947.

Shelley, Percy Bysshe. *The Complete Known Drafts of Shelley's "Prometheus Unbound."* Edited by Lawrence John Zillman. Ann Arbor: University Microfilms International, 1978.

_____. *The Complete Works of Percy Bysshe Shelley.* Vol. 6, *Prose.* Edited by Roger Ingpen and Walter E. Peck. The Julian Edition. New York: Scribner's Sons; London: Benn, 1929.

_____. *Essays, Letters from Abroad, Translations, and Fragments, by Percy Bysshe Shelley.* [Edited by Mary Shelley.] 2 vols. London: Edward Moxon, 1840.

_____. *The Letters of Percy Bysshe Shelley.* Edited by Frederick L. Jones. 2 vols. Oxford: Clarendon Press, 1964.

_____. *The Mask of Anarchy by Percy Bysshe Shelley.* Facsimile of the holograph copy. Introduction by H. Buxton Forman. London: Reeves and Turner for the Shelley Society, 1887.

_____. MS. Notebooks. Bodleian MS. Shelley adds. c. 4, e. 6, e. 11, e. 12; Shelley e. 1, 2, 3, 4. Huntington (HM; formerly Bixby) 2176, 2177, 2178. Pforzheimer *Philosophical Reform* notebook.

_____. *Notebooks of Percy Bysshe Shelley, from the originals in the library of W. K. Bixby.* Deciphered, transcribed, and edited with a full commentary by H. Buxton Forman. 3 vols. Boston: printed for Bibliophile Society, 1911.

_____. *Shelley's Poetry and Prose.* Edited by Donald H. Reiman and Sharon B. Powers. A Norton Critical Edition. New York: Norton, 1977.

_____. *Shelley's "Prometheus Unbound": A Variorum Edition.* Edited by Lawrence John Zillman. Seattle: University of Washington Press, 1959.

_____. *Shelley's "Prometheus Unbound": The Text and the Drafts.* Edited by Lawrence John Zillman. New Haven: Yale University Press, 1968.

_____. *Shelley's Prose, or The Trumpet of a Prophecy.* Edited by David Lee Clark. 1954. Reprint. Albuquerque: University of New Mexico Press, 1966.

_____. *The Works of Percy Bysshe Shelley.* Edited by H. Buxton Forman. 8 vols. London: Reeves and Turner, 1880.

Shelley, Percy Bysshe [and Mary Shelley]. *History of a Six Weeks' Tour* through a part of France, Switzerland, Germany, and Holland; with Letters descriptive of a Sail Round the Lake of Geneva and of the Glaciers of Chamouni. By Percy Bysshe Shelley. London: T. Hookham and C. and J. Ollier, 1817.

Sherwin, Paul. "Dying into Life: Keats's Struggle with Milton in *Hyperion*." *PMLA* 93 (1978): 383–95.

Slote, Bernice. *Keats and the Dramatic Principle*. Lincoln: University of Nebraska Press, 1958.

Smitten, Jeffrey R., and Ann Daghistany, eds. *Spatial Form in Narrative*. Ithaca: Cornell University Press, 1981.

Southey, Robert. *The Life and Works of William Cowper*. Vol. 15. London: Baldwin and Cradock, 1837.

Spencer, Jeffrey. *Heroic Nature: Ideal Landscape in English Poetry from Marvell to Thomson*. Evanston: Northwestern University Press, 1973.

Sperry, Stuart M. *Keats the Poet*. Princeton: Princeton University Press, 1973.

_____. "Necessity and the Role of the Hero in Shelley's *Prometheus Unbound*." *PMLA* 96 (1981): 242–54.

Stephenson, William C. "The Performing Narrator in Keats's Poetry." *Keats-Shelley Journal* 26 (1977): 51–71.

Stillinger, Jack. *The Text of Keats's Poems*. Cambridge, Mass.: Harvard University Press, 1974.

Stovall, Floyd H. *Desire and Restraint in Shelley*. Durham: Duke University Press, 1931.

Swift, Jonathan. *A Tale of a Tub, to which is added The Battle of the Books.* . . . Edited by A. C. Guthkelch and D. Nichol Smith. 2d ed. Oxford: Clarendon Press, 1958.

Swinburne, Algernon Charles. "Notes on the Text of Shelley." In *The Complete Works of Algernon Charles Swinburne*, edited by Sir Edmund Gosse and Thomas J. Wise. Bonchurch Edition. 20 vols. London: William Heinemann; New York: Gabriel Wells, 1925. 15:348–97.

Tayler, Irene. *Blake's Illustrations to Gray*. Princeton: Princeton University Press, 1971.

_____. "Blake's Laocoon." *Blake Newsletter* 10 (1976): 72–81.

Taylor, Peter Alan. "Providence and the Moment in Blake's *Milton*." *Blake Studies* 4 (1971): 43–60.

Thomson, George. *Aeschylus and Athens*. 3d ed. 1966. Reprint. New York: Grosset and Dunlap, 1968.

Thomson, James. *The Complete Poetical Works of James Thomson*. Edited by J. Logie Robertson. Oxford Standard Authors. 1908. Reprint. London: Oxford University Press, 1963.

Thorpe, Clarence. *The Mind of John Keats*. New York: Oxford University Press, 1926.

Thurston, Norman. "Shelley and the Duty of Hope." *Keats-Shelley Journal* 26 (1977): 22–28.

Todd, Ruthven. "William Blake and the Mythologists." In Ruthven Todd, *Tracks in the Snow*. London: Graywalls Press, 1946. Pp. 29–60.

Todt, Wilhelm. *Lessing in England, 1767–1850*. Heidelberg: Carl Winters Universitätsbuchhandlung, 1912.

Tolley, Michael J. "Blake's Songs of Spring." In *William Blake: Essays in Honour of Sir Geoffrey Keynes*, edited by Morton D. Paley and Michael Phillips. Oxford: Clarendon Press, 1973. Pp. 96–128.

———. *"Europe*: 'to those ychained in sleep.' " In *Blake's Visionary Forms Dramatic*, edited by David Erdman and John E. Grant. Princeton: Princeton University Press, 1970. Pp. 115–45.

Tomory, Peter. *The Life and Art of Henry Fuseli*. New York and Washington: Praeger, 1972.

Trelawny, Edward. *Recollections of the Last Days of Shelley and Byron*. In *The Life of Percy Bysshe Shelley*, edited by Humbert Wolfe. London: Dent, 1933.

Trickett, Rachel. "The Augustan Pantheon: Mythology and Personification in Eighteenth-Century Poetry." *Essays and Studies*, n.s., 6 (1953): 71–86.

Tunnard, Christopher. *A World with a View: An Inquiry into the Nature of Scenic Values*. New Haven: Yale University Press, 1978.

Twitchell, James B. "Shelley's Metaphysical System in Act IV of *Prometheus Unbound*." *Keats-Shelley Journal* 24 (1975): 29–48.

Van Ghent, Dorothy. "Keats's Myth of the Hero." *Keats-Shelley Journal* 3 (1954): 7–25.

———. *Keats: The Myth of the Hero*. Rev. ed. Edited by Jeffrey Cane Robinson. Princeton: Princeton University Press, 1983.

Vitoux, Pierre. "Jupiter's Fatal Child in *Prometheus Unbound*." *Criticism* 10 (1968): 115–25.

Vogler, Thomas A. *Prefaces to Vision: The Epic Venture of Blake, Wordsworth, Keats, and Hart Crane*. Berkeley and Los Angeles: University of California Press, 1971.

Wasserman, Earl R. *The Finer Tone: Keats's Major Poems*. 1953. Reprint. Baltimore: Johns Hopkins University Press, 1967.

———. "The Internal Values of Eighteenth-Century Personification." *PMLA* 65 (1950): 435–63.

———. *Shelley: A Critical Reading*. Baltimore: Johns Hopkins University Press, 1971.

Watson, J. R. *Picturesque Landscape and English Romantic Poetry*. London: Hutchinson Educational, 1970.

Weaver, Bennett. *Prometheus Unbound*. Ann Arbor: University of Michigan Press, 1957.

———. *Toward the Understanding of Shelley*. 1932. Reprint. New York: Octagon, 1966.

Webb, Timothy. *Shelley: A Voice Not Understood*. Manchester: Manchester University Press, 1977.

———. *The Violet in the Crucible: Shelley and Translation*. Oxford: Clarendon Press, 1976.

Weiskel, Thomas. *The Romantic Sublime: Studies in the Structure and Psychology of Transcendence*. Baltimore: Johns Hopkins University Press, 1976.

Wellek, René. *A History of Modern Criticism*. Vol. 1, *The Later Eighteenth Century*; Vol. 2, *The Romantic Age*. New Haven: Yale University Press, 1955.

[West, Thomas]. *A Guide to the Lakes in Cumberland, Westmoreland, and Lancashire.* 6th ed. London: W. Richardson, 1796.

White, John. *The Birth and Rebirth of Pictorial Space.* 2d ed. Boston: Boston Book and Art Shop, 1967.

Wicker, Brian. "The Disputed Lines in *The Fall of Hyperion.*" *Essays in Criticism* 7 (1957): 28–41.

Wicksteed, Joseph. *Blake's Vision of the Book of Job.* 1910. Rev. ed. New York: Dutton, 1924.

Wilkie, Brian. *Romantic Poets and Epic Tradition.* Madison: University of Wisconsin Press, 1965.

Wilson, Milton. *Shelley's Later Poetry: A Study of his Prophetic Imagination.* New York: Columbia University Press, 1959.

Wilson, Mona. *The Life of William Blake.* Rev. ed. New York: Nonesuch Press, 1932.

Wimsatt, William K., Jr., and Cleanth Brooks. *Literary Criticism: A Short History.* New York: Knopf, 1962.

Winckelmann, Johann Joachim. *Histoire de l'Art Chez les Anciens*, traduit de l'Allemand, avec des notes historiques et critiques de differents auteurs. [Translated by Huber, revised by Jansen]. 2 vols. bound as 3. Paris: Bossange, Masson et Besson, 1802.

_____. *History of Ancient Art.* Translated by G. Henry Lodge. With Johann Gottfried Herder's essay "Winckelmann." Translated by Alexander Gode. 4 vols. in 2. New York: Frederick Ungar, 1968.

_____. *Reflections on the Painting and Sculpture of the Greeks. . . .* Translated by Henry Fuseli. 1765. Facsimile reprint. Menston, Yorks.: Scolar Press, 1972.

Wittreich, Joseph Anthony, Jr. *Angel of Apocalypse.* Madison: University of Wisconsin Press, 1974.

_____. "Opening the Seals: Blake's Epics and the Milton Tradition." In *Blake's Sublime Allegory*, edited by Joseph Anthony Wittreich, Jr., and Stuart Curran. Madison: University of Wisconsin Press, 1973.

_____. "William Blake: Illustrator-Interpreter of *Paradise Regained.*" In *Calm of Mind: Tercentenary Essays on "Paradise Regained" and "Samson Agonistes" in Honor of John S. Diekhoff*, edited by Joseph Anthony Wittreich, Jr. Cleveland: Press of Case Western Reserve University, 1971, 112–17.

———, ed. *Calm of Mind: Tercentenary Essays on "Paradise Regained" and "Samson Agonistes" in Honor of John H. Diekhoff.* Cleveland: Press of Case Western Reserve University, 1971.

———, ed. *Nineteenth Century Accounts of William Blake.* Gainsville, Fla.: Scholars' Facsimiles and Reprints, 1970.

Wittreich, Joseph Anthony, Jr., and Stuart Curran, eds. *Blake's Sublime Allegory.* Madison: University of Wisconsin Press, 1973.

Wolfflin, Heinrich. *Principles of Art History.* Translated from 7th ed. by M. D. Hottinger. 1929. Reprint. New York: Dover, n.d.

Woodman, Ross Greg. *The Apocalyptic Vision in the Poetry of Shelley.* Toronto: University of Toronto Department of English Studies 12, 1964.

———. "Shelley's Changing Attitude Toward Plato." *Journal of the History of Ideas* 21 (1960): 497–510.

Wordsworth, William. *A Guide Through the District of the Lakes.* Edited by W. M. Merchant. London: Rupert Hart-Davis, 1959.

———. Unsigned introduction. In Joseph Wilkinson, *Select Views in Cumberland, Westmoreland, and Lancashire.* London: R. Ackermann, 1810.

———. *The Poetical Works of William Wordsworth.* Edited by Ernest de Selincourt and Helen Darbishire. 5 vols. Oxford: Clarendon Press, 1940–1949.

———. *The Prelude: 1799, 1805, 1850.* Edited by Jonathan Wordsworth, M. H. Abrams, and Stephen Gill. A Norton Critical Edition. New York: Norton, 1979.

Wright, John W. *Shelley's Myth of Metaphor.* Athens: University of Georgia Press, 1970.

Wyatt, David M. "The Woman Jerusalem: *Pictura* versus *Poesis.*" *Blake Studies* 7 (1974): 105–24.

Yates, Frances A. *The Art of Memory.* 1966. Reprint. Harmondsworth: Penguin, 1969.

Zaehner, R. C. *The Teachings of the Magi: A Compendium of Zoroastrian Beliefs.* London: Allen and Unwin, 1956.

Index

Adams, Hazard, 66
Aeschylus: *Prometheus Bound*, 147, 167, 195; and initial sculptural figure, 25; and dramatic form in *Prometheus Unbound*, 136–39, 153
Architecture, gothic, 112
Aristotle, 74, 79, 138
Arts: rivalry among, 29–36; redemption through, 30; in Blake, compared to Keats, 68
Ault, Donald, 44, 48, 59

Bate, Walter Jackson, 12, 69; and sculptural massiveness in Keats, 79
Beaumont, Sir George, 60
Blake, William: illustrations to *The Book of Job*, 32; to Dante, 32; to Milton, 32; and knowledge of scenic picturesque, 34–35; and contrast with Burke, 89; and expansive moment, 106, 128; and criticism of Wordsworth, 113; and Gothic sculpture copied, 127; sympathy, compared to Prometheus', 151; illuminations, compared to Shelley's sketches, 159; visionary chariots, compared to Shelley's, 163; *Paradise Lost* illustration compared to *Prometheus Unbound*, 187
—*Annotations to Reynolds*, 58
—*The Book of Los*, 62
—*The Book of Thel*, 32
—*The Book of Urizen*, 62
—"The Crystal Cabinet," 121
—*Descriptive Catalogue*, 35, 55
—*The Four Zoas*, 32, 48, 49, 62
—*Jerusalem*, 61, 193
—Lambeth prophecies, 169
—*Laocoon*, 55, 60–61
—"London," 148
—*The Marriage of Heaven and Hell*, 100, 173
—*Milton*, 2, 3; and sculpturesque-picturesque contrast, 5–6; and stationed feet, 19; initial static figure confronted, 25–28; analyzed, 29–67; origins of, 35; stationing, technique of, 35; prefatory stanzas, 16–19, 21, 51, 113; metaphors of sculpting in, 61–67; compared to *Hyperion*, 68, 82, 93; compared to *The Fall of Hyperion*, 102, 103, 118, 131; and post-obit revelation, 104; discrepancy of scale, 111; Urizen and Keats's Titans, 129; compared to *Prometheus Unbound*, 138, 158–59, 172, 174, 175, 176, 182; compared to "Notes on Sculpture," 144; self-recognition in, 190; stationing as criticism of Milton, 191–92; redemption through arts, 192–93
—"Public Address," 35
—*The Songs of Innocence*, 32
Blazon, 120
Bloom, Harold: and poetics of influence, 3; and sculptural stance, 51; and Keats's epic

257

ambitions, 69; and Moneta's speech, 100; and orientation in *The Fall of Hyperion*, 109; and Moneta's dialogue, 114–15; on Demogorgon's chariot, 157

Brisman, Leslie, 51

Brisman, Susan, 145

Brown, Charles Armitage, 10, 13

Burke, Edmund, 30, 77, 89, 100, 147. *See also* Sublime

Bush, Douglas, 69, 108

Byron, George Gordon Lord, "Prometheus," 160

Calvinism, 41–42

Caves, in *Prometheus Unbound*, 177–79

Chariot: in *Milton* stanzas, 18; in Blake and Milton, 21; in Keats, Milton, and Ezekiel, 83; in *Prometheus Unbound*, 157, 185; in Shelley's sketches, 163; and moon in Shelley and Coleridge, 181–82

Chaucer, Geoffrey, 102

Clairmont, Claire, 140

Class, term in Blake's *Milton*, 41–44

Classicism, romantic, 31, 50, 52, 109

Coleridge, Samuel Taylor: and metaphysical picturesque, 5, 117; and development from sculpturesque to picturesque, 57, 60, 70–71, 81; and debt to Schlegel, 75–76; and Milton as musical poet, 77; and spirit of poetry, 87, 95; "Dejection Ode," 103, 173, 181; "Kubla Khan," 157, 178; and reconciling imagination, 174, 175–76; and reconciliation of contraries, 195

Contraries: in painting, 71; in metaphysical picturesque, 87–90; Moneta's face as symbol of, 117–122; Empedoclean, 141, 142–43; in *Prometheus Unbound*, Act 4, 175–89; reconciled, 195

Corinthians I, 186–87

Cumberland, George, 57, 59

Dante: and vortex, 48; and dream-vision, 102; and Garden of Eden, 106; as modern writer, 136

De Luca, Vincent, 63

De Quincey, Thomas, 58

Development of consciousness: sculpturesque to picturesque in *Hyperion* poems, 68–72; naive to sentimental, 70; English sources for Keats, 75–78

Demi-urge, 144

Demogorgon: and voice from abyss in "Ode to Liberty," 19; and disfigurings of process, 28; and answer to Asia, 172–75; and final speech, 186–89

Descartes, René, 47

Disfiguring, 6, 21–24, 190; of Moneta, 26; of Prometheus, 27; of process, and correction through stationing and statuary, 28

Dream, 194

Dreamer, 114–16

Dream-vision: and contrast with epic, 96–101; background, 102

Dyck, Sara, 145

Earth, transformation of in *Prometheus Unbound*, 176–80

Empedocles, 141, 142–43

Enargeia, 34

Energeia, 34

Erdman, David, 54

Ezra, 18

Fall, fortunate, 81

Farington, Joseph, 60

Feet, in *Milton*, 36

Firkins, Oscar, 145, 147

Flaxman, John: and sculpture as ideal image, 57–58, 73, 79; and romantic classicism, 52; and painting of sculpture, 119; and funeral monuments, 127

Focal point, in *The Fall of Hyperion*, 99

Fogle, R. H., 134, 148

Form, term used in *Prometheus Unbound*, 144–47

Forman, H. Buxton, 140, 142

Fox, Susan, 45

Freud, Sigmund, 66

Frosch, Thomas, 48, 50

Frye, Northrop: and brief-epic model for *Milton*, 36; and narrative syncopation, 46; and vortex, 48; and epic structures in romanticism, 53

Fuseli, Henry: sketch, *The artist in despair*, 51, 111; and *paragone*, 57; as translator of Winckelmann, 57–58; and discussion of Lessing in Royal Academy lectures, 58–59; and expressive moment, 60, 127; and sculpture as emotional feeling, 59; as illustrator of Aeschylus, 135

Gilgamesh, Epic of, 38
Gilpin, William: and scenic picturesque, 8, 10, 99; and role of observer, 12; and Blake, 34–35; and Milton as musical poet, 77

Hagstrum, Jean, 33–34
Harris, James, 58
Haydon, Benjamin Robert, 75
Hayley, William: as Satan in Blake's *Milton*, 41; and sculpture as art of feeling, 57, 59; and knowledge of Winckelmann, 58
Hazlitt, William: and review of Schlegel, 76; and progressive development in arts and sciences, 76–77; on epic objects, 77–78, 135; on Milton's sculpturesque effects, 77–78; on metaphysical picturesque, 78, 174; on indefinite in modern consciousness, 89; and historical consciousness, 94; and "romantic" consciousness, 100
Herder, Johann Gottfried, and sculpture as tactile art, 57, 58–59
Homer, *Odyssey*, 24, 27, 80, 134, 149, 178
Horace, 34
Hughes, Daniel, 145–46

Image, as term in *Prometheus Unbound*, 144–47

Jack, Ian, 69
Johnson, Joseph, 60
Jones, John, 68

Keats, John: marginal note to *Paradise Lost*, 2, 22, 24, 105, 190; trip to Lake Country, 10, 12–13; use of "station" in own poetry, 11; "station" in letters, 11–12; attack on scenic picturesque, 88
—*Endymion*, 68, 91–92, 108, 122, 181
—*Eve of St. Agnes*, 97
—*Epistle to John Hamilton Reynolds*, 85–86
—*The Fall of Hyperion*, 2, 3; and development from sculpturesque to picturesque, 5–6; and "stationing" in "Psyche," 16; and stationed central figure confronted, 25–28; disfiguring of Moneta, 26; "stationing or statuary" in, 68–69; analyzed, 96–133; integration of epic fragment, 96–97, 99; induction, 101–4; scene 1 analyzed, 104–8; scene 2, 108–14; Moneta's dia-

logue, 114–17; Moneta as emblem of contraries, 117–22; scene 3, 122–32; scene 4, 132–33; compared to *Prometheus Unbound*, 150, 160–66 passim, 173–79 passim, 181–82; and self-recognition, 190; and redemption through arts, 194–95
—*Hyperion*, 2, 3; and development of consciousness, sculpturesque to picturesque, 5–6, 96; "stationing" in "Psyche," 15; and clouded chariot in *Milton* stanzas, 18; and initial sculptural figure confronted, 25–26, 28; analyzed, 68–95; and "stationing or statuary," 68–69; narrative action in, 73; response to Hazlitt's "power," 76; Oceanus' sculptural ideal, 78–87; compared to *The Fall of Hyperion*, narrative viewpoint, 101, 125; changed perspective on Titans, 110, 122, 123, 126–27, 130; and absence of progress in *The Fall of Hyperion*, 119, 124; absence of overarching scheme in *The Fall of Hyperion*, 131–32; and sculptural form in *Prometheus Unbound*, 134; and observer in *Prometheus Unbound*, 148; and natural limits in *Prometheus Unbound*, 158–59, 168–69, 180; and unshaped spirits in *Prometheus Unbound*, 150, 176; and self-recognition, 190; and redemption through arts, 193–94
—*Lamia*, 97
—"La Belle Dame Sans Merci," 120
—*Letters*, 11–12, 68, 69, 104, 107, 111
—"Ode on Melancholy," 107, 116
—"Ode to Psyche," 15–16, 21, 103, 113
—*Sleep and Poetry*, 2, 12
—Sonnets on Elgin marbles, 75

Landscape: gardens, 2; studied by Shelley, 158–64; hierarchical in *Milton*, 31, 36–39; hierarchical in *Prometheus Unbound*, 168
Larrabee, Stephen, 145
Leonardo da Vinci, 23, 57
Lessing, Gotthold Ephraim, *Laocoon*: and *ut pictura poesis* debate, 57–58, 61, 73–74, 75, 80, 100; and English translations of, 58; and moment in Blake, 60, 65; and moment in Keats, 127
Lévi-Strauss, Claude, 103
Little, Judy, 76, 78, 91
Longinus, 34, 143

McGill, Mildred, 171, 177
McLuhan, Marshall, 33–34
Mark, Gospel of, 42
Medwin, Thomas, 140, 141, 142
Mellor, Anne Kostelanetz, 30–31, 109, 120
Michelangelo, 30
Miles, Josephine, 32
Milton, John: and internal vision in "Ode to Liberty," 21; as musical, not picturesque, poet, 77; praised by Hazlitt for sculpturesque effect, 77; criticized by Keats's Moneta, 101; and ambiguous syntax in *The Fall of Hyperion*, 103; compared by Keats to Wordsworth, 111; as modern writer, 136; defined as sculpturesque by Keats, Shelley, 192
—*L'Allegro* and *Il Penseroso*, 11
—*Paradise Lost:* stationing or statuary in, 1–2, 71; romantic revisions of, 3; use of station as term in, 7–8; quoted in West's *Guide*, 9–10; and bower in "Psyche," 15; Pandemonium and Shelley's Athens, 20; Satan observed by Uriel, 22–24, 68; as structural model, 22–28; and statuary in epic structure, 24; and change of perspective, 26; as narrative model for *Milton*, 37–39; and fallen Titans in *Hyperion*, 80; Ezekiel's chariot compared to Hyperion's, 83; and narrative structure in *Hyperion*, 94; and inductions, 104, 113; and gardens in *The Fall of Hyperion*, 106; and visions of history, 119; and *spectator ab extra*, 124, 130; as sculptural form in *Prometheus Unbound*, 136; and scenic structure of *Prometheus Unbound*, 137, 168; and shapelessness in *Prometheus Unbound*, 147; and chariots, compared to Shelley's, 164; and design of creation in *Prometheus Unbound*, 164, 170; and falling in *Prometheus Unbound*, 170, 172
—*Paradise Regained:* station as term in, 8; structural model for Milton, 36–37
Mitchell, W. J. T., 31, 32, 47
Monk, Samuel, 13
Murray, E. B., 140
Murry, John Middleton, 69, 71

Nehemiah, 18
Newton: and natural law, 5, 30; and three-dimensional space, 31, 44, 48, 49, 50, 192; and single vision, 34; and Blake's Satan, 40, 50; and vortex, 47; and moment in physics, 59
Nietzsche, Friedrich, 69
Nurmi, Martin, 48

Ovid, 80

Painting: as analogue for picturesque modern consciousness, 70–71, 88; in *Hyperion*, 83; portraits in *Hyperion* poems, 90
Paragone, 56–57
Park, Roy, 74
Peacock, Thomas Love, 140
Perkins, David, 96
Personification, 155; and sculpture, 2, 23, 187–89
Petrarch, 120
Phidias, 141, 157, 158
Picturesque: origins of term, 4; and relation to romantic imagination, 14–15
—Metaphysical: defined, 5; in Hazlitt, 78; in *Hyperion*, 90–95; and portrait-like expression in *Hyperion*, 92–93; and contraries in *Hyperion*, 94; in *The Fall of Hyperion*, 98; in Moneta, 100; as Poesy, 104; in *Prometheus Unbound*, Act 2, 137, 159, 174; in *Prometheus Unbound*, Act 4, 138, 159, 175–89
—Scenic: defined, 9–15; attacks on, 13–14, 88; Blake's knowledge of, 34–35; in *Hyperion*, 92, 95; in *The Fall of Hyperion*, 98–99, 105, 112, 117, 118; Shelley's knowledge of, 159–61; in *Prometheus Unbound*, 159, 167
Piranesi, Giovanni Battista, 51, 110
Plastic, 68; as sculpturesque classical consciousness in Schlegel, 72, 88; as malleable quality of language in Shelley, 139; and internal form in *Prometheus Unbound*, 150, 156
Plato, 73, 80, 145–46, 155, 173, 195
Point of view, 6–7
Pottle, Frederick, 137
Powers, Sharon, 173, 188
Praxiteles, 141, 143, 153, 156, 157, 165
Price, Martin, 13, 14–15, 167

Rajan, Tilottama, 69–70
Raphael, 71

Redemption of Milton's vision, 195–96

Reiman, Donald, 137, 146, 158, 173, 188

Revelation, Book of, 186

Reynolds, Sir Joshua: correspondence with Gilpin, 34–35; grand style and general nature, 35; and sculpture as ideal, 57–58, 79

Richardson, Jonathan, 30

Ricks, Christopher, 68

Rogers, Neville, 162

Romantic: term used by Schlegel, 72; consciousness in Oceanus' speech, 81. *See also* Picturesque

Rosenblum, Robert, 31, 52, 109

Schiller, Friedrich von: and development from naive to sentimental consciousness, 70; and sculptural consciousness, 107, 110, 131

Schlegel, A. W.: and development of consciousness, sculpturesque to picturesque, 25, 70–72, 136, 191–93; and Blake, 60; and unity of tragic action, 74, 128; read by Haydon, 75; in *Hyperion*, 81–82; read by Shelley, 136, 140–44; analysis of Aeschylus' *Prometheus Bound*, 136

—and metaphysical picturesque: defined, 5, 87–90; optimism of, 28; in facial portraits, 90; in Moneta, 100, 117; and picturesque dramatic structure, 137; in *Prometheus Unbound*, 138, 170, 174–76, 181

—and sculpturesque consciousness: defined, 72–75; in *Hyperion*, 80; in *The Fall of Hyperion*, 97, 107, 110, 125, 126, 131

Schopenhauer, Arthur, 70

Sculptor: Shelley's Liberty as, 21; Blake's Milton as, 30, 65–67, 192–93; Blake's Los as, 61–65

Sculpture: Elgin marbles, 2, 75; *Farnese Hercules*, 2, 56; as tactile art, 6, 30, 33, 58–59, 67, 124, 129, 144; Donatello *David*, 22; colossus of Constantine, 51; as redemptive metaphor in Blake's *Milton*, 54–67; as art referred to in Blake's works, 55; *Laocoon*, 55, 72, 75, 89, 140–42; *Apollo Belvedere*, 56, 75, 140; *Venus de Medici*, 56; as ideal image of general nature, 57; *Niobe*, 72, 89, 142–44; as analogue in *Hyperion*, 78–87; archaic Greek style of, 79; Egyptian style of, 79, 126; Phidian *Athena*, 120; analyzed

by Shelley, 139–44; Monte Cavallo *Horse-tamers*, 140; Arch of Titus, 140

Sculpturesque: analogy for classical culture, 60; defined in Schlegel, 72–75

Shakespeare, and picturesque drama in Schlegel and Coleridge, 70–71

Shape, term in *Prometheus Unbound*, 144–47

Shelley, Mary, 136

Shelley, Percy Bysshe: A. W. Schlegel, reading of, 136; Winckelmann, *History*, reading of, 136; and sketches in notebooks, 159, 161–64; and knowledge of picturesque theory, 159–61

—"The Colosseum," 160–61

—*The Defence of Poetry*, 139–40, 145, 166, 173

—*Julian and Maddalo*, 160

—*Letters*, 140, 159–60

—"Notes on the Sculptures of Rome and Florence," 140–44, 165

—"Ode to Liberty," 19–22, 113, 160

—"On Love," 173

—*Prometheus Unbound*, 2; and sculpturesque-picturesque development, 5–6; and Shelley's correction of Milton, 22; and initial sculptural figure confronted, 25–28; and imagelessness in Hazlitt and Schlegel, 89; compared to *The Fall of Hyperion*, 102, 118; analyzed, 134–89; dramatic structure, sculpturesque to picturesque, 134–39; and sculptural vocabulary, 144–47; sculpture as torture in Act 1, 147–53; sculpture as redemption in Act 3, 153–58; and arguments from design, 164–75; Demogorgon's answer to Asia, 172–75; and self-recognition, 190; and redemption through arts, 195

Sophocles, 72

Spenser, Edmund, 32, 164

Sperry, Stuart, 78

State, use of term: in Blake's *Milton*, 44–45; in *Jerusalem*, 45; in *The Vision of the Last Judgement*, 45

Station, use of term: as viewpoint for picturesque landscape, 4; origins, 6–15; in Milton, 7–8, 36; in Thomson, 8–9; in Gilpin's scenic picturesque, 8, 10; in West's scenic picturesque, 8–10; in Wordsworth, 10–11; in Blake's *Milton*, 31, 36, 39–42; in Shelley, 160

Stationing, technique of: in *Paradise Lost*,
1–2; in Keats, marginal note to *Paradise
Lost*, 2, 39; in three prefatory lyrics, 15–
22; in "Ode to Psyche," 15–16; in Blake's
prefatory stanzas to *Milton*, 16–19; in
Shelley's "Ode to Liberty," 19–22; in *Milton*, 29–33, 35–36, 45; with vortex, 50;
with feet, 50–54; in *Hyperion*, 84–89 passim; in *The Fall of Hyperion*, 99, 105, 109,
123, 125; in *Prometheus Unbound*, Act 4,
138, 146, 176, 182, 187; in Act 1, 148; in
Acts 2 and 4, 159, 195; in Act 2, 166–67;
in "The Colosseum," 161; in Uriel's view
of Satan, 190–91; as narrative structure in
Blake, Keats, Shelley, 191–96
Stationing or statuary, in Keats's marginal
note, 2, 22
Statuary: use of term, in Keats, marginal
note, 2; in gardens, 2–3; and expressive
gesture, 23; in epic structure, 24–28; Urizen as, 29
Sublime, 13, 30; egotistical, 113. *See also*
Burke, Edmund; and Monk, Samuel
Synaesthesia and sister arts, in *Prometheus
Unbound*, 155

Thomas, James, 8, 32
Titian, 71
Turner, J. M. W., 135

Ut *pictura poesis*, 2, 4, 15; and sculptural
expressiveness of personifications, 23; in
Paradise Lost, 30; Longinian, not Horatian,
33–34; in Blake's *Milton*, 54, 192; and
Laocoon debate, 57; and Los's sculpting,
63; and expressive gesture, 64; and Blake's
Milton as sculptor, 65; and expressive moment in Milton, 66, 67; criticized by Lessing and Burke, 88

Van Ghent, Dorothy, 69–70, 98
Vico, Giovanni Battista, 46
Virgil: *Aeneid*, 24, 27, 38, 80, 104, 134;
Sixth Eclogue, 108
Vortex: in Blake, 36, 45–50; in Shelley, 160

Wasserman, Earl, 174
Watson, J. R., 112
Webb, Timothy, 140, 148
West, Thomas, 8–10, 12
Wicker, Brian, 97–98
Winckelmann, Johann Joachim: and ut *pictura poesis* debate, 57–58, 61; and cultural
contrast, 72; and sculpture as serene ideal,
73–75, 79–81, 98, 135, 140–50 passim,
193; and sculpturesque to picturesque de-
velopment in Shelley, 136; Shelley's read-
ing of, 136, 140–44
Wölfflin, Heinrich, 14
Wordsworth, William: and station, use of
term, 9–11; and role of observer, 12; and
attack on scenic picturesque, 10, 13–14,
88, 95, 190; and Shelley's landscape
sketches, 163
—*The Excursion*, 11, 78, 112
—*Ode: Intimations of Immortality*, 111
—Lucy poems, 177
—*The Prelude*, 13, 103, 111, 116, 169
—*The Recluse*, 111–14, 116, 121
—"Lines Written Above Tintern Abbey,"
14, 111–12, 167
Wren, Christopher, 109

Yeats, William Butler, 46

About the Author

Nancy Moore Goslee teaches English and is the director of graduate studies in English at the University of Tennessee-Knoxville. She received her bachelor of arts degree from Smith College and her master of arts degree and doctorate from Yale University. This is her first book.